Red Chicago

AMERICAN COMMUNISM AT ITS GRASSROOTS, 1928–35

Red Chicago

Red Chicago

AMERICAN COMMUNISM
AT ITS GRASSROOTS,
1928–35

RANDI STORCH

UNIVERSITY OF ILLINOIS PRESS
Urbana and Chicago

Publication of this volume was supported
by the State University of New York
at Cortland.

First Illinois paperback, 2009
© 2007 by the Board of Trustees
of the University of Illinois
Manufactured in the United States of America
1 2 3 4 5 C P 5 4 3 2 1
∞ This book is printed on acid-free paper.

The Library of Congress cataloged the cloth edition
as follows:
Storch, Randi
Red Chicago : American communism at its grassroots,
1928–35 / Randi Storch.
p.   cm. — (Working class in American history)
Includes bibliographical references and index.
ISBN-10 -0-252-03206-3 (cloth : alk. paper)
ISBN-13 978-0-252-03206-6 (cloth : alk. paper)
1. Trade Union Unity League (U.S.) 2. Communism—
Illinois—Chicago—History. I. Title.
HX83.S78   2007
331.88'6097731109043—dc22   2007016991

PAPERBACK ISBN 978-0-252-07638-1

For Merrill, Merrill Anne, Henry, and
my parents, Hyman and Adrienne

Contents

Acknowledgments

It has taken over ten years for this project to transform from an idea to a book. Along the way, I have had the support of key people for whom I feel a deep sense of gratitude.

I will be forever indebted to Jim Barrett, who introduced me to the world of working-class history and socialist politics. Despite his busy schedule, Jim always made time to listen to a new idea, critique chapters (over and over), and suggest ways to make my work better. Through his balanced commitments to family, friends, history, and politics, Jim has been an incredibly important role model for me. This book has benefited from his attention to detail and his passion for good history, and I have benefited from his lessons on life.

At the University of Illinois at Urbana-Champaign, Jim led an inspiring dissertation committee (Mark Leff, Leslie Reagan, Diane Koenker, and Steve Rosswurm), whose members sent me off to the real world with excellent critiques and ideas for revision. Special thanks to Steve, who opened his home and his heart to this project; his generosity continues to be unceasing. Illinois also provided me with lifelong friends who help keep me grounded. Thanks to the gang (Kathy Mapes, Toby Higbie, Steve Vaughan, Lisa Gatzke, Tom Jordan, Julia Walsh, Caroline Merrithew, Robert Merrithew, Loretta Gaffney, Steve Jahn, and Mary Vavrus) who nurtured me with their intellect, good humor, love for home cooking, and Graduate Employees' Organization adventures. Kathy, especially, has continued to be the backbone of my support structure, reading everything I write, telling me what I really mean, and sharing her humanity through the highs and lows that come with new life and tragic death.

Researching and writing this project allowed me to work with people who are incredibly good at their professions and generous with their time. Some stand out. The late Archie Motley and the staff at the Chicago Historical Society made doing research enjoyable and easy. Jeffrey Janusch's open-door policy and love for Chicago and its working-class history made research trips affordable and entertaining. I was particularly lucky to meet Michael Flug at the Carter Woodson Library. Michael knows just about everything about Chicago and happily shared ideas for sources and leads. Joy Kingsolver and the staff at the Spertus Library kept me abreast of new acquisitions and accommodated my hurried visits. Galina Khartulary and Valery Klokov helped me get past the armed guards at the Russian archives and once inside to comb through party collections. Heather Coleman got me out of a number of jams along the way and made excursions outside of Moscow fun. Eric Fenster's study-abroad program made it possible for me to live in Moscow and attend cultural and educational events with ease. Daria Lotareva helped me locate materials once I returned to the States. The folks at the University of Illinois Press, and especially Laurie Matheson, have been patient, kind, and calming forces throughout this process.

Steve Rosswurm's first piece of advice was to start interviewing people yesterday. I was lucky to speak with several activists who participated in the events described in this book. Some opened their homes; others talked over the phone. Thanks especially to Vicky Starr, Herb and Jane March, Yolanda and the late Chuck Hall, Les Orear, Molly West, Mimi Gilpin, Earl Durham, Gus Vavrus, Helen Balskus, Richard Criley, the late Gil Green, and the late Jack Spiegel.

I was fortunate to have feedback from a number of scholars. Many people read all or parts of the manuscript, listened to ideas for chapters, gave a tip on a source, and/or offered suggestions for revisions. Special thanks to David Montgomery, Bryan Palmer, Ken Fones-Wolf, Maurice Isserman, Beth Bates, Kathy Mapes, Julia Walsh, Caroline Merrithew, Heather Coleman, Toby Higbie, Mary Mapes, Steve Vaughan, Tom Jordan, Karen Pastorello, the late Steve Sapolsky, Paul Buhle, Glenda Gilmore, Tom Gugliemo, Rick Halpern, Roger Horowitz, Toni Gilpin, Dan Letwin, Paul Young, Robert Cherny, Rosemary Feurer, Don Watson, Dan Katz, and the two anonymous readers for the press.

SUNY-Cortland affords me supportive colleagues. Thanks especially to Girish Bhat, Gigi Peterson, Sandy Gutman, Brett Troyan, Kevin Sheets, Laura Gathagan, John Shedd, Luo Xu, Frank Burdick, Roger Sipher, Don Wright, and Judy Van Buskirk for reading some or all of the chapters, sharing strategies for balancing teaching and research, and making me proud to be a historian. Don needs to be singled out for his incredible work ethic and willingness to help me edit line by line—he is that good. Judy took me under her wing, cheered me along, and came over to play with the kids just because she wanted to. I am also fortunate to know Howard Botwinick in economics, who has shared with me his library, stories, and progressive vision. Susan Wilson, in recreation and leisure studies, wishes I were a presidential historian but still regularly asks about Chicago's

Communists and makes really good pretend pancakes out of our kids. Betsy Meinz and George Manning share my passions for research methods, teaching strategies, politics, parenting, and cooking. Matt Lessig and Mary Patroulis helped by sharing the magic that was Illinois and the GEO over good wine and grown-up conversation. Through Cortland's history department, I also had the good fortune of working with excellent research assistants. Daniel Smith, Anthony Natale, and Michael Archambault stand out. Martin Smith from the University of Illinois graciously offered his time as well. David Miller, in geography, introduced me to his student Lezlie Button, who worked tirelessly on the book's maps. Dawn Van Hall kindly digitized and cleaned up many of the book's photos. Bella Gorelaya fine-tuned my Russian reading skills and prepared me for my second research trip.

I was also able to fund much of my research, travel, and production costs through SUNY-Cortland's various in-house grants as well as the generosity of the dean of arts and sciences, provost, and president. Our faculty union, the United University Professions, helped with grants, travel funds, and a Nuala Drescher Fellowship. The National Endowment for the Humanities' International Research Exchange Grant made it possible for me to return to Moscow's archives and complete the research for the book. Other support for this project came from the Newberry Library, the University of Illinois, and the Illinois State Historical Society. The views expressed in this book, however, are my own.

My family has always helped me keep things in perspective. My parents, Hyman and Adrienne, and my sister, Jenelle, have been cheerleaders and financial supporters during each stage of this long journey, even though none of us was sure where it would lead. My in-laws and the whole Miller clan have graciously welcomed me into their pack and their pinochle games. Merrill is my biggest critic and most loving supporter. He has read every word I have written, talked through the arguments, and reminded me that the glass is half full. He has given new meaning to the notion of being on a team. That partly has to do with the expansion of our own team. In the time I have been working on this book, Merrill Anne and Henry have become their own people with incredible hearts and minds. I only hope that by the time they come of age, they will inherit a spirit of struggle and in their own ways work to make a better tomorrow.

Red Chicago

Introduction

On a January evening in 1934, approximately six thousand Chicagoans gathered in the city's large Coliseum Hall to celebrate and remember Lenin. It was the kind of evening that brought out the complexities of Communism in the city. "In behalf of the American Communist Party," the main speaker declared, "I say that the one program which will bring unity to the American people is the program of Lenin."[1] The audience included a contingent of five hundred children among the thousands of grown women and men, half of whom were African American and the other half of whom were a mixture of native-born whites and first- or second-generation immigrants from various ethnic communities. They represented a number of occupations, including skilled and unskilled industrial workers, artists, intellectuals, and students. In a sense, this occasion honoring Lenin's memory had already begun the work of unifying American people across the lines of age, sex, ethnicity, and occupation.

And yet Communists clearly had their work cut out for them. American Federation of Labor leaders, the speaker warned the crowd, equated Lenin's program with "'a Russian program—not one for the United States.'" And even though the hall was decked out in Soviet-styled pageantry, complete with red flags of all sizes and banners displaying such slogans as "Down with Imperialist War," "Defend the USSR and the Chinese People," and "Hail Dimitroff—Leninist Fighter for the Working Class," the night's speaker triumphantly reported to a sea of applause and cheer, "*We* say that the program of Lenin is *the* program of the working class."[2] What did this diverse grouping of Chicagoans find relevant about Lenin and the Communist party? How are students of American history supposed to reconcile these two seemingly contradictory images: one of an organization that celebrated Soviet leaders, co-opted Soviet symbols, and embraced revolutionary Marxist-Leninist ideology, and the other a somewhat popular American social movement comprised of a wide array of otherwise ordinary people? This book closely examines American Communism in a local context and explains how this radical movement was experienced in the United States. I argue that by the mid-1930s, Soviet control remained incomplete, and local cultures still shaped the movement.

Red Chicago focuses on the years between 1928 and 1935, thought to be the most sectarian period in party history. The scholars Irving Howe and Lewis Coser, for example, argue that these years represent a time of unified thought and action throughout the party. "Year by year," they claim, "the totalitarian symptoms grew more distinct."[3] Their conclusion is supported by the general outline of Communist teaching during these years. Beginning in 1928, Communist theorists predicted, postwar development was entering its "Third Period"—a time when capitalism's collapse and imperialism's end were certain.[4] Once the Depression hit and unemployment mounted, these predictions seemed prophetic, and Communists embraced their calling to lead workers in what they thought was bound to be a second American revolution. To speed the system's ruin, they exposed what they saw as capitalism's contradictions, focusing on the conflicts of interest between America's workers and its capitalist class and exposing non-Communist liberal and leftist groups as "social fascist" betrayers to the workers' cause. Using direct and confrontational tactics, Communists promoted welfare, civil rights, inclusive and militant unions, and anti-imperialism.[5]

Some scholars argue that these Soviet-inspired tactics lent themselves to ultra-revolutionary rhetoric and behavior that alienated American workers and made the American Communist party irrelevant, but it was during these years that Chicago's party experienced its first substantial growth in membership, when tens of thousands turned out for Communist rallies and the city's Communists developed lasting structures in its neighborhoods and factories. One of the themes carried throughout the following chapters is that some of the character that historians identify with the period of the Popular Front (the years between 1935 and 1939) existed in Chicago during the Third Period. It was in these years that Communists learned how to work with liberals and non-Communists: they developed successful organizing tactics and fought for workers' rights, racial equality, and unemployment relief and against imperialism. Chicago Communists appealed to an assortment of followers—African Americans, ethnics, students, artists, writers, workers, and women—and began to move away from sectarianism in all of their major campaigns, before any orders to do these things arrived from Moscow. Party leaders in Moscow and New York decided on and disseminated party policy. In Chicago, a great diversity of people lived it, but not always by the book.

Until now, a lack of local Communist party sources has encouraged some scholars to assume that the priorities of international Communist leaders were those of the ranks and that whatever party leaders ordered, local activists served. Those in this school interpret all aspects of the party's organization and structure as determined by Moscow and therefore not relevant to people and politics in the United States. They remove Communists from their neighborhoods, workplaces, and networks in order to show, with condescension and disdain, that Communists in the United States acted as Soviet puppets.[6] Theodore Draper, writing in 1960, determined that by 1929, "nothing and no one could alter the fact that the American Communist Party had become an instrument of the Russian Communist Party."[7] Such beliefs led him to the conclusion that "a history of the Communist Party is chiefly a history of its top leadership." Echoing Draper nearly four decades later, Harvey Klehr, John Earl Haynes, and Kyrill M. Anderson argue that "the dictates of the Comintern almost invariably superseded policies offered on the basis of local conditions."[8]

Revisionist scholars in the 1980s and 1990s collected oral histories, combed published party records, and studied party-influenced organizations' archives to create a more nuanced approach to the study of American Communism. These scholars contextualized the American party and wrote some excellent studies that used social-history methods, fleshing out how individuals and groups experienced Communism in places as disparate as the midwestern shop floor, southern farm, and eastern city; but in their enthusiasm they tended to romanticize the Communist movement, understate the party's bureaucratic structure, and downplay the movement's sectarianism. They also emphasized the party's Popular Front heyday, when the culture of the movement supported their broader arguments.[9]

Lurking behind these various methodologies and interpretations are assumptions about Stalinism and how it operated in the United States. Revisionist scholars downplay Stalinism's effect and depict Communists as idealized, organic radicals. Draper and those writing in his tradition see Soviet Russia's domination over the American Communist project as the only relevant piece of the story and the fact of Soviet control as a foregone conclusion. More recently, Bryan Palmer, a socialist historian, has challenged Draper's teleological argument and yet agrees that, in the end, foreign domination fundamentally shaped the American party. To him, Stalin's brutal control of the Soviet party and the international movement destroyed revolutionary socialism, narrowed the Communist project to revolution in one country, and dominated the priorities of the Comintern and its international parties. "Only if we are capable of seeing Stalinism's degenerations, and how they registered in the transformation of Soviet politics and the role of the Comintern over the course of the 1920s," Palmer argues, "can we appreciate what was the foundational premise of the American revolutionary left."[10]

Of course, Stalinism *did* matter to the American Communist movement;

Communists followed the Marxist-Leninist hierarchical style of organization, and they required members to follow party policy. For these reasons, this study pays careful attention to political and institutional matters. The party line shaped the activity, language, and structure of Chicago's local party. These lines and policies that leaders in Moscow and New York sent down damaged the party (when it went on purging campaigns against its own members) and the Left more generally (when Communists taught that all non-Communist leftists were the enemies of working people everywhere). Such other lines as class revolution and racial equality brought on the wrath of the state and its police force but were more in line with a leftist movement and revolutionary thought. And yet, *Red Chicago* argues that to fully understand American Communism, one must move beyond these Stalinist policies to more concrete questions. Who were Chicago's Communists? How, when, and why did they implement Third Period policy? What did they actually do in the city's neighborhoods and industries? How did they understand the party line? When and why did they reinterpret it? Many in Chicago's party were proud Communists. They believed in the Soviet Union, the Comintern, and party policy. But they did not always follow the rules. Some of these rule breakers were newcomers, others were longtime party leaders, and still others—ethnic leaders, African Americans, professional lawyers, elected union officials, and student activists—had their own bases of power that party leaders had to share. Each had their own reasons for stepping out of line: outright defiance, willful ignorance, traditions of their radical past, sensitivity to the particular people they organized, or the politics of party subcultures. Even though some were not compliant, they *were* party members. American Communism embraced Stalinist stalwarts *and* their less-disciplined troops. This mix best explains the experience of Communism in the United States.[11]

To reorient the story of American Communism and provide an alternate perspective, *Red Chicago* relies on previously classified local American Communist records in Moscow open to Western scholars only since the 1990s. The Russian State Archive of Social and Political History (RGASPI) includes more than four thousand files on the Communist Party of the United States for 1919 through the early 1940s, with its richest materials relating to the period between 1928 and 1935. It also houses thousands of other files that pertain to the Profintern, which coordinated industrial organizing, and the Comintern, which oversaw the entire international operation. These formerly untapped documents (including membership statistics, disciplinary hearings, field organizers' reports, neighborhood meeting minutes, pamphlets, newsletters, shop papers, and leaflets) produced by rank-and-file members as well as party officials detail Chicago party activities and reveal local Communist cultures and decision-making processes. These sources place activists in particular workplaces, neighborhoods, schools, and clubs, fleshing out Communists' social networks and political trajectories.

They put a human face on American Communism and thus allow scholars to tell a detailed story that places the personal and political choices Communist activists made into the social and political context in which they lived.[12] Many of the recent studies that use Soviet records emphasize Communist espionage and intrigue with an eye toward rehabilitating the tactics of red hunters, like Joseph McCarthy.[13] And while spying did occupy some party members between the years 1935 and 1945, and *may* have during the Third Period, Chicago's local records do not reveal espionage. Instead, they record Communists' daily struggles facing police repression, mobilizing mass organizations, and raising workers' political consciousness. Instead of intrigue, local sources reveal the efforts of this revolutionary party to make itself relevant and provide a clearer understanding of the way the majority in its orbit experienced American Communism.

While Moscow's sources provide a uniquely candid view of party life, they are best interpreted when supplemented with newspapers, published records, and Chicago's own archival sources. The combination helps explain the period's broader social and political context and calls attention to the social, political, economic, and cultural forces that shaped American working-class life from the 1920s through the mid-1930s. It also helps explain another central theme of this book: why and how ordinary people became radicalized. On the one hand, these questions are essential to understanding the local character of American Communism: they draw attention to the ways individuals understood Communism, the circumstances that brought them to the movement, and how they lived it. On the other hand, they go beyond party history and place Communism in the broader context of working-class history. How people make a living, their social ties, their neighborhood politics, their workplace cultures, and their political outlets shape their ability and desire to create social change. Between 1928 and 1935, the nation underwent significant shifts between Herbert Hoover's laissez-faire administration and Franklin D. Roosevelt's New Deal, between prosperity and Depression, between balanced budgets and deficit spending, and between individualist, private solutions and collective, national ones. The effects of these changes made their way into homes, workplaces, and street corners throughout the nation. Excellent studies examine how America's workers responded to these changes but often dismiss as less viable their most radical choices.[14]

A community study allows for a more comprehensive understanding of American Communism than is possible using other methodologies.[15] The inclusiveness of a community study allows one to compare experiences across the sexes, industries, neighborhoods, and ethnic groups that inhabit the city and to recognize local quirks, personalities, and cultures in ways that are difficult to see from a national perspective or by studying one group of people. It also allows one to consider how (in)completely national and international policies, structures, cultures, and institutions made their way down to the ranks.

If a community study is best suited to study working people's encounter with American Communism, Chicago is an ideal environment. The city was the second largest industrial area in the nation during the interwar years. In 1930, thirty-eight railroads and twenty-three trunk lines terminated there, contributing to the city's distinction as the world's leader in the production and distribution of food staples and in the manufacture and distribution of meat, meat products, agricultural implements, dry goods, railroad supplies, and foundry products. The union stockyards, steel plants, railroad yards, garment factories, and farm-equipment industries gave Chicago its working-class cast and appealed to Communists, who were especially interested in organizing mass-production workers, who they judged would be more inclined to support a socialist-styled revolution. Chicago was also one of the most heavily unionized cities in the country, yet these mass-production workers had been unable to build lasting unions, a problem Communists hoped to fix. The Chicago Federation of Labor (CFL) held together an assortment of mostly craft workers. In the aftermath of failed industrial organizing campaigns in meatpacking and steel, CFL leaders still supported a fairly radical agenda, including third-party politics and anti-imperialist movements. But almost a decade of employer-led open-shop drives depleted its member unions' enthusiasm to build industrial unions. Communists believed the time had come for the city's mass-production workers—first- and second-generation Eastern European immigrants, black migrants, Mexicans, and Mexican Americans—to create interracial and multiethnic unions. Stretching their reach into distinct neighborhoods, Communists set up, used, and/or co-opted ethnic clubhouses, restaurants, newspapers, and theaters to get their message out.

Although gaining adherents was a struggle, Communists found supporters who agreed to rethink segregated and divisive relationships in their workplaces and communities and who were willing to move toward a newly gendered, interracial, and interethnic strategy of organizing and relating to others. Whether in community organizations, workplace settings, or street-corner meetings, many laboring people in Chicago listened to, debated, thought about, and occasionally acted in support of Communist campaigns. Such behavior suggests how a diverse mix of Americans imagined a new world should be. Why they did not see their ends realized is as important to examine as it is to understand why they believed a revolution was possible and what they were willing to do to accomplish it. The methods of social history help us achieve such an understanding. Looking down Chicago's streets and into its schools and factories makes it easier to see that the connections various groups made to radicalism were dependent on personal experiences, which in turn were shaped by America's Depression-era political, social, and economic conditions. Chicago's Communists were most successful in the densest industrial areas and working-class neighborhoods in

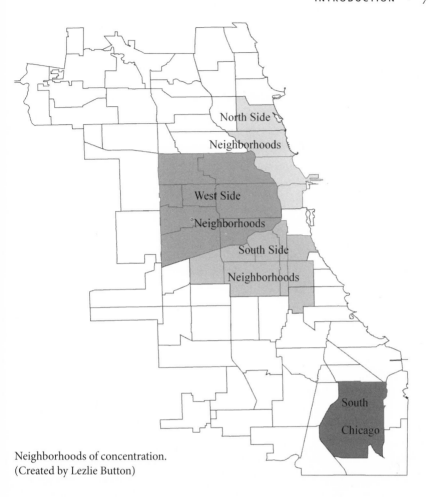

North Side
Neighborhoods

West Side
Neighborhoods

South Side
Neighborhoods

South
Chicago

Neighborhoods of concentration.
(Created by Lezlie Button)

Chicago's West Side, the Black Belt, Packing Town, the North Side, and South Chicago, where the Depression's effects hit with devastating force.

Chicago's Communists were heir to the city's radical traditions. The city was the site of the 1886 Haymarket tragedy, the eight-hour movement, and the 1894 Pullman Boycott, as well as the birthplace of the Industrial Workers of the World and the American Communist party. In what ways did Chicago's party represent continuity with radical movements of the past? What challenges did Chicago's radical past present? Chicago's Communists built on local, leftist cultures and developed their own enclaves that dotted the city's working-class neighborhoods. In some important cases, individuals followed the historical trajectory of radicalism in America and moved to the party after stints in other leftist organizations. They brought with them a commitment to a workers' revolution and lots of other political baggage. Rather than a unified and completely Stalinized movement, the following chapters show how difficult it was for disciplined party members to get others to follow—even, and sometimes especially, when the others were seasoned radicals. In these early Depression years, Chicago's party successfully held together and built upon a group of otherwise loosely affiliated activists, and did so with a limited ability to micromanage, decide, and direct.

Red Chicago argues that at the local level, a wide variety of Communists coexisted in Chicago. Some, even among the lowest-ranking members, were Stalinized, but they organized, socialized with, and married Communists who were not. Working in a community with as many neighborhoods, industries, and ethnic groups as Chicago, the party encountered all kinds of people, with various priorities and interests. The Soviet Union and party policy mattered a great deal to these people, but neither precluded their acting in ways that also made sense in their local union, community, or club meetings. The international Communist movement was centered in Moscow, ruled over by Stalin, and governed by Leninist principles. But these facts leave much of the story of the Communist experience in a place like Chicago untold. *Red Chicago* is an attempt to explain how Communism came to matter to a wide assortment of people and how they experienced this particular version of American radicalism.

1

Sam Hammersmark's Chicago

It was 1938 when Michael Gold, the veteran Communist newspaper columnist, referred to Sam Hammersmark as "that old Rock of Ages . . . the original model of Jimmie Higgins, the rank-and-filer who keeps plugging and plugging until the battle is won."[1] Hammersmark's determination placed him on the front lines of the nation's leftist and labor movements. Given his predilection to fight for working people, it was fitting that his path of radical activity originated in Chicago. By 1882, the year he arrived, the city already had some of the nation's strongest labor, socialist, and anarchist movements, and it would serve as a harbinger of workers' radical sentiments into the twentieth century. Raised in this worker-oriented environment by his Norwegian father, a skilled carpenter, and Norwegian mother, a rug weaver, Hammersmark found himself in the center of the city's and the nation's major leftist movements. Moving in and out of anarchist, labor, and socialist organizations, Hammersmark developed contacts and friendships with an array of activists struggling to find their own answers to the problems they saw inherent in the capitalist system. These people taught lessons that caused many to rethink their ideologies, switch organizational camps, and join new movements. So it is not surprising that when a Communist party formed in the United States in 1919, some of its first members were from Chicago. The party proved to be an organization to which many, including Hammersmark, would remain loyal for the rest of their lives and one that would become the dominant leftist organization in the city and the nation into the 1950s.

Chicago's radical past provided members of its nascent Communist movement a context full of hope and a history of working-class militancy. It also held lessons of state and employer repression and organizational challenges. Heady and emboldened, Chicago's newly minted Communists had great hopes of overcoming the hurdles that stymied radical movements of the city's past and worked to unify Chicago's labor militants and working-class ethnics under the Communist party's banner. They would find, however, that in the initial process of affiliating themselves to the international Communist movement, Soviet leaders—and the policies they set—alienated Chicago's Communists from their non-party labor allies and encouraged an inwardly focused, factional feud.

Chicago's Early Growth and the Development of Radical Traditions

Chicago's rich labor and radical traditions that greeted Hammersmark and thousands of others like him were inexorably tied to the city's heritage. In the short time between 1774, when Jean Baptiste Point DuSable, a Haitian trader, became the first non-Indian settler to the city, and Hammersmark's arrival in 1882, Chicago had grown into a thriving industrial center. Opened to the Erie Canal in 1825 by mostly Irish hands, Chicago developed into a center for trade, slowly at first and then with increasing speed when railroads arrived. Its access to the West made Chicago the nation's railroad center in 1856: its nearly one hundred daily train arrivals helped attract all manner of industry to this rapidly growing city. The 1871 fire caused havoc, homelessness, and destruction but also stimulated a wave of industrial development. By the time Hammersmark arrived, Chicago had become not only the Midwest's commercial and transportation center but also one of the nation's leading manufacturing centers, dominating the agricultural-implement, livestock, lumberyard, and sawmill industries. In terms of number of employees, total wages, capital invested, gross value of products, and value added in manufacturing, only New York and Philadelphia had Chicago beat.[2]

Employers' insatiable need for labor attracted a fast-growing population of working people to this once swampy trading outpost. When it was incorporated in 1843, the city housed under five thousand people, but by 1860, it had 109,260 residents and would multiply to 503,185 in 1880, only to double again in the next ten years, making it the third largest city in the nation. Such immigrants as Hammersmark and his family caused the city to brim with foreign-speaking newcomers, many of whom arrived with little but the willingness to work. By 1890, 78 percent of the city's residents were either immigrants or their children. From the 1880s through the early 1920s, newer arrivals from Italy, Greece, Lithuania, Poland, Russia, and the American South joined older settlements of Germans, Irish, Scandinavians, and Czechs, distinguishing Chicago as a working-class city of immigrants and black migrants.[3]

Such diversity made unified activity among these working-class ethnics difficult. In fact, from the earliest days of settlement, immigrants nestled into familiar ethnic enclaves, insulating themselves from native-born Chicagoans and people hailing from different lands. Whether it was the North Side Germans who congregated east of the river among Diversey, Devon, and Lincoln Avenues; the Southwest Side Bohemians who claimed Pilsen; the Irish of Bridgeport and Canaryville; or the Swedes who developed Swede Town between Erie and Wells on the Chicago River, ethnic Chicagoans' particular language differences, churches, schools, newspapers, restaurants, and cultural institutions segregated one group from another. Ethnically identified parishes and neighborhood institutions provided comfort and support to newly arrived peoples but also promoted insularity and at times intolerance.[4]

Chicago's government policies further exacerbated ethnic tension and division in the city. In the 1850s, for example, Germans fought local laws to close their beer gardens and to raise licensing fees on liquor stores. At one point, a vigilante committee used firearms provided by the mayor to stop German socialists from getting to city hall. The force Chicago's police used in putting down worker-related protests would become notorious the world over. In the meantime, anti-immigrant policies regulating alcohol and foreign-language instruction in the schools would keep Chicago's ethnics on the defensive.[5]

Because particular jobs, crafts, and trades were linked to certain ethnic groups, shop-floor divisions between skilled and unskilled positions translated into ethnic resentment. Older, more settled groups like German cigar makers, Swedish wood workers, and Irish butchers saw the mechanization and reorganization of their work between the 1870s and the early 1900s as a threat to their work culture and livelihood. Even if the more established skilled workers had wanted to unite with unskilled workers newly arrived to the city who took jobs for whatever pay employers offered, working-class unity across skill, gender, and language barriers would have been difficult to accomplish.[6]

Employers relished and exacerbated these divisions. This was particularly true in large industries, like meatpacking, where workers were already divided along skill, gender, and ethnic lines. Philip Armour, the leading packinghouse industrialist, was aware of how Eastern Europeans held off unionization. He openly explained that they did so "'by displacing experienced and perhaps disillusioned employees . . . who might have been contaminated by contacts with union organizers.'" Swift's employment office antagonized ethnic differences among their workers by hiring and firing entire groups of ethnics in front of one another. One employment officer explained, "'We change among different nationalities and languages. It prevents them from getting together. We have the thing systematized.'"[7] Employers' ability to play different ethnicities off one another would make such future ethnic migrations as the Great Migration of African Americans during World War I a particular organizational challenge for labor and the Left. Given ethnic groups' residential insularity, the state's willingness to repress organized protest, and employers' determination to divide employees along ethnic lines, workers found it difficult to see past their own ethnic differences, unite along class lines, and demonstrate against political and economic forces threatening their work cultures.

But such a tradition began to show in the city as early as the railroad strike of 1877. When employers for the Baltimore and Ohio Railroad in Pennsylvania and West Virginia announced a 10-percent wage cut, a strike wave developed along the railroad lines. When it finally reached Chicago, ethnic and native-born laborers joined railroad workers in laying down their tools and walking off their jobs. Workers refused to run streetcars, left ships idle, and walked out of furniture, cabinet, and tailor shops and lumber yards. Soon ironworkers, brass finishers, carpenters, brick makers, stonemasons, glaziers, and painters joined in. At one point, five hundred stockyard butchers marched—sporting cleavers, bloody aprons, and a banner that read "Workingmen's Rights." Although ultimately suppressed by excessive government force, Chicago's workers demonstrated their ability to act in solidarity against capitalist forces encroaching on their established work cultures.[8]

The willingness of Chicago's organized workers to flex their muscle appealed to a small but influential group of Socialists in the city who had their own roots in Chicago's past. A group of German Socialists who fled Germany after its 1848 failed revolution put out Chicago's first Socialist newspaper, *Der Proletarier*, in 1854, but not until the post–Civil War period could a core of agitators and workers develop a coherent Socialist movement. This movement created organizations between the 1870s and 1880s—including the workingmen's associations and parties of the early 1870s, the Socialist Labor party (SLP) of 1877, and the International Working People's Association (IWPA) in 1883—that had strikingly similar compositions. Rather than membership, what changed for these organizations was the structure of modern industry and the questions each addressed, such as the role of politics in fomenting revolution and whether revolutionaries should promote worker militias.[9]

By the 1880s, one of the most pressing issues facing Chicago's radicals was the relationship between trade unions and revolution. In Chicago, a trade-union-focused group of anarchists pushed for dynamic and militant unionism as the key to revolutionary change and gained more influence among workers than in any other city. Their concept, later known as the "Chicago idea," represented a unique blending of anarchist and revolutionary trade-union ideology that would resurface in slightly altered form as members of different radical organizations came to appreciate trade unions' potential to make revolutionary change. At its height, between 1885 and 1886, the IWPA had three to five thousand members and fifteen thousand supporters throughout the country.[10] Chicago, the heart of the movement, was home to fifteen different language groups, representing

English, German, French, and Czech workers. Chicago anarchists, the largest such concentration in the country (roughly a thousand, with five or six thousand sympathizers), supported a vibrant social life of picnics, parades, dances, and concerts. Most members were either skilled or unskilled workers and were led by craftsmen and independent artisans.[11]

As new arrivals filled the city and competed for work, anarchists' lively culture, disdain for the ballot, and encouragement of direct action attracted a growing number of people, including Sam Hammersmark. In Europe and America, it was men like Hammersmark's father, a skilled tradesman, who populated anarchist movements. They saw the aggregation of wealth and power created through industrial capital, the use of mechanization benefiting employers while exploiting workers, and the dehumanization associated with the deskilling of trades and crafts. Professions being modernized by factories and machines had strong representation among Chicago's anarchists. The Pullman railroad-car factory and McCormick and Deering agricultural-machinery plants were sites where anarchists regularly set up soapboxes and drew crowds.[12]

As members of local unions, Chicago's anarchists and Socialists nurtured the indigenous militants in the ranks of the city's labor movement. In 1884, that labor movement was divided into three organizations: the Knights of Labor, the Trade and Labor Assembly, and the Central Labor Union. Reflecting workers' fragmentation by ethnicity, skill, and ideology, each represented various work and ethnic cultures. Generally speaking, skilled Anglo-American workers supported the Trades and Labor Assembly, while Irish Americans dominated the Knights. Other semiskilled and unskilled European immigrants with connections to socialist and anarchist groups formed the Central Labor Union. Despite this organizational division, over time the membership of these groups overlapped, and they occasionally cooperated openly. In 1886, there were 307 strikes in the city, a ninefold increase from each of the prior five years, showing that Chicago's workers were more organized and militant than they had ever been.[13]

Instead of 1886 inaugurating a new era of labor activism, however, the radical potential of the year's militancy was squashed in light of labor's demand for an eight-hour day. What began as a powerful and united labor movement of about eighty thousand demonstrating publicly in Chicago for an eight-hour day ended two days later when an unknown person threw a bomb into a crowd of protesters and police in Haymarket Square, killing seven police officers and four workers. In the bomb's aftermath, tremors of fear and hysteria rocked the nation, shaking Chicago with particular force. Police rounded up labor and anarchist leaders, shut down labor and radical presses, and arrested eight suspects for what would become an internationally followed trial resulting in the suicide of one, the acquittal of three, and the hangings of Adolph Fischer, George Engel,

Albert Parsons, and August Spies, a group who became honored in Left circles as the Haymarket martyrs.[14]

People such as Hammersmark were deeply affected by the state killings of these labor radicals and joined with thousands of the city's labor boosters, including singing societies; members of the carpenter, baker, saddler, wagon maker, cooper, brewer, and furniture-worker unions; unorganized groups of workers; sections of the city's Central Labor Union; and bands, in a march to protest their hanging, but such a display of sympathy for radicals was to become unique during the repressive months that followed. Quickly and with force, the city's clergy, newspapers, and public opinion turned against labor agitation of all kinds. Meanwhile, the Knights of Labor and Trades and Labor Assembly took strong stands against anarchism, driving a wedge between Chicago's more traditional labor unionists and those who hoped to spark militancy. For a time, radical movements and their adherents in the city seemed defeated.[15]

Hammersmark was one among several who spent the following years looking for answers outside of organized labor and radical movements. From 1889 through 1893, he studied in a seminary. As it turned out, though, religion was not for him: just before becoming ordained as a minister, he did an about-face and joined a generation of Chicago's working-class radicals in declaring himself an atheist. In his continuing search for answers, Hammersmark began mingling with Chicago's progressive literary world. The written word and its distribution would become the focus of his activism for years to come, joining him to those throughout the country who maintained this labor and leftist tradition.[16]

In the midst of Hammersmark's soul searching, the 1894 Pullman strike again focused the nation's attention on Chicago's labor movement. This time Hammersmark joined anarchists and Socialists, who watched from the sidelines as skilled and unskilled workers united against Chicago's industrial magnate George Pullman. Thousands of Chicago workers in and around the railroads ensured that at least between June 29 and July 8 no trains left the city. As in the railroad strike of 1877, the power of the government through the military eventually subdued their efforts, but this time workers had managed a greater feat, as the thousands of skilled and unskilled workers represented a broader ethnic mix. The potential of workers from different ethnic and skill backgrounds to join and challenge industrial capital would carry into the imagination of labor radicals of the next century.[17]

Before then, strength returned to the Socialist movement when workers began to rally behind such new leaders as Eugene V. Debs, who, fresh from the Pullman conflict, directed militant workers toward the revived Socialist Party of America. With such activity, Chicago remained at the center of radical gatherings, and new labor movements formed. Hammersmark made his contribu-

Samuel Hammersmark, early 1930s.
(Chicago Historical Society, ICHi-
39208, photographer unknown)

tion to the rebirth of the Socialist movement through his creation in 1904 of
the Hammersmark Publishing Company. He printed and distributed works by
Clarence Darrow, Edgar Lee Masters, and John Altgeld, the governor of Illinois
who pardoned the last of Haymarket's victims. And he eventually made his way
to Washington State to help Lucy Parsons, the widow of the Haymarket martyr
Albert Parsons, put out *Why?* from Tacoma. In the few years he spent in Tacoma
before returning to Chicago, Hammersmark extended his activities and interests, like the Haymarket anarchists before him, to include the labor movement.
He helped organize retail clerks in Seattle and Tacoma and eventually became
head of Tacoma's trade council.[18]

In 1905, Hammersmark reinforced his interest in labor by attending the
founding convention, in Chicago, of a new anarcho-syndicalist organization, the
Industrial Workers of the World (IWW). This convention brought together the
nation's leading labor radicals: Bill Haywood, secretary of the Western Federation of Miners; Eugene V. Debs, leader of the American Socialist party; Mother
Jones, the fighter for miners' rights; Daniel De Leon, the leader of the Socialist Labor party; Lucy Parsons; and hundreds of others from various Socialist
and anarchist organizations. The IWW's purpose was to launch a dual form of
revolutionary unionism that would challenge the American Federation of Labor
(AFL), the main labor federation dedicated to the organization of skilled craft
workers. That radical workers were frustrated with the AFL was not surprising.
Even though some AFL locals had a Socialist presence, the AFL as an organiza-

tion lacked interest in the unskilled, unorganized, and nonwhite. These IWW members hoped to build a separate, competitive, militant labor organization open to workers of all backgrounds and skill levels.[19]

As an IWW "Wobbly," Hammersmark met labor radicals who disagreed with the IWW's dual-unionism strategy. These activists believed that the IWW's tactic of creating militant unions in opposition to AFL unions isolated militants, confused rank-and-file workers, and hampered the ability of activists to inspire workers to action. One of the leading advocates of the need to work within established AFL unions was William Z. Foster, a future leader of the American Communist party. Unable to convince the IWW's leadership of dual unionism's futility, Foster abandoned the IWW in 1912 and formed a new organization modeled after a revolutionary syndicalist organization he had seen at work in France a few years earlier. With a core of labor radicals, Foster launched the Syndicalist League of North America (SLNA) in Chicago, where the heart of its membership was based. SLNA members, about two thousand of whom were drawn from the IWW and fledgling anarchist organizations, joined local AFL unions and focused on organizing the unorganized.[20]

Meeting William Z. Foster made an imprint on Hammersmark and affected his political future.[21] Hammersmark quickly joined Foster and became friendly with his SLNA group, a core of whom, like Hammersmark, had connections to the Haymarket revolutionaries of 1886. Other former Wobblies from the city brought the "Chicago Idea," so prominent among Haymarket anarchists, with them into the new organization.

The SLNA only survived two years before its overly decentralized structure disintegrated. It was followed by an equally fleeting organization, the International Trade Union Educational League (ITUEL). Although small and ineffectual, these organizations succeeded in important ways. They brought together a core of activists who had experience in Chicago's distinct radical labor milieu and were committed to making established unions militant centers of revolutionary activity. They found themselves in the center of what would be some of the nation's biggest wartime labor conflicts. When they finally joined the Communist party, their leadership, contacts, and experience in Chicago's labor movement offered Chicago's Communists a bona fide opportunity for a mass base in the unions.[22]

In the meantime, these activists' poor record in the SLNA and the ITUEL in no way readied them for what was to come, first in the packing industry and then through the nation's steel mills. Part of their success was certainly due to the economic and political context of the wartime period, but credit for Chicago's wartime labor activity also needs to extend to the support of the CFL and the leadership of John Fitzpatrick. In his writings, Foster credits ITUEL militants with making the CFL "the most progressive labor council in the United States."

Certainly people like Johnstone and Hammersmark helped. At various times, the CFL assigned Hammersmark as an organizer to the rubber workers, candy workers, and bakery and confectionery workers. But leaders in the federation established their own path of progressive labor leadership even before the ITUEL militants came on board.[23]

Fitzpatrick had joined with Edward Nockels in taking control of the CFL from "Skinny" Madden and grafters from the building trades.[24] Once in charge, Fitzpatrick joined other progressives in helping organize the Amalgamated Clothing Workers and the International Ladies' Garment Workers. From 1917 through 1919, CFL activists under Fitzpatrick's leadership filled the Chicago Coliseum for a rally protesting the frame-up and imprisonment of California Federation of Labor's left-wing leader, Tom Mooney. They started their own local labor party, helped create a national one, fought against imperialism, and began an effort to bring unions within the railway industry into a single organization. Fitzpatrick was even willing to challenge the entrenched AFL leader Samuel Gompers, which resulted in the CFL losing its charter from time to time. That Fitzpatrick and his federation were willing to fight for Chicago's workers was not in question. What was unknown was whether he and the CFL were willing to cooperate fully with Foster and his group.[25]

In the summer of 1917 such questions began to dissipate when Fitzpatrick and the CFL supported Foster and about a dozen local unions with jurisdiction over packing workers, rail workers, and machinists to join a Stockyards Labor Council (SLC) and hash out a strategy to organize the city's packinghouses. Foster brought militants from his SLNA and ITUEL, including Hammersmark, to work tirelessly to bring workers to union organizations. The campaign initially focused on Chicago's five biggest packing plants and eventually grew to embrace cooperating packinghouse unions across the country into a national organization with Fitzpatrick as chairman and Foster as secretary. The threat of a national strike brought thousands of workers into previously moribund unions and attracted the attention of President Woodrow Wilson and his Federal Mediation Commission, whose members stepped in and provided arbitration for packinghouse workers throughout the country. By early 1918, the government agreed that packers needed to grant their workers an eight-hour day with ten hours' pay, overtime, wage increases, a guaranteed five-day workweek, and time off with pay for lunch for workers laboring in eight-hour shifts.[26]

With such a huge victory for packinghouse workers, Foster turned to the steel industry, where again he introduced a resolution to organize an industry of workers. This time his resolution called for a nationwide AFL joint campaign of unions with jurisdiction in the steel industry. CFL delegates unanimously supported the effort, only this time, organizers would not be as successful. Bucked by AFL leaders from its onset, the campaign to organize steel had a slow start, beginning only in Chicago and the Calumet region rather than in the fifty or so steel towns in which Foster had hoped to organize. In Chicago and Calumet, steel workers turned out to mass meetings, signed union cards, and showed the promise of a winning campaign. But its slow start, the end of the war, and steel industrialists' determination to keep their industry largely unorganized resulted in a stunning defeat. Despite the fact that the 1919 steel strike resulted in over 365,000 steel workers striking in fifty cities around the country, state violence and employer intimidation resulted in the strike being called off with few victories.[27]

The ability of the steel industry to stave off union organization hinted at the successes industrialists were to enjoy in the 1920s. Corporate welfare policies and company unions put a damper on the ability of militant unionists to make change through labor organizations. The Palmer Raids, named for Attorney General A. Mitchell Palmer, were government attacks on Socialist and union offices and homes and resulted in the deportation of suspected foreign-language-speaking threats. These federally mastered events, like the repression following Haymarket, quieted militant voices in political movements and union organizations alike and provided the context for the underground orientation of the Communist party in the early 1920s.[28]

Employer and government efforts to stomp out militancy and unionism were furthered by conflicts among workers themselves. In the summer of 1919, Jack Johnstone, on behalf of the SLC, organized an interracial march from the neighborhood adjacent to the stockyards, the Back of the Yards, through to the neighborhood populated predominately by African Americans, the Black Belt. Unfortunately for labor militants, this event's success was short-lived. Three weeks later, a race riot exploded on the city's South Side. Even though the riot started in response to violence on a beach rather than in a factory, racial tensions spilled over with devastating effects on interracial militancy in the labor movement. At the same time, patriotic fervor and nativism tore at the progressive CFL leadership, quieting any hopes of new, ambitious campaigns.[29] So defeated and divided for a time they might be, but Chicago's labor radicals, symbolic of the tradition of labor militancy that characterized the city, were not obliterated.

The Birth of Chicago's Communist Party

Just as Hammersmark spent the years between the Pullman strike and the birth of the IWW rethinking and operating in new political circles, a core of Chicago's labor militants spent the 1920s regrouping and readying for upcoming battles. They would do this through a new organization that many of them helped build. Like many of the radical organizations before it, the Communist Party of the

United States was born in Chicago. Inspired by the triumph of the Bolshevik Revolution, members of the Socialist party's left wing organized an American Communist party. These left-wing Socialists, dominated by semi-autonomous foreign-language federations, came to American Communism with their own newspapers, cultural groups, institutions, and willingness to quarrel. Their early enthusiasm to create an American Communist party quickly disintegrated, however, into wrangling over the timing of the new organization's birth. One group, which included most of the foreign-language federations, argued that an American Communist party must be established immediately in June 1919. The other, which included more native-born radicals, wanted to wait ten weeks until the Socialist party's convention, in hopes of gaining its support. Resentment, hubris, and personality conflict resulted in the formation of two parties in 1919: a Communist party and a Communist Labor party. Through 1923, their members seemed to do little else but disagree over internal questions facing their organizations. Moving from the issue of unification between the groups to the feasibility of maintaining an underground organization, those interested in creating an American Communist party remained a small, internally focused bunch. By 1923, with the aid of Communist leaders in the Soviet Union, American Communists settled on an above-ground organization called the Workers (Communist) Party of America, a name they would use until 1929, when they switched to the Communist Party of the USA.[30]

Once in the party, recruits found an elaborate, hierarchical structure awaiting them, which fit them in at its bottom while connecting them to a leadership in the Soviet Union, who sat at its top. There stood the Communist International, or Comintern. Founded by Lenin in 1919, the Comintern was the international headquarters of the Communist movement, the place where party leaders the world over met to make strategy, solve problems, and receive orders. Stalin's rise to power in the 1920s consolidated Soviet government control over the Comintern and the policies of Communist parties around the world.[31] The American party, with its offices in New York, was always one of the smallest and less significant of the international movements. Regardless, its leaders maintained the same organizational structure found in other party headquarters. A Central Executive Committee (CEC, known as the Central Committee from 1929 on) represented the party's top national leaders. A smaller committee, the Political Committee (or Polcom), oversaw party policy between CEC meetings, and an even smaller secretariat ran the party's daily activities. Small departments in the national office oversaw such specific activity as women's work, propaganda, and organizational efforts. Jay Lovestone led America's Communists as the general secretary from 1927 through 1929, when he was expelled and replaced by Earl Browder, who served in that capacity through the Popular Front period.

Lovestone's expulsion dramatizes James R. Barrett's observation that "until the mid-1930s, power on the Central Committee derived not from the authority of one individual but from a series of shifting alliances."[32]

Directly under the national party's command were eighteen districts, each representing cities. Chicago was the headquarters of the party's Eighth District, second in size to New York. In addition to Chicago, the district included industrial areas in Indiana, Wisconsin, and southern Illinois. Delegates voted at district conferences for anywhere from fifteen to nineteen party members to lead them. Once picked, the district committee elected an executive committee of three to seven leaders, whom they called the secretariat or buro. The secretariat then divided various office responsibilities among themselves.[33]

Under the district leaders were leaders of city sections, regions of a city that in turn were organized by neighborhood and shop groups, known as nuclei or units. Delegates to section conventions, picked from among their best unit leaders, chose a section organizer and an executive committee of nine to eleven, who in turn were supposed to elect a buro of three to four. Representing the most capable organizers coming out of the rank and file, section leaders participated in the activities carried on by their nuclei as well as the work organized by leaders at the district level. From 1928 through 1935, the number of sections increased from five to thirteen, reflecting the party's increase from an organization with just over six hundred members to one with over three thousand.[34]

The nucleus or unit was at the structure's lowest level. Shop and street nuclei, units of ten to fifteen people, were to bring Communist ideals to factories, schools, and residential areas throughout the city. Members in good standing elected three to five leaders from the active, capable, and willing—the number depended on the unit's size. The leaders then met and selected which of them would be their agitation and propaganda director (in charge of explaining party campaigns to the masses and raising members' political awareness through readings and discussion), their financial secretary, and their lead organizer. As such different issues as women's rights and black equality pressed on the party, national leaders would send word all the way down to unit leaders, directing them to elect one of their own to take charge of these initiatives. In addition to providing opportunities to lead, units were responsible for educating each other about Marxism and their movement; selling party literature; circulating petitions; doing face-to-face organizing; and reporting to section leaders, higher in the party's hierarchy.[35]

When Communism came to Chicago, Hammersmark had been experimenting with Foster's Trade Union Educational League (TUEL).[36] Its purpose was similar to the SLNA and the ITUEL, but TUEL activists had the advantage of international support. As it turned out, Lenin's writings confirmed the TUEL's tactics of working to radicalize established unions from the inside, as mem-

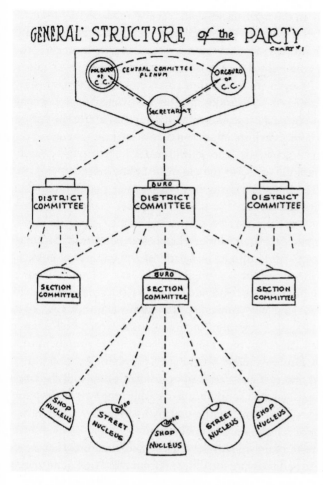

General structure of the American Communist party as illustrated in the April 1931 issue of the *Party Organizer*.

bers of these unions—Communists referred to this activity as "boring from within"—and the Communist International's Red International of Labor Unions (RILU) supported the strategy at its first congress. These encouragements gave Foster and his TUEL more authority in radical circles than they previously could muster on their own. They also made Foster and his cohort of labor militants more disposed to Communism. Still, before they joined, each activist had to be convinced that the party's focus on revolutionary political action was correct. Coming from a syndicalist framework that valued economic action above any other kind, Foster and his fellow labor militants needed time to reconsider their political assumptions.[37]

Even before attending the RILU conference in Moscow, Foster had begun to rethink the value of political action. He remembered, "As a result of my own experience, especially in the meat-packing and steel campaigns, the need for political action had been gradually dawning upon me and I began more and more to feel that it was not a wise policy that tried to restrict the struggle of the workers solely to the economic field."[38] Before leaving for Moscow, Foster joined the Chicago-centered movement for a Labor party. Watching the weakening of syndicalism in Europe; the collapse of the London Triple Alliance among miners, railroaders, and transport workers; the success of the Russian Revolution; and syndicalists' and anarchists' attacks on the Soviet government and the RILU when he was in Moscow, Foster secretly joined the party in the summer of 1921 and waited until the spring of 1923 to make public his move.[39]

Back in Chicago, Hammersmark was also unsure of Soviet Communism. Moving in CFL circles and having also served as the secretary of the Cook County organization of the Farmer-Labor party when Fitzpatrick ran for mayor as a Farmer-Labor candidate, Hammersmark, like Foster, had already begun to question his purely syndicalist attitudes and had tested the waters of political activism by the time the American Communist party was founded. In Farmer-Labor party circles, Hammersmark befriended Charles Krumbein, a product of the Socialist party's left wing, who joined the Communist Labor party in 1919 and worked with radical Chicago unionists to build the Farmer-Labor party. A future delegate to the CFL from the Plumbers' Union, it was Krumbein who most effectively made Hammersmark "see the need for political action."[40] Discussions like this and observations like Foster's resulted in most of the labor TUEL militants joining Chicago's Communist party, where they would continue their project, which was undermined in the aftermath of World War I, of bringing a multiethnic workforce into multiethnic unions.

Initially, American Communism represented a conglomeration of leftist cultures, traditions, and experiences not too different from those that came before it. "The Bolshevik revolution in Russia of November 1917," writes Theodore Draper, "did not immediately displace these older traditions."[41] This was the case in Chicago, where TUEL militants mingled with an assortment of ethnic and native-born radicals. Alfred Wagenknecht, the son of a German shoemaker, fled from Germany with his family to avoid antisocialist laws. Joining the left wing of the Socialist party, Wagenknecht played a crucial role in forming the Communist Labor party, the United Communist party, and finally the Workers (Communist) party. Nicholas Dozenberg, an immigrant from Riga, Latvia, and a member of the International Association of Machinists, became business manager for the Communist paper *The Voice of Labor* in 1921. They were joined in the party by Joseph Podulski, a former member of the Socialist party in Poland and the United States, who was also a member of the International Ladies Garment Workers Union. Ellis Chryssos, born in Turkey to a family whose members became refugees in Greece, edited *Empros*, a weekly organ of the Workers party's Greek Federation, and acted as the federation's secretary. Arne Swabeck, a Danish immigrant and former IWW and Socialist party member, became a leader in Seattle's 1919 general strike before coming to Chicago. Swabeck served as head of Chicago's Workers party at the same time that he acted as a CFL delegate from the Painters' Union. Vittorio Vidali came to Chicago in the early 1920s fresh from antifascist battles in Italy and eager to become involved in the Italian American Communist movement.[42]

Vidali commented on the diversity of experience he found in Chicago. One cold and snowy morning, he made his way into the party's main office on North State Street: "The desks were scattered around the room without any definite plan. The Yugoslavs, the Greeks and the Latin-Americans were next to us Italians. The richer sections which had their own headquarters in Chicago or in New York, daily paper and periodicals, such as the Russians, the Jews, the Finns, the Poles and others, had their own desk also in this big room where all the nationalities were represented. In one corner sat the general secretary of the Party, C. E. Ruthenberg with his secretary. There was a constant buzz of voices in all the languages of the world, sometimes interrupted by a laugh, exclamations and the clicking of the typewriters."[43]

The international buzz among the city's national leaders hinted at the clamor audible whenever Communists assembled at their citywide social gatherings. Communist events, like the one organized in Wicker Park for about fourteen hundred Scandinavian and Jewish people in 1923, represented the international unity and cultural dynamism that Soviet Communism represented to many of its adherents and sympathizers. Here, in the words of a *Scandia* reporter, "a string orchestra, consisting mostly of mandolins, played revolutionary music." Next, the *Freiheit* singing society, a group of one hundred, sang classical Jewish songs. These musical numbers culminated in the reading of "The Last Revolution," a text written by Michael Gold that was musically accompanied by a Jose Ramirez score.[44]

By the time of Vidali's visit in 1923, the party's national headquarters had moved from New York to Chicago, where it would remain until 1927. In Chicago, working-class ethnics with their own cultural connections to leftist movements were joined by a core of veteran American trade unionists, some of whom had made their way from labor struggles in the West. Earl Browder had been active in Kansas City's labor and socialist organizations since 1907 and had recently served a prison sentence for resisting the draft. William Dunne worked as a union organizer for the International Brotherhood of Electrical Workers on the West Coast before becoming involved in a strike near Helena, Montana, where he was a leader on a strike committee and editor of the Montana State Federation of Labor's newspaper. After the strike's defeat, Dunne was elected as a state legislator on the Democratic ticket. He also served as vice president of the Montana Federation of Labor and in 1919 became a charter member of the Communist Labor party.[45]

With party headquarters in the city and leaders' focus on trade-union militancy, Chicago's party attracted radicals from far and wide. Manuel Gomez, an experienced representative of the RILU from the Latin American Bureau, arrived in Chicago in 1922 with a desire to be known among Chicago's party members as a rank-and-file worker rather than a party leader. After securing a job at Sears Roebuck as a mail-order correspondent, he sought out the city's Communists. Doing a "bit of probing," he came upon a newsstand on West Madison that sold the *Voice of Labor*, a once-independent paper that was now under the party's aegis, immediately putting him on the trail. Making his way to the paper's office, he met the editor Jack Carney and the columnist Tom O'Flaherty and was brought by these two Irish immigrants to his first Chicago meeting. After answering questions about his background, Andrew Overgaard, whom Gomez remembered as "a scrawny Scandinavian," invited him to a meeting of the "real Party."[46]

Chicago's proletarian reputation and trade-union orientation overshadowed the intellectual character of its members. It was common for members of New York's largely college-educated leadership to describe Chicago's activists as "trade-union idolaters and inferior Marxists."[47] And while most of Chicago's leaders were self-educated, blue-collar workers active in trade-union movements, they were also intellectuals. Foster was a prolific writer who was well versed in Marxist theory. Hammersmark mixed labor organizing with intellectual endeavors as he mingled with progressive literary types and published and distributed socialist writings. The milieu in which Chicago's worker-radicals operated made this combination fairly common. In the early 1920s, this was especially true on Chicago's Near North Side, where an eclectic mix of pickpockets, literary figures, labor leaders, radicals, intellectuals, and prostitutes mingled in Jack Jones's Dil Pickle Club while they read poetry, watched dramas, and debated political questions of the day. Foster and other Communists were regulars at the club. They also participated in the lively intellectual banter that carried on just outside of the club at Bughouse Square, a public site where debaters, soapboxers, and eclectic thinkers harangued hecklers, onlookers, and ideologues.[48]

Hammersmark straddled this proletarian/intellectual divide by helping found the party's official English-language newspaper, the *Daily Worker*. Gil Green, a future national party leader, remembered the excitement that met the paper's birth: several thousand supporters packed the Ashland Auditorium for the *Daily Worker*'s inaugural rally and proudly walked across the stage dropping money into a barrel to raise operating funds. Eventually, the paper's offices would move to New York, leaving Hammersmark behind to establish Chicago's Modern Bookstore, which became a party hangout and center for the distribution of Communist literature. Until then, Hammersmark helped the *Daily Worker* publish party documents and theses, establishing it as the official voice of American Communism.[49]

The creation of an English-language paper occurred on the heels of the party's 1925 reorganization, when Communist leaders attempted to change its structure from one based on the Socialist party's foreign-language units into one organized by neighborhoods and factories. Party leader Steve Nelson recalled, "[O]f a membership of some seventeen thousand, fewer than two thousand were involved in English-speaking groups, and it was seen as imperative to get beyond the language barrier."[50] Leaders hoped that by grouping members where they lived and worked rather than by the language they spoke, they would nudge them closer to Americanization and the American labor movement. At least initially, it looked like Chicago's party was experiencing success. A 1925 report indicated that out of 930 registered members, 340 were in trade unions. The unions most represented by the factory groups included clothing, machinists, printing, railroad, and steel industries. Other lesser Communist trade-union outposts included building trades, the teachers' federation, United Wallpaper trades, egg inspectors, laundry workers, musicians, watch- and clockmakers, cigar makers, milk drivers, IWW window washers, janitors, leather workers, newspaper drivers, butchers, and coopers. Regardless of union, party leaders were interested in creating a connection to the city's workers. Even when reporting on the street nuclei, party leaders were concerned with their potential to reach out to workers. Chicago's head of party organization made this point well: "We are by no means underestimating the importance of the street nuclei, but we are at the same time emphasizing to them that the street nuclei must be transformed or developed into a shop nuclei."[51]

Martin Abern, Chicago's organizational secretary during restructuring, initially reported that reorganization enlivened Chicago's Communists and better prepared them to connect to fellow American workers. Nine out of ten former dues-paying members re-registered in Chicago as Communists following the reorganization, a significantly higher proportion than the national average of 50 percent.[52] Foreign-language-speaking Communists reported satisfaction with the "change which makes it possible for them to learn the English language and really participate in the American labor movement." In the street nuclei, Communists reported that they "cannot be so lax as they have been in the former language branches. Work is being demanded of them."[53]

Even in his enthusiasm, however, Abern hinted at the problems reorganization created. Members of this heavily foreign-born organization did not mingle easily outside their ethnic enclaves. Communists in the steel industry had the greatest difficulty because no English-speaking comrades worked there, bringing Communists to exist in "very much mixed national units" and complicating the ability of activists to communicate and act together. In addition, Abern admitted that not all of the language federations supported the reorganization: the Finnish and Lettish groups opposed openly.[54]

Party leaders also found that despite their attempts to Americanize their membership, street organizations still tended to group Communists according to ethnic background. Czechs, for example, populated seven different street branches, including one exclusively for women. Their organization was matched by the Lithuanians, who also maintained seven neighborhood branches. The Scandinavians organized three, including a former Socialist club known as their Karl Marx branch, one in Lakeview, and one on the South Side. Two Polish branches met, one on the North Side and one on the South Side. The Ukrainians also maintained two branches. Russians, Armenians, Rumanians, Spanish speakers, and Bulgarians each maintained one branch in a neighborhood where each had a dominant presence.[55]

As it turned out, Abern's initial reports of ethnic enthusiasm proved hollow. Communist party leaders, who worked diligently to keep these formerly Socialist nationality-based groups within the party, recognized their persistent independence. A tenuous bind held Armenians to the party, and records show that Czech number 3 was "not extremely convinced but follow[ing] along." At one point in 1925, party leaders conceded they had lost their Italian connections, but by the year's end, the situation had improved. In the Eleventh Ward, twelve of eighteen members agreed to stay in the party, and almost 70 percent of those in the Nineteenth Ward agreed to remain Communists. Others in the Thirty-first Ward and in Cicero still had to be contacted individually.[56]

Establishing strong connections between this heavily ethnic and foreign-born community and the American labor movement became a central concern of party leaders and one that overshadowed the fluctuation of women in the party. It was not that women were inactive at the dawning of Chicago's Communist movement. The names of Helen Kaplan, Lydia Beidel, Dora Lifshitz, Clara Rodin, Elsa Bloch, Ethel Flegel, and Lydia Gibson dot pages of party reports, minutes, and letters. In these early days of party organization, however, women's participation was not a central concern of the male leaders. Most pioneer women Communists, such as Lifshitz and Rodin, were active in garment or needle trades. Some, such as Lydia Gibson, were married to party leaders. Others, such as Flegel, continued the work they had done in Socialist federations, only now under the Communist party's banner.[57]

A mix of men and women, including Tom O'Flaherty, Harrison George, and Helen Kaplan, coordinated women's political work. Plans for new efforts to reach women focused on industry. In one instance, planners discussed working through the Women's Trade Union League to form a Chicago Federation of Working-Class Women. Little resulted from their efforts, and when housewives dropped away from the movement during the party's reorganization, leaders were not overly concerned. One report indicated that in 1925 about 50 percent of the members from two Chicago Finnish branches had come into the newly reorganized party. The report's author indicated that 50 percent is "what we can expect at best . . . since these two branches had a far greater share than did any other branches, of housewives members, who were merely attached to the former language units because their husbands were."[58]

Equally marginal to the central concerns of this early party were the handful of African Americans who attended its meetings. The majority came out of the African Blood Brotherhood (ABB), an organization whose members expressed national revolutionary ideas and rallied in opposition to Marcus Garvey and his pro-capitalist United Negro Improvement Association (UNIA). Those twenty-five or so in the ABB who gravitated to Communism had a strong presence among black building tradesmen, plumbers, electricians, bricklayers, and stockyard workers. Edward Doty, a plumber, led Chicago's ABB and had already organized the American Consolidated Trades Council, a federation of black unions in the building trades that collaborated with Foster's TUEL. He was joined by Herman Dorsey, an electrician; Alexander Dunlap, a plumber; Norval Allen, Gordon Owens, and H. V. Phillips from the stockyards; and Otto Hall, a railroad porter. Some had spent time in the Garvey movement; others were associated with the Free Thought Society, an organization that held forums and participated in a political challenge to the old-guard Republicans in the city. Harry Haywood remembered first seeing these black Communists at open-air forums and at the Dil Pickle Club. According to Haywood, African Americans who joined the party "were the types who . . . kept abreast of the issues in the Southside community and participated in local struggles."[59]

When they got to the party, however, blacks found that its members did not recognize their problems as being any different than those of white workers. Public support won by the UNIA and prodding by members of the ABB encouraged white Communists to rethink the connection between capitalism and race. But it was leaders in Moscow who really gave the American party a push. With support from the Soviet Union, American Communists focused on the building of the American Negro Labor Congress (ANLC), an organization dedicated to organizing black workers. American party leaders hoped to build an organization led by black workers and open to whites with connections to civil rights groups throughout the black community. The organization hobbled along into the early 1930s but never reached a level of stabilization or success. From the onset, organized labor and conservative black leaders attacked the ANLC as Communist and therefore duplicitous. Black Communists did not help matters. At the ANLC's opening meeting in the heart of Chicago's black neighborhood, a Russian drama group performed a play in Russian. There were no black performers on the program. Robert Minor and his wife, Lydia Gibson, kept the ideal of interracial organization alive by opening their South Side apartment to serve as what Harry Haywood remembered as a "virtual salon where Black and white friends would gather to discuss the issues of the day."[60] But as for the ANLC, its Chicago membership, one of the largest in the country, hovered around fifty members.[61]

Thus, the diversity of opinion and culture that grew from its members complicated efforts to build a Communist movement in Chicago. Compounding the problem was the Soviet party and its leaders' authority in settling conflicts and setting priorities. In its earliest days, the Comintern did not have much effect on American Communists. "Except for references to 'Soviets' and 'dictatorship of the proletariat,'" writes Theodore Draper, the American party's programs "still reflected more of the movements of the past—socialism and syndicalism—than of the movement of the future, Communism." But by the summer of 1920, the Comintern established itself as the ultimate authority on political questions and began issuing orders to the American party to unify its members and begin working within the AFL.[62] The increasing role of the Comintern in settling differences and setting priorities distinguished American Communism from the radical movements that preceded it. In the early 1920s, the American party's relationship to the Comintern resulted in systematic consideration of the "Negro Question" in the United States, but it also fanned factional flames among party leaders and isolated Chicago's trade unionists from their former allies.

William Z. Foster and Chicago's group of trade-union activists were at the center of these early factional fights. From Foster's earliest days as the leader of the party's trade-union efforts, a major split developed, pitting Foster and his proletarian supporters against Charles Ruthenberg, Jay Lovestone, Bertram Wolfe, and other intellectuals based largely in New York. In the decade to come, party leaders understood all manner of differences of opinion between members to be a result of one's alignment with the "majority" or "minority" groups. One Chicago party member explained, "Charlatans have a hold of our Party. All matters of the Party are considered by them from the point of whether or not the present majority will benefit." Viewing each political assignment and leadership appointment through the perspective of factionalism, one Communist pleaded with Lovestone to "find some way of settling down this district. This transition period is not very healthy and should not be prolonged unnecessarily."[63]

These factional struggles complicated Communists' relationship to Chicago's labor movement. The main debacle centered on the formation of a Farmer-Labor party. Successful unions throughout the country developed the idea for a national party at a November 1919 Chicago conference. By 1922, John Fitzpatrick, who had become a leader in the Farmer-Labor party movement, invited Foster and his trade-union activists to participate. Along with Foster, the Communists

Jack Johnstone, Arne Swabeck, Charles Krumbein, and Earl Browder responded positively. But what began as a unified effort between party and non-party labor activists quickly broke down due to Communist tactics and pressures from an increasingly repressive environment. The formal split occurred when Fitzpatrick asked for a delay in a 1923 Farmer-Labor party convention in order to better organize a following. While Foster and his supporters understood the need for mass support, the Communist party's New York leadership saw no reason to wait. With Comintern backing, they engineered a split between Chicago's Communists and Fitzpatrick. The convention, which initially seemed to be a success, resulting in the formation of a nationally federated Farmer-Labor party with Communists in control of most positions, ended as a fiasco with little support outside of party circles. Without Fitzpatrick's support, Chicago's Communist trade unionists became exposed to conservative attacks from Gompers and AFL unionists who shared their leader's disdain for Communists. Foster and James Cannon wrote, "In Chicago, which was once our chief stronghold, our alliance with the progressives has been broken. . . . [O]ur comrades are largely isolated and face a united front of all other elements against them."[64]

The Bolshevik Revolution sparked the imagination of liberals and radicals throughout the United States. Immediate postwar uprisings across the country suggested the possibility that the revolutionary fervor that swept Russia might enliven American workers. Militants rooted in Chicago's Socialist, anarchist, and militant trade-union traditions were swept into the American Communist movement and believed that their activity had a new urgency. This new radical organization, peopled by militants of older movements, quickly became the target of government attack and AFL animus. To most party members, this was the stuff of radical political undertakings. What was new, however, was the depths to which their leaders were now entangled in the realities of a centralized organization where priorities were set and disputes settled in Moscow. The willingness and enthusiasm of American Communists to hitch their movement to the Soviet Union might seem nonsensical to the twenty-first-century observer, but to many Chicago labor radicals it seemed the only rational course. The Soviet Union was the site of the only successful workers' revolution in the world and the only country predicting a continuation of their revolution in other nations. It was the home of the Comintern, an international arena for revolutionaries to meet and plan, and the only nation willing to support revolutionary education and training of its party's ranks. And for Hammersmark and his close allies in the party, Communist leaders in the Soviet Union were the only ones on the left who supported the kind of militant labor activism they believed most likely to lead workers to revolution.

In December 1927, five thousand people packed Chicago's Ashland Auditorium, listened to Communist speeches, and celebrated the ten years of struggle that had ensued since the Russian Revolution.[65] No revolution had so far developed in the United States, and yet the core of Chicago's Communists who stuck with the party, such as Hammersmark, had been raised in an environment where radical movements had their highs and lows. As members of the American Communist party, heirs to the workers' revolution that transformed the Soviet Union, and protectors of Chicago's militant labor traditions, they believed that revolutionary change was surely right around the corner. As it turned out, the party's current funk that kept its members at odds with one another and isolated from American workers was about to be challenged. While no socialist revolution ensued, the years 1928 through 1935 witnessed a rebirth of Chicago's party, inundating its rolls with newcomers and sparking militant activity among workers. To veterans such as Hammersmark, it would be worth the wait.

2

Revolutionary Recruitment: Numbers and Experience

On September 6, 1931, Bill Gebert, Chicago's leading Communist party official, stood before the city's most active party members and in his heavy Polish accent outlined his vision of a mass Communist movement in Chicago. By 1931, leaders such as Gebert believed that the city's Communist party was on the verge of a mass influx of members that would mark the beginning of a second American revolution. Although in hindsight this vision seems overly ambitious, at the time his prediction had some basis. That August, party activists successfully organized a demonstration where one hundred thousand black and white workers protested against Chicago's police, whose officers had shot and killed three African American, unemployed activists. Proudly recalling the attendance at the event, Gebert hinted at the local appeal of Chicago's party. Those at the demonstration were not all unemployed, he remembered. Instead, "Many of them are employed and many of them probably never came to any of our meetings before. They came as a result not only of our protest against shooting but as a protest against evictions, unemployment, wage cuts, because this demonstration signaled all this."[1]

Gebert found inspiration in the fact that employed people, with what he imagined were broad political interests, had found their way to a party demonstration. He hoped that improvements in the party's structure would result in increased recruitment among these employed workers, a category who party leaders in New York and Moscow believed, once radicalized, would serve as the vanguard in the upcoming workers' revolution. Gebert's observations reveal his preoccupation with the party's appeal among the employed and hint at party leaders' obsession with categorizing people. "Employed" and "unemployed" represent only two of these groupings; such others as "Negro," "unionist," "women,"

Bill Gebert, ca. 1936. (Chicago Historical
Society, ICHi-39210, photographer unknown)

"youth," and various foreign-language-speaking people figured prominently in
each party plenum, recruiting bulletin, and organizational outline.

The way Communists categorized people offers a sense of whom they favored and attracted. Local records make clear that Chicago's Communists were
disproportionately unemployed, foreign-born or African American, and male.
The party wanted to bring in women, youth, and employed workers but never
succeeded to the extent they believed possible. Occasionally they attracted unintended groups, such as intellectuals. And like intellectuals, Jewish recruits concerned them because Jews and intellectuals were not generally thought to work
in industry, where party leaders hoped to recruit their highest numbers.[2]

Party cataloging tells something of leaders' priorities and Communism's allure
among certain groups, but the party's statistics and categories do not provide
an adequate picture of its members. What appeal did Communism have for
people who were unemployed and ethnic, for example? Where were the party's
bases of support during the Third Period? To answer these questions, one can
turn to rich, individual stories to complement statistics and gain insight into
not only who became a member but also, occasionally, why.

Between 1928 and 1935, numbers of Chicagoans who joined the Communist party jumped from hundreds to thousands. Their composite profile never
met leaders' mandates, but it did reflect the demography of the city, its traditions, and the struggles of its activists. Chicago recruits were rooted in ethnic

groups, traditions, workplaces, neighborhoods, and causes. They were a diverse bunch. Held together by party structures, Chicago's Communists were anything but monolithic. Their varied interests, backgrounds, temperaments, and (un)willingness to devote themselves to party demands would result in large membership turnover and frustration among leaders, who pushed for recruitment but also wanted retention, particularly of employed and native-born workers. Chicago's leaders found that many roads led to Communism and that many different kinds of people traveled them.

Communist Recruitment: Goals and Reality

In Chicago, John Williamson assumed the main responsibility for Communist recruitment. He had immigrated to the United States from Scotland in 1913 at the age of ten after losing his father to a workplace injury. Leaving school after the eighth grade to help support his mother, Williamson worked as a press feeder, an apprentice shop's draftsman, and by the age of fifteen, as an apprentice pattern maker. The English and Scottish craftsmen he worked with took Williamson under their wing and taught him about "life, . . . trade unions, politics, and socialism." Williamson's initial foray into radical politics brought him to De Leonism and the Socialist Labor party, but once the Russian Revolution succeeded and Williamson began reading Lenin, Nicolai Bukharin, Karl Liebknecht, and Rosa Luxemburg, his loyalty waned. Through his activity at the Seattle Labor College, Williamson came in contact with numerous speakers, including William Z. Foster, whose new ideas about socialism and the revolution caused Williamson, at age nineteen, to leave the Socialist Labor party for the Communist party. Finding his way to Chicago, Williamson rose to be the Chicago party's second in command and its organizational secretary, and from 1930 through 1933, he worked closely with Gebert.[3]

Part of Williamson's job was to relate economic trends to organizing possibilities. The worsening Depression eased that task. From October 1932 to March 1933, when the economic crisis reached its greatest depths, between twelve and seventeen million workers found themselves unemployed, and another thirteen to seventeen million workers could only find part-time jobs. As business activity continued to decrease, industrialists threw thousands more out of work. By 1933, nearly one-third of the American labor force was unemployed, and by 1934, two and half million people had been unemployed for two or more years, and six million more had been jobless for one year. Even those who had jobs saw their pay decrease 20 to 30 percent.[4]

Chicago, with its broad industrial base, felt this crisis acutely. Company payrolls shrank one-quarter from 1927 to 1933, and only half of the people employed in manufacturing in 1927 still had a job in 1933.[5] Employers fired black

John Williamson, 1960s.
From *Dangerous Scot*, by John
Williamson. (Used with permission
by International Publishers)

workers so disproportionately at the Depression's start that by the end of 1932, 40
to 50 percent of workers concentrated in Chicago's Black Belt were unemployed.
Other neighborhoods were hit hard as well. In the Back of the Yards, Polish,
Lithuanian, and Mexican neighbors saw their local banks fail, businesses go
under, and small stores close. The Polish local soup kitchen, run by the St. John
of God Church, could not keep up with the hungry. A 1931 study by officials
at the Chicago Commons settlement, located on the West Side in a Polish and
Russian neighborhood near a number of light manufacturing plants, showed
that half of the 472 unemployed families from the neighborhood were headed
by men in their prime work age, below forty. The experience of unemployment was new for many of these families; most had never received any form of
charity before. School administrators' findings also raised concerns about the
Depression's effects. Before a Senate subcommittee, Chicago's education officials
reported that throughout the city children came to school without breakfast
and were anemic through "lack of proper nourishment."[6]

Williamson believed that Depression conditions would double Chicago's party
membership easily, so he pushed recruitment activity and included quotas in
citywide organizational newsletters, plans of work, and recruitment bulletins.
The "Lenin recruiting drive," a name given to an effort in 1931 and others like it

over the years, emphasized recruiting new members as part of all party activity. "What is necessary now," Williamson directed, "is to intensify the recruiting drive and keep it in the forefront of all activities." Leaders assigned each city section a quota of new members and reminded all low-level leaders that recruitment numbers "must be checked up at every nucleus meeting."[7]

To Williamson's dismay, in the early 1930s, Chicago's party never approached his recruitment goals. In an August 1932 organization letter, he warned that early results of a recruiting drive "don't show the slightest sign of an intensive drive for members."[8] If they were going to double their numbers, everyone had to act. But quotas were hard to fill because the extraordinary expectations of party leaders were based on the unrealistic assumption that an economic Depression would turn workers into revolutionaries. Workers' need for employment during the early Depression years discouraged many from publicly protesting their conditions, and even those willing to protest were not necessarily proto-Communists.

And yet, compared to previous years, enormous growth in membership characterized Chicago's Third Period. In 1928, Chicago had 650 members. In 1930, the number grew only slightly, to 683, despite increased recruiting. By 1931, the Lenin recruiting drive and small successes organizing among the unemployed brought the party its first leap, to 1,963 members. This total made Chicago home to almost one-quarter of the nation's Communists, second only to New York.[9] In 1932, membership in the party's neighborhood and shop organizations grew again, this time reaching 2,513 members and causing national leaders to recognize Chicago as the party's "most important district."[10] By 1934, the city's membership had increased five times from its 1928 size, and the number of sections in the city grew from six to thirteen. In November 1934, 3,303 people paid party dues in Chicago.[11]

National and city membership statistics obscure the actual number of people who joined the Communist party over time, since turnover was great.[12] Chicago felt this acutely. In 1930, the district issued nearly two thousand membership books from January through September but only received a third of that amount in dues sales in September.[13] In 1930, half of all new party applicants remained members less than a year. From July 4, 1931, through November 28, 1931, monthly turnover ranged from a low of 30 to a high of 97 percent. The greatest number of those leaving were new recruits; a good number of them would become vocally anti-Communist, but the majority would serve as allies and, ironically, even future recruits.[14] Party leaders took turnover seriously. Williamson called the city's high fluctuation rates "the most scandalous situation that could exist in the Party."[15]

Recruitment methods sometimes caused such high turnover. Nathan Glazer found on a national level that "when the Party made the strongest efforts to get

Table 2.1. Communist Party Membership, 1928–35[1]

Date	National	Chicago
1928	—	650
1930	7,500	683
1931	8–9,000	1,963
1932	12–14,000	2,513
1933	16–20,000	2,417
1934	24,500	3,303
1935	31,000	—

1. This table is intended to give a general overview of party growth. For Chicago's figures, I have used dues payers from 1928 through 1935. For national figures, I used Nathan Glazer's table in *The Social Basis of American Communism* (New York: Harcourt, Brace, and World, 1961), 92. For Chicago's numbers, I consulted "Letter to the CEC," n.d. [1928], the Russian Center for the Preservation and Study of Documents of Recent History fond (f.) 515, opis (op.) 1, delo (d.) 1334, listki (ll.) 43–45; Letter to Hathaway, 2 September 1930, d. 1956, l. 48; Party Registration—1931, n.d., d. 2464, ll. 93–104; Organizational Status of the CPUSA, 1932, d. 2618, l. 95; Analysis for Recruiting and Dues for the Month of November 1934, n.d., d. 3591, l. 39.

members, the members it got were the least satisfactory."[16] Chicago's recruitment drives reflected this phenomenon. One Chicago bulletin complained, "[C]omrades approached recruiting merely to make a record, regardless of whether the worker was the best type for the Party or not. Others handed in application cards which had never been written by the worker whose name appeared on it but by a friend. . . . The entire atmosphere was a hectic one, with everyone working to make records—with the result that we recruited application cards but not class conscious workers."[17]

Even when class-conscious workers were legitimately recruited, they were sometimes lost in the party's bureaucratic shuffle. Chicago's leaders pointed to the bad experience of one city section, where out of 178 applications received over a few months of 1932, the party made members out of only twenty. No report existed for 101 of the applicants; four could not be located; twenty-three moved; and five changed their minds. The remainder were "no good for the Party," "working nights," transferring to another party section, or, oddly, "too old to join."[18] Even when workers signed application cards, they did not always become members.

Those who did join sometimes quickly reversed their decision for the same reasons found in party districts throughout the country. According to Williamson, unsatisfactory political life within party units plus poor recruitment methods added up to 90 percent of their problem. Units where new recruits were supposed to have their first formal contacts with the party were not yet oriented toward the neophyte. They were notorious for not starting on time and for running well after 11 P.M. They were also known for not engaging members on concrete daily issues but instead for focusing on technical work that needed to be accomplished. Williamson complained: "[I]n one unit, a sincere and well meaning new member, only a few months in the Party, is made organizer, but the Section Committee never gave the nucleus personal attention. . . . The meeting is called for 8 but there are only three members plus the District Representative present at 8 P.M. Gradually others come and the meeting opens at 9 P.M. The Section Representative finally arrives at 9:30 and another 'leader,' the District Woman's Director, also does the nucleus a 'favor' by coming in at 9:30. A fine example. The nucleus organizer brings in an agenda of 15 points—all dry routine. No political content to the proposals—just a mere presentation that such and such must be done."[19] Unit members were also known to talk about party issues and campaigns in shorthand, using party lingo, and did not, according to Williamson, discuss "the content and basis of [a] campaign as well as all various aspects and also the political questions connected with it."[20]

If 90 percent of the problem had to do with recruiting methods and the life of the unit, perhaps the remaining 10 percent involved joiners talked out of party membership by what leaders referred to as "hostile influences." Certainly there might have existed any number of these influences discouraging new members from keeping their membership active. One organizational bulletin instructed Chicago's members to "[f]ind out what hostile influences he has around him which might drive him away from Party. Carefully help him overcome this."[21] And while instructions in the bulletin emphasized helping "him" overcome these influences, female recruits also had pressures from family and friends to spend less time with the party. A letter from a member of Chicago's ranks explained how a combination of these internal and external problems made itself felt: "I will be criticized next Tuesday night at the organizers' meeting because the unit is not larger; because I have not done more; because I did not attend some meeting or other. I work hard every day in a building as a painter. . . . I have a few there who read the *Daily Worker* and subscribe to it. I cannot break down the Catholic faith there and start a shop unit. I do the best I can. However no matter how much I do, I always hate to show my face because there are things I do not do that I was told to do. Directives, directives, directives. . . . I am getting tired. I am just as much a Communist as ever, but I am not 10 Communists. . . . I must sleep sometimes. . . . My wife won't stand for it either."[22] In dealing with these frustrations, those who stayed had to be particularly committed. In 1931, 73 percent of the party's members had joined within the past year, 12 percent between 1925 and 1929, and 15 percent between 1919 and 1924.[23] With only 27 percent of its membership base stable in this early period, many more Chicago workers shuffled through the Communist party than simple membership statistics suggest.

These high turnover rates troubled party leaders, especially when they reflected the loss of American-born workers. After all, if the American Communist party was supposed to be the vanguard of the American working class, then the people who joined and stayed should have been American working people. Nationally, though, scholars have determined that the organization failed to meet these goals and that during the Third Period, the party was overwhelmingly composed of the unemployed and foreign-born.[24]

The Chicago party's own records show that its membership matched these national trends and also reflected some of the city's unique population. Williamson and Gebert kept tabulations of what they believed to be Chicago Communists' most important characteristics. Such records obfuscate certain identities. "Jews" were the only religious group mentioned, even if it was done to identify a particular ethnicity rather than religious belief. Intellectuals were not officially recorded because they were not particularly valued for their creativity. Despite such shortcomings, the party's simplified categories help identify Chicago's Communists.

Looking over recruitment reports, Williamson was disgruntled to find that Communist recruitment was most successful among the city's unemployed. If national unemployment in 1932 and 1933, the worst years of the Depression, was running as high as 25 percent, Chicago's figures were significantly higher, and those in its black community higher still. In 1931, Chicago's overall unemployment rate reached 30 percent. One year later, the city's black workers faced an unemployment rate of 40 to 50 percent. But in a two-month period in 1931, the party brought in unemployed people at a rate of four unemployed to one employed person. In 1931, half of those in Chicago's party were unemployed. The effects were even greater on Chicago's black South Side, where unemployment was more concentrated. There, in 1933, 79 percent of party members, mostly African Americans, were without work. This trend of recruiting the jobless at a much greater rate than the employed continued even after Williamson left the district, through 1934. In October of that year, 72 percent of Communist recruits were unemployed. In part a reflection of the economic crisis and in part caused by the ensuing organizing initiated by Communists, the unemployed filled party ranks in Chicago throughout the period.[25]

In the early years of the Depression, Chicago's Communists were also largely proletarians. According to the 1931 district registration of its 1,963 members, only seventy-eight people described themselves as professionals or small businessmen, and 103 as housewives. The rest identified themselves with a variety of wage-earning occupations.[26] Most were from metalworking, building, and needle trades. These figures show that party members identified with particular occupations even though many were unemployed and therefore removed from the culture of the workplace, where they might be able to recruit fellow workers.

REVOLUTIONARY RECRUITMENT · 39

Unemployment also probably prevented many from keeping up dues payments to their individual unions. The sketchy figures available suggest that Chicago's members belonged to unions at a higher rate than the national party average, even though most of them did not belong to unions. Of those who listed occupations in the 1931 registration, 189 belonged to the party's "revolutionary" trade unions, and 207 joined other "reformist" trade unions. The national party average was only 15.9 percent, compared to Chicago's 23 percent. Contrary to national trends, however, more Chicago party unionists joined the reformist AFL than the party-sponsored Trade Union Unity League (TUUL). Party leaders were unhappy with low TUUL figures, but in fact, Communists' participation in the AFL provided them with wider contacts among Chicago's workers and more chances to influence the Chicago Federation of Labor, an important power base in the city.[27]

A minority of proletarian and union activists was American-born, but a high number of these were African American. The disproportionate number of African Americans in Chicago's party always helped soothe leaders' fears that their recruitment efforts among American-born workers were failing, even if they agreed that party organizers should be doing even better among "Negroes." Of all the cities in the United States with a large concentration of African Americans, Chicago was most successful recruiting blacks into the party.[28] In 1930, 233,903 African Americans lived in Chicago, 6.9 percent of the city's population, dominating a small region on the South Side. In 1932, however, 24.3 percent of party members were African American. These 412 black Communists represented the highest number of black party members concentrated in any city in the United States, including New York, where in 1932 seventy-four party members were African American.[29]

To the party's dismay, though, Chicago's black members followed national trends by drifting in and out of the party.[30] In 1932, the South Side section with the most concentrated black membership had over half its members join in the past year. By 1933, 58 percent of members in the section had joined in 1932, and only 10 percent before 1930.[31] Nathan Glazer suspects that this high turnover was because blacks "entered with the lowest degree of indoctrination, with the least commitment, with the least knowledge."[32] Certainly some African Americans fit these characterizations, but many who left were informed and committed but incensed over racial conflicts within the party.[33]

Immigrant Communist leaders regularly expressed disappointment at the party's ethnic composition. Organizing in Chicago's working-class neighborhoods and around its industries, Communists recruited from those areas with a disproportionate number of foreign-born workers, many of whom had connections to radical traditions. Chicago was an immigrant city, and its party reflected that character. The 1930 census shows that of 3,376,438 Chicagoans,

24.9 percent had been born in another country, while 52.3 percent of Chicago's party members were foreign-born.[34]

From available figures, it is clear that Russians, South Slavs, Lithuanians, Hungarians, and Finns were overrepresented, while Poles, Germans, Italians, and Mexicans were underrepresented.[35] Activities and traditions among some groups of ethnic workers made their membership in the Communist party more likely than others'. Charles Karenic, for example, a Slovak machinist, had been a member of the city's Socialist party. Already a politicized worker, Karenic became a Communist in June 1925. Knowing he had worked in industry since he was twelve, party leaders encouraged Karenic to help them organize there. While Karenic willingly extended his party activism out of his ethnic workers' clubs to industry, others were less eager to do so. Karenic also worked with fellow fraction members within his Slovak Workers Society to bring new recruits to the party. These fractions, consisting of members who worked together in mass organizations to voice party policies and positions, were the party's lifeline to all of its mass organizations.[36]

Table 2.2. Nationality Breakdown of Chicago's Foreign-Born Population and Foreign-Born Communist Membership, 1930–31[1]

Nationality	Chicago's Foreign-Born	Chicago's CP Foreign-Born
Russian	9.1%	14.5%
South Slavic	1.9	10.4
Lithuanian	3.6	9.9
Polish	17.3	6.5
Hungarian	1.8	6.5
German	12.9	5.5
Italian	8.6	5.3
Finnish	0.3	1.8
Mexican	2.2	0.6
Jewish	N/A[2]	22.0
Misc.	42.4	17.0

1. This table looks at each nationality's percentage of the total foreign-born population listed in the party's 1931 membership registration and compares it to the corresponding percentage of foreign-born in Chicago's population listed in the 1930 U.S. Population Census. Jewish members were identified in the party's registration and were treated within the party as a nationality rather than as a religious group.

2. The category "Jewish" does not appear in the 1930 Census. However, according to Irving Cutler, in 1931 approximately 16 percent of Chicago's population was composed of foreign-born Jews. He estimated that 45 percent of the Jewish population of three hundred thousand was foreign-born. See Irving Cutler, *The Jews of Chicago: From Shtetl to Suburb* (Urbana: University of Illinois Press, 1996), 126–27.

Leaders praised Karenic's willingness to organize in industry more than they did his essential foreign-language work among working people for whom English was a second language. The Communist activist Steve Nelson recalled, "[W]e had a lot of autonomy in our work in the [ethnic] lodges, for the main attention of both the district and national leadership of the Party was toward the trade union work."[37] And yet, despite the attention party leaders extended to industrial work, they still relied on these members of mass organizations at the party's fringes to mobilize people for rallies, demonstrations, and mass meetings.

Members of mass organizations, always more numerous than party members, were often sympathetic to Communist activities. These organizations provided rich recruiting grounds and allowed Chicago's workers to support particular pieces of the party's agenda without the same commitments required of party members. Some of the organizations that became known as Communist mass organizations, like the foreign-language groups involved in cultural, sport, and fraternal activities, predated Communism, while others were new. The International Workers Order (IWO), founded in 1930, provided insurance as well as a social outlet for ethnic working people and offered an additional arena for party activists to raise political questions and organize. In 1931, 1,444 party and non-party workers belonged to the IWO's branches (of which thirteen were Jewish, six youth, five Polish, four Ukrainian, one Greek, one German, and one Rumanian).[38]

In addition to those mass organizations related to ethnic groups, Communists joined civil rights groups and educational organizations that supported their general agenda. Once they became members of these groups, Communists, through their fractions, were supposed to nudge each organization's priorities toward those of the party. Such conformity was never perfect, but generally speaking, these organizations did not need much prodding. For example, the International Labor Defense (ILD) provided legal support to causes related to social justice. According to one party leader, Communists believed that "every worker on trial for radical or labor activity was a political prisoner." So party members participated in this organization to "teach the public as well as to preserve our valuable organizers," activities that were in line with the ILD's overall mission.[39] The Friends of the Soviet Union (FSU) was an organization designed to promote the country and defend it against slander in the United States. While the focus of the organization fit well with party loyalists, at times the lack of proletarians in the group's membership frustrated Communist leaders and gave party members in the FSU goals to work on.[40] Importantly, Communists did not numerically dominate these organizations. For example, in the FSU, only twenty of its 250 members were in the party, and only 150 of the ILD's 2,520 crossed membership rolls.[41] Such auxiliary organizations suggest a much wider support base than membership numbers allow.

Once in mass organizations, Communists were expected to engage in political work. No doubt, Communists in the party's John Reed Clubs believed they were doing just that. Thirty clubs around the United States beckoned proletarian writers and artists to gather, read, and publicly discuss and display their work, and an estimated 1,200 members throughout the nation rose to the call.[42] One article from Chicago's club newspaper explained how these activities were fundamentally different than one could expect from mainstream writers and artists: "At the bourgeois Art Fair, the artist is forced to become a petty shopkeeper. At the revolutionary exhibit, he becomes an active propagandist, revolutionary painter, and mass pedagogue."[43]

Chicago's John Reed Club met on the second floor of 1427 Michigan Avenue, just south of the Loop, where a room littered with cigarette butts and decorated with colorful murals depicting proletarian scenes greeted about a hundred members each Tuesday evening for discussions and each Saturday night for talks by invited speakers, some by such established writers as James T. Farrell.[44] Its members published their own magazine, *Left Front,* and sold the national leftist journal *New Masses* in the club office. Over time, the Chicago club would boast of its own accomplished leftist literary and visual artists, including Richard Wright, who at the time was beginning to publish in *New Masses* and another leftist journal, *The Anvil;* Nelson Algren, whose gritty depictions of Chicago's proletarian underworld would appear in novels, short stories, and on the pages of the *New Republic;* Howard Nutt, a poet and future editor of *Direction;* Meridel Le Sueur, a writer of short stories, poems, a novel, and essays that appeared in *American Mercury, Dial, The Anvil, New Masses, New Republic, Scribner's,* and *Yale's Review;* and Jan Wittenber, whom Algren's biographer described as "a painter with a Christ-like air whose work exalted the unity of the proletariat and appeared regularly in *Left Front.*"[45]

The John Reed Club provided a space for leftist writers and artists to support one another's work, to nourish leftist ideals, and to share these ideals with a wide audience. Meridel Le Sueur recalled, "'It was a very hard time to live to be a writer. The left was very severe on you. It had its own orthodoxy. . . . But it also summoned us forth. . . . We wouldn't have tried without them . . . the Communists gave us light and even love.'"[46] Wright, who later left the party angry and disheartened, recognized Chicago's club as his "first contact with the modern world." It also served as the vehicle to bring out his ideas. Wright wrote, "Indeed, we felt that we were lucky. Why cower in towers of ivory and squeeze out private words when we had only to speak and millions listened? Our writing was translated into French, German, Russian, Chinese, Spanish, Japanese. . . . Who had ever, in all human history, offered to young writers an audience so vast?"[47]

Wright was "impressed by the scope and seriousness" of the club's activity.[48]

The pages of *Left Front* reflect this ambitious agenda. Club members wrote essays and poems dealing with proletarian life and revolutionary hope. They also reported on political events of interest to revolutionary intellectuals, such as the French author Henri Barbuss's visit and speech in downtown Chicago on fighting war and fascism, and the Midwest John Reed Club conference held in Chicago's office.[49] Articles also departed into journalism, covering unemployment rallies and campaigns for racial equality in the city. Reports, poems, and articles reflected the political struggles in which Chicago's club members engaged. In its May–June issue of 1934, Chicago's club reported that members Mitchell Siporin and Ray Breinin created Public Works art murals, Henry Simon designed and painted scenery for a Chicago Workers' Theater production, Morris Topshevsky's drawings appeared in *Farmer's National Weekly,* and Jan Wittenber traveled around southern Illinois with the ILD.[50] Like club members in cities around the country, Chicago's members examined questions of justice and humanity as they set up art exhibits, wrote strike pamphlets, and participated in union pickets, party rallies, and neighborhood protests.[51]

Chicago's Communists organized as a fraction within the club and pushed party policy. Occasionally conflicts emerged between those with party connections and those without. Wright recalled that the painters in Chicago's club dominated the leadership and club policies; they were also the ones with party connections. The non-party group, dominated primarily by writers, thought the party made too many demands. Not only did the club have to sell the *Daily Worker* and the *New Masses* at each meeting, but the party taxed the clubs' resources for money, speakers, and people to paint posters. According to Wright, non-Communist club members learned how to use the party's lines against Communist club members. One time they successfully ran Wright—a non-Communist at the time—to lead the club, knowing that Communists would not vote against an African American. There were some things, however, that non-party members could not influence; even though club members preferred putting their energies into building *Left Front,* the party did not support it and eventually insisted that it be dissolved. Under Wright's protection, it continued through 1934, longer than most other cities' publications.[52]

Club members knew that party leaders valued industrial organizing more than the work of painters and writers. A Chicago club member, Abe Aaron, wrote to the writer Jack Conroy "'that the J.R.C. is regarded disdainfully and with tolerant amusement by a great number of comrades.'"[53] And while a few party club members, like Jan Wittenber, enjoyed time on the front line of class struggle, most were reluctant to participate in the party's work among the masses and were happier keeping their energies focused and contained in the artistic world. Algren, for example, never seemed comfortable at party meetings. "'Going to a meeting seemed to be painful for him,'" Meridel Le Sueur commented. "'He would be hanging around in back as if about to disappear.'"[54] Those who felt like Algren were more comfortable at the small weekly gatherings of party and non-party activists in the poet Larry Lipton's Near North Side house, where a much more "bohemian, emotive atmosphere than at the John Reed Club" prevailed. Lipton explained, "'Those who came to the house were brought under the influence of this more tender, artistic kind of love attitude . . . and some of them were influenced in that direction, although they felt guilty. It was against the Party line.'"[55]

It was likely this tendency that drove most working-class Communists to look down on these intellectuals as what one scholar describes as "effete, namby-pamby types who read 'bourgeois books' and who were therefore 'class traitors.'"[56] Abe Aaron made the difficult decision to abandon writing to become a labor organizer. In a letter to Conroy, Aaron expressed his ambivalence: "'Will I write, or will I continue as an active section functionary? When I told the committee how I felt, saying, was it a question of writing or of the section committee, I must choose writing, I was accused of individualistic tendencies. Hell, I tried to explain, it's not a question of giving up Party work but, rather, of giving up one type of Party work. It didn't go over so well.'"[57]

Such suspicion of purely intellectual types had a long tradition in Chicago, dating back to the party's earliest days. According to Harvey Klehr, this disdain was matched by national party leaders. Even though an unprecedented number of prominent non-Communist intellectuals supported William Z. Foster's 1932 bid for the presidency, ideological differences following the campaign between key non-party supporters and national party leaders ended the initiative and confirmed, at least to party leaders, that intellectuals were simply not sufficiently committed to Communism. One of Chicago's party members told Wright as much: "'Intellectuals don't fit well into the Party.'"[58]

More consistently active and aspiring Communists were members of the Young Communist League (YCL), a training ground for youth, the key to the party's future. Yet the ages of Chicago's members made clear that youth did not dominate. Of the 1,078 party members who reported their age in 1931, 11 percent were over fifty, 28 percent were between forty and fifty, 39 percent were between thirty and forty, 15 percent were between twenty-five and thirty, and 7 percent were twenty-five or younger. Only 22 percent of the party was under thirty, alarming leaders who understood the importance of bringing in young members to replenish the party's forces and who witnessed firsthand the militancy of young recruits they could claim.[59]

Problems with recruiting youth were matched by the difficulty in attracting women to the party. Communist teachings explained that women were oppressed as low-wage laborers and used by capitalists to undermine the male wage worker. Party leaders were supposed to view women as an important component of their organization and recruit them through shop work and neighborhood organizing.[60] *Working Woman* addressed specific problems of women, and Chicago's leaders encouraged their members to use it as a recruiting tool.[61] In neighborhoods, the party also set up the Working Women's Federation, an organization designed to mobilize working women from a variety of women's organizations, and had some success building on the federation's work. On March 8, 1930, for example, a thousand women showed up for the party's International Women's Day rally. Women organizers also brought thirty-nine women together for the Trade Union Unity League's first conference of working women. Half of them non-party, these women came from Western Electric, Majestic Radio, and various clothing, food, and chemical plants.[62]

These supportive showings turned out to be one-time events, though, because Chicago's party never put its resources into women's organizing, nor did the momentum to organize women ever build in this period. A 1931 city membership tally showed that only 262, or 15.5 percent, were women. Of these, 126, or 48 percent, identified themselves as working women. Williamson and others desired a better representation among working women, but the support women felt in the party, as women, varied. Often men participated in the women's department and on women's committees, but women found that they themselves were the only ones with enough interest to keep projects going.[63] Women like Anna Schultz criticized district leaders. She thought that as far as they were concerned, women could stay in the "toilet and play with the baby." Consistent placement of women's articles and reports next to youth pages and reports in newspapers and at meetings confirmed the secondary role women played in Chicago's party. Their representation in party iconography as hard-edged, industrial, masculine fighters betrayed the realities of the majority of them. And the fact that older and more respected men, like Alfred Wagknecht, were known in certain circles as womanizers made clear the reality of women's second-place status in the party.[64]

Not that organizing women was an easy task. Most working women lived outside early 1930s union culture.[65] AFL unions organized relatively small pockets of them, and Communist membership, heavily male, did not have many connections with women's departments in industrial workplaces. Party membership, moreover, became superfluous to women involved with Unemployed Councils or other party-affiliated groups because their spare time was already spent. Regardless, the party's male presence and style, through its language, iconography, and agenda, left a legacy that women activists would fight against through the next period of the Popular Front.[66]

Surprisingly, in their categorization schemes, party leaders did not distinguish ethnic or racial characteristics among their female recruits. Certainly, Chicago's African American women, for example, participated in Third Period party activity, but little is recorded about them as a group. Party leaders ran Dora Hucklberry as state representative in 1934. On a party election pamphlet, workers learned that Hucklberry was a "militant Negro woman. Arrested many times for her participation in struggles against discrimination and unemployment. A fighter for Negro rights." The *Negro Champion* advertised the Communist candidate for congressman-at-large, Elizabeth Griffin Doty, as a "militant fighter for the interests of workers" who led a date and fig worker strike in the city. In 1934, Romania Ferguson ran for superintendent of public instruction. Nothing of her background is offered in the campaign literature, but Ferguson was an important leading Communist activist. In 1929, city leaders added her to the Negro department. One year later, she was doing so well that she was released from all work except the district's Negro department, her section's Negro department, and as lead organizer of her nucleus. Ferguson returned from a trip to the Soviet Union in time for the 1932 elections, for which Chicago's secretariat assigned her to speak on behalf of the party's electoral campaign and to visit organizations in its name; they also brought her into meetings of the district buro and involved her in its members' political discussions.[67] Marie Houston is even harder to know from party materials, even though the party sent her to Moscow to study at the Lenin School, and upon her return she ran classes on Marxist economics in Washington Park, where "hundreds of Negroes attended each day, listening intently for two hours [at a time]."[68] The park, a large green space that bordered the Black Belt, Packingtown, and Hyde Park, became the central organizing grounds for Chicago's Communists during the Depression. It was here that the unemployed, homeless, and curious gathered to hear all manner of speakers riff on political and social topics of the day. Not only might Garveyites, Wobblies, and Communists take center stage, but preachers, academics, and local politicians were known to climb on soapboxes, debate, and harangue. Occasionally, talks turned to rallies and rallies to demonstrations.[69] Houston's willingness to participate in this public oratory made her a valuable asset. And yet, despite party leaders' cultural and political inclinations to support black women like her, they continually compartmentalized "Negroes" and "women," rarely talking about black women as such.

Chicago's Neighborhoods and Representative Individuals

If categories like "Negro," "woman," "unemployed," and "trade unionist" reveal which groups of people listened most intently to the party's appeal, they oversimplify the recruits' backgrounds, say nothing about their reasons for joining, and obscure their temperaments, personalities, and experiences. Remarkable variety was a hallmark of those who joined the Communist party or traveled in circles with its members, and reasons why it appealed to one or another differed with the individual. Examination of the Chicago neighborhoods where most Communists lived in the late 1920s and early 1930s and of a few individuals from these regions who were involved with the party suggests the messy and complex story of who Chicago's Communists were and what attracted them to Communist ranks.

The greatest number of recruits came from the section on Chicago's South Side that embraced the Black Belt and Packingtown. In 1931, this section recorded 342 members.[70] At hunger marches in the stockyards, hundreds of demonstrators turned out to support efforts against unemployment and for food rations from the packers. In the 1932 presidential election, the Communist vote was most concentrated (at 7 percent or higher) in the area directly north of Washington Park, and from Forty-third to Pershing between Wentworth and State. In these areas, votes for the Communist party not only reflected people's support for its black vice-presidential candidate, James Ford, but also recognized work the party did in these neighborhoods.[71]

This work centered on organizing employed workers and extended into unemployed organizing, campaigns for racial equality, and Marxist education. Black Belt shop work included Ben Sopkins and Sons clothing factories, the community's Capitol Dairy plant, and local laundries, whereas Packingtown activity centered on the stockyards and was only secondarily channeled into the Crane Company, just west of the Back of the Yards. The two neighborhoods were racially divided, but many blacks populated the stockyards workforce, encouraging Communists to push for interracial activity in both communities. They advocated that whites travel into black neighborhoods in the South Side and march with blacks during hunger marches, funeral processions, and Labor Day demonstrations. They also embraced local community institutions by calling their meetings in both the Odd Fellows and Forum halls and holding their public protests at local parks, such as Washington Park, where traditions of open-air political discussion and debate ran deep. For those stimulated by Communist speeches and activism, a Workers' Book Store on Indiana and Forty-third, at the heart of the black community, provided supporting literature.[72]

The party was also successful in these areas because they were two of the poorest and most segregated communities in Chicago. The Black Belt had some of the most unhealthy conditions. Located three miles from many of their co-workers in the Back of the Yards, blacks, who made up 30 percent of the packinghouse workers in 1930, lived in a world separate from white Back of the Yards. By 1930, 90 percent of all of Chicago's blacks lived in census tracts where more than 50 percent of the inhabitants were black. Bordered by Thirty-ninth Street on the north and Sixty-fifth Street on the south, Wabash on the west

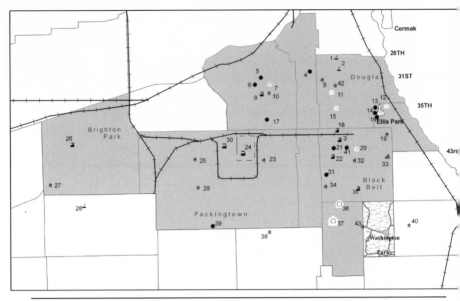

Party Schools 🚩
1.   28.
2.

Factories 🏭
3. Sopkins and Sons 42nd. St. Plant   24. Union Stockyards
9. Omaha Packing   26. Crane Company
18. Sopkins and Sons 39th St. Plant   30. Packing Plants
22. Capitol Dairy   35. Alfred Decker and Co.

Meeting Halls ⌂
7. Lithuanian Auditorium   20. Forum Hall
11. South Side Community Center   36. Royal Circle Hall
15. Pythian Hall   37. Odd Fellows Hall

Party and Mass Organization Offices and Meeting Sites •
4. Section Meeting Site   21. Section Meeting Site
5. Section Meeting Site   31. Trade Union Unity League Section Office
6. *Vilnis* Office   33. South Side Metal Workers' Industrial Union
12. Karl Marx Hof   39. International Labor Defense Office
13. Section Meeting Site   41. Party Book Store
14. League of Struggle for Negro Rights
    Headquarters
16, Section Meeting Site
17. Section Meeting Site

Sites of Interest/Party Events 🚶🚶
8. Site of Antilynching Conference   32. James Ford Dance
10. Open Air Meeting   34. Tag Days
19. 100th Anniversary of Nat Turner Rebellion 38. Post Office
23. Site of *Daily Worker* Sales   40. University of Chicago
25. Site of *Daily Worker* Sales   42. Mock Trial of Mayor Cermak
27. Polonia Grove, Site of Party Picnics   43. Washington Park Forums
29. Open Air Meetings

Communist party sites of activity, South Side neighborhoods. (Created by Lezlie Button) and white, middle-class communities such as Hyde Park on the east, the Black Belt housed an astonishing thirty-five thousand people per square mile. Allan Spear explains that in the core of the Black Belt, between State and Wentworth, "two-story frame houses, devoid of paint, stood close together in drab, dingy rows, surrounded by litters of garbage and ashes." Here, residents living in run-down and overcrowded apartments and kitchenettes paid exorbitant rents. Spear found that "ordinary conveniences were often non-existent: toilets were broken or leaked; electricity was rare; heating and hot water facilities failed to function." In the more affluent section of the Black Belt, east of State, housing was better, but Spear explains that many homes "had begun to deteriorate and frequently were in need of repair or lacked necessary sanitary facilities." Residents of sur-rounding neighborhoods violently enforced segregation. With separate and unequal facilities, blacks struggled to maintain their own segregated schools, hospitals, recreation facilities, movie theaters, restaurants, and taverns.[73]

The Back of the Yards also had poor housing and environmental conditions, but here, white ethnics and Mexicans peopled the dilapidated area, bordered on the north by the Belt Line Tracks and on the east by the stockyards. As part of an industrial belt that ran through the city's southern edge, the Back of the Yards offered residents poor living conditions. The pungent odor of the stock-yards, pollution, and congested housing led to high rates of infant death and tuberculosis. Unskilled Slavs and Mexicans lived in decaying and bug-infested two-story wood homes where loud noises and the stench-filled air continually reminded them of their proximity to cattle arriving daily for slaughter. Only skilled and semiskilled Slavic workers could afford to live in brick or better wood-constructed homes south of Forty-seventh Street, just below the neigh-borhood's worst area. Scott Nearing found in 1928 that little had changed in the twenty-two years since Upton Sinclair exposed these poor conditions in *The Jungle*: "the same stench," dirt, and dilapidated housing still existed.[74]

In addition to sharing poor living conditions, both neighborhoods had their own subcultures of activism that the party tapped. In the black community, spontaneous, direct-action mobilization; a Garveyite movement; and such in-dependent community institutions as the National Association for the Ad-vancement of Colored People (NAACP), the Urban League, churches, and the *Chicago Defender* provided experience and structures that the party built on and organized through. Here, antilynching meetings and Scottsboro rallies drew on a large activist population. In the Back of the Yards, Mexicans and Mexican Americans identified with radical movements in Mexico and brought these traditions into the party. Whereas most Polish skilled workers attended Catholic church rather than join the party, a small group actively responded to the party's actions against unemployment in the Yards.[75]

With such a mix of workplaces, ethnic groups, and political traditions, it is no wonder that one section would turn up such different kinds of people. Party records place Harry Haywood, Richard Wright, David Poindexter, and Claude Lightfoot all in the category "Negro." But who they were beyond that descriptor and how they came to Communism reveal different stories.

Haywood, the youngest of three siblings, was born in Nebraska on February 4, 1898, to former slaves. As a youth, he worked a number of jobs, including as a dining-car waiter on the Chicago and Northwestern Railway and as a waiter at the Tip Top Inn. In 1917 he joined the Eighth Illinois Black National Guard Regiment and developed a sense of racial pride. Having read about the existence of greater racial fairness in places like France, Haywood admits that patriotism was the least of his motivations for enlisting. Sailing to Europe in 1918, Haywood and his regiment were integrated into the French army and found that "the French treated blacks well—that is, as human beings. There was no Jim Crow."[76]

On his return from battle, the force of racism in America hit him head-on. July 28, 1919, Haywood and ten other black workers stepped warily out of the dining car on which they worked and onto Chicago's Twelfth Street Station. The previous night they received word that a race riot had broken out in the city. On the platform, a white trainman told them not to leave by Michigan Avenue but to take the tracks by the lake because some black soldiers had been killed, and the riots were taking place on the avenue. Hurrying home, the twenty-one-year-old Haywood started to think he had been "fighting the wrong war. The Germans weren't the enemy—the enemy was right here at home."[77]

What sparked the riot were white youths throwing rocks that killed the black seventeen-year-old Eugene Williams, who was swimming off the city's Twenty-sixth Street beach. Apparently he had swum too close to the imaginary line separating white waters from black. Police refused to arrest any of the whites involved. Fighting that began on the beach spread across the city and lasted over six days. In the end, thirty-eight people were dead, over five hundred injured, and over one thousand homeless. This event was "the great turning point" in Haywood's life.[78]

Shortly after the riot, Harry's brother Otto joined the Garvey movement, the IWW, and the African Blood Brotherhood. By 1921, he found his way to the Communist party. Otto introduced Haywood to Marx and Engels, Henry Lewis Morgan's *Ancient Society,* and John Reed's *Ten Days That Shook the World.* In the meantime, Harry secured employment at Chicago's post office, where he met other young blacks who were also questioning American society's racism. A discussion group formed with a dozen or so vocal members, including, Haywood remembers, "aspirant intellectuals, . . . students of education, . . . and some intellectually oriented workers."[79] For three months the group held bimonthly meetings at people's homes and apartments. They picked a topic, such as ways to counter white racism with scientific truth, and then gave volunteers a week to prepare a report.

After a few months, talk was not enough. Leading members of the group, including Haywood, wanted to get more involved in broader political activity. After attending open forums in Washington Park, Haywood wanted to connect to larger movements. He also kept reading—*The Communist Manifesto,* Engles's *Origin of the Family,* and Marx's *Value, Price, and Profit.* He recalled, "The first stage of my political search was near an end. In the years since I had mustered out of the Army, I had come from being a disgruntled Black ex-soldier to being a self-conscious revolutionary looking for an organization with which to make revolution."[80]

In the spring of 1922, Harry decided to join the Communist party. He liked the black Communists he knew, such as the Owens brothers and Edward Doty in addition to his brother Otto, and was impressed by such white leaders as Jim Early, Sam Hammersmark, and Robert Minor. But what sold Harry and others on the party was its relationship to the Bolshevik Revolution. Even though the party was mostly white in its composition, Harry believed "that it comprised the best and most sincerely revolutionary and internationally minded elements among white radicals and therefore formed the basis for the revolutionary unity of Blacks and whites. . . . [I]t was a part of a world revolutionary movement uniting Chinese, Africans, and Latin Americans with Europeans and North Americans through the Third Communist International."[81]

Harry Haywood sketched by Bob Brown. From *Black Bolshevik,* by Harry Haywood. (Used with permission by Bob Brown)

The negative attention that the Bolshevik Revolution received in the white press further convinced Haywood that it "couldn't be all bad." Harry was first accepted into the African Blood Brotherhood, the YCL, and then finally the Communist party, where he was groomed for leadership and sent to study in Moscow. Spending four and a half years in the Soviet Union and then three and a half more in New York writing policy and theory, Harry found that he had little experience with the masses. His itch for face-to-face organizing led him to return to Chicago in 1934. He became the leader of the city's South Side, where new recruits found his political approach, in a word, irritating.

Perhaps no other Communist despised Haywood as much as Richard Wright, who depicted him as the character Buddy Nealson in *Black Boy*. Nealson/Haywood had a "furtive manner," "greasy, sweaty look," with "thick lips." Haywood's asthma caused him to "snort at unexpected intervals." Such a characteristic must have exaggerated Haywood's own depiction of his personality as "hot-tempered."[82] In an instant, Wright disliked Haywood. Haywood's insistence that Wright do community organizing for the party rather than spend his time writing exacerbated Wright's dislike. But Haywood was simply applying party discipline, which he was trained to follow to a tee.[83] The conflict between Haywood and Wright concerning what it meant to be a Communist was representative of those that occurred throughout Chicago's ranks.

Wright came to the party less interested in its discipline than in the outlet its John Reed Club offered his intellect. Initially, Wright regarded the club with skepticism. At open forums in Washington Park, he had greater affinity for the Garveyites and their racial pride than for the Communists, whose professed atheism, Wright believed, alienated black people. Rather than come to the party through the front door, Wright entered through an alternative route. While working at the largest post office in the city, he stumbled upon a group of friends who regularly met in Abe Aaron's room at the Troy Lane Hotel on the South Side. Aaron, a tall, lanky Communist who grew up in the only Jewish family in a small coal-mining town in Pennsylvania, was an aspiring writer who had already published in proletarian publications. As a member of the Communist party, Aaron became Wright's gateway to Chicago's John Reed Club.[84]

Wright's desire for intellectual interaction with writers overcame his concern about party control over the clubs. Besides, Aaron assured him he would not have to join the party to be a member of the club. Skeptically climbing the club's stairs on South Michigan Avenue, Wright wondered, "What on earth of importance could transpire in so dingy a place?"[85] He was sure that racism would sour his experience. Instead, he found whites interested in blacks' experiences. Reading poetry and short stories from such leftist journals as *New Masses, International Literature,* and *Left Front,* Wright learned that these writers were interested in the problems of common people. Through his interactions at the club with the likes of Nelson Algren, he discovered that many of the writers were also poor. Hooked by his creative drive and the intellectual energy of the club, Wright became one of its most avid members. Only when he was elected to the position of executive secretary was he taken aside and told that as a leader of the club he would have to join the party. Convinced that his leadership in the club would serve as his party duty, Wright signed on and found out that he was expected to do more.[86]

The anguish Wright experienced at his first Communist party meeting demonstrates a strain of anti-intellectualism that persisted through the party's ranks and speaks to the alienation he and other writers and artists experienced. In his suit and tie, Wright sent awkward ripples through the room of a few working-class whites and approximately twenty southern blacks with less then three years of education among them. When Wright pulled notes out of his pocket and read them, snickering and giggling became audible. As if his suit were not enough, Wright introduced himself as the executive secretary of the John Reed Club and as a writer who was published in a number of proletarian literary magazines. Wright did not realize that many in the ranks thought of the club as a "playground for white artists."[87] So even as one of its members, Wright remained skeptical of the party.

One member whom Wright and others found inspiring was David Poindexter, a southerner who brought with him to Chicago the chilling experience of having witnessed a lynch mob in Nashville, Tennessee. Poindexter hoped one day to take revenge on whites, but working with them on odd jobs in Chicago and Detroit, he began to see white workers as his "'class brothers.'"[88] This vision took time to develop. Like Wright, Poindexter first gravitated to the Garveyites, but, listening to debates in Washington Park, he eventually found Communists more convincing. William Patterson, an African American party leader, recalled that the party's belief that blacks and whites needed to work together ultimately caused Poindexter to leave the Garvey movement.[89] Once there, Poindexter proved "fearless," even "reckless." Harold Gosnell explained, "His face was scarred as a result of rough handling by the police, but his spirit was unbroken. He was clearly a masochist type seeking martyrdom, since most of the injuries which he received might have been avoided if he had been less hot headed."[90] Claude Lightfoot, a fellow African American party leader, remembered Poindexter as "'a frustrated preacher.'" As it turned out, Poindexter grew up in the Baptist church, "'could talk pretty well,'" and led a protest at a National Baptist convention before becoming a party member. Spoken before unemployed crowds, Poindexter's words took on a life of their own. Lightfoot recalled, "'[W]hen he got through preachin' everybody'd be ready to go on into the lake with him. That's how much power he had over people.'"[91]

Poindexter's charisma almost overwhelmed Lightfoot. A young African

American Democratic party activist, Lightfoot joined the Communist party when Poindexter convinced him that a socialist revolution was imminent. As a foot soldier for the Democrats, Lightfoot had witnessed the power of direct action. In September 1930, hundreds of blacks, Lightfoot among them, marched from Washington Park to a city transportation work site and successfully demanded jobs. Now the Communists promised they could deliver a revolution on Chicago's South Side.[92] Lightfoot reflected that if anybody asked why he joined the Communist party, he would have said it was "for idealistic reasons, to help the poor, the downtrodden and oppressed people all over the world." These factors were partly true. But in retrospect, he admitted, "After having gotten up on the soapbox and cursing out the police and then march away triumphantly with the workers, well, from that day on I was a man. I was no longer that timid little boy that used to go to an all-white school and the white kids used to beat the devil out of me, and then I went to the all-black school, the blacks beat me, too. So I was one of those little kids, scared of his shadow, so to speak. Now I'm somebody. 'There goes Claude Lightfoot. He's the one that cursed out the police the other day over there, you know.'"[93]

United by the party's organization on the South Side, these new black recruits represented diverse backgrounds, political leanings, interests, personalities, and levels of commitment. They lived the unemployment, racism, and oppression white Communists discussed and debated. For a time they would agree to join the party and overcome their differences.

Rivaling the South Side's 342 members were the West Side units, which claimed 240 members in 1931. In West Town, a neighborhood bordered by Humboldt Park on the west, the north branch of the Chicago River on the east, West Kinzie Street on the south, and Bloomingdale on the north, unemployed organizing received widespread attention and support. Here the party used community institutions as the settings for their meetings, such as the Labor Lyceum Hall and the Ukrainian People's Auditorium. Relying on the fact that this neighborhood was home to the largest Polish community in the city, party organizers called meetings of the Polish antifascist committee in this neighborhood. They also drew heavily on the large Jewish community and organized gatherings at the Jewish Club. With so many of the residents in this area on relief (22.88 percent), Communists successfully recruited many to their protests at the Humboldt Park relief station and their Unemployed Council meetings at the Folkets Hus, a cultural meeting hall in the area owned by non-party but sympathetic residents.[94]

Levels of Communist support in West Side neighborhoods can best be understood by recognizing the varying levels of poverty there. These neighborhoods contained pockets of manufacturing and industry, including the Chicago and Northwestern Railroad, a few dairies, and machine shops. During the Depression, jobs were hard to come by, and destitution was widespread. West Town housed unskilled laborers, a majority of whom were Poles, Italians, Jews, and Norwegians. They shared frame cottages, shanties, and dilapidated apartment buildings. In 1935, 302 buildings needed repair, and 502 were recommended for demolition. In 1934, 22.88 percent of the families in this neighborhood were on relief. Near West Side workers of Italian, Russian, Greek, Polish, and German descent lived in multifamily units. This neighborhood included a large Jewish population that supported eleven synagogues. Hit hard by the Depression, 43.74 percent in the Near West Side were on relief in 1934. A less run-down and poor area, the Lower West Side was composed mostly of Czechs and Yugoslavs. Poles, Lithuanians, Italians, and some Germans also lived in the area. Only 18.54 percent of the Lower West Side's residents collected relief in 1934, but the residential area was congested.[95]

In addition to living conditions, leftist traditions in several of these ethnic communities help explain party successes. Ukrainians and Poles brought socialist traditions to Chicago, and for both the plight of their homeland figured prominently in their activities. Rather than join community churches, these Socialists and Communists identified with the secular and ethnic cultures leftist movements offered. The West Side Ukrainian People's Auditorium, one of the Chicago party's most important meeting halls, competed with the Ukrainian churches and fraternal organizations for activists. Polish Communists had an even tougher battle against the Polish church, which had considerable sway over Chicago's Poles. In 1929, the party held a counterdemonstration in Wicker Park's Schoenhaffer Hall to protest what party leaders called the "fascist Pulaski day celebration." With sixty thousand attending the official Pulaski Day event, the party's four hundred protesters demonstrated the challenges Communists faced in the Polish community.[96]

Like Ukrainian and Polish Socialists, Jewish Socialists brought their beliefs and culture with them on their journey to the United States, developing a rich leftist enclave complete with newspapers, theaters, and restaurants. Building on Jewish interests and populations on Chicago's West Side, Communists, beginning in 1929, held meetings on the question of Palestine, the issue on which much of the party's antifascist work began in 1933. Whereas many West Side religious Jews responded to calls from philanthropic organizations, working-class Jews often responded to socialists' and Communists' pleas: 196 registered with the Communist party in 1931.[97]

Mollie West, a Polish-born Jewish immigrant from the town of Soklov, settled with her family on Chicago's West Side and was taken by the modern luxuries available in the United States. In Poland, about twenty of Mollie's family members plus a boarding watchmaker and violin player occupied a small three-story house with no running water or central heating. Her father was an Orthodox

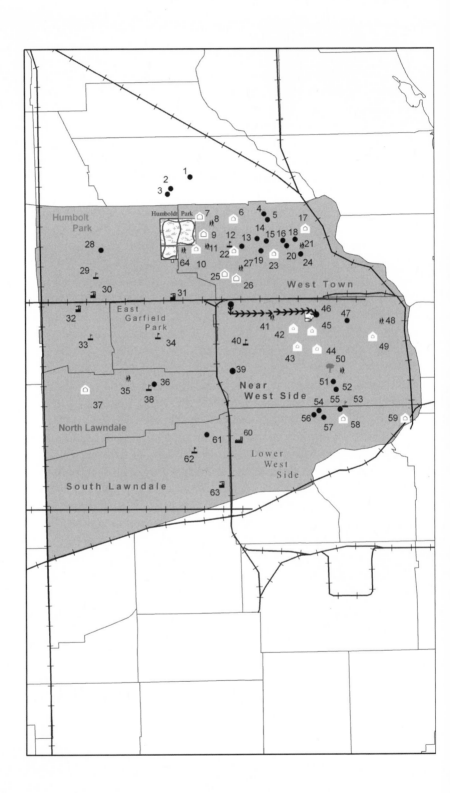

Party Schools ⚑
29.
33.

38.
53.

City Schools ⚑
12. Tuley High School
34. Marshall High School

40. Crane Prep School
62. Harrison High School

Factories ▰
30. Capitol Dairy
31. Bowman Dairy
32. Northwestern Railroad Yards

60. International Harvester, McCormick Reaper
63. Tractor Works

Meeting Halls ⌂
6. Northwest Hall
7. Labor Lyceum
9. Workers' Lyceum/Folkets Hus
10. Jewish Workers' Club
17. Schoenhoffen Hall
22. Mirror Hall
23. Hungarian Hall
25. Ukrainian People's Home
26. People's Auditorium

37. Workers' Center
42. West End Women's Club
43. Temple Hall
44. Carmen's Hall
45. West End Club
49. Musicians' Hall
58. National Hall
59. Coliseum

Party and Mass Organization Offices and Meeting Sites •
1. *Scandia Press*
2. Young Communist League Office
3. Unemployed Council of Cook County
4. Hungarian Workers' Club
5. Financial Meeting Site
13. Antifascist Polish Committee
14. District Office, 1930
15. *Northwestern Shop News*
16. Unemployed Council Meeting Site
18. Trade Union Unity League Offices
19. Workers' Bookstore
20. Agitprop Meeting Site
24. AFL Machinists Fraction Meeting Site
28. Young Communist League Office

36. *Freiheit*
39. Party Section Meeting
47. *Daily Worker* Publishing Company
51. Unit Meeting Site
52. District Office, 1931
54. *Ludowy Rennik*
55. Jugoslav Labor Defense
56. Slovak Workers' Society and *Rovost L'udo*
57. Language Office
61. Jugoslav Buro Office

Sites of Interest/Party Events 🚶
8. Needle Trades' Bazaar
11. Blue Inn
21. Russian Cooperative Restaurant
27. House Party
35. Open Air Meetings

41. Dance Site
46. Union Park, Rally Site
48. Haymarket Square
50. Jefferson Park, Rally Site
64. Dance Site

Communist party sites of activity, West Side neighborhoods. (Created by Lezlie Button)

Jew who regularly passed between home and the synagogue to pray while her mother and the rest of the family's women did housework and ran a small shop that sold staples. Mollie's uncle Yacov was the only family member to take an interest in politics.

The year 1929 was rough for Mollie. Her family moved to Chicago's West Side, the Depression hit, and she was enrolled in a school where her German, Polish, and Yiddish did her no good. Mollie also stood out because of a complication that occurred when she was born, causing her to have a painful limp. After two years, she graduated from the lower school into one of the city's largest high schools, Marshall, which was 95 percent Jewish at the time. It was here that Mollie's radicalization began. Not only did Marshall High have a strong academic record, talented sports teams, and other extracurricular activities, they also had radical students and teacher mentors. Lessons from fellow students and teachers were complemented by the vibrant political tussles that occurred in her neighborhood on Roosevelt Road. Mollie remembered, "It changed my life, that street. Our recreation was to be outside. And there was great turmoil, fights between the Communists, the Social Democrats, and the Trotskyists. I was still naïve about it all, but I was learning about the trade union movement and all kinds of social problems. It was still possible to walk the streets. We would just walk and go in and have an ice cream or a corned beef sandwich and talk and listen. We would just *shpatzir* [wander about]. It was a real community like you don't see today. It gave meaning to my life."[98]

Lessons learned on the street led to Mollie's first political rebellions. When Mollie criticized a stenography teacher for dictating racist material, she was promptly removed from class and threatened with a failing grade. Only after several teachers came to her defense did she receive a passing mark. In 1934, the school's budget was tight, and the school board threatened to cut music, art, and physical education from the curriculum. As a blossoming French-horn player, Mollie decided to call a strike. She organized a committee and began making banners, but the night before the strike was to begin, Chicago police arrested the committee. As the event's leader, Mollie was taken to a juvenile detention center, where her father refused to come get her. An avid Zionist, he was anti-Communist to the core. Mollie waited until her mother and a neighbor picked her up. These early organizing experiences prepared Mollie for active membership in the YCL.

While party membership was high on the West Side, it grew to be higher on Chicago's North Side. During most of the Third Period, the North Side fell behind the South and West Sides in terms of membership, but in 1931 they outnumbered the West Side's 240 members with 267 of their own. North Side Communists usually rated first in the amount of dues that they paid because of the number of their high-wage skilled workers. Communists' North Side labor organizing focused on the Stewart Warner plant, on the neighborhood's Deering plant, and among building-trades workers at various sites. Activists planned demonstrations at Washington Square Park, known as Bughouse Square, a free-speech park on North Clark where bohemians, radicals, and any interested passerby had an open invitation to get up on a soapbox and riff. Communists also held meetings in the Finnish Hall and Viking Temple and participated in the numerous ethnic social organizations of the Scandinavians and Ukrainians living in the area. A few were even known to pass some time at the Dil Pickle.[99]

Varying levels of wealth and employment again help explain the mixed response to the party in the North Side, which included the most economically diverse neighborhoods in the city, encompassing affluent blocks as well as the tenements in "Little Hell." Extending northward, this section included Lincoln Park, which was wealthier than the Lower North Side and had only 18.65 percent of its residents on relief, compared to 26.08 percent on the Near North Side. Lincoln Park housed Germans, Yugoslavs, Hungarians, Rumanians, Irish, Italians, Poles, Russians, English, and Swedish. Above Lincoln Park was Lake View, a mostly German enclave where Scandinavians played a particularly important role in the building trades, which were hit hard by the Depression.[100]

Wealthy neighborhoods exaggerated the miserable experience of poverty and unemployment in this region and fed its residents' political traditions, especially those with connections to radical Scandinavian culture. The Denmark native Nels Kjar was one of these. In the first decade of the twentieth century, Kjar was active in the Norwegian-Danish Karl Marx Club. Linked to the American Socialist party, the club functioned as a social and political outlet for Scandinavian workers, sponsoring a library, dances, bazaars, and concerts. The prominent Scandinavian Socialist Charles Sand hailed from this region. Sand arrived in the United States from Sweden in 1895 and became an active unionist, Socialist party leader, and newspaper editor.

Kjar left Sand and Socialism behind for the promises of the Communist party. By July 1920, Kjar and other club members successfully gathered funds to purchase their own meeting hall, Folkets Hus (People's House), a later meeting place of the Unemployed Councils. After World War I and the Russian Revolution, Chicago police cautioned all hall owners not to rent space to radicals, but the Fulkets Hus's management proudly rented to "whoever [they] wanted."[101]

A carpenter by training, Kjar found his niche in the party's industrial work and became a leader in Chicago's Trade Union Educational League, a militant trade-union group that coordinated activities among its sympathizers in AFL unions. Although never formally affiliated with the party, the TUEL generally followed the party's industrial policies, and in Chicago, Kjar and his fellow TUEL members comprised the most important radical opposition in the city's labor movement. As the party's emphasis shifted from organizing within the AFL to working through separate revolutionary unions, the TUEL was abandoned and a new set of revolutionary unions founded and affiliated with the party's new industrial arm, the Trade Union Unity League. Through the TUUL, Kjar got involved in organizing unemployed workers and found his sphere of activity broadened. By 1932 he had become a leader of the party's unemployed orga-

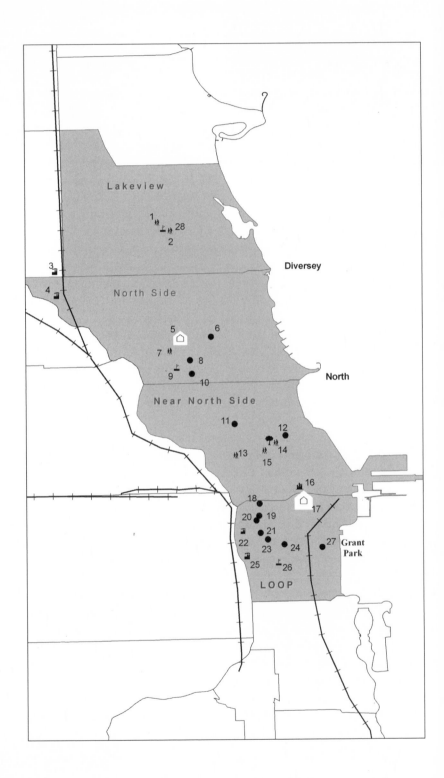

Party Schools ⚑
  2.   26.
  9.

Factories 🏭
  3. Stewart Warner Plant   22. Hart, Schaffner, and Marx
  4. Deering Plant   25. Alfred Decker and Company

Meeting Halls ⌂
  5. Imperial Hall   17. Sons of Israel Hall

Party and Mass Organization Offices and Meeting Sites •
  6. North Side Trade Union Unity League and   20. Committee for the Protection of the Foreign Born
      Offices   and Unemployed Council
  8. *Radnik*   21. *Armour Young Worker*
 10. Adria Printing Co   23. District Office, 1935
 11. German Speakers' Fraction Meeting 24. American Youth Congress
 12. John Reed Club   27. John Reed Club
 18. American League Against War and Fascism
 19. National Counter-Olympic Organizational Committee

Sites of Interest/Party Events 👥
  1. Play Performance, "Steel Strike" 15. Washington Square Park, Open Air Meetings
  7. House Party   16. Chicago Tribune Tower
 13. Shoe Strike Headquarters   28. Open Air Meetings
 14. Dil Pickle Club

Communist party sites of activity, North Side neighborhoods and the Loop. (Created by Lezlie Button)

nization. Military intelligence records report "Kjar had the reputation of being one of the most rabid of the radical leaders."[102]

Kjar and other first-generation ethnic radicals mingled in the party with those of the second generation, including sons like Jack Spiegel. The child of Jewish immigrants from Poland, Spiegel's hopes of attending the University of Chicago's law school were dashed when the Depression hit in 1929. Taken by North Side neighborhood discussions of Marxism and the depiction of workers' equality and socialist justice in the Soviet Union, Spiegel soon disappointed his parents' wishes for him to become a lawyer. Instead he joined the Communist party.[103]

With the nation's economy seeming on the brink of collapse, Spiegel became convinced that Communists had the answers to society's problems. This belief and party education led him, as he recalled, to become "overzealous," "militant," and a bit "too sectarian," as he was swept up in the fight to bring justice to unemployed Chicagoans. A regular sight at relief offices on the city's North and Northwest Sides, Spiegel was the target of many a swung police club and a regular occupant in Chicago's jails. As he recalled, some party members did not mind spending the night in jail because that meant they would at least get one free meal. Since he received no pay from the party for his efforts, Spiegel's wife, a garment worker and fellow party activist, supported his work as a revolutionary with her own wages. Such dedication resulted in Spiegel's becoming the leader of the party's unemployed organization, the Unemployed Councils, on Chicago's North and Northwest Sides.[104]

But not all Jews had the same path to Communism through educational disappointment. Instead of youthful hopes of attending law school, Jack Kling had to work. Born Jack Klinghoffer in 1911 on the Lower East Side of New York, Kling was raised among Jewish working people. The oldest of five children, he grew up in an Orthodox home, the son of a fur worker who was a strong unionist and regularly voted for Socialist candidates but did not identify himself as a political person. Lacking interest in school, Kling got involved with the Pineapple Gang, a group of Jewish youth who fought Polish gangs, raided peddlers, and eventually mugged and stole from people. Kling believed that the YCL helped him "get [his] head on straight."[105]

Kling was introduced to the YCL at a 1928 May Day parade in New York. He had landed a job as a sewing-machine operator, joined the Needle Trades Workers' Industrial Union, and held the union's banner as part of the large contingent that showed up for the march. Kling recalled, "Young Communists were in the line of march, speaking to young people on the sidewalks and inviting them to join the Young Communist League. I was impressed, and decided to join. So I signed a card on that Day—May 1st, 1928, right at the demonstration—for me, an historic day."[106] John Williamson, the presiding party official in New York at the time, signed off on Kling's card and marched next to Kling in the parade.

Believing Kling to be a natural leader, party superiors eventually sent him to a national YCL school in Cleveland. After a short stint organizing in New York, Kling was asked to go to Chicago to work with the YCL. Arriving with no money or place to stay, Kling slept in Grant Park with other homeless people. When party leaders learned of Kling's accommodation, they arranged for him to stay with a party family, the Boyers. For several years he shared a room with their son, who was also active in the YCL. He ate at a Russian cooperative restaurant on Division near Ashland run by party sympathizers who offered party activists one free meal a day.[107] In 1931, at age twenty, Kling was elected YCL organizer for Chicago's district. With only seventy-eight of Chicago's party members listed as twenty-five or younger, Kling had his work cut out for him.[108]

These individual narratives show that other stories lay beyond party statistics, strongly rooted in time, place, and experience. Some of Chicago's Communists were influenced by their family's politics, others by the books they read. Orators and teachers drew in some members. Others shuffled in when leftist groups were folded into the party or when clubs started. Some were true believers in the Communist revolution and the Soviet Union, while others cared more about racial equality or reading. Chicago's Communists came from different countries, states, and locales. Rooted in various progressive struggles, ethnic

Jack Kling and Claude Lightfoot. (Chicago Historical Society, ICHi-39210, photographer unknown)

clubs, and political and social groups, they offered their varied temperaments, dispositions, and personalities to the party. Held together by the party's structure and the culture it exuded, Chicago's Communists were able to look out at a striking assortment of people in any given party demonstration, picnic, and mass meeting. Some marveled at the diversity and solidarity among its followers. And yet, the various ways they lived Communism chafed those in charge.

On the one hand, throughout the Third Period, questionable recruitment techniques, stifling party bureaucracy, and overwhelming demands proved too challenging to all but the most committed of Chicago's Communists. A vast majority who signed up quit after the first year. Those who stayed were overwhelmingly male, unemployed, proletarian, and ethnic. Even though leaders hoped for native-born, employed industrial workers, they took what they could get and instructed their newly minted members to bring party policies to the masses within the city's ethnic, unemployed, labor, cultural, and leftist organizations. Those who stayed, some assume, must have been the most hardened and committed Communist revolutionaries.

The problem for party leaders, however, was that Communism meant different things to those who came through its ranks. Just because someone was "unemployed," "native-born," or "ethnic" did not mean that they would understand the party and its policies in the ways that its leaders expected. People's life histories, experiences, and cultural connections shaped the reasons they came and stayed and the way they lived Communism.

3

"True Revolutionaries": Chicago's Party Culture in Thought and Action

David Poindexter, an African American Communist active in unemployed and civil rights work, was popular with the party's rank and file. He was also a thorn in the side of city leaders, regularly criticizing them at party meetings. Sometime in 1934 he apparently took his independent streak too far for Harry Haywood. The national party leader, trained at Moscow's Lenin School and newly arrived in Chicago, brought up Poindexter on charges of promoting anti-Communist ideas at a public forum.[1]

Poindexter's trial, held in a hall that accommodated an interracial group of party leaders and followers, lasted over three hours. It began with four different leaders speaking on world fascism; the dangers of Germany, Italy, and Japan; the success of a Socialist Soviet Union; the weakness of capitalist America; and inequities on Chicago's South Side. Once the speeches finished, charges brought by the party's rank and file, Poindexter's friends and comrades, proceeded. After these comrades spoke their concerns, Poindexter took the floor. In one account of the trial, a "distraught" Poindexter admitted, "Comrades, I'm guilty of all the charges, all of them." In another, Poindexter's testimony took on an edge. Above shouts of "yes," "tell it," and "amen," Poindexter stated: "'If my Party sees fit to sever me from the revolutionary movement, which I have served faithfully, so be it. If I soiled Communist principles while leading the unemployed, while fighting for relief, while standing at the citadels of power and demanding justice for the working class—while [voice rising] comrade Haywood was studying at the Lenin School, so be it, so be it.'"[2] The trial ended when Haywood rescinded the charges. After all, Poindexter had proved his ability to be "self-critical."

Most likely Poindexter's testimony reflected a combination of the two accounts. Since Haywood dropped the charges, Poindexter probably admitted some guilt. Given his predilection to call party leaders to task for their own transgressions, though, Poindexter likely did point out his own years of commitment to Communist causes while Haywood either studied abroad or led from New York, far away from "the masses," a point about which Haywood was particularly sensitive.[3]

Regardless of the version, the fact that party trials existed, the expectation that comrades would submit to criticism, the belief that justice was being carried out, and the way accusers and accused confirmed Communist principles all reveal a unifying culture of beliefs and behaviors. Trials were only one place where Communists' convictions and conduct became apparent. Attitudes toward the Soviet Union, education, and gender also revealed a dominant party culture that some embraced and others policed. Daily activism further reinforced the party's dominant culture. Through party activity, Communists were to learn how to relate to the masses, deal with police, accept party discipline, and think about race and the non-Communist Left. Drawing on symbols, practices, and policies of the American Left and international Communism, Chicago's Communists created a party culture that shaped members' clothing and language as well as their ideology and behavior. Some scholars have viewed this cultural co-optation as evidence that American Communists were isolated from America's workers. In Chicago, these political and cultural practices did alienate large groups of people; they also connected Chicago's party to the world's only successful Socialist revolution, convincing others of its legitimacy.

As the spontaneous outbursts at Poindexter's trial suggest, Chicago's party culture also reflected the behaviors, understandings, attitudes, and beliefs of its individual members and was therefore rarely lived in any uniform way. High turnover was one response to leaders' revolutionary expectations, but even those who stayed did not practice Communism in a uniform fashion and still found ways to blend their beliefs and dispositions with party expectations and remain loyal, even if the mixture proved unsavory to those in charge. In Chicago's parks, neighborhoods, and workplaces, people identified themselves as Communists, many enthusiastically. Yet they lived within the party on terms different from those laid out in New York and Moscow. Chicago's leaders regularly battled the reality that their members came to Communism for various reasons. Through the Third Period, they were unable to build a uniform entity. Instead, Chicago's leaders ruled over a loose amalgamation of individuals and subcultures. Which activities and ideas united Chicago's Communists? Which policies created cleavages in the movement? How did rank-and-file party members experience Communist culture, and to what extent was it a product of their own creation?

A Singular Vision

The relationship of the CPUSA to the Soviet Union made Communism in the United States different from other American social and political movements. Beliefs about and behaviors determined by the Soviet Union provided one defining feature of party culture at all levels of the party. A letter to John Mackovich, the head of Chicago's Czech buro, from party member Fero Bury conveyed the sentiments of other Slovak immigrants. "Russia is OURS," Bury wrote. "[W]e Slovaks have always looked upon Russia as to our savior, as to our strong brotherly protector." Now Bury was writing to inquire about sending a delegation of Slovaks to Russia because he believed that "newborn Russia in its progress, in its famous ability of action will bring regeneration to the whole world so that all antagonism of the enemies of poor people will be in vain."[4]

Carl Hirsch, a writer born and raised on Chicago's West Side, remembered the importance of the Soviet Union to him as a young party recruit. Communist friends gave him books that described Russia as a country without unemployment. He recalled reading that "[i]t was a planned society and all of these things could be planned out." With their economic problems solved, Hirsch read, Russia's citizens shared better mental health than was possible in capitalist societies. Through the Depression's early years, Hirsch watched his half-dressed and unemployed father sit in the family's living room day after day rather then dress and head out to find employment. His mother regularly was in tears. This was a stark contrast to the Russia of his reading—a more perfect, planned society, where human relations were on a higher plane.[5]

Bury and Hirsch were not alone. Communist memoirs and internal party records allude to members' admiration of the Soviet state, its leaders, and its people. Some admirers even took to mimicking Russian dress and speech. Richard Wright, for example, recalled his frustration with some of Chicago's black Communists, who "in order to resemble Lenin, . . . turned their shirt collars in to make a V at the front, and turned the visors of their caps backward, tilted upward at the nape of the neck." "When engaged in conversation," Wright recalled, "they stuck their thumbs in their suspenders or put their left hands into their shirt bosoms or hooked their thumbs into their back pockets as they had seen Lenin or Stalin do in photographs." Lovett Fort Whiteman was probably one of these who so annoyed Wright. Tuskegee-schooled and trained in the IWW and in Harlem's Socialist party, Whiteman by 1924 was a leading black member of the American Communist party, confidently writing angry protests to Soviet party leaders from Moscow's Lux Hotel because they had not yet convened a World Negro Congress. As a delegate to the Fifth Congress, Whiteman established himself as a rising star in American party leadership. His enthusiasm for the Soviet Union was apparent in his dress. In August 1932, the *Chicago Tribune* featured a photo of him walking Chicago's streets in tall, tight boots, riding pants, and a Russian-styled coat and hat.[6]

Wright remembered that a few black party members even "rolled their r's and mispronounced some words, like . . . they heard in the Party."[7] Black comrades were not the only ones to use Russian speech patterns. All party members

This photo of Lovett Fort Whiteman appeared in the *Chicago Tribune,* August 4, 1932. While it is not credited, the picture was likely taken by a member of the city's Red Squad.

borrowed from Russia when they referred to such organizational units and functions as "buro," "nucleus," and "agitprop," and experienced types flaunted their comfort with such jargon as "proletarian," "vanguard," and "bourgeosie," to the discomfort of newcomers. Carl Hirsch recalled when he first heard this last term at a party meeting when a leader from another part of Chicago spoke "a good part of the evening . . . about something he called the BoorGois." The guy "talked and talked about the BoorGois and," according to Hirsch, "nobody in the room knew what the hell he was talking about."[8]

John Williamson was concerned about such confusion, so at a gathering of city leaders, he offered pointers in the use of Soviet terminology. He was disturbed that in one case party ranks called their nucleus meetings "shock troops," a loose reference to Russian troops trained for engagement and assault, and in another members called every Sunday organizing activity a "Red Sunday," a term that should have been set aside for specific days of concentrated work. Williamson told his peers that in the first case the term confused those who did not know what shock troops were, and in the second case the use of "Red Sunday" was simply incorrect.[9] He assured his comrades, "[T]here is nothing wrong with [transporting terms from the Soviet Union]." He simply wanted to be sure it would be done correctly. Such action showed the pervasive belief that the Soviet Union was worth modeling. In fact, emulation of things Soviet gave confidence to those who saw Russia as a model, just as it disturbed those who saw such a connection as strange and foreign.[10]

Emulation of the Soviet Union was not enough for some party loyalists who wanted desperately to visit. Party offices became so inundated with requests to transfer to the Soviet Union that American leaders developed an elaborate application process. After compiling a detailed biography and accounting for their labor and party activities, applicants were required to find people to vouch for them in front of the district committee, whose members would make a recommendation to New York's Central Committee.[11] City and national party leaders hoped that such barriers would discourage applicants. One mandate from Chicago's leaders, which was to be read at all nuclei meetings, explained, "While the Soviet Union needs a few skilled mechanics, they are not in need of Communists. Therefore if you happen to be a good mechanic and also a Communist, then you stay in the USA. The Soviet Union needs the mechanics but America needs the Communists."[12] Regardless, Chicagoans contacted Soviet individuals, hoping to make arrangements for work. Some sold their belongings, while others joined Soviet cooperatives.[13] A few followed the rules and applied. Clara Rodin explained that her mother was in Russia and ill. J. Podgorny wanted to travel to Siberia, he wrote, for the "better climate." Julius Peck desired work in a Soviet laundry cooperative.[14]

More common than those applying to leave were those wanting to remain in the United States where they could defend the Soviet Union. Ben Gray, a Ukrainian Jewish immigrant, believed the Soviet Union had to be defended "because it was the only socialist country in existence at the time and . . . because [of] the constant danger that the Soviet Union was in of being attacked by the imperialist world in the actual sense."[15] Because they believed in the importance of the Soviet Union as a countermodel to American capitalism, Gray and others added phrases to their leaflets and literature about defending it. He reluctantly remembered, "[I]n some cases it was really tragic because we did it in a very mechanical manner, whether it belonged or it didn't belong, it seemed that every leaflet had to have some reference to the fact that there was a danger of the Soviet Union being attacked, that the Soviet Union must be defended."[16]

With the Soviet Union as an ideal and Marxism-Leninism as a guide, in many minds, the successful Soviet Revolution was sure to come to the United States at any moment. In the context of massive unemployment and mobilization of workers, the belief inspired Communists to continue their struggle. When David Poindexter recruited Claude Lightfoot out of the Democratic party, he could honestly believe what he stated: "A revolutionary change will take place in the next five years. The country can't go on five more years the way it is now. In fact, it could change this year, this winter."[17] Carl Hirsch actually postponed personal decisions due to the impending revolution. "It was as though any day now life was going to change so drastically. . . . So don't plan . . . what you're going to do 10 years from now or 20 years from now. . . . There were few . . . committed Party people who had insurance—or who bought homes or anything of that nature."[18] With such dedication, people like Ben Gray admitted that they were "completely and totally sold on the idea that the Communist Party ha[d] the answer."[19]

Chicago's Communists' connection to the revolutionary Soviet Union created a sense of superiority among Communist recruits as they prepared to lead America's workers to socialism. Their mission created a loyalty to and confidence in the Soviet Union that was unrivaled by other groups in the city.

Another aspect of party culture—reading and education—further defined how people felt about the Soviet Union. Chicago's leaders outlined an educational mission for members in order to instill a Marxist perspective. Williamson believed that "[i]n early days of the life of a new member, he must devote less time to practical work and more time to study." The reason, he argued, was that "if he gets a general theoretical idea of what the Communist Party stands for, then our problem of involving him into work is much easier."[20] To this end, books, newspapers, journals, and pamphlets in twenty-one languages rolled off party presses around the city and country and made their way into the hands of Chicago's workers through bookstores, street meetings, and factory-gate sales. In October 1930, reports indicated that 5,789 copies of the *Daily Worker* circulated in the district.[21]

In addition to readings, there were classes for new members, leaders, and interested folk. As early as 1929, Chicago's leaders taught classes out of party headquarters. This district "school" allowed new members to share their impressions of the party and its functions with veteran members. Current-events classes and sessions for full-time party leaders could be found here as well.[22]

By 1932, Communists' emphasis on formal education resulted in the district school changing its name to the Chicago Workers' School, widening its appeal, and broadening its offerings.[23] Internal party memos indicate that all workers were encouraged to participate in the school, but "workers in important industries and factories were recommended."[24] The *Workers' Voice,* a newspaper for Chicago's unemployed, advertised the school to the non-Communist public. In addition to more specialized classes on Marxism-Leninism, leaflet and shop-paper writing, strike strategy, and "fundamentals of class struggle," workers could take "elementary education for foreign born workers," or elementary or advanced English. For fifteen cents, workers could attend weekly forums to complement their other classes.[25] Such classes and party forums reveal the importance Communists placed on Americanization, workplace struggles, and alternative educational models as correctives to state-supported curricula that prepared workers to accept their lot in life without question.

Beginning in 1932, new party members no longer had their introductory sessions at the Chicago Workers' School. Instead, within each city region, Communists operated schools on a smaller basis to integrate new members and introduce them to basic skills necessary to Communist activity. A neighborhood in South Chicago, for example, offered four courses: workers' correspondence, elements of Communism, trade unionism, and public speaking. On the West Side, Communist leaders offered similar classes and a course on the fundamentals of class conflict. Italian Communists in the city also held beginning and advanced classes for organizers.[26] By January 1933, military intelligence turned up over eighty-six workers' schools in Chicago.[27]

Educational opportunities in Communist party meetings complemented neighborhood schools. In January 1930, city leaders instructed each neighborhood gathering to discuss Lenin, Leninism, and current conflicts in Illinois's coal mines.[28] They hoped to sharpen members' political understanding in order to create more effective Communists. Neighborhood meetings also held occasional speakers' conferences and study circles with hopes of enabling members to understand and speak about the workings of capitalism.

Not surprisingly, workers' schools and neighborhood meetings did not always go as planned. Chicago party leaders complained that while the schools filled a "definite need in the Party," they tended to attract "a large number of intellectual elements." Most agreed that school organizers should emphasize "getting more workers."[29] A West Side party group, facing problems filling its classes, worried openly that "we will not be able to supply speakers to open forums."[30]

Despite such problems, many recruits who would eventually find themselves in leadership positions could remember the specific pamphlet, book, or other writing by Lenin, Marx, or William Z. Foster that confirmed their suspicion that the Communist party was the answer to most problems. Formal classes, assigned readings, and informal political discussions helped workers understand that they were not to blame for their economic position and that workers had played important roles in the history of other societies. In addition to providing a theoretical base, Communist education developed organizing skills: how to collect signatures, or how to become an open-air speaker. The party expected members to participate in these practical classes and then use their skills in the city's streets, parks, and union halls.[31]

Educational opportunities were also important to Chicago's party because through these experiences, teachers identified students with potential and marked them for further training in schools across the Midwest. The most talented spent three weeks at the party's national school in New York, and some even went on to Moscow's Lenin School. With such training in the science of Marxism-Leninism, Communists believed revolution was possible. And while those like the Moscow-trained Haywood might have believed in the possibility more fervently than others, the idea permeated even the party's lowest levels.[32]

Besides providing formal education, party classes, newspapers, and magazines also reveal an internal struggle in the Depression's early years to define the party's position on femininity.[33] Lenin, Engels, and Marx supported women's emancipation; and during the Depression, Communists stood for women's rights to equal pay, fewer hours, sanitary work conditions, and birth control. Yet, despite the party's formal advocacy of women's emancipation, its self-image and priorities were decidedly masculine, mirroring the hypermale construction Eric D. Weitz finds in his study of German Communists, among whom street battles, competition with Nazis, the presence of paramilitary groups, and the historic connection labor and socialist movements made between work and masculinity translated into images of skillful, strong, and armed male workers. In the United States, Communist gender construction focused less on a romance with militarism and weaponry and instead emphasized male workers as the source of America's great wealth; they were usually drawn as muscular, brawny, and confident, symbolic of the party's strength and fortitude. Like Germans, American Communists borrowed from their country's labor and socialist tradition of imagining the idealized worker as a strong male.[34]

Despite plans and resolutions on behalf of women's issues, the party's imagery of women paralleled Weitz's findings in Germany: "notably diffuse, even contradictory."[35] On the one hand, Communists imagined women's struggle in purely class terms, presenting them as workers in their own right challenging low wages, unsafe work conditions, long hours, unemployment, and racism. They also emphasized women's supportive roles during men's labor struggles: taking blows from police, walking picket lines, and feeding striking and unemployed workers. In hand-drawn sketches, these women look more like men in drag—sporting broad shoulders, muscular arms, short hair, shirts, and occasionally heels. This depiction fit with the party's understanding of class in male terms and identified women's struggles with those of their male, working-class comrades. And yet despite these overly masculine and generally unrepresentative visions of women workers, the party's support of women's wage work occurred at a time when U.S. politicians and unionists advocated laws intended to push women out of the workplace and into the home. Communists were among a minority who advocated for women wage workers.[36]

Alongside its image of women workers as strong, determined industrial fighters, the party's press also presented working-class women as passive, degraded victims of capitalist exploitation. The historian Van Gosse argues that the party's emphasis on the crisis of unemployment allowed its rhetoric to shift from industrial struggles (coded as male) to household and neighborhood ones, understood and depicted as the realm of women.[37] This shift broadened the notion of the spaces women could legitimately occupy, and yet the press's treatment of women as mothers, housewives, and consumers remained diffuse and contradictory. As mothers, women could be downright helpless. Above a photo of a woman and two babies on the front page of an April 1931 issue of the *Working Woman* appears the caption, "Fathers Deported; Children Starve," suggesting that the woman is helpless to do anything about her situation. From 1930 through 1935, mothers' helplessness and their children's vulnerability were key images the party—ironically—used to appeal to women.[38]

Yet other images presented mothers in strong and active roles. As Annelise Orleck argues, the party increasingly politicized women's roles as mothers, housewives, and consumers in the 1930s.[39] Mothers occasionally led other women and children in the fight for lower bread prices and rents, and it was such mothers as those of the young African American men accused of raping two white women in Scottsboro, Alabama, in 1931 who appealed to other mothers to organize against racism and state brutality.[40]

The party's varied image of femininity speaks to the Communists' difficulty squaring members' own gender bias with the formal positions set by party theorists and policy makers. And yet Communists strongly believed that working women would be best served by its brand of socialism rather than by middle- and upper-class feminist groups. The party's press distanced working-class women from their middle- and upper-class counterparts while emphasizing the shared interests of working women and men. The part of its program that emphasized women's issues—the fight for a seven-hour day, the demand for equal pay for equal work, the protest against night work and wage cuts, and the support for women's right to birth control—straddled positions offered by middle-class feminists, who pushed for women's equality, and Progressive Era, middle-class reformers, who sought working women's protection.[41] In the context of Third Period revolutionary language and behavior, however, Communists discouraged women workers from joining others on this issue or that. Instead, images and articles in the press emphasized class differences between working women and those portrayed as fatter, more comfortable, and lazier, identified with progressive and feminist movements.[42]

Gendered notions of propriety also shaped the way the party disciplined Communist women. Chicago's leaders never told a man he spent too much time at dances and social affairs, but they cautioned Edith Miller not to do so and "not to bring the movement into her personal affairs." Hanging out with a new recruit, whom some had deemed a bad character, caused a stir in her family as well as in her local unit. When her party-member stepfather objected, her fling became party business. And while Chicago's leaders found it necessary to admonish Miller, there is no record of their calling any man to task for being promiscuous or spending too much time at socials. Party leaders also felt free to charge women for being "gossips." Men simply spread rumors.[43]

Yet despite women's differential treatment and the difficulty the party had in constructing a unified feminine ideal, Communists created one of the few public spaces for working women to lead, learn, and advocate a radical agenda. While their numbers were small, the women who participated bravely challenged the place that mainstream society had created for them. Dora Lifshitz led the party's fight in Chicago's International Ladies Garment Workers' Union against David Dubinsky and other anti-Communist union leaders. She was one of the few women elected to Chicago's district committee and its secretariat. John Williamson remembered that not only did "many a policeman's truncheon hit her head," but she often directed her "sharp tongue for fellow leaders if she felt they were wrong, and especially if they appeared to be swellheaded."[44] Katherine Erlich was a similarly feisty woman who, like Lifshitz, organized women workers, suffered police beatings, and challenged male party leaders. In an interview, Erlich revealed what drew her and most likely the cohort of women who joined with her: "The thing that impressed me the most was the stress on education, culture, respect for others, devotion to a movement that would by its example win the masses to the cause of Communism."[45] Such women were not motivated by feminism. And yet, by becoming active in the party and its campaigns, they would begin to develop a feminist critique of Communism, its leaders, and its program, bringing them to build a network of women's activists that would sustain them in the years to come.[46]

In addition to the lessons Communists learned about gender, socialism, and class through reading, discussion, and schooling, they also picked up party beliefs and behaviors through participation in Communist activities. Watching veteran members, new recruits got tips on organizing, socializing, and discipline.

With the belief that each party event might be the one to tip the scales, Bill Gebert and John Williamson encouraged others to think big every time they planned a demonstration, and they were regularly planned. Williamson instructed members to stencil sidewalks; to sell special-edition newspapers, buttons, pamphlets, and leaflets; and to talk about each event's political significance at neighborhood and mass meetings. For example, Gebert reported that preparation for 1930's May Day demonstration, while not as thorough as it might have been, resulted in the distribution of more than two hundred thousand leaflets and shop papers and ten thousand *Daily Worker* newspapers. He was glad to report that party members also held a number of shop and street meetings. May Day was an internationally celebrated holiday begun in Chicago and, in theory, familiar to Chicago's workers. But Chicago's Communists pulled out the stops regardless of the occasion's obscurity. The sociologists Harold Lasswell and Dorothy Blumenstock found that in the first five years of the Depression, Chicago's party "led, organized, or participated" in 2,088 mass demonstrations.[47]

On the day of this typical May Day demonstration, rank-and-file Communists learned how to reach the masses. Marchers moved in what Gebert reported to be a "military manner," carrying "plenty of banners" and guarded by a specially selected "defense corps," entrusted with keeping the lines in order. Gebert estimated that there were thirty-five thousand marchers. It ended inside Ashland Auditorium, where Gebert gave a speech, followed by those by party leaders in charge of work among blacks, youth, the unemployed, and the International Labor Defense. One non-party speaker was Lucy Parsons, the widow of Albert Parsons, who had been executed by the state for his alleged participation in the

Under this May 2, 1930, *Chicago Tribune* photo read the following caption: "Chicago Reds' May Day Procession, under police supervision, proves peaceful affair. Communists marching west on Maypole Avenue from Ashland Avenue on their way to the Ashland Boulevard auditorium on Ashland Avenue and Van Buren Street, where the paraders and others listened to addresses which were comparatively tame." (*Chicago Tribune* file photo. All rights reserved. Used with permission.)

Haymarket affair of 1886. Connecting their movement to Chicago's traditions of labor struggle, Communists like Gebert pushed Chicago's workers to see the party as the natural heir to lead workers forward.[48]

Unfortunately for party leaders, Chicago's police were more interested in the comings and goings of party activists than were most workers. While this uninvited state interest convinced some that the party was on the right track, police raids and harassment proved a nuisance for leaders. Police intervention punctuated Communists' daily work, creating confusion, disruption, and a defensiveness about shortfalls in party recruitment. It also convinced some members of the need to have an underground, or at least secretive, arm of the movement.

A special police force, the Red Squad, had its origins in Chicago as early as the Haymarket incident. The squad constantly surveyed party offices, leaders, and members and kept detailed records. Undercover agents attended party meetings, took notes, and arranged for taps on phones and at gatherings. Before big events, officers raided party offices and destroyed furniture and records.[49]

To compensate for such intrusions, leaders organized an "illegal" or "semi-legal" apparatus based on the Bolshevik model and comprised of leaders who agreed to take control of party operations during periods when police took to arresting leaders. During these times, substitute leaders directed the party through an underground structure that controlled the interaction between them, leaders who stayed public, and their rank-and-file members. In the case of the 1930 May Day raid, Gebert assured national party leaders that organizational results were so low because a police raid occurred in the days leading to the demonstration, and the "shadow apparatus" was unable to make "sufficient contact with the lower ranks of the Party and district leadership." As May Day approached, the functioning of the underground organization improved, but Gebert admitted that the party was not prepared when they met five hundred Chicago police officers armed with machine guns. Underground leaders sent instructions to defend the parade, and the defense corps had been chosen, but Gebert conceded that if the police wanted them dispersed, they easily could have done so.

Despite the existence of underground structures, party leaders taught their members that illegality was a final resort. Throughout the period, Chicago's leaders desperately wanted a public party whose members could shepherd workers to the impending revolution. To that end, they worked to develop organized, legal resistance to police repression. Williamson announced a "monster meeting against activities of police and [the] Red Squad" held under ILD auspices that would occur at the Coliseum in October 1931. In a letter to party members, Williamson emphasized the importance of having an overflow crowd to show "working class resistance to police terror."[50]

In addition to such gatherings, Communists tried to curry workers' support in the midst of party activity. One example involved Herbert Newton. An African American leader sent to Moscow for training, Newton was the only black member of the "Atlanta Six," a group of Communists charged under Georgia's Insurrection Act. The group faced the death penalty for involvement in an antilynching and unemployed demonstration. By 1932, Newton had become a member of the national party's Central Committee and an organizer on Chicago's South Side. One afternoon Newton was speaking at a black forum in Ellis Park when Chicago police arrived and tried to stop him. By all accounts, Newton scampered up a nearby oak tree, and no police were able to follow him. With the aid of a megaphone, Newton kept talking to the crowd until the fire department arrived. Even though he was eventually arrested, the police did not physically harm him, and the park remained open to speakers, becoming, in party parlance, "Newton Forum Park."[51] Perhaps this story is often retold because it portrays what party leaders predicted would occur with worker support. Rather than having to go underground, leaders believed that workers, in witness to party activity, would protect them from police. Even though Newton's arrest technically silenced him, police beat no one and allowed the forum to continue.

During times of police suppression and public demonstration, Communists did not overlook the importance of social activity. As an alternative to company picnics and sporting events or church dances and bazaars, Chicago's Communists created a social world intended to foster solidarity and emphasize party values. Communist symphonies, picnics, chorus performances, socials, and dances carried political significance. A "symphony conference" for miners' relief promised "struggle and good music"; workers could witness a mock trial at a "red singing competition." Dances and picnics were also ways to raise money for the *Daily Worker* and ethnic presses. Socials to raise funds for the Soviet Union's defense promised tea from a Russian samovar; and parties to raise money so that unemployed, working students, and party hopefuls could attend workers' schools were complete with choruses, music, refreshments, games, and, in at least one case, a popularity contest. Party games played on Communist themes, like the one celebrating revolution that was enjoyed at socials in the 1930s: "The comrades are seated in a circle. They are furnished (secretly) with names of various countries, one for each comrade. A comrade stands at the center of the circle and calls for revolutions in two countries. The comrades with the name of these countries try to exchange seats, the comrade at the center of the circle attempting to take one of the seats. Sometimes world revolution is called for and everybody tries to get a new seat. It was explained at one game that Russia was not given because 'there can be no revolution in Soviet Russia.'"[52]

Whether they organized or played, Communists were to follow Third Period teachings, particularly about race. Communist leaders in Moscow, with the aid of such American blacks as Haywood, formulated the official position on race, and local party leaders enforced it. The policy—known as the right to self-determination—was based on the nationalities policy of the Soviet Union.[53] Southern African Americans, the argument went, composed a dispossessed nation with unfulfilled rights to land and self-government. The fight for self-determination in the region was seen as a fight for black nationhood, thus tying the anticolonial freedom struggle of southern African Americans to the work of making working-class revolution. In the North, African Americans would not push for a separate nation but would work toward interracial solidarity.[54]

With this mandate on race issues, Chicago's white Communists were supposed to bring blacks into the fold. Compared to any other progressive group in the city, Chicago's Communists stood alone in their efforts to include African Americans.

The Scottsboro Boys' defense was the most visible campaign the party launched among blacks. The 1931 case resulted from two young white women accusing nine young black men of rape in a boxcar in Alabama. After two weeks and questionable testimony, an Alabama court sentenced the young men to death. Communists rallied in their defense and promoted their case as a symbol of the terror carried on in the South against blacks. Some of Chicago's members, like Newton and a Jewish man named Herb March, who would make a name for himself as a union leader in Chicago's stockyards, were active in campaigns against lynching in other cities. But the Scottsboro case would galvanize the entire party as news spread of the trial and sentence. Chicago party leaders instructed members, "[O]n us [Communists], first of all, rests the responsibility for the lives of the Scottsboro Boys."[55]

In typical Third Period fashion, Chicago Communists made elaborate preparations for a Scottsboro demonstration in 1933. Leaders held three predemonstration street meetings in the Black Belt, and on four separate nights they sent members house to house with leaflets. Through street meetings, speeches at churches, and door-to-door mobilization, the party spread the word of the injustices against the young men in Scottsboro and received a warm reception from the city's black community. In Chicago, according to St. Clair Drake and Horace Cayton, "[T]housands of Negro preachers and doctors and lawyers, as well as quiet housewives, gave their money and verbal support to the struggle for freeing the Scottsboro Boys."[56]

In addition to campaigns that focused on racial injustice, Communist leaders organized interracial picnics, dances, and social events where black and white Communists learned from one another and occasionally developed strong relationships, a rarity in 1930s segregated Chicago. In December 1933, the YCL in Englewood held a dance with some new black recruits in attendance. One party member, P. Camel, told of how "a Negro girl were [*sic*] teaching a white boy a new dance step."[57] It was inevitable that from such social opportunities came interracial couples. David Poindexter and Herbert Newton, for example, were both married to white women. In Jane Newton's case, the marriage caused a stir. Her wealthy father, Col. John C. Emery, never approved of her union and actually forced her to undergo psychiatric testing because of her marriage to a black man. The couple eventually moved to Russia with their two children.[58]

Such commitment to black and white social relationships made an impression on non-party Chicagoans. In response to a question about Communism on the editorial page of the *Chicago Defender,* one race-conscious reader explained: "My knowledge of Russia convinces me that the Negro element can more easily fit in there than it can in this land of sainted bigots and thinly veneered barbarians who appreciate us only when we are in our places, wherever that may be." Dempsey Travis brought these observations home. Growing up on Chicago's South Side, Travis believed that any white person who talked to a black person was a Communist.[59]

If organizing and socializing were intended to unify the ranks, so was party discipline.[60] Whether old-timer or novice, African American or immigrant, leader or follower, through reading, word of mouth, and at formal party gatherings, Chicago's Communists learned that success hinged on discipline. A key to Communist discipline was members' willingness to subject themselves to criticism. Party members were to regularly examine their roles to make sure they were living up to the party's principles and ideals, and they were expected to call each other to task. A leading Chicago Communist explained, "[I]t is necessary for the various individuals who comprise the Party and particularly the individuals that have been responsible for leading work to subject themselves to a searching self criticism. Not only must our policy—our work be criticized but . . . individuals can be singled out, placed on the platform and their weaknesses exposed."[61]

This application of Leninism to party work occurred at all levels. Ben Gray, a member of Chicago's YCL, recalled that even rank-and-file Communists were supposed to be part of "a highly disciplined, well-organized and dedicated group of people who considered themselves revolutionaries." After participating in an action, party members would gather with others from their neighborhood or shop group to review what occurred. "If somebody stepped out of line or maybe was provocative in their dealings with the police or in carrying forward unnecessary actions which only hurt the movement," Gray remembered, "they would be severely criticized and be educated in the form of drawing lessons."[62] Through evaluation, critique, and analysis, individuals would learn how to become better Communists. All city party members also participated in the process. Minutes of one meeting of the political committee record that "comrades got up and showed the weakness of the comrades, their defects, their strong points." Bill Gebert proudly announced at a citywide meeting, "Today it is a living example that Party comrades understand what self-criticism means, and they fully and completely exercise it. We must make self criticism the instrument for cleansing the Party."[63]

The idea of such strict party discipline originated in the Soviet Union with Lenin's emphasis on verifying whether comrades followed instructions. Moscow's party heads assigned these responsibilities to an international Control Commission. Communist leaders in cities throughout the United States established local Control Commissions and directed their members to enforce not only party ideology but also the keeping of sound financial records and ethical operations. Members suspected of wrongdoing in any of these areas were called before their city's Control Commission and subjected to disciplinary action.[64] Individuals or groups could bring charges from anywhere within the party's structure, and Chicago's Control Commission listened even when non-party members brought charges. Units in neighborhoods and factories lodged the most common complaints, and section leaders usually supported them. When not emanating from an individual's unit, complaints sometimes came from his or her fraction. Discipline in the local context meant that close friends and political allies were responsible for keeping one another in line.[65]

That such duties would get mired in personality conflict as well as ideological difference is no surprise. Once someone brought charges, it was up to the various party units to make a recommendation on which discipline to enforce. The most common rulings involved dropping members from party rolls or expelling them. A member might be dropped from the rolls for inactivity, not paying dues for more than three months, or not showing up at unit meetings. Once dropped, this individual might still be considered a "good sympathizer and left winger" and still be relied upon in trade-union work and mass organizing. If their former units approved, these people might even be readmitted when prepared to invest more time. Acts of expulsion were more severe and implied that party members had done more than shirk activity, payment, and attendance. Some of the expelled were considered "anti-party elements" and became pariahs who were forced to sever former friendships, social networks, and political ties. Others might still be useful to the movement if they came around on this or that point. Like rehabilitated criminals, they might be encouraged to reapply after a period during which they would have to show they were redeemed and worthy.[66] Sections and units were not allowed to expel members on their own. This serious gesture needed the support of the city's Control Commission.[67]

Through their Control Commissions, local party leaders had the responsibility and power to see that their members pushed priorities and followed policies articulated by higher-ranking Communist officials. It is no wonder that during the Third Period, Control Commissions were occasionally used for factional purposes. The roots of Third Period factionalism originated in the aftermath of the 1923–24 Farmer-Labor party debacle. John Pepper, a Hungarian Comintern representative, won the body's support and forced William Z. Foster, against his better judgment, to lead a Communist takeover of the Farmer-Labor party, causing a rift between Communist party trade unionists and mainstream, progressive labor activists. The ensuing battle to win control over the party's future direction pitted Foster and James P. Cannon against Charles Ruthenberg and Jay Lovestone, two leading American supporters of Pepper's positions. While different visions of Communist policy drove the leaders and some members of the two factions apart, some of Chicago's Communists aligned themselves with personalities. Al Glotzer, a youth organizer in the city, remembered siding with the Foster-Cannon group. His reasoning was "perhaps because of proximity . . . I tended to lean to groups that were more American and more Chicagoan, people who were midwesterners." Portraying the Ruthenberg-Lovestone group as "smart New Yorkers, big college New Yorkers, not working-class types," Glotzer aligned with Foster. Glotzer was joined by entire language fractions in the factional bitterness. According to city leaders, "instead of making themselves instruments of the Party to mobilize for Party work," foreign-language fractions also "made themselves instruments of a faction to mobilize against the Party leadership."[68]

The Comintern finally stepped in when antagonism between factions escalated to a fevered pitch. In 1925, the Comintern established a Parity Commission to settle questions of party control. Even though Foster's faction had a majority of the delegates at the convention and hoped to consolidate their control of the party, the Comintern ruled for Ruthenberg. Foster and his supporters could either submit to the decision or leave the party. They submitted. Ruthenberg took control and began to install his supporters on key committees throughout the party's hierarchy, but divisions persisted at the local level. Chicago's party leaders continued to identify as members of "majority" and "minority" groups and to interpret committee appointments and policies as factional acts.

These divisions simply worsened in 1928 when the Communist party expelled Leon Trotsky, and the American leader James P. Cannon rose to his support. In *The Draft Program of the Comintern International: A Criticism of Fundamentals*, Trotsky had leveled a fundamental critique of the Comintern's Stalinist direction and its effect on the party's European and Far Eastern policies. "It was the document," Cannon recalled, "that hit us like a thunderbolt."[69] The details of his attack focused on theory and international concerns, but the visceral appeal of Trotskyism to people like Cannon was the belief that Trotsky—not Stalin—was right and by following Stalin's lead, Communists were actually betraying the revolution and Lenin's wishes. What to Cannon was a revelation screamed of heresy to the unconverted. Turning on his former ally, Foster brought charges against Cannon, whom the party expelled in October 1928. Fewer than one hundred members left with Cannon, but Chicago lost about a dozen, including such key union and party activists as Arne Swabeck, the former district organizer, and Martin Abern, a Rumanian Communist active among youth, the city's leadership, and the ILD.[70] These defections exacerbated older divisions between those identified as "majority" and those identified as "minority." As the national party attacked Cannon, the majority faction within Chicago's Political buro pointed to "a dangerous manifestation of Trotskyism" among its minority members. In response, minority leaders banded together and denied these "wild accusations," arguing that it was members of the majority who needed to be self-critical and better follow Comintern policies.[71] In this battle, neither side wanted to be painted as a follower of Trotsky, and both asserted their loyalty to the Comintern.

When they were not pointing fingers at one another, Chicago's leaders sent word to members at the nuclei level to fight against Trotskyism and Cannon's followers. Joe Giganti, a barber by trade and head of the city's ILD, remembered attending a North Side nuclei meeting during the party's purge of Trotskyists. It was one of many meetings held to spread the word that the party stood against Trotskyism. Giganti remembered the speakers railing "against the dire criminality of the Trots and their collusion with the bourgeois and the counter revolution." He was not sure what to think. A few weeks later, his indecision brought him expulsion. Denying his support for Trotsky and his American followers, Giganti sent a protest to the city's leadership, which he hoped they would publish in the party's press to clear his name. It was one thing in 1929 to be expelled for not having issue with Trotskyists and another to be a known Trotskyist.[72]

Citywide meetings continued in February 1929. That month, the city's leadership pledged to combat all "Trotskyist manifestations" in the district. Holding more meetings, especially in Jewish and Russian neighborhoods, where interest in the issue was strongest, party leaders instructed members to be firm with "Trots": no fraternizing, no audience, no contacts.[73]

Chicago's Communists continued to scorn followers of Trotsky even as Comintern politics began to shift battle lines. Stalin turned his attention away from the Trotsky issue in 1929 and toward a "right danger" in the Soviet party. Nicolai Bukharin became associated with this danger, and in America, national party leaders found their "right danger" in the person of Jay Lovestone, who took charge of the majority faction after Charles Ruthenberg's death in 1927. Lovestone made the mistake of aligning himself with Bukharin. The two supported the notion of American exceptionalism—the idea that class relations in the United States were unique and that revolution was less likely because of the stable nature of American capitalism. With the official Third Period line being that capitalism was in crisis and that revolution was imminent, Lovestone, Bukharin, and American exceptionalism became party pariahs.

Gebert enforced these policies ruthlessly and was joined by the other district-level leaders Sam Don and Clarence Hathaway, who supported Foster's caucus. They used expulsions and their threat to remove Lovestone's and Trotsky's sympathizers from the party's ranks to move against anyone who was not prepared to move to the left in their thinking and actions.[74] In the city's political committee, Hathaway, Don, and Gebert exposed the "right" mistakes of fellow leaders Cline, Held, and Feingold and pointed out others who lurked at lower levels of the hierarchy. Ensuring distance between themselves and Trotsky, Cannon, and now Lovestone, Chicago's Communist leaders hoped to make it clear to America's workers that the Communist party was the only leftist group capable of providing revolutionary leadership.[75]

For this reason, Communists quickly broadened their attack outward, from the deviants in their midst to those reformist and Social-Democratic forces outside the party. These groups were called "social fascist" because Communists believed them to be "socialist in words and fascist in deeds."[76] American Communists modeled their social-fascist campaign on Comintern teachings that directly linked Germany's turn to fascism with Social-Democrats' counter-revolutionary nature. In the early years of the Third Period, Chicago's Communists scorned any non-Communist leftist and liberal organization that spoke on behalf of American workers because, they argued, these groups distracted workers from the real class fight, just as Social-Democrats had in Germany. A "class versus class" slogan became popular during the period and left no room for any non-Communist group in the struggle between the working class, led by Communists, and the bourgeoisie, led by capitalists.[77]

Instead of making alliances with social fascists, party leaders promoted a deceptive tactic that they called "the united front from below." It required party members to create coalitions with workers in Socialist and other non-party organizations in an attempt to win them over to the party and to turn them against those in charge of their group. The leadership of other organizations was bankrupt, Chicago Communists argued; the Communist party alone possessed solutions to workers' problems.[78]

The party loyalist Jack Spiegel took this task to heart. Successfully disrupting non-party meetings of the unemployed, Spiegel heckled Socialist and reformist leaders and "exposed" the fact, as he believed, that "when the chips are down and we [workers] have a confrontation with the enemy, they won't be on our side." To Spiegel, the leaders of other "lesser" parties were not "genuine," not "true revolutionaries," and as a Communist he needed to reveal their ulterior motives to workers everywhere.[79]

Party newspapers furthered the fight. One issue of the *Northwestern Shop News* railed against the Socialist party, arguing that it was not a workers' party but one of "petty shopkeepers, longhaired intellectuals, and wealthy morons." The paper exposed one machinist, John Collins, as a Socialist and a person to be disregarded. Like others in the Socialist party, the paper argued, Collins "never comes to the front when there is a fight against railroad bosses for better wages or working conditions." It was the Communists, the writer insisted, who stood up against "police clubs and blackjacks" to lead workers.[80]

Foreign-language Communist papers also carried the fight against social fascists. *Radnik* exposed the "Jugoslav Educational Association leadership as one that supports the Republican Party and is counterrevolutionary." Its editors offered proof that the association was not a worker's organization but "the tail end of the most corrupt bourgeois Party in America." A later edition discredited Hrvatski Radisa and Srbski Privrednik, two organizations established to raise money to care for orphans of the First World War in Serbia and Croatia that, *Radnik* accused, "corrupted" their initial mission. Including quotes from students in Serbia, the paper accused the organizations of forcing children to slave for masters in an unquestioning and brutal fashion.[81]

Occasionally, non-party foreign-language papers turned the tables on Communists and exposed party tactics to their non-party readers. A Hungarian paper, *Otthon*, revealed Communist attempts to take over the Rakoczy Sick Benefit Society. "They [Communist members] started a whispering campaign against the officers of the Rakoczy with the intention of getting them suspended from office and enabling them to put their satellites in place." In another case, a Russian paper belittled Communists' "revolutionary spirit" when about two hundred party members stood on the platform of an elevated train and waited for columns of Ukrainians demonstrating against "Soviet terror" in their home country to pass below them. As they did, they felt "a sudden hail of rocks, bricks, and pieces of iron . . . fall upon their heads." *Rassviet* applauded the Ukrainian counterattack that ensued and successfully gave the Communists "a good whipping." Just imagine, the paper asked, "how many victims there would have been among innocent people if the Communist hooligans had been superior in number?"[82] Such thoughts and tactics convinced many that the Communist party was not for them and bolstered anti-Communist sentiments throughout the city. Communists justified such actions because they were convinced that it was their duty to lead workers away from such organizations and their leaders and toward the Communist party, the only party actively defending the Soviet Union.

Ideas about the Soviet Union, education, activism, race, party discipline, factionalism, and social fascism sat at the intellectual center of Chicago's party culture. They reveal positions of party leaders that were occasionally embraced by those lower in the ranks and make left-wing anti-Communism during this period understandable. Viewed together, they help create a picture of party activists in the Third Period as idealistic, committed, militant, serious, and ambitious. Of course, they also show Communists to have been sectarian, pompous, and overeager to please Comintern and national leaders. At the neighborhood level, party culture embraced all of these tendencies and encouraged others. In park forums, neighborhood meetings, language fractions, and shop groups, where most Communists experienced the party, an even more diverse set of behaviors and attitudes coexisted and sometimes contradicted those modeled and envisioned at the highest levels, revealing Chicago's party's quirks and particularities and the inability of its leaders ever to stamp them out.

True Revolutionaries

Communist leaders imported Soviet-styled organizational structures, hoping to organize America's ranks in a disciplined manner, but on American soil their structure never worked exactly as the Soviets intended. During the Third Period, Gebert and Williamson, and those sent to Chicago to replace them, did not impose the level of discipline on their members that they were supposed to. Directions from above structured their work and coordinated their activity, but mundane problems were forever interfering with the most reasonable and seemingly rational party directives. Individual Communists, moreover, decided which piece of party ideology they would follow, sometimes quietly ignoring the rest and at other times drawing leaders' attention their way. Whether caused by organizational problems, the independent stance of various national groups, or individual resistance, Chicago's leaders oversaw an organization with a lively, contentious, and varied local party culture where individuals and groups emphasized, ignored, or resisted different aspects of the party's dominant culture.

Communists received weekly letters from Williamson's department that laid out weekly and monthly work and emphasized party directives that sections and units were to adapt to their neighborhoods and factories. But section and unit members did not always read the letters. Some did not even pick them up at the district office. In September 1930, Williamson called attention to the one nucleus whose members did not read his past letters: "This particular nucleus did not even know that the nuclei meetings had been changed to Thursdays."[83]

As a backup measure to ensure the passing of information, personal contacts happened intermittently. Section leaders assigned themselves to nuclei to guide and encourage their work but often sent decisions on paper instead of attending themselves. Leaders insisted that the more personal contacts they made, the better chance they would have to retain new members and increase meeting attendance, but throughout the period, district leaders complained that too little contact occurred among the party's tiers. A 1930 organization department letter argued that district leaders had made mistakes in coming "in touch mainly with the section committees" while ignoring the nuclei.[84] With little personal contact, district and section leaders consistently lacked basic information about the neighborhoods. In the party registration of 1931, 90 percent of the city's section leaders were unable to tell the district which revolutionary trade union or AFL local existed in their section and which fractions "worked."[85]

Williamson, in vain, reminded section and unit leaders to carry through organizational directives. For over a month, district leaders tried to collect money for the national office from section members. Rather than responding, one frustrated section leader wrote, "[I]f you want the assessment in a hurry, send someone to collect them [sic]."[86] This attitude was carried over into other areas of activity, including sending reports, mobilizing for party functions, selling literature, and attending meetings. In October 1930, the party's section that included part of the West Side was in a bad state. Even though its minutes showed that its leaders addressed party issues, its members neglected at least half of the section's decisions. The section buro rarely met to plan the work of the section committee, and the committee meeting started about an hour late and lasted until midnight, by which time all workers had left.[87] In the summer of 1931, 50 percent of the city's unit members disregarded district leaders' warning against taking more than two weeks' summer vacation, nor did they find replacements to take over their responsibilities or pay their dues in advance as instructed.[88] Throughout this period of revolutionary hope, leaders and members at all levels were pulled between expectations of revolutionary responsibility and everyday economic and social realities, which sometimes caused them to falter.

Inefficient departments and changing leadership added to the confusion. Department leaders among youth and women at the section level sometimes called meetings only to find that their counterparts did not exist at the unit level. City leaders of the anti-imperialist committee refused to meet, causing district leaders to replace them. Confronted with the lack of work at the lowest levels, some section leaders would just "shrug [their] shoulders and say what can I do?"[89] Even when leaders were in place, individuals moved around and sometimes dropped out. In 1932 the district complained that one section changed its unit functionaries without explanation. In 1933 the secretariat criticized another section for changing its functionaries and committee members without holding elections, and when another section did not produce results in 1930, district leaders called a section conference to elect a new committee.[90]

Rookie and veteran leaders struggled with the amount of work that party responsibilities required. Often unit members faced too many meetings and obligations. The district constantly demanded a reduction of meetings, but the problem continued.[91] The district hoped that each person would hold only one leadership post, but this was seldom the case. One nucleus member held six job titles in 1930.[92] Not surprisingly, these overloaded people ignored some work. In 1934, the leaders in one section focused so heavily on their union work that they neglected their section duties, and the district leadership eventually replaced them.[93] Instead of balancing study groups with activism, some units cut out political discussion entirely and concentrated on action.[94]

While the party's internal problems generated conflict, negligence, and confusion, they also created opportunities for members to circumvent party orthodoxy. One member held unit meetings in his home that were continually interrupted as he sold bootleg liquor to supplement his income. In 1934, a section committee voted down a motion that Herbert Newton, a leader from the Political buro, act as its section organizer.[95] One member lied about another member's family finances so that the family could pay reduced dues; he did not think that they should have to pay the full amount. When district leaders held an internal investigation of one of their sections, they found that section leaders hid information that the district wanted. Other section leaders, who had to fill newspaper sales quotas set by the district, ordered larger bundles of reading materials than they could sell in an effort to show the district that they could reach their goals, then failed to pick them up. Some sections independently dropped members who did not pay dues in order to convince the district they were doing well with collections. These actions show that Chicago's Communists resisted party hegemony and hint at a local culture cultivated by the party's ranks.[96]

At times this local culture of resistance extended from basic organizational issues to those related to policy. Ethnic Communists were some of the worst offenders. The diversity of people in the party confirmed to some that it was a truly international organization with the right answers for the world's workers. But the international and diverse nature of the party also created strains and stresses for party leaders. In the sense that people from all over the world came together under the banner of Soviet Communism, internationalism made Chicago's leaders proud. Statements of support to the revolutionary movement in Lithuania during a Lithuanian buro meeting, or plans of Chicago's Yugoslavian buro to correspond with Yugoslavian Communists in Vienna, confirmed such international ties.[97] But white ethnics' lack of party discipline, particular international loyalties, and prejudices violated party policies and suggest that ethnic subcultures existed in Chicago's party.

The party's own structure supported these subcultures. Beginning in 1925, national Communist leaders created a campaign of "bolshevization" in part to move their organization away from the foreign-language-federation model of the Socialist party and toward the streets and shops of America's workers. In 1929, party leaders decided to modify the organization once again and this time organized each language group into its own buro, with representation at the national, city, and neighborhood levels. Language-buro leaders at the city level assigned rank-and-file ethnic counterparts to work in fractions. As editor of *Radnik* and leader of the city's language groups, S. Zinich liked to remind Chicago's Communist ethnics, "Fractions are organs of the Party within non Party organizations. They are not independent, fully authorized organizations but are subordinate to the competent local Party committee." As fraction members, ethnic Communists were to gear these mass organizations toward the issues and activities Communists supported, like union building, protection of foreign-born activists against deportation, and unemployment campaigns, while fighting social-fascist tendencies among their leaders and all the while bringing foreign-language masses "closer to the American revolutionary labor movement."[98]

One of the problems in seeing these tasks through was that many of Chicago's ethnic Communists came to the party from the Socialist party's foreign-language federations, organizations that functioned autonomously from the Socialist party's English-language organization. Within their federations, foreign-language-speaking Socialists talked about their own concerns, handled their problems internally, and became involved in whatever activity they chose. "Federationalism" frustrated Communist party leaders. They regularly tried to rid their ranks of its tendencies and to bring foreign-language members closer to party discipline, party activity, and self-criticism.

But federationalist tendencies persisted. Party records reveal leaders' frustration with the Greeks for being "hard to control" and with the Czechs, who were unable to shift from a federationalist way of organizing themselves. "I doubt if [the Czechs] have re[a]d the instruction sent to them from here," one party leader complained.[99] In one case, the leader of the Finnish buro got into a battle with a worker who was new to the Communist party, but who had been a member of the Socialist Finnish federation. Each blamed the other for deviating from the party line and causing disruption in the federation. The battle had its roots in a struggle back when they were members of the Socialist federation. Such internal debate carried on in the Jewish buro as well, particularly around the question of Palestine.[100]

As late as 1931, groups of Lithuanians were violating party policies. Before a meeting of party and non-party shareholders of the party's Lithuanian paper, *Vilnis,* a group of Communists tried to convince those assembled that the party had wrongfully expelled one of their fellow ethnic comrades and that accusations made concerning the danger of racism at the paper and among Lithuanian Communists were exaggerated. Lithuanian-language leaders saw this airing of dirty laundry among non-party members as a "gross violation of Party discipline." Differences among loyalists escalated to such a degree that national leaders agreed to send a delegation of Lithuanians to Moscow, where they would have their positions heard and decided upon by a Comintern commission.[101]

Historic divisions and conflicts between Communist ethnics were also known to turn Communists against one another. In an attempt to create united committees against fascism, for example, Chicago's party ran up against a wall when it came to its Yugoslav and Balkan comrades. Historic prejudice between these ethnic workers kept them from wanting to join together for any cause. In this case, party leaders were unwilling to reprimand individuals. A letter from the national language committee to a leader in Chicago stated, "It is impossible to draw in all the mass organizations that are building a united front on jugo slav issues also into the Balkan committees, . . . because the problem is to some extent new for them because of the national prejudices." Understanding the historic hatred that existed between certain groups, party leaders encouraged starting slowly with a few individuals who showed leadership on the issue.[102]

While historic hatred among white ethnics might be tolerated, white-on-black prejudice was usually taken more seriously. When a group of Lithuanian Communists proved unwilling to get in line with the party's campaign to expose and eliminate racist tendencies (its white chauvinism campaign), they learned the consequences. Party leaders understood black and white unity as a precondition for black liberation and socialist revolution. If they wanted to usher in the revolution, then Communists had to publicly and actively promote black liberation and bring up those who refused on white-chauvinist charges.[103] Meanwhile, a small group with Strazdas, a member of *Vilnis*'s editorial staff, as their leader, refused to take a stance against the fight to keep blacks out of the white-ethnic neighborhood of Bridgeport. They also thought that an editorial against racism in Detroit was too harsh, and they defended the Lithuanian workers' cooperative against accusations that it supported racist policies. Strazdas was annoyed that the party so openly questioned him and his Lithuanian comrades and believed that such questions "should have been settled among ourselves [the Lithuanians]." Party leaders formally expelled Strazdas, an action which he largely ignored as he continued doing party work.[104]

Party leaders removed highly visible racist ethnic leaders such as Strazdas from their membership rolls, but other examples of racist attitudes among language-group members persisted within party ranks. A letter to the *Daily Worker* from P. Camel, a concerned black party member, dealt with racism among the party's white ethnics. Russian comrades in the city canceled an affair because, according to the author, a few black Communists planned to attend. The Russians knew better than to use black attendance as the reason for the cancellation and instead claimed that they feared a police shutdown of their Mutual Aid Society building, where they held a school for Russian children.[105] Such action resulted in the party losing six new black recruits. Sam Ptasek, a Russian party veteran of ten years, became the scapegoat, and after appearing before an open trial, arguing that his bad English was the cause of the mishap, he was expelled in the fall of 1933 "with the right for readmission after six months." By May 1934, Ptasek was reinstated. His fellow comrades unanimously supported his application. While it is possible that Ptasek rid himself of racist beliefs, he probably did not. More likely others in his group shared his racist views and supported canceling the dance but were never brought up on charges.[106]

In the context of a rigidly segregated city where race relations were generally bad, white ethnics who challenged racial mores had their work cut out for them.[107] Party leaders hoped that their white ethnic members would rise to this challenge, and they did make examples of people, such as Ptasek, when cases became public. But sometimes lower-ranking leaders refused to report violations, allowing some of Chicago's Communists to keep their racist attitudes below higher-ranking leaders' radar.

Details of Camel's experiences support this observation. At a YCL dance, a leading white member of the YCL, according to Camel, accused a white boy of "falling" for "*crow jam*" when he danced with a young black female member. This comment shocked Camel and the other black attendees. Leaving the event, the YCL leader gathered "every hoodlum she could get and had them line up" outside the dance hall. When black members came out of the hall and walked down the street, "[T]hey were call all kind of *names* and some of *our* old Party member had to guard these negro home [*sic*]." While such racist behavior disturbed Camel and the other black recruits at the dance, more upsetting was the fact that the incident was never reported to city leaders. Even when the issue "was taken up with some of the leading YCL members" in the neighborhood, Camel reported in anger, "they suggested we forget about it."

Camel believed in the party's racial program and wanted it and the YCL to "be clean of hiding white chauvinism," but a lack of reporting and leniency meant that such a cleansing was impossible. Camel wrote about a man who would "walk up to you and put his arm around you and pat you on your back and say com[rade]. *You* know we Communists must stick to*gether. You* know there arent *any* different in me and *you* [*sic*]." But when this man's daughter fell in love with a black man, married him, and had a baby, the man had a change of heart. Camel wrote, "I *know* not any of her family ever come to see her. And the Bad Part of it is that her dad and brother are Party *members* [*sic*]."[108]

Racism endured among some Communist groups because leaders largely focused their attention away from them. It was not that Williamson, Gebert, and other party leaders did not care about the character of their ethnic members, but they were even more concerned with recruiting native-born industrial workers, which meant that language work, in particular, got short shrift. With Chicago's party leaders offering more lip service than actual supervision and oversight, it was up to S. Zinich and others on the city's language buro to oversee the daily checking up on and supervising of ethnic work. But three to five people could not handle the work alone, especially when, in Zinich's estimation, "many Party officials are not considering this [language] work as important."[109] The result was that subcultures were allowed to coexist within Chicago's Communist party.

As party leaders diverted ethnic ranks into general party work, more isolated and independent language groups were left behind. In July 1934, members of the Scandinavian fraction complained about the way Chicago's party leaders raided their fraction, assigning their members to work among the unemployed and unions and perform other nonlanguage party work, leaving nobody to carry out fraction work in the Danish-Norwegian Karl Marx Club. "The anarchistic method now exercised by sections, units, etc., in the appointments of comrades to other duties must stop for the good of the movement." The authors noted that the few Communists who remained active in language work had party responsibilities heaped on them. Many became overwhelmed, inactive, and the subject of talk among non-party club members who began to question Communists' leadership skills.[110]

Such realities meant that leadership was a general problem for ethnic Communists. Gebert himself had been plucked from the Polish buro, leaving a glaring hole that leaders found impossible to fill. One report from the language buro stated that the Yugoslav buro was "politically clear" but had "little forces left." John Mackovich, the leader of the party's Czechoslovaks in Chicago, had more troubling problems; his small number of leaders were politically unclear at best, and yet he counseled caution when disciplining them: "I advise the greatest tact with dealing with their unCommunist stand. They are loyal workers of the Communist Party. . . . At present would be very hard to fill the place of anyone. The lack of leadership is a very burning issue in our fraction. The two speakers what we have, are not much closer to the line of our Party than the socialist. The worst thing is that they have a real following in the mass organization. The workers naturally believe them to be the best Communists."[111]

With a scarcity of trustworthy leaders, Communists expressed independence. When city buro and language leaders demanded that Comrade Hohol, the business manager of the Ukrainian Labor Home and manager of its soda-fountain store, stay in his positions, Hohol refused and resigned. Another competent party manager took over the home, but the store, a party headquarters of sorts where Communists left literature and made phone calls, was sold to a non-party member. City leaders agreed that Hohol did not "understand discipline," yet his blatant disregard of party leaders' direction only resulted in his being "severely criticized" and "warned" that he must "become subject to Party discipline at all times." In another case, J. Semashko, a member of a Polish fraction and Unemployed Council, found that his fellow comrades filed numerous complaints against him. A report reads that Semashko ignores his unit leaders, "styles himself as an 'Old Bolshevik,'" and thinks himself "above" them. In one case he led a group of unemployed workers to an eviction without any plan. City leaders agreed that his actions created a problem, but not one big enough for expulsion or even suspension. In the end, Semashko was simply "criticized for the attitude and action he has taken."[112] In these cases, the decision not to expel left behind individuals who willfully defied the rules.

In addition to individual resistance, entire foreign-language fractions marched to their own tune. In 1930, John Williamson counted approximately sixty language fractions in the city. He labeled their functioning "still insufficient and in some cases weak."[113] His negativity was justified. The South Slavic fraction faced a wide field of possibility, with more than two hundred thousand workers in ethnic organizations and a majority of those employed in mass industry, but party fractions were disorganized, did not support party campaigns among South Slavic workers, and did not promote the party paper, *Radnik*.[114] The Yugoslavs, in particular, did not understand fraction work and had to be reminded that Communists "are not in these mass organizations to take up the inner questions but to connect them up with the problems of the class struggle."[115] The South Slavs were not alone. The Lettish buro reported that its fractions were "functioning very weakly; are not taking a real hold of Party campaign, and are losing membership instead of gaining it."[116] Lithuanian Communists were not active in general party work, and in Gebert's words, they refused to "carry on real Communist work in the mass organizations."[117] As late as 1935, Polish fractions also were reported to be "functioning very badly, meeting irregularly," and not providing "real political leadership."[118]

Chicago's ethnic party members shared problems with those elsewhere. Harvey Klehr found that across the country, "foreign-language groups, which monopolized many members' time and energy, were insular and inward-looking." In a 1930 Organization Conference, leaders in Michigan, New York, and Pennsylvania lamented the exclusiveness of their language groups. Some were afraid of outsiders, while others were simply more comfortable working with their own. Regardless, party leaders had a hard time getting their foreign-language-speaking members to extend their interests into nonlanguage work.[119]

In general, Zinich reported, Chicago's foreign-language-speaking Communists were active in language organizations but violated the Third Period's revolutionary spirit. He saw these tendencies as part of larger "right wing" problems that language members needed to "liquidate." Examples included fractions that were "afraid to come openly as a fraction but hid themselves and in that way lose the respect of the progressive workers who have much confidence in the Party." They also included ethnic Communists who were "afraid to insult the feelings of non-progressive workers [in mass organizations] with Communist speeches, motions, literature, press, or with politics." Some foreign-language Communists even argued that "fraternal societies usually are nonpolitical."[120] Perhaps these "right wing" behaviors were why some foreign-language-speaking Communists were so well respected in non-party groups. Regardless, they signaled to party leaders that their ethnic comrades did not accept Third Period policies.

Not only were foreign-language-speaking Communists occasionally unwilling to carry out party campaigns in non-party organizations, they also were unwilling to participate in section committees or unit meetings. This compartmentalization concerned city and national leaders, especially when it came to financial matters. City and national leaders hoped for loans and financial support from foreign-language buros for party campaigns. Chicago's foreign-language leaders assigned a person from each language buro to attend ethnic affairs and bring back 10 percent of the earnings for the party. This person was also assigned to "[g]et a list of sympathizers and . . . well-to-do people who can be approached for donations."[121] Language groups were also expected to support the party nationally. When the Czechoslovakian buro had lapsed in their support, the district suggested that John Mackovich "take off part of the pay of Party members who are employed by our organizations and give that to the center, as many other buros had done."[122] More often than not, city and national leaders found themselves scolding language groups for their refusal to support campaigns and comply with financial directives.

The party leaned on language groups for money in part because finances were strained throughout the city's organization. Beginning in 1929, Chicago's leaders complained that the local party organization could no longer exist on a "shoestring" as it had in the past. Paid functionaries often did not receive their paltry salaries, and the city's party could not pay for the number of organizers it needed. On a more practical level, money was often unavailable for basic necessities. Unable to afford mimeograph machines for their units, Communists fought over workspace in the party's trade-union office.[123]

Party leaders hoped that the sale of ethnic newspapers would raise awareness among workers about party causes and potentially lead to their support. But they found that ethnic editors, like foreign-language Communists more generally, were not always willing to follow the line set out for them. In one of his examinations of foreign-language papers in the city, Zinich found that "most . . . are not conducting Party campaigns especially against the right danger in the language fractions, as they should." He reported to Alpi, the national language leader, that some fractions, like the Armenian, Greek, and Spanish, did not even know about language directives. He reported that others were of the opinion that "they can passively reject such articles because they are afraid of 'undermining' the paper," or more simply because "the editors do not agree with them."[124]

Instead of party directives, the contents of party papers reflected the interests of foreign-language-speaking members. The Ukrainian newspaper printed a thesis that did not mention the TUUL or the Worker's International Relief organization but did include a discussion of comrades concerning an international Ukrainian Emigration Congress. Zinich doubted "whether the CEC knows anything about this thesis."[125] While the Ukrainian comrades debated an international congress, Polish Communists printed advertisements from religious publications and for "capitalist candidates for mayor in the city of Hamtranck." When called on this lapse of good Communist acumen, Kowalski, the paper's editor, stated that he simply disagreed.[126] Ethnic papers also balked when asked to lend money to the party. In one case, members associated with *Rovnost Ludu* agreed that they could not give the party money while their paper was in such a bad condition.[127]

This incident and others like it suggest that party control was never unilateral and always had to be negotiated with particular personalities. Even when leaders had the power to relieve editors like Kowalski, which they did when he continually proved politically unreliable, they still decided to keep them on the membership roles. Gebert always believed that Kowalski, for one, could be "saved."[128] In this case, Kowalski's independent behavior was not enough to cause him to be expelled, suggesting that there was a place in the party for people who strayed.

In addition to recalcitrant ethnics, there was room in Chicago's party for those who were ambivalent about the social-fascism policy. Communists' social-fascist line taught that Communists were the only true revolutionaries capable of leading workers to revolution. But non-party papers pointed out that occasionally—like the time that party members attacked Ukrainians from the elevated tracks—Communist activity involved "assaults upon workers."[129] If Communists were supposed to be the leaders of these workers and not their assailants, such assaults probably made some Communists uncomfortable. Evidence exists that Communists, even at the highest level in the district, were conflicted about this policy. They sometimes left it out of their relationships with other workers and their organizations, and their behavior was reflected in the ranks.

Albert Goldman explained to party leaders that he agreed that members should act in accordance with Communist decisions, but he wrote, "[I]t does not demand the Party members believe in accordance."[130] Some did neither. In 1933 the Communist leader of the party's antifascist committee refused to retreat from his position that when in coalition with non-party groups, Communists should not expose social fascists. Party leaders removed him as the committee's lead organizer but allowed him to remain in its larger leadership circle.[131] Goldman scorned a fellow comrade for railing against leaders of the Socialist party at a mass rally against a relief cut. Goldman was later expelled, but only after one whole year of haranguing against the party's position in the Communist classes he taught. The decision to expel him probably satisfied party leaders, but the fact that it took so long meant that classrooms of activists met at least one party representative who disagreed with the social-fascist line. Another was Alfred Loge, a Communist and president of the Maywood branch of the Nature Friends, an eco-friendly group with roots in nineteenth-century Vienna. He would not let the party use his organization to promote activity among German workers in the fight against social fascism.[132]

Rank-and-file Communists regularly saw their leaders resist party policy. In 1928, Carl Sklar, a young district leader, was sent to Milwaukee to organize an electoral campaign under the Communist banner. He refused these orders, organized for the Socialist party, and opened Communist headquarters to a "capitalist" candidate for office, whose flyers party members distributed. His fellow district leaders found him to be "tactless" and "incompetent," but factional fighting in the city's leadership allowed even these kinds of blunders to be protected by those in Sklar's faction at the city's highest levels. By 1930, he was reassigned to another part of the country, and his Chicago comrades reported that he was doing "good work."[133] In another case, a debate between a party leader and a Trotskyist resulted in the leader making "serious" ideological mistakes. Instead of showing how "entirely opposite" the Trotskyist's "bourgeois pacifism" was, the leader made the point of showing how similar the two positions were.[134] In 1931, party leaders were setting counterexamples once again. Gebert reported that "in the old traditional way, *in spite of the definite decisions of the district buro,* comrades Browder and Hammersmark" rounded up ten "typical liberals" and brought them as spokesmen to a party protest at city hall. Arthur Maki, a carpenter and member of the district Control Commission and the Communist party since its founding and the Socialist party before that, made the same blunder. At a state convention of the unemployed, Maki was responsible for allowing George Voyzey, a Trotskyist, to speak openly.[135]

Party leaders' wavering actions affected the kinds of people allowed to remain in the party. In 1928, William Kruse sent Lovestone a list of Cannon's supporters in the city. It included fifteen names and five others who "lean in that direction." Yet that year, only five members were expelled. Party leaders did not go on an expulsion spree; they only picked off the most vocal, or least hopeful, members of the opposition. Leaders' inconsistent enforcement of this policy allowed members to continue identifying as Communists even if they were not completely convinced of social fascism. For example, four party members attended a functionary meeting and "publicly protested" expulsions of Trotskyists, calling for "full freedom" in the expression of Trotskyist views in the party. At first, the four were not even called before the city's Control Commission but instead were invited to a meeting with a few party leaders. Only when leaders learned that three of the four were circulating an anti-party petition did they agree to suspend (and not expel) them. The fourth agreed to make a statement against Trotsky in his nucleus meeting. For this reason and the fact that he was a "rank and filer," no action ensued.[136] Another rank and filer, however, was expelled for selling the Trotskyite paper *The Militant.* Party leaders admitted that no one objected to that expulsion for the arbitrary reason that "everyone knows he is a nut."[137]

Relations between Communists and social fascists continued informally. At a Communist New Year's party in 1929, a recently expelled Trotskyist sold drink tickets in the place of the unit's financial secretary because the party members "didn't think her Trotskyist view would hurt anyone."[138] Trotskyists were also known to hang around the party's bookstore and various headquarters throughout the city. Local party leaders insisted that Communists needed to crack down on these contacts.[139] The ranks needed reminding.

Despite the priority put on party discipline and the fight against social fascists, there were surprisingly few expulsions for this behavior in Chicago. David Bentall, in charge of expulsions in the city, carefully monitored members who were brought up on charges but only expelled those he believed could not be won back to the party. Bentall's Control Commission examined each case separately and considered personal factors in making its decisions. In 1930, the party expelled eleven for following either Lovestone or Trotsky, but by 1932 the fervor had died down: only one Trotskyist sympathizer was expelled in 1932 and two in 1933.[140] Once expelled, people were not forever severed from the party, and a few were readmitted. When the Political buro readmitted one former renegade, it agreed to do so based on his trade-union work and swallowed the fact that he had not completely fallen back in line.[141] Some complained about the weak actions of the Control Commission, but party leaders did not want to lose promising members. It was not that leaders did not apply Third Period formulations, but they did so selectively and were ineffective in rooting out all the shades of noncompliance in their ranks.

This was particularly true among African Americans, who were recruited from such race-based organizations as Marcus Garvey's United Negro Improvement Association. In the early 1920s, Communist leaders were impressed with Garvey and the lower working-class composition of his following. There is even evidence that Garvey's notion of black nationalism influenced party leaders' conception of black self-determination.[142] But in the context of the Third Period and Communists' open competition with Garvey for an African American following, party leaders threw Garvey and Garveyites into the same scorned group as Trotsky and Lovestone. Whereas the latter two had come out of Communist traditions, Garvey was easily seen as an evil capitalist and outright betrayer of the black masses. His Black Star line was the essence of capitalist enterprise, and his Back to Africa program, however vague, was particularly troubling to party leaders, who encouraged an interracial struggle for black freedom within the United States.[143]

The bitterness that characterized American Communist leaders' feeling toward Garvey did not penetrate to Chicago's ranks. This was particularly true among Chicago's African American Communists, who were recruited from Garvey's UNIA. Once in the party, Garveyites came into conflict with its leaders. Sol Harper, a leading member dealing with "Negro issues" and an ex-Garveyite, argued that Garvey had duped black workers and stolen from them. A debate ensued within Chicago's party over the meaning of Garveyism in the party. The Communist members Anna Schultz and Marie Houston argued that the movement may have wronged blacks, but they were still fond of Marcus Garvey the man. These ex-Garveyites and newly made Communists believed that the party would help them achieve racial equality, but they were not willing to betray Garvey, a man who they felt had awakened their political consciousness. The feud resulted in one section losing several former Garveyites. Interestingly, though, those Garveyites who left remained neutral to the party, and relations between the groups continued. In fact, relations were so good between some Communists and members of other groups that the party leaders had to continually remind members to distinguish between those in the party and those who were not when passing on confidential information.[144]

While those who were offended by the party's treatment of Garvey left, the party never ridded its black units of African American religious culture. Within one of their organizations, the American Negro Labor Congress, party members and sympathizers prayed and sang hymns. And on the South Side, Michael Gold described the experiences of black cadre: "At mass meetings their religious past becomes transmuted into a Communist present. They follow every word of the speaker with real emotion; they encourage him, as at a prayer meeting with cries of 'Yes, yes comrade' and often there is an involuntary and heartfelt 'Amen!'"[145]

Beginning in the early 1930s, Chicago's Communists organized in black churches around the Scottsboro case and against unemployment. One section, composed mostly of black members, called a meeting for those who attended church. Thelma Wheaton taught and trained women workers out of Chicago's South Parkway branch of the YWCA. In an interview with Beth Bates, she recalled, "I never knew a Communist who was not also a Christian. I'll bet over a third of my church was Communist." While perhaps an exaggeration on both accounts, Wheaton's memory is revealing of Communists' efforts in black Chicago. The district's political committee was so concerned about members' church activity that it ordered the agitprop department to organize special classes to make black comrades "clear on the question of religion."[146]

As religious influences became part of black party gatherings, the party's own formulation of self-determination shielded those who pushed less for interracial action than for a black nationalist perspective. Rallies for Nat Turner were held on the South Side, alluding to an armed rebellion with nationalist overtones. Rank-and-file Communists like Henry Ray, who joined the party in 1930, were attracted to these displays of nationalism. According to David Bentall, the leader of the city's Control Commission, Ray professed nationalist ideas and "fostered distrust of Negro workers against white workers." He also accused an entire section of the party leadership of being white chauvinists without providing evidence. Yet, typically regardless of such transgressions, Bentall and others viewed Ray as a "capable comrade," and rather than expelling him, they simply encouraged him to "overcome his weaknesses." The party member Oscar Hunter had a similar experience when he referred to blacks as "my people" when appealing to white party leaders on the South Side. A black party member came to reprimand him. "So he comes right out and says what is this shit MY PEOPLE. . . . There's no such a goddamn thing."[147] Hunter believed that there was a difference between the interests of white and black workers and that he represented the black ones. According to party mandates, he was wrong. He took his scolding but did not change his mind.

Another telling display of a black party subculture occurred in 1932, when members in a mostly African American section rejected the district's ruling on interracial leadership and insisted on all-black leadership. Because white party members wanted blacks in the party and in leadership roles and actively sought to rid their ranks of prejudices, district leaders explained to their secretariat why they overruled them and agreed with their black members. A leading comrade explained that "from the formal point of view this was incorrect, but this question cannot be looked upon formally, but from the point of view of the realities of the situation." And in 1932 the realities were that interracial leadership would not always work in majority black sections.[148]

Not all black Communists were overeager to identify as "Negro," however. Some, in fact, resisted the party's insistence on seeing all blacks as "Negroes" rather than as simply native-born Americans. It is no wonder that when asked to fill out a registration survey in 1931, some blacks registered as "American" instead of "Negro." Others resented whites' use of the term "Negro." One black unit voted unanimously to use the word "colored" instead, demonstrating that some challenged the party's homogeneous idea of Negroes as an oppressed nation.[149]

Chicago's Communists brought with them shades of commitment and varieties of experiences, attitudes, and behaviors. Instead of acting as a small army, whose members followed orders without question, Chicago's party operated on a more contingent basis, with its leaders having to take account of their members' varied backgrounds, experiences, and beliefs. Party leaders believed that to bring about socialism, they needed both a disciplined membership prepared to lead workers and a high level of commitment to the revolution. Segments of Chicago's party bought into this vision and carried out party policy as best they could. Other large segments—including white ethnics, African Americans, and leaders at various levels—bought in and yet experienced the party on their own terms. In Chicago, from 1928 through 1935, things did not run as smoothly as planned. Despite this fact, or more likely because of it, Communists managed to develop effective community and labor organizers, and their numbers grew to over three thousand by the end of the period.

And still, from 1928 through 1935, Chicago's Communists were unable to lead their members in a complete turn toward the revolutionary agenda envisioned by the Comintern. The difficult task they set for themselves was beset by the attitudes and beliefs of their members, who failed to spark a socialist revolution among Chicago's workers but who managed to make headway in their work among unemployed and unionized workers.

4

Red Relief

In *Left Front*, the publication of Chicago's John Reed Club, Edith Margo reiterated the sequence of events in 1931 that led Chicago's police officers to kill three eviction protesters. On August 1, 1931, Oscar DePriest, a congressman and "millionaire Negro landlord," and other white and black landlords and politicians met at the W. H. Riley real estate office and resolved to demand that Chicago's chief of police take more severe measures to stop the anti-eviction activity of the city's Communist-party created Unemployed Councils. On August 3, the police acted.[1]

Early that morning, police arrested a leader of the Unemployed Councils, Charles Banks, at the site of an eviction and warned others, "If any of you go out on any more evictions today you're goin' to get drilled." But Banks and other council members took this as "an invitation to battle," according to Margo. The Unemployed Councils, as the militant leaders of jobless workers, could not ignore it.[2]

Council members discussed Banks's arrest and future actions they might take in Washington Park, a half-square-mile recreational area where all manner of people had traditionally gathered to talk, listen, protest, sleep, and occasionally act. Washington Park forums promoted lively discussion and debate among radical, liberal, and conservative employed and unemployed blacks, whose cacophony of voices and ideas sometimes inspired impromptu action. On this day, the group decided to march together to the 5000 block of South Dearborn Street, the heart of Chicago's African American neighborhood, and replace the furniture of an evicted seventy-two-year-old woman, Diana Gross. A council leader, Joseph Gardner, led between five hundred and four thousand people (estimates vary) out of the park and down Fifty-first Street to Dearborn. Abe Grey, "one of the best Negro organizers in the Party," was among the crowd and found himself geared up for what he believed was going to be the start of the revolution on Chicago's South Side. "If there is shooting," Grey reportedly said, "I expect to be killed, because I shall be on the front rank."

After the procession reached Gross's residence, police arrested council leaders, including Gardner. Just as the police car he was in turned a corner, Gardner heard gunshots. In a letter to the national party leader Earl Browder, Bill Gebert explained that Grey and others had disarmed and beaten three policemen, causing other police to attack and fatally shoot Grey in the arm. After being shot, Grey threw a police revolver into the crowd, calling on the people to continue fighting. An eyewitness Margo interviewed told a less heroic story: Police tried to arrest Grey, but he escaped and began to lead the group after Gardner and other leaders were arrested. At one point, Grey had his hand in his pocket, which caused the police to jump to the "conclusion that he had a gun and [they] shot him five times."

Two other deaths soon followed. In response to Grey's murder, John O'Neil, an unknown African American man who had joined the group at the park, took a gun from a police officer or picked one up that was dropped (as several were) and tried to shoot. If not for the safety, he would have fired. Instead, a policeman shot him. Frank Armstrong, Grey's close friend, was also killed, but witnesses do not recall his being slain at the demonstration. Late that night, some neighbors found his body in Washington Park, "shot through the head and badly mutilated." To party members, the conclusion was clear: "[Q]uite evidently he had been taken for a ride by the police."[3]

Within twenty minutes, word of the first two murders reached downtown party headquarters, where Gebert and a few others were working. Eight of them hurried to the South Side to learn details while the rest stayed to plan a meeting for top party leaders. While leaders planned, neighborhood organizers acted. The South Side party members David Poindexter, Squire Brown, Claude Lightfoot, and Marie Houston joined at least fifty-three council sympathizers, organized a neighborhood meeting, and turned out seven to ten thousand people that night in Washington Park. The following week, Washington Park forums ran every evening with between five and ten thousand sympathizers listening, questioning, and cheering as Communists and others struck verbal blows against the capitalist state, racism, and police violence. By the following Tuesday, Communists and sympathizers set up a committee to arrange a mass funeral.

With council support, the group made the slain workers' funeral a huge demonstration that brought Communists' critique of the city's administration (and capitalist state power more generally) together with their advocacy of such issues as civil rights and racial equality. Party members distributed fifty thousand party leaflets, seventy-five thousand funeral leaflets, twenty thousand League of Struggle for Negro Rights leaflets, and twenty thousand Unemployed

Council leaflets. For three days leading to the funeral, the bodies of Grey and O'Neil lay in state at the Odd Fellows Hall to, as organizers explained, "give the outraged masses an opportunity to view the bodies." Party members guarded them in twelve-hour shifts. Behind the corpses, a spotlight drew observers' eyes to a picture of Lenin, paintings of white and black hands clasped together, and murals of upraised fists. Twenty-five thousand came during the first two days of the viewing and thousands more on the next three.[4] On the day of the funeral, Gebert explained, "[T]he 100,000 workers felt power and took possession of the street." Behind a red flag, sixty thousand discontented workers (40 percent of them white) paraded carrying sheets on which forty thousand onlookers (90 percent of them black) threw coins to help defray the families' funeral expenses.[5]

These moments enhanced Communists' conviction that they would successfully lead the impending revolution. In their view, the capitalist system would

View down State Street of the funeral procession for three men killed by police during a rent protest. The caption in the *Chicago Tribune*, August 9, 1931, in part read, "Hundreds of policemen guarded the funeral and the parade, but no communistic outbreaks occurred." (Used with permission from AP/Wide World Photos.)

not be able to sustain itself while granting the kinds of socialist remedies they demanded. This overriding idea provided a rationale for Communists throughout the country to put to work Third Period beliefs about capitalism, race, and fascism. Throughout the Depression they did so by connecting their convictions about capitalism's imminent decline, the system's racist tendencies, and the threat of fascism to the problems of the unemployed. In work through a group of their own making, the Unemployed Councils, Communists perfected the fight to improve conditions for the unemployed and their families by tailoring their tactics to the problem at hand. This meant that from city to city, council activity varied. In Detroit, councils organized unemployed autoworkers and built an organization within the auto unions, while in Birmingham, councils focused on women's activism and blacks' rights.[6] Chicago's councils responded to the unemployed neighborhood by neighborhood, causing their structure and solutions to reflect the variety of the city's population and their problems.

Although such events as those that occurred in early August show the considerable support that Unemployed Councils and the Communist party received in Chicago, to party leaders, the results from their unemployment campaigns were decidedly mixed. Most people who participated in Unemployed Council activity shuffled in and out of the movement and never joined the party. To these people, reforms won at the flophouse, relief station, and in city government were sufficient, undermining party leaders' Third Period assumptions. Women did not participate in Unemployed Council activity as much as leaders pushed, and leaders were unable to translate their sense of widespread support into electoral victory. Lizabeth Cohen's study found that in the early Depression years, Chicago's working people changed their views concerning government's role.[7] Their shift from relying on private institutions in periods of crisis to expecting government assistance was revolutionary. It was not the kind of revolution that Communists envisioned, however. And yet Communists were a part of the force that brought about these changes.

If this situation was not grim enough for party leaders, new members' political bent caused them further concern. As the events of August 3 suggest, Communists and their councils brought people into the party's orbit who were not born and bred on socialist politics. How much were Unemployed Councils creatures of Communism, and how much did they represent an indigenous movement? How did Communists affect the activity and character of the councils, and how did council activity affect the character of the party? During the Third Period, Unemployed Councils become the main arena for recruitment, and overall Communist membership numbers followed the pattern of unemployed-campaign successes. As a result, Communists found it easier to recruit in the hardest-hit areas of the city than in other neighborhoods, but such trends concerned leaders who wanted stronger recruitment among the employed. Unemployed Councils won specific victories as members returned furniture to an evicted person's apartment, cut through red tape at a relief station, turned on someone's electricity, or temporarily improved homeless-shelter conditions. But some leaders worried that this "grievance approach" to organizing—where council members focused on practical problems, daily struggles, and immediate relief—tended to take them away from more theoretical approaches.[8] Through councils, Communists also successfully tapped into existing cultures of resistance and broadened their base with people who had no issue making Popular Front–style coalitions with non-party leftists and who sometimes behaved as reformers instead of as revolutionaries. In these ways and more, Unemployed Councils forecast changes that would come during the Popular Front. Many of those trained through council activity stayed on to become some of Chicago's leading party members and most-skilled trade unionists in this later period.

Those who became involved in the party through the Unemployed Councils often expressed themselves and interpreted party directives as they saw fit, occasionally to the chagrin of Chicago's Communist leaders. Once there, they joined more veteran members who sometimes defied party policies and supported local cultures that did not fit Stalinist visions created on high and that at times bucked the party apparatus altogether. Their attitudes and activities suggest the importance of understanding American Communism as a sum of its diverse parts rather than as a reflection of party mandates and leaders' desires.

Building a Structure

In 1929, a few cities, including Chicago, created an early form of Unemployed Councils, but it was a year before the Communist party worked out its nationwide structure. The initial councils borrowed from the pre-revolutionary Russian model, grouping people in "revolutionary centers" based on where they worked (or had worked). Since work was the center around which these councils would organize, it made sense to party leaders to place them under control of the Trade Union Unity League, a party-created union structure formed in 1929 to organize workers, employed or not. In Chicago, party leaders created a steering committee within the TUUL composed of section leaders, trade-union activists, and nationality-group leaders. Its members included the garment worker Dora Lifshitz; the carpenter Nels Kjar; Joe Dallet and John Meldon of the Steel and Metal Workers' Industrial Union; Steve Rubicki of the International Labor Defense; Paul Cline of the Young Communist League; Irving Gersh of the Journeymen Tailor's Union; the editors of *Vilnis* and *Radnik,* the Lithuanian and Serbo-Croatian party papers; and the unemployed leader Bill Holloway.[9]

These men and women wanted a mass movement. Resolutions passed at citywide Communist gatherings suggest optimistic directives ordering Chicago Communists to join the TUUL through their former or present places of employment. "It is precisely the building of the TUUL," party leaders believed, "which will become one of the most important means of closing the gap between the growing political influence of the Party and its organizational isolation."[10]

The limited nature of the TUUL dashed these inflated hopes, however. Instead of working to build a mass movement uniting the city's employed and unemployed workers, early council leaders focused on workplace issues and the membership of small, revolutionary unions. Occasionally delegates from fraternal groups, homeless workers, and residents of flophouses joined elected delegates from the TUUL to discuss the unemployment situation, but concrete action rarely followed. Unemployed Communists were supposed to work in TUUL councils, but few party or non-party unemployed workers were attracted to them through mid-1930.[11]

The one exception was the first national Communist-organized response of the unemployed on March 6, 1930, initiated by the Comintern and dubbed International Unemployment Day. "The economic crisis in the United States is part of the world crisis of capitalism," one party paper explained, "and as a result of it over 17,000,000 workers are unemployed in the capitalist countries." In a call to action, the TUUL and its affiliates called on "American working class employed and unemployed to demonstrate in solidarity with the workers in all capitalist and colonial countries."[12] Local conferences of delegates from TUUL unions and fraternal groups culminated in a regional meeting in Chicago, where Bill Gebert announced the March 6 action. Gebert estimated that thirty to fifty thousand marchers participated in the demonstration and that another two hundred thousand watched in sympathy from factory windows or sidewalks. While city papers estimated marchers in the hundreds rather than thousands, the turnout was successful enough to get the attention of Chicago's city government.[13]

Due to party members' organizing inexperience, the TUUL's preoccupation with industry, and most workers' lack of interest in becoming members, however, leaders were unable to turn this outpouring of response into a membership base for the councils, let alone the party. A report of the event reveals other weaknesses from the perspective of Third Period expectations. Party members did not shout slogans into the crowd; they did not raise up speakers at different points in the demonstration; and instead of convincing people on the sidewalk to join the marchers, they called them "scabs" and "yellow." Most disheartening was the low turnout of the party's own numbers: only three hundred Communists showed up. Even some group captains did not appear, and those who did failed to hold together their groups of eight. Communists in charge of the demonstration got separated from one another, and a few ignored non-party members who assembled for the rally. This demonstration revealed the need for new organizing structures and tactics if the party was going to lead Chicago's unemployed workers.[14]

Despite the problems this march uncovered, Chicago could boast that it had twelve councils with one thousand members, the largest outside of New York. Councils in Milwaukee, Duluth, and Indianapolis were only beginning to grow and already differing from those organized by the TUUL. Instead of working on an industrial basis, they organized members around neighborhood issues. In Chicago, some early councils were based in existing ethnic and fraternal organizations rather than the workplace. Steve Nelson, a national party leader sent to organize in Chicago, attended his first Unemployed Council meeting at a Greek workers' club on Halsted Street, with Greek furriers, garment and stockyard workers, waiters, cooks, and busboys in attendance. According to Nelson, "[A]lmost all were single and very militant. Actually, they knew what to do better than I."[15]

Similar experiences in seventeen other states led to preliminary talks among party leaders, members, and sympathizers concerning the formation of a national organization. The result of these talks brought 1,320 delegates to Chicago in July 1930 to organize the Unemployed Councils of the USA. The convention adopted a program that highlighted the councils' demand that federal relief and unemployment insurance come from funds appropriated for the military and that representatives of the unemployed administer relief. At the convention, delegates declared their opposition to racism and pushed for black and white organizers to work within black neighborhoods. As a final act, the convention created a new council structure.[16] From this point forward, the Unemployed Councils' structure would be separate from the TUUL and the Communist party. From the Comintern in Moscow to the party's district office in Chicago, leaders agreed that unemployed activity had more potential to reach a wider audience through neighborhood councils than through Communist trade unions.[17] Within Chicago, the new councils first organized the unemployed within branches, covering areas of the city similar to the ones organized by party sections. By 1931, council members were building block committees within each branch to mobilize around neighborhood issues. Block committees covered residents in neighborhoods hardest hit by the Depression. Chicago's *Hunger Fighter,* a biweekly publication of the city's Unemployed Councils, explained: "A block committee is composed of three or more workers who canvass the block, going from house to house to get the support of the workers, employed and unemployed, for the relief of the desperate cases in the block. The block committee calls the neighbors together to decide what action to take when some family in the block is to be evicted or is starving. . . . If the committee needs assistance or the advice of more experienced workers, they can go to the neighborhood council to which the block committee sends delegates."[18] The *Hunger Fighter* highlighted the ease with which these committees could be built, reporting on such successful cases as the one in April 1932, when a woman organized twenty-one men and women on her block in one day.[19]

Even though the Unemployed Councils had a separate structure and localized base, city party leaders were directly involved in council policy and personnel questions. Chicago's executive committee of the Unemployed Councils, composed of delegates elected from neighborhood councils, had ample Communist representation. Steve Nelson was put in charge of organizing at its first meeting and was eventually elected secretary of the city's Unemployed Councils.[20] District leaders worked with Communist council leaders to pick future representatives from the party's ranks. They handed down decisions that changed the councils' structure, creating a city center responsible for coordinating activity and block councils that would increase neighborhood concentration. They organized citywide rallies and conferences, staffed councils with unpaid Communists, suggested slogans for councils for rallying support, and organized a signature campaign for the passage of unemployment insurance in the councils' name.[21]

But citywide leaders were not always able to implement their decisions because only rarely were they involved in the councils' day-to-day work. Most party members working in councils were unhappy with their leaders' hands-off approach and encouraged them to become more directly involved. Occasionally Communists in councils questioned their leaders' commitment to unemployed work. In February 1931, city leaders responded to such criticism by hiring Nels Kjar to oversee council work and report to them on it. They paid him when they could with funds raised jointly by the party and the TUUL.[22]

Kjar proved to be an effective, if short-lived, organizer. Jack Spiegel, a lower-level council leader, remembered Kjar struggling with police and relief officials on the third floor of a Milwaukee Avenue relief station. During the skirmish, Kjar and his wife held tightly to the railing as unemployed delegates and supporters occupied the stairway. "The police had a hell of a time dislodging us," Spiegel recalled.[23] As a result of Kjar's militant action, he was arrested, held for eighteen months, and then deported to Denmark.

More than party district leaders or their appointed council representatives, then, it was Communist section leaders and unit fraction members who were most involved in the councils' day-to-day functioning. Section leaders assigned rank-and-file Communists to work within the councils; and when they noticed that council work had fallen off in their area, they asked their respective unit leaders to check with Unemployed Council fraction members, who were supposed to meet regularly to discuss the political education of unemployed workers. Of course, although section leaders were supposed to keep close tabs on council fraction members, contact frequently broke down.[24] At the end of 1931, 75 percent of all councils had an active party fraction working in them, providing many rank-and-file Communists their first experience of mass organizing.[25]

Communists involved in unemployed work blurred the lines between council and party organizations. The party section organizer Katherine Erlich went to the party's city leadership for bail money after the arrest of an entire block committee of a council within her section. In another case, an announcement for the Roseland Unemployed Council to send delegates to a city unemployed meeting appeared in a Communist section newsletter. Sometimes lower-level Communists working in councils did not focus enough on party recruitment, causing leaders to send directives, like the ones circulated on the South Side, ordering members to make more of a "distinction" between party work and the councils. Other times, like during socials, picnics, and films cosponsored by a particular party unit and Unemployed Council branch, party members were purposely melding the two groups for potential socializing and recruiting.[26]

Communists within Unemployed Councils were supposed to raise party directives during council discussions, talk about them with council members, and then have them adopted through a vote. Sometimes Communist leaders themselves would attend council meetings to push through party decisions, but fraction members did not always accommodate them. When party leaders came to one of Erlich's council meetings and tried to get their demands passed, the members unanimously voted them down. At an enlarged district committee meeting, Erlich explained, "If any decision is to be made the comrades should come and have some discussion with the Party fraction and executive committee."[27]

While party leaders did not appreciate this lack of support, they did encourage councils to create their own campaigns and understood that to organize a mass movement, councils had to have various approaches to the city's problems and people. Signing off as G. P., one North Side activist explained, "[I]n order to build Unemployed Councils and to speed up the organization of the unemployed, it is necessary for us to be flexible and adopt proper demands that will fit in for the territory in which we build."[28] Nelson pushed the city's Communist leadership to ensure that councils "take up everyday problems of the workers."[29] In early 1931, the district resolved that there would be "no general plans for all Unemployed Councils because in the different localities . . . there are different problems confronting us and therefore various tactics and methods must be adopted."[30] The party's ability to adapt its structure to address the variety of problems facing Chicago's unemployed eventually made the councils popular and difficult to control.

Organizing the Unorganized

This pliant structure also allowed lower-level Communist activists and jobless workers to use them for shelter protests, relief-station rallies, anti-eviction work, interracial activity, and centers of antifascist propaganda. Tied together by a national organization and Communists' determination to expose the futility of the American welfare system, Chicago's councils carried through party direction in various ways, while developing their own character and bringing new faces, personalities, and inclinations into Chicago's Communist party.

ORGANIZING IN FLOPHOUSES

Ben Gray was six years old in June 1914 when he, his mother, and three siblings landed on Ellis Island. Born to an Orthodox Jewish family in Kiev, Gray retained his religious practices in the United States. When his father died in 1925, Gray attended synagogue three times a day for an entire year. It was not until Ben's brother Dave went into business with a "fast operator" who was also "philosophically . . . a Communist" that Ben encountered any political thinking. This partner shared his ideas with Dave and Ben, and soon Ben found himself connecting these teachings with his own work experiences. Before long he was radicalized.[31]

By the time the Depression hit, Ben Gray had surrounded himself with friends who were "attuned to what was going on." So when he heard that nine black young men had been sentenced to death in Alabama for raping two white women and that it might be a frame-up, Gray attended a protest meeting in Grant Park. Reading the protest signs and listening to speakers, Gray got caught up in the rally, and "all of a sudden [he] had the sign [he was holding] framed over a policeman's head." In jail, Gray met YCL and Communist party members. He "made up [his] mind that this is what it means to . . . not having liberty to express yourself or declaring your protest against what you thought was wrong, that there really must be something wrong with things in this country and perhaps these Communists were right [sic]." Somebody gave Gray a YCL card, and he signed on the spot.[32]

As an unemployed worker in Depression-era Chicago, Gray found himself looking for shelter in Chicago's municipal lodging houses. Within a half-mile west of the Loop, they dotted the streets along with pawnshops, secondhand clothing stores, taverns, and poolrooms. Twenty-three percent of shelter residents were casual workers, migratory laborers, and homeless who claimed this area of the city as their permanent residence. What stuck out most in Gray's memory, however, was that "those flophouses which ordinarily housed the 'bowery bums' and those people, found people with college degrees, former engineers, college professors, people like that who were really down and out."[33]

It was among these people that Gray and others like him began an intense effort to organize. Timing was important. Lawrence Moen, a council organizer in one flophouse, reported, "We don't give a damn for a man after he has spent six months in the flophouse. It does things to him. He loses his guts. He doesn't care. He forgets who he used to be. His scrap is gone."[34] Before their inhabitants lost their spirit, Gray, Moen, and other council members hoped to channel their energies into protest.

One recruit, Car Kolins, a former steam-shovel operator, was the kind of person they sought. He had only been in a city shelter for four weeks and already had a "great hobby" in following party activity. Repeatedly offering "Communistic principles . . . gleaned from the *Daily Worker,* which . . . he always carried a copy of," Kolins was convinced that Chicago's mainstream papers had it wrong. "To read the *Tribune,*" he argued, "you would think Communism was a kind of deadly poisoning. . . . They've got all the money they want—that's why they don't want Communism or a liberal government. They want to keep us on the bum." A University of Chicago student deemed Kolins "not a type to mix well with people," but fellow council members likely thought differently.[35]

Flophouses provided lodging, meals, facilities for recreation, and ample cause for complaint. According to one war veteran, at his flophouse "you are handed a circular tray caked with rust on top and covered with a black smudgy smear on the bottom." The cornbread hash, he claimed, was made from bread brushed off tables with a broom that was also used to sweep the floors.[36] At 1210 South Morgan Street, all beds touched one another. Thirty-seven men had to be removed from a Salvation Army flophouse on Union Street due to an influenza outbreak. In June 1932, the city forced flophouse residents to work on county roads if they wanted to stay in the shelters.[37]

According to Gray, these concerns made it "very easy to organize a demonstration because all you had to do was send word through the flophouses that something is taking place and inside of a half hour you had ten thousand people out in the streets."[38] While probably an overstatement, large demonstrations did flow from the city's shelters. On one occasion in January 1932, five thousand men left their flophouses and marched to the Clearing House for Men at Monroe and Grant Streets to present demands.[39] Not all demonstrations were so dramatic. Most often, Unemployed Council committees won official recognition from a shelter's staff, who would then listen to council members' demands. While such a hearing may not seem like much, it often resulted in concessions. In one case, an unemployed committee was given the right to hold daily meetings, to have three meals a day, to get free medical attention, and to use tobacco twice a week.[40]

Sometimes the stakes were higher. In May 1932, a Morgan Street shelter was closed, shutting out four hundred homeless people. Organized by the Unemployed Councils, they sent delegations to the Central Clearing House for Men and to emergency relief offices. A writer for the *Hunger Fighter* reported that Robert Beasley, in charge of men's shelters, realized that workers would not be "bulldozed" so easily and offered to take them all back.[41]

Unemployed workers should not be punished, council members explained, for problems created by capitalism. When the city threatened to close another shelter, a delegation of council members drawn from the city's shelters met behind a closed door with state representatives and Beasley. "They were not going to sleep in the streets," the *Hunger Fighter* reported. "They had nothing to do with the Depression. . . . [B]osses, like [Samuel] Insull and [Ogden] Armour, would have to come across and provide for the homeless and unemployed."[42] Insull and Armour had no intention of providing for the needy as council representatives intended, and this meeting did not change their views. Still, council members succeeded in articulating the view that Chicago's wealthy owed their fortune to the city's workers, who were not lazy, as these state representatives believed, but simply victims of a failing economic system.

The party and its council members wanted workers to embrace the notion that they had created the wealth of the rich, and therefore taxes on the wealthy were rightfully due to the unemployed. While this logic attracted some, the draw for most councils was the specific benefits won. When trucks from the county highway department carted men from shelters to work for their keep, Unemployed Council members tried to sabotage the effort. They believed it unjust to make victims of the Depression work for shelter, and to them, forced labor seemed ludicrous at a time when so many needed a paycheck. Two thousand congregated at one protest, but only five hundred willingly rushed the crews. A few threw projectiles at what they viewed as misguided workers who boarded the trucks, but in the end their efforts were unsuccessful. As one report indicated, "[F]rom that day there was definitive diminution in the council's activities within the shelters."[43] Former council members admitted that their recent failure in winning concessions was the reason they lost interest and let their memberships lapse, but certainly the physical attack on those willing to work alienated groups of workers from the councils and the party, making enemies among those who were only doing what shelter officials instructed them to do. To Communists, they were betraying their class. But at least some of those willing to work must have been relieved at the idea that they would be allowed to be productive.

Council activity in and around shelters brought Communist ideals to homeless people gathered in facilities scattered throughout Chicago's downtown. In April 1932, party leaders reported that 1,700 homeless people held memberships in flophouse committees.[44] Questions ranging in importance from whether residents could smoke to whether the city should support a shelter's existence became the fodder that fed council activity. Council and party activists did not always win, and occasionally their aggressive tactics gained them new enemies. Most often their encounters created a supportive following among shelter residents, who could then be counted on to demonstrate at relief stations throughout the city. One unemployed demonstration in Union Park brought ten thousand workers, gathering flophouse residents with workers leaving their jobs in the neighborhood.[45]

ANTI-EVICTION WORK, BLACK ACTIVISM, AND INTERRACIAL ORGANIZING

Whereas shelter activity was concentrated downtown, anti-eviction activity spread in neighborhoods throughout the city, notably on Chicago's South Side, where the spiraling economic downturn caused relentless suffering. According to the 1931 Unemployment Census, in one area of the South Side over 85 percent of the people ten years and older who were employed in 1930 were unemployed in 1931. By comparison, the average rate of unemployment in Chicago's 147 districts excluding its African American communities was 28 percent. Between August 11 and October 31, 1931, 38 percent of cases before the renters' court were filed against African Americans. A quarter of all relief cases in the city involved African Americans, who made up only 6.9 percent of the city's population.[46]

In Chicago's black community, councils built on African Americans' institutions and history of resistance to establish trust in the community. To do this, they began meeting at Washington Park, where African Americans had traditionally mobilized. When word came there in September 1930 that the city council had given a streetcar company the right to expand its lines to the edge of the black community and that the company employed white immigrants for the job instead of black workers, anger burst into a spontaneous protest. During these "streetcar riots," hundreds of blacks marched from Washington Park to a city transportation work site and demanded jobs.[47]

By 1932, Communists were speaking daily at the park to crowds that sometimes reached between two and five thousand. Describing an encounter at a Washington Park forum, Michael Gold observed, "Fathers, mothers, grandmothers from the deep south, and scores of children—all the generations were at the forum, this Communism has become a folk thing. They have taken Communism and translated it into their own idiom."[48]

According to Claude Lightfoot, by the time the councils came on the scene, "black people were in a stage of transition from old methods of struggle for their rights." Beth Bates refers to this cohort of Chicago's African Americans who increasingly embraced a militant protest style as "a new crowd." Unconvinced by the NAACP's focus on legal avenues to fight for civil rights or the Democratic party's promise of leadership, party and non-party blacks who participated in Washington Park activities provided the basis for this new crowd and for Unemployed Council membership. Lightfoot, a former member of the Garvey movement whom local Democratic and Republican politicians tried to recruit to help with their campaigns, converted to Communism through his Unemployed Council activity, which began in Washington Park.[49]

At this juncture, when black activists were looking for leadership, Communists reached out to the African American community through their campaign to support the Scottsboro Boys, which converted Ben Gray. When Communists went into churches and met with large gatherings, they connected the trial of the "Scottsboro Nine" to discrimination against blacks in Chicago. Through meeting with ministers and church congregations and speaking before large groups, party members recruited and began to develop a trusting relationship with the community. James Samuel and Richard Tate first learned about Unemployed Councils through a church meeting, where they decided to get involved. Both later became active unionists in Chicago's meatpacking industry.[50]

Building on these community contacts and the spontaneous actions that made Washington Park an activist center, by the summer of 1931, council members joined park regulars in working to prevent evictions in the black community. Black militants, many of whom were party members or would later join the party, led groups from the park to the homes of evicted families to put them and their furniture back in their houses or apartments. Jane Newton remembered seeing David Poindexter in demonstrations of Unemployed Councils on the South Side. Newton recalled that "Dex" had a "'volatile disposition'" and "'a ready flow of speech.'" He often put himself in dangerous situations, and in one meeting, Newton recalled, he did not stop talking "'until a policeman took him by the collar and cracked his head as if it were an egg.'"[51]

When Washington Park's council members and supporters did not leave from the park, council organizers acted on tips left at Unemployed Council meeting halls. Harold Lasswell, a contemporary sociologist, described the sequence of events that followed. A person would show up at the hall and announce that a few blocks away a landlord was evicting a family. "Their indignation aroused, the men would march in a group down the street, adding the sympathetic and the curious to their number as they marched, until by the time they reached the scene of the eviction, the crowd would have grown in size and temper. The furniture of the unfortunate family would be replaced and the crowd, delighted with its success, would disperse gradually, in small groups."[52] In African American neighborhoods, jobless workers were so disgusted with their predicament that within a few weeks of establishing councils, organizers reportedly could mobilize as many as five thousand workers in half an hour to stop an eviction.[53]

Although evictions consumed organizers' time in black neighborhoods, the councils also turned on gas, electric, and water in apartments where unemployment prevented their occupants from paying the bills. The signs they left, reading "Restored by the Unemployed Councils," helped councils' popularity grow in the black community. By August 1931, council membership on the South Side numbered one thousand, 90 percent of whom were black.[54]

Within councils, African Americans became leaders. One party report in 1931 announced, "'[T]he only mass organization where the Negro workers have been organized and feel at home is the Unemployed Councils. Approximately 40 percent of the workers in the unemployed movement in Chicago are Negro workers, and they are in the leadership.'" Lizabeth Cohen estimated that by 1934 Chicago's blacks provided 21 percent of the Unemployed Councils' leadership and 25 percent of their membership.[55]

This high rate of African American participation stood in contrast to Socialist organizations, where blacks made up only 6 percent of their leadership and 5 percent of their membership. Harold Gosnell, a University of Chicago scholar, explained that there was no one in Chicago's Socialist circles who "could keep hammering away steadily on the Socialist objectives [of racial equality]." The national Socialist party platform condemned racial inequality, but Socialist unemployed organizations neither tackled race as an issue nor took their action to the streets. They focused on discussion groups, especially in the early Depression years. Their efforts to reach black members were stymied by their lack of African American leaders and their inability to formulate a solution to the black community's crisis that addressed racism, the problem that explained the disproportionate amount of suffering in the black community.[56]

Not surprisingly, blacks began to trust the councils and, through them, the Communist party. Marxist-Leninist ideology may not have appealed to the majority of African Americans in Chicago, but it did not prevent their supporting particular aims of the party and the councils.[57] Black newspapers supported Communists' goals of bettering living conditions and ending segregation. Even the conservative *Whip* recognized the inroads the party had made in the African American community: "'The Communists have framed a program of social remedies which cannot fail to appeal to the hungering, jobless millions, who live in barren want, while everywhere about them is evidence of restricted plenty in the greedy hands of the few.'"[58] Such attitudes made their way to the grassroots. The sociologists Horace Cayton and St. Clair Drake write that it was not unusual, when parents feared an eviction, for them to tell their children to "run quick and find the Reds!" Cayton writes that one woman cried and thanked God "loudly and dramatically" for the presence of council members.[59] James Yates, an African American member of the Unemployed Councils on the South Side, expressed the party's significance to him: "I was a part of their hopes, their dreams, and they were a part of mine. And we were a part of an even larger world of marching poor people. By now I understand that the Depression was worldwide and that the unemployed and the poor were demonstrating and agitating for jobs and food all over the globe. We were millions. We couldn't lose."[60]

City authorities expressed concern that Communists were gaining influence in the black community and that "fundamental institutions of the country" were in jeopardy. Examining these accusations firsthand, Cayton joined an "unkempt"-looking group that was marching in a "serious and determined fashion" through the heart of the Black Belt. "Instead of trying to destroy our splendid and glorious institutions," Cayton reported, "these poor black folks were simply going over to put a fellow race member back into the house he had been unceremoniously kicked out of. This was indeed a come-down for one who had expected to witness the destruction of constitutional American principles, such as, for example, 'due process of law.'"[61] After the group returned a woman's "miserable belongings," Cayton observed another black woman speaking to the group from a soapbox. Rather than offering empty phrases or Marxist theory, he reported, she talked the "talk of a person who had awakened from a pleasant dream to find that reality was hard, cold, and cruel." Before the woman could finish, Chicago's Industrial Squad arrived and began beating the observers, who ran in fear for their lives. Such an experience made Cayton wonder if American institutions were not in trouble, but for different reasons than he had when he began his investigation. He also wondered if this incident, like many others, would be billed as a "red riot."[62]

The black community's response to the councils' activities heartened Communists, who did not let public attacks bother them too much. Instead, they worried about the predominately black composition of the Black Belt's councils.[63] An unemployment demonstration on February 10, 1931, where councils mobilized four thousand white workers to march down South State Street from Thirty-third to Forty-third Street, was encouraging. What began with twenty whites to one black ended in a mass rally, half white and half black. Party leaders pushed councils to organize future interracial demonstrations in other communities.[64]

They had particular success in the Back of the Yards, where men, women, and children lived in some of the city's worst conditions. Stockyard pollution fouled local creeks, and wafting odors filled the air in the congested streets. The Yards' business cycles gave an ebb and flow to employment of the resident Lithuanians, Poles, and Mexicans.[65] In the Back of the Yards, interracial councils combined anti-eviction work with demands to help unemployed packinghouse workers. The council that began meeting regularly in the neighborhood toward the end of 1930 organized a march on the stockyards to demand jobs, the abolition of labor spies in the plants, and weekly supplies of meat for unemployed yard workers. In April 1932, the *Hunger Fighter* reported that some twenty thousand black and white workers participated in a "mighty hunger march" where over six thousand marched for three miles, the first interracial rally in the area since the pre–race riot "checkerboard crowd" that had gathered in 1919 when Communists worked to organize stockyard workers. The party proudly recognized that this was the first time that black workers had marched into the white territory around the Yards in such large numbers.[66]

This emphasis on interracial work brought blacks and whites together in Chicago's councils, often for the first time. Lowell Washington, an African American member of the Unemployed Councils, remembered, "'[I] never really even talked to a white man before, and I certainly hadn't said more than two words to a white lady, and here I was being treated with respect and speakin' my mind and not having to worry about saying something that might rile 'em up. . . . Let me tell you it changed the way I thought about things.'"[67]

The frequent, unprecedented displays of interracial solidarity on Chicago's streets sparked the city's administration into action. After the shootings and arrests of August 3, 1931, the municipal court bailiff temporarily stopped serving eviction warrants. City officials seemed to begin to recognize the high rate of evictions that had been carried out for some time.[68] After meeting with business leaders and welfare officials, city officials arranged for three hundred people to work in the city's parks. Mayor Cermak, who had told workers that demonstrators would be arrested, now acquiesced to a "moratorium" on rents. Tenants began hanging signs reading, "We Do Not Pay Rents" and "Please Do Not Ask Us to Pay Rent."[69]

These were temporary measures, and the desperate situation accelerated throughout the city in 1932 as landlords began turning off gas, water, and electricity to evict tenants in arrears. Jobless workers found it increasingly difficult to find housing because landlords refused tenants on relief. State funds released in March 1932 loosened relief agencies' purse strings and even specified shelter as an acceptable form of relief, but charities continued to delay rent payments until eviction was "imminent," and even then, fund distribution remained at the agent's discretion.[70] Regardless, the Communist party and their Unemployed Councils succeeded in raising people's expectations regarding government support, and they made an inroad into Chicago's African American community. Ben Gray remembered that if you walked on the South Side and wanted to hand out a leaflet at someone's home, all you had to do was say "'hello comrade' when you never saw the person before . . . that was the 'open sesame,' you said you were from the Unemployment Council or the Communist Party. 'Hello comrade,' that was the password."[71]

RELIEF-STATION PROTESTS AND POLICE VIOLENCE

Anti-eviction and shelter activity gave council members a record of victories, but with welfare payments threatened, they did not have time to rest and praise themselves. By 1932, public-relief stations were the places Chicago's unemployed were expected to go if in need of rent, food, clothing, coal, or utility money. Outside of the South Side, they became the main focus of council activity.[72]

Relief stations were an easy target because the hastily created welfare system they supported was unnecessarily complex and unnerving for its clients. A 1932 letter to Chicago's social-welfare agents makes clear how time-consuming and frustrating was the process of obtaining welfare. No fewer than fifteen district offices across the city dealt with unemployment relief (and these, therefore, provided the stage for much Unemployed Council activity). Fourteen other offices dealt with public welfare (but not for disabled veterans, who were rerouted to the American Red Cross). Jewish families were expected to go to Chicago's Jewish Social Service bureau, unless they lived in the area between Fullerton, Chicago, Ashland, and Washtenaw Avenues, which had its own special office. Fourteen different district offices of the United Charities accepted all families with one member under twenty-one as long as other agencies had no responsibility over them, and the Catholic Charities of Chicago referred all Catholic families to their parish priests, while the Salvation Army dispensed family welfare at five locations. More specialized offices like those for the aged and "non-family women" also were available. That Chicago's Council of Social Agencies prohibited the letter's public circulation, that the letter reminded its restricted group of readers that all offices were completely full, and that it contained instructions to offer carfare for those who were sent from office to office and to tell people that it may take time to get to the right office suggest how overwhelmed the system was and how ill treated were Chicago's needy through the heat of the Great Depression.[73]

With this as a backdrop, Unemployed Councils built a following at relief stations. Through block committees, council members represented clients at these stations, demanding money for rent, food, clothing, and utilities. One demonstration planned by the North Side Neighborhood Council called for a demonstration at the Ravenswood and Montrose Avenue relief station, where a committee of ten planned to present "minimum demands" to the agents. Interested folk were to march with council members from the corner of Belmont and Wilton, increasing their numbers as they proceeded to the station. North Side council leaders also promised demonstrations at the neighborhood's two United Charities and one Joint Emmerson relief station.[74]

Once at the relief stations, council representatives found that not all station agents were willing to deal with them. But the councils had an ally, at least initially, in Joseph Moss, the county's director of public welfare. Moss agreed that council members brought his agents more work, but he believed that the contact with council representatives had "made it possible . . . to anticipate certain criticisms and also keep on our toes."[75]

Moss was so committed to gathering constructive criticism that he set up neighborhood conferences to find ways to improve the city's welfare system. Wicker Park conferences, held in the Chicago Commons settlement house, were attended by "all workers' committees in this district," including the neighborhood's Unemployed Council. From July 1932 through the beginning of 1933, council members met with the head of the Wicker Park relief station, Moss, representatives of the district's settlement houses, and other representatives from workers' committees to suggest ways to improve the system. Rather than have an open confrontation at a demonstration, council members sat and worked through the bureaucratic minutia necessary to get welfare clients their due. Party leaders raised concerns in September 1932 about this "disastrous tendency of substituting legal 'gentlemenly' methods in our relation with relief station for form of mass struggle, mass delegations, etc." But the conferences continued into 1933.[76]

For a time, Moss was open to hearing from council leaders, but conflict was not long in coming. At the Union Park relief station, where agents would only see council representatives on Fridays, neighborhood leaders wanted more open access. A South Side branch demanded abolition of special times set aside for receiving council members (and their having to wait outside until admitted), as well as immediate relief for all the committee's clients. Moss agreed that agents must accept written complaints at all times and report in writing within twenty-four hours. He authorized weekly conferences of grievance committees also, but the specifics of relief would always vary among cases. These bureaucratic layers, intended to control council activity, simply frustrated council leaders, who continued to demand immediate attention.[77]

Over time, council members became effective in shepherding clients through red tape and getting results. In addition to sitting in conferences with welfare officials and staging relief demonstrations, members searched out the most needy cases from their block committees and organized the rest to join them at a relief station, where they would demand the kind of relief their client needed. Sometimes at these gatherings, council leaders put relief agents, agencies, and city officials on trial for the inadequate provisions and poor treatment they offered, and these brought results. In the March 12, 1932, edition of *Hunger Fighter,* a West Side council representative reported that the council had 396 members and a number of block committees. In one month, they successfully attained relief in thirty cases taken to the Humboldt Park relief station. The branches' eviction cases, taken to United Charities and the Jewish Charity, were also successful. The council also succeeded in keeping an elderly man from being sent to a flophouse by convincing social-service agents to send him to an "old folks' home" instead. Relief workers' records also show effective council work. In at least two cases, council leaders brought uncooperative caseworkers to management's attention, with satisfactory results.[78]

Sometimes Communists saw victories merely in exposing racism. In March 1932, the council called a protest at Fourteenth and Loomis against the station's practice of discriminating between black and white box rations. Later in the year, after workers at the Emmerson relief station refused to pay unemployed workers' rent and an official at the station slapped a black client, council members called for a large demonstration. They brought together demands to stop relief cuts and to start rent payments with demands for the removal of the offending official. Collecting demonstrators from local shelters and pool halls, councils mobilized a thousand blacks and whites, including a number of youths. When station officials refused the demands of an elected committee, an unemployed crowd pushed its way into the station, facing the clubs of twenty-eight police. When she tried to speak, police knocked down and arrested Edith Miller, a YCL member. After the police arrested the leaders, council members mobilized other block captains and branches to march to the courthouse. Meeting them on arrival, police began making mass arrests. The YCL leader Jack Kling explained to national party leader Gil Green that the event's interracial character caused police to roam black neighborhoods, making the streets appear as an "armed camp."[79]

Whether they won concessions or not, council members always had to prepare for violence. Even before the August 1931 killings, city officials brought in firehoses to break up a crowd of eviction protestors on the South Side, and then police repression escalated.[80] In November 1932, councils secured a permit to protest "administrative abuses and inadequacy of relief distribution." The demonstrators wanted a hundred of their ranks (about one-third of the crowd) to enter the station. After the police allowed two dozen to enter, they began beating people in the crowd. A Chicago Civil Liberties Committee member reported that sixty-year-old Martina Knutsen, partially paralyzed, "was given so severe a blow on the chest that she fell to the sidewalk. The police beat her and dragged her on her knees across the car track to the patrol wagon, refusing to pick up a shoe that she lost on the way." Police also struck a twelve-year-old girl who tried to protect the woman. When a Mrs. Gold yelled for an officer to stop hitting a young boy she believed to be her son, police struck her over the head. Another observer recalled seeing a police officer "strike down a woman who was pushing a baby carriage, the carriage was overturned, and the baby fell out." A man was then hit by an officer and carried to a wagon, where another officer yelled, "'You God-damned red, you're one of the leaders,' and struck him on the leg with a baseball bat." Testimony from sixteen witnesses corroborated the protestors' stories, but the police denied that any violence had occurred.[81] Upset about the overwhelming brutality of the incident, Joseph Moss wrote to the police commissioner, James Allman, complaining about his officers' unnecessary brutality.[82]

Chicago police attack Unemployed Council protestors at the Humboldt
Park relief station, March 11, 1932. (From *World Revolutionary Propaganda: A Chicago Study,* by Harold D. Lasswell and Dorothy Blumenstock,
copyright 1939 by Harold D. Lasswell and Dorothy Blumenstock. Used by
permission of Alfred A. Knopf, a division of Random House, Inc.)

Communists tried to avoid violent altercations by regularly applying for police
permits. Make Mills, the head of the Industrial (or Red) Squad, was responsible for deciding whether these permits should be issued or denied, normally
denying them only when the location or issue seemed volatile. One example
was the case of an October 1932 demonstration on String Street, where protest
had recently led to violence. At the October event, police shot and killed Joseph
Sposob, a homeless man from a nearby shelter protesting relief conditions. Mills
permitted no warrants in the area for the next year.[83]

The ability of demonstrations to be "legal" encouraged Communists to hold
them more often, increasing from 408 in 1931 to 566 in 1932, but while they
were technically legal gatherings, police regularly arrested demonstrators and
took out their aggression on the crowds. In most cases, the Communist-inspired
ILD came to their rescue. Irving Meyers was one of the ILD lawyers assigned
to council cases. Growing up in the Jewish neighborhood of Lawndale, Meyers
remembered listening to Socialists and Communists speak on street corners.
After graduating from law school and passing the bar in 1930, Meyers met the
ILD activist Bill Browder, Earl Browder's brother, who inspired him to work
for the ILD even though Meyers was not sure what it was.[84] His first case was

to defend twenty demonstrators arrested at Elmwood Park's relief station. His legal partner, David Bentall, an old-time Swiss Communist who ran a farm in Minnesota during the growing season and otherwise led the Chicago party's Control Commission, chewed tobacco and spit liberally in court when he did not like what the judge was saying. In the Elmwood Park case, Bentall convinced the judge to throw out the case by delaying proceedings long enough to gather community support. Meyers's time with the ILD taught him that the organization's work went beyond legal assistance. When police shot into a demonstration in Melrose Park, nine demonstrators, including John Jacob Jacobsen, the editor of *Hunger Fighter,* were seriously injured. After the shooting, Jacobsen was nowhere to be found. Bentall and Meyers later found him in a hospital ward suffering from gangrene. Through the ILD, Bentall got Jacobsen in touch with a party-friendly surgeon who saved his leg.[85]

Through his work, Meyers found out that Communists ran the ILD. He remembered being asked if he would have a problem representing them in court. He did not, but he also was not interested in becoming a member himself because, he later claimed, he feared it would keep him from doing other business. As it turned out, he never had other business anyway. A devoted Marxist and regular reader of the *Daily Worker,* Meyers preferred to participate in party activity as an outsider, as did the majority of those involved in relief demonstrations.[86]

ROADBLOCKS, SHIFTING TACTICS, AND REVOLUTIONARY APPEAL

Just as council members used the ILD to protect them from police prosecution, Joseph Moss, the director of public welfare, increasingly felt that he and his welfare agents needed protection from council members. After Sposob's murder in 1932, council demands became increasingly difficult to answer. Within relief stations, council members were resisting local agents' talk and demanding words with Moss. In one case, James Allen threatened relief workers and "obstructed office routine by entering case workers' offices." In another, a Mr. Huszar of the council refused to wait in line and had to be removed by police. When council representatives did meet with Moss, they were, in his words, "no longer satisfied with my statement that certain matters are beyond my jurisdiction."[87]

In December 1932, Moss received a report from an Unemployed Council member who was upset with the character of his fellow council members. Louis McCann, the author, insisted that of the seven hundred members in his branch, 70 percent were not radical and only went to the council when they had grievances. Communists exploited the situation, according to McCann, and hooked people on the party once they solved their problem. Three different Communists approached McCann and asked him to join. He refused and then asked Moss for support in the creation of an alternate organization, which McCann thought at least four hundred would immediately join. There is no evidence that Moss endorsed such an organization, and it is impossible to verify McCann's claims. His letter does suggest, however, that in his neighborhood organization, Communists worked with hundreds of non-Communists in building their local council and attempted to recruit party members from its leadership. If his numbers are correct, it would mean that over two hundred of them were "radical." Placed on its head, McCann's plea hints at a local Depression-era phenomenon whereby his neighbors were becoming politicized. Their local Unemployed Council was the main organization in that neighborhood competing for their attention and loyalty.[88]

By January 1933, Moss had had enough of the council's tactics and admitted it was no longer possible to deal with them effectively because their members were "one hundred percent obstructive." As a result, district offices no longer fielded complaints. Instead, all activity was centralized into a single office in the city. Communists were particularly upset with this changed policy, and in Elmwood Park one hundred people rushed the relief station, refusing to let relief workers leave. One of the workers fainted, and another clerk deserted the office and refused to return. At the Lawndale relief station, demonstrators fought against police with rocks and stones. Buckshot from one officer's shotgun seriously hurt four demonstrators.[89]

The centralizing of the procedure was a hard blow for council activists, since they would no longer be able to assist such a varied population in a public manner. Also, for a time, the police would not let council members hold as many public demonstrations as they would have liked. Relief-station activity attracted thousands of Chicagoans to the councils as rent, utilities, and food bills got paid. Communists not only began to prove their ability to lead and stand up against racism but also succeeded in providing humanitarian assistance. If some took advantage of their newfound power by charging for their services or threatening relief workers, the majority were happy simply to point to the holes in the system that they could begin to fill.

Communists were pleased with the attention they received in shelters, among renters, and at relief-station rallies, but as the Depression wore on, they looked for new ways to organize the unorganized. In neighborhoods like Cicero, little council activity had taken place as late as September 1931.[90] In this neighborhood, where families tended to own small bungalows, party organizers needed a new hook if they were going to raise any interest. By the end of the year, they found it and began advocating an end to mortgage payments for small homeowners who suffered from the Depression.

The campaign to organize small homeowners was small and largely ineffective, but it did have some successes. Communist papers asked homeowners to "think it over." After all, workers were "asked to borrow, or in plain words, to jeopardize the homes they have saved and scrimped to get." Councils asked homeowners to organize to "force the city and state to grant a moratorium on tax and mortgage payments! No Foreclosures!" To a group of revolutionaries who largely did not own homes themselves, this appeal was a stretch. Not much effort went into the campaign, and yet, according to police files, at least one branch formed in Berwyn to deal with foreclosures, and the Back of the Yards group took on the issue as well. In both cases, little resulted, short of increased education and membership numbers.

Despite such setbacks, council membership throughout the city confirmed in many Communists' minds that their party was the true leader of Chicago's workers. A party registration in 1931 showed that the city had seventy-eight branches and 104 block committees, representing 11,234 council members, 442 of them Communists. No strict accounting appeared again, but council activity strengthened throughout early 1933, bringing thousands more into its membership. This large representation meshed with Third Period expectations and encouraged council members onto soapboxes, into apartments of the evicted, and through relief-station doors.

Large membership numbers also reinforced party activists' Third Period belief that Communist-backed organizations were the only organizations that represented workers' interests. When other organizations tried to speak for the unemployed, Communists' Third Period teachings prepared them to attack. The most important Chicago group the party faced was the Chicago Workers' Committee on Unemployment (CWC), led by Karl Borders until 1934 and then by Frank McCulloch. About twenty-five members from the League for Industrial Democracy, a Socialist party offshoot, began this group in 1931.[91] At first mainly meeting to talk about issues, the CWC later formed locals in settlement houses, organized an advisory committee of professionals, and began holding meetings in 1932 on living conditions of the unemployed, advising relief stations, and calling conferences of relief workers. If the Unemployed Councils were displeased with the encroachment, the CWC's leadership found the councils equally irksome.[92]

As their locals grew, Communist party and CWC leaders developed a tense working relationship. At times it was not clear whether the groups were more upset with each other or the paltry system of welfare. But events like the October 1932 march against the 50-percent relief cut suggest they could overcome group rivalry.[93] As soon as Cook County announced a 50-percent cut in relief payments, all representatives of the unemployed realized a great organizing potential, and they worked together. In what even military intelligence marked as an "unusual feature" of the planned demonstration, the CWC and Unemployed Councils joined forces and marched with an estimated fifty thousand demonstrators through the Loop, stopping traffic for an hour.[94]

Not that all contact between the groups was easy. In typical Third Period fashion, Communist leaders felt determined to discredit the CWC and win the loyalty of its members. In a session with seven hundred party and non-party delegates, John Williamson read from a prepared speech that denounced the AFL and Karl Borders as betrayers of the working class. Williamson and other Communists in attendance also insisted that councils be allowed to carry political banners in the march, and even though conference attendees voted down the banners, Communists showed up to the march with signs.[95]

Despite such impolitic behavior, the union between the two organizations proved to be a success, and the groups' leaders planned future united actions. Although the party encouraged attacks on Socialists and liberal reformers, Communists found that they sometimes needed to work with these other groups. In addition to such party veterans as Bill Browder, Sam Hammersmark, and Arthur Maki working publicly with liberals and Trotskyites, even sectarians such as Jack Spiegel remembered at times reaching out to Borders and leaders of other groups because he needed their support.[96]

Protestors gather downtown for the Hunger March of October 31, 1932, cosponsored by the Communist party's Unemployed Councils and the Chicago Workers' Committee on Unemployment. (Chicago Historical Society, ICHi-20955, photographer unknown)

Throughout their ranks, Communist leaders found that their members were not consistently following their line against working with liberals and Socialists. In South Chicago, council members burst into a meeting of the CWC, denounced the leadership as "misleaders, hypocrites, capitalists in disguise, liberals, socialists, etc.," and urged spectators to join the councils and find out the "truth about everything."[97] But council members often turned up working with these same "misleaders." On the South Side, party members recruited in churches and met with leaders of reformist groups. This was especially true in places like Washington Park, where relations with community leaders ran hot and cold. On the North Side, when a council tried to present the alderman and vice president of the Chicago Federation of Labor, Oscar Nelson, with a list of demands, police stymied the action. Leaders of the Swedish National Society responded by agreeing to work with the council on issues involving meal tickets and housing, and the council accepted the offer. While Communist party leaders castigated the offer as a "demagogic trick," council leaders saw things differently.[98] Liberal supporters also helped to obtain parade permits for the party and helped get people out of jail.[99] These institutions and leaders were important gateways to masses of workers, and rank-and-file Communists were not always willing to scorn them. Party leaders recognized that the Depression brought them a "new" party and that they could not expect the same discipline from these new members as from older ones.[100] But they were continually aggravated by their members' willingness to work with people whom party leaders viewed as social fascists.

Mingling with liberals was only part of party leaders' problem. New recruits simply demonstrated less commitment to party discipline. Expulsion records reveal cases of individuals who lived as Communists on their own terms. Some were expelled; others were permitted to remain. Through most of the Depression years, such independent thinkers represented the face of Communism to Chicago's unemployed workers and demonstrated its shades of red. One report for October and November 1932 tells of Charles Banks, an Unemployed Council leader and party member who for a year was the subject of his comrades' complaints of carrying on "activities on his own hook" and remaining "isolated from the Section." Banks even disagreed publicly with his section leader and made the leaders' decisions "matters of debate amongst individual Party members and in his unit." Since Banks was "sincere, devoted, and [a] fearless fighter," party leaders agreed not to suspend or expel him.[101]

In South Chicago, L. Reuter, a machinist and former member of the Social-Democratic party in Germany and current Communist party member in Chicago who rose to leadership in the South Chicago Unemployed Council, continually questioned party decisions and exposed party weaknesses in public. While his campaign against the party began in September 1932, he was not

brought before the discipline committee until April 1933. Disciplinary committee members gave him three weeks to shape up. He decided not to and was
finally expelled. In March 1933, another council/party member, an electrician,
used the "prestige of being a Party member amongst the masses" to develop
an individual racket, charging two dollars for each light he illegally turned on.
Six months after this behavior began, the party expelled him.[102] Whether they
were "isolated," combative, or crooked, individuals joined the party and acted
in the councils in ways that did not fit party notions of discipline. This was
especially true on Chicago's South Side, where Unemployed Council recruitment was the highest. Chicago's Control Commission warned these members
that their numerous acts of "financial irresponsibility and drunkenness, loose
talk and general Party irresponsibility" caused a surge in disciplinary cases.[103]
While leaders were not happy with the political level of these new recruits or
their lack of discipline, they were pleased that they were the first interracial
organization to reach into and mobilize the city's black community.

Communists also made limited inroads into mobilizing women. Through a
maternalist model that argued for women's political demands on the basis of
their roles as mothers, leaders encouraged women to join the protest.[104] In this
capacity, women existed in the twenty or so women's committees, which were
established in 1933 and coordinated by an executive committee that included
three party women borrowed from Cook County's Unemployed Council executive committee. They varied their struggles between demanding pots and pans,
bed linen, and clothing from relief agencies for families with schoolchildren
and organizing neighborhoods for strikes against rising prices.[105]

As a rule, the Comintern and national party did not permit separate women's
councils, but in Chicago, some councils did not draw women into leadership and
instead used them for technical work or for house-to-house canvassing, causing
groups of women to organize separately. In the October 1932 demonstration
against the government's proposed 50-percent cut in relief, nine women's committees of the unemployed sent delegates to the conference that planned the
demonstration to convince other organizations "to help in the fight around the
schools for the bettering of the conditions of our children." Yet, while breaking
party rules in terms of their willingness to organize separate women's committees, these women's committees followed party policy when it came to Third
Period ideas against social fascism. "Karl Borders' [socialist] movement," reads
a letter from a women's committee leader, "[has] . . . proven to be nothing more
nor less than a faker, in the United Front for the fight against hunger." The letter
urged "all women in the City of Chicago as well as in the whole of the United
States, to affiliate with the Unemployed Councils, and help carry on the fight
against hunger."[106]

In addition to populating the enclaves of women's committees, some women in the South and West Sides worked arm-in-arm with their male comrades. Kate Erlich, Marie Houston, Romania Ferguson, and Dora Hucklberry appear in police or party reports as "militant" participants in eviction protests, and other reports suggest women's participation at relief-station rallies. For some women, council work provided a place to learn the basics of mass organizing, and women's participation, attitudes, and beliefs began slowly to change the character of Chicago's party.

The historian Van Gosse argues that Unemployed Councils rhetorically opened a new space for women activists. Yet while Chicago party leaders prodded Communists in councils to "embrace" women, young workers, and children, a July 1932 report recognized that Chicago's unemployed movement was "primarily based on adult men workers."[107] While the movement's language may have been more woman-friendly, in Chicago, council activity never took this turn as sharply as it might have, and the party was not able to translate what women's unemployment activity there was into an increase in female membership to the same degree that they were in black and white male unemployed communities. Margaret Keller, the party's director of women's work in 1933, complained, "[I]t is terrible difficult work among the women, they are very narrow, due to the majority being housewives and can't see anything else but the relief, we hope through education to convince them this is a political struggle. It is slow but we will get there. The interesting part is that we have very few Party members among these women and yet I am sure they will eventually be very loyal to our movement, provided they are handled carefully."[108] Chicago's party and council members were keen to involve women in children's relief, but they were unable to offer these women, whose primary concern was household issues, a role to play with issues of the employed. Women with children, moreover, could not devote time to party work, and time was what party activists needed.

These were not the concerns of Chicago's male party leaders, who largely ignored the councils' problems reaching women and instead focused on their belief that unemployed activity would result in support for Communists at the polls. Beginning in 1932, the party increased the number of their candidates run in elections. Whereas Freeman Thompson, running for U.S. Senate, was the only candidate in 1930, Communists in 1932 ran candidates for president and vice president, senator, governor, lieutenant governor, secretary of state, auditor of accounts, state treasurer, attorney general, and representative in Congress. Thompson polled only 1,325 votes in the city in 1930, but Communist candidates in 1932 polled between 11,879 and 8,359, with most receiving over nine thousand votes. And while most Communist candidates did not fall too far behind Socialist candidates, who averaged about fifteen thousand votes, the Communist candidates for president and vice president fell behind the Socialist vote for Norman Thomas's ticket by almost twenty thousand votes. In any case, Communist candidates failed miserably in comparison to Democrats and Republicans and fell short in terms of party leaders' expectations.[109]

Chicago's workers wanted a better welfare system, but this sentiment did not translate into political backing for Communist candidates. Yet 1932 returns show that in the neighborhoods where unemployment activity was most intense, on Chicago's South Side, Communist party votes were most concentrated. Whereas Communist candidates averaged nine hundred votes each in the city's second ward, Claude Lightfoot, the African American Communist party candidate for Congress, won thirty-two thousand votes in this district. In West Side neighborhoods, returns varied from six hundred in the Thirty-first Ward to over three hundred in the Thirty-second. In the Near North and North Side neighborhoods, candidates polled just over two hundred votes per candidate, and in South Chicago between three and four hundred.[110]

A New Era

By 1934, the sharp edge of hard times had dulled as state welfare programs were lessening individual suffering. The Illinois Emergency Relief committee approved rent payment as an integral part of relief budgets, which resulted in a decrease in the number of Writs of Restitution from their 1932 height of 63,152 to their 1934 low of 8,876. Although this was twice the number served in 1929, relatively speaking, workers felt less under attack. They also had a newly inspired hope in President Franklin Delano Roosevelt. His inauguration in 1933 marked the beginning of the New Deal and a sense of optimism. By the summer of 1933, the New Deal's Federal Emergency Relief Act (FERA) was providing additional money, and by 1934 a slight economic recovery took the edge off workers' crises. By the end of 1935, FERA had allocated $3 billion to relief.[111]

Moreover, by 1935, fewer welfare decisions were being made at the local level, leading Communists to rethink their approach to unemployment. Many in Chicago thought Unemployed Council work was at a dead end, with the city's grievance offices centralized and many in their ranks finding new jobs in industrial work and on WPA work sites. So instead of community work, national party leaders encouraged more political organization and citywide mobilization. Since the Socialists' unemployed program included lobbying, meeting with relief administrators, and putting pressure on national leaders, Communist leaders realized that the more organized and focused agenda they were now pursuing would duplicate Socialists' activities unless there was unity. Pushing for council members to merge with other unemployed organizations, leaders hoped to create a powerful force that could require the government to stay in the business of offering relief.[112]

In addition to working locally on government projects, the Communist party hoped to work with non-party groups to get support for its unemployment and social-insurance bill, introduced to Congress on February 2, 1934.[113] Even though non-party leaders were hesitant to act in unity, their local branches were less inhibited. Several former CWC locals participated with the Unemployed Councils in a 1934 May Day rally, and others agreed to work with the Unemployed Councils afterward. Joint pickets tried to prevent the closings of a River Grove relief station and North Side WPA project. And a year later, a joint committee on relief action, created by members of both organizations, unanimously authorized a letter to the Illinois Workers' Alliance and the Illinois Unemployed Councils urging a united-front demonstration in Springfield. Communists were determined to smooth over past problems and create a powerful, united movement.[114] Work like this led the way to an eventual merging of the two organizations in 1936 to form the Workers' Alliance of America.

* * *

The party and council member Lydia Bennett, speaking before a labor council gathering in 1932, reported the party's intention of showing the inability of the system to support its citizens. She apparently believed that such exposure would result in its collapse. But ironically, in their daily work Communists helped Chicago's unemployed navigate the shaky welfare system, and their individual victories for the needy diminished any resolve these people might have had to launch a revolution. Instead of a revolutionary movement, then, Communists and council members, working closely with needy people as they experienced personal devastation, developed organizing skills and widened the Communist movement. More than a few party council members would eventually build on their organizing skills in the labor movement: the council leader Joe Weber would find his way into steel, Jack Spiegel would work with the boot and shoe union, and James Samuel and Richard Tate organized packinghouse workers. Herb March recalled borrowing tactics from unemployed organizers when he and others built the packinghouse workers' union in Chicago. One evening a week, employees forced their employer to set aside time to deal with their grievances. "Beginning at 4 or 4:30 P.M., one by one a hundred or so aggrieved workers would take their turn confronting the plant bosses with their problems." Their focus was now on employers rather than relief workers, but their line was the same: "Nobody's getting out until we settle all these cases. These guys have all been waiting here all this time and you can't treat us this way."[115]

Unemployed Council activity occurred in multiple venues, called for various measures, and incorporated a wide array of people with different backgrounds and dispositions. Some, like Louis McCann, who worked with Communists, were repelled by party tactics and alerted authorities to their activity. Others, like Irving Meyers, also remained outside the party while working with councils but, unlike McCann, developed a strong admiration for Communists' bravado and their network. Still others, like Ben Gray and Claude Lightfoot, found their commitments to Communism confirmed by their council activity. And a few women, both black and white, like Marie Houston and Katherine Erlich, had the unique opportunity to speak in public to audiences of men and women, to stand up to Chicago's police, and to rail, with others in support, against relief agents who treated them poorly.

Party teachings had varied effects. Militant positions on race attracted skillful and dedicated black organizers and increased sympathy within the black community. The party also provided one of the only places in the city where black and white activists could discuss, socialize, and protest together. But ideas about social fascism generally proved divisive, alienating leaders at settlement houses and workers loyal to non-party organizations and leaders and delaying the unification of unemployed organizations. Council success occurred despite these social-fascist teachings and because some Communists were willing to bend the rules.

The structure of Unemployed Councils made them easier for Communists to influence, and yet the relationship between the councils and the party did not preclude council activity from reflecting the diversity of Chicago's neighborhoods; nor did it prevent lower-ranking Communists from shaping activities that were pertinent to particular communities and individuals. Council work proved an important training ground for new activists, who shifted their attention once the momentum of council work had slowed from unemployed to union work.

5

"Abolish Capitalism": The Trade Union Unity League's Potential and Problems

On August 30, 1929, a convoy of automobiles left Chicago for Cleveland, draped with signs and filled with trade-union delegates en route to a convention where Communist party officials would announce the formation of a new labor federation, the Trade Union Unity League. Party leaders imagined that the system of capitalism would soon collapse and that workers would enthusiastically support an organization dedicated to building revolutionary unions in industries where established unions neglected vast groups of workers.[1]

Communist leaders also realized that some industries, such as garment, transportation, and construction, had entrenched unions, so they instructed Communist trade unionists in these industries—whether they carried independent or AFL union cards—to continue agitating from within against their leaders and when possible to promote unemployment insurance, militancy, and democratic union policies. In other words, they were to win away craft workers from reformist leaders for the program of the TUUL, while remaining members of their particular AFL or independent union.

From the time of the TUUL's launch, Bill Gebert was convinced that Chicago's workers were ready for revolutionary unions. At a 1931 gathering of the city's Communist leaders, Gebert stated, "[T]his is the most important district in the country from the point of view of industry." Like others in the city's party leadership, he believed that if TUUL organizing was going to work anywhere, it was going to be in Chicago. "Surely," he pleaded, "we can carry this campaign."[2]

From Communists' perspective, the potential for radical union growth in Chicago was great. Syndicalist impulses within Chicago's party survived the 1920s anti-union backlash, and union militants remembered, rehashed, and waited to relive the 1919 mass-production organizing drives in steel and meatpacking. In the late 1920s and early 1930s, they looked at AFL leaders' resistance to rebuilding Chicago locals and to starting new organizing drives as both a crime and an opportunity. Employers' open-shop drives through the 1920s devastated many of the city's unions, but the percentage of unionized workers in Chicago—22 percent in 1929—was twice that of the nation.[3] The majority of the city's unionists were clustered among construction trades, transportation, and public-service workers. Semiskilled and unskilled factory workers had almost no organization. The most important manufacturing industry in Chicago, metal products, showed only 8,900 union members out of 142,000 workers, a miserly 6 percent.[4] A majority of black men were employed in packing, steel, and the building industry. Racially exclusive AFL unions in packing and steel and only small pockets of mixed-race AFL locals in a few building trades meant that as a group, African American men were largely untouched by unions. Black and white women in domestic work and manufacturing also suffered from a lack of representation. Women in the garment industry did have some union representation, but from the party's perspective, the International Ladies' Garment Workers' Union (ILGWU) left much to be desired.[5] With such a largely open field, party leaders predicted that their organization would spark a radical resurgence among workers.

Despite party leaders' resolve and their belief that the TUUL would dominate Chicago's labor scene, the TUUL faced an uphill battle. Only two months after it formed, the stock market crash hinted at hard times to come. The city's construction industry had been in decline since 1927, but the rapid closing of mortgage banking houses hastened the slowdown. In 1930, only 23 percent of the 8,500 carpenters who replied to a union survey were employed in the trade. An arbitration award reduced their union scale from a high of 97.5 cents an hour to the low that year of 62.5 cents. A few strong voices among contractors wanted it even lower, at 40 cents. Unemployment and assaults on pay hurt union morale. In such bad economic times, some thought it wrongheaded to fight back.[6]

Party leaders like Gebert could not disagree more. The crisis was exactly the sign Communists looked for as the beginning of capitalism's end. They believed there was no better time to organize workers into militant unions and to promote revolutionary agendas in established AFL and independent unions. Communists believed they would simply need to explain how the TUUL differed from the more mainstream labor organizations, and Depression conditions would ensure that workers would flock to the revolutionary unions. Through the TUUL, Communists were to "organize the widest masses of workers on the basis of struggle to improve their conditions and to resist the attacks of the bosses on their wages, hours, conditions, etc."[7]

Year after year, party trade-union strategy sessions pushed the same goal of getting out the message, but results were not what party leaders had hoped.

One problem was that rank-and-file Communists were not unified behind the TUUL's goal of organizing unorganized workers into revolutionary unions: some opposed dual unions, others preferred working with Unemployed Councils rather than with revolutionary unions, and still others were unwilling to do the difficult, daily work of union organizing. Chicago's party leaders would also eventually confront another issue: even when Communists were enthusiastic, focused, and committed, they had a very difficult time gaining the trust of Chicago's workers, whose interests in union militancy and Communist leadership waxed and waned in relation to their own personal, political, and economic calculations, the culture and climate of their particular workplace, and the historical and political context in which their grievances arose. In 1933, when Franklin Delano Roosevelt suggested his support for union organization, more workers in Chicago's large and small industries joined unions. They did not, however, choose the TUUL as the organization to represent them as often as they turned to the AFL. By that year, some of Chicago's Communists already had begun reconsidering the TUUL as the most effective tactic; within two years, the Comintern abandoned it altogether.

In the context of a raging economic depression and an injured union movement, plans to build the TUUL seem quixotic. And yet, Communists' unyielding belief in revolutionary unions and persistent plans to see them through resulted in several breakthroughs for the party and industrial trade unionism. They made inroads into unorganized sectors of Chicago's workforce, pushed for interracial, industrial organization, and reached out to women workers. The TUUL became a training ground for union activists, who learned practical lessons about how to organize workers; and through it, Communists laid groundwork in several of Chicago's major industries by listening to workers' grievances and promoting racial equality. Through TUUL newspapers, Communists shared shop news, grievances, and shop-committee successes with wide audiences, preparing workers to expect responsive and democratic unions, and in these ways laid important groundwork for the Congress of Industrial Organizations (CIO) and industrial unionism. That the party officially disbanded the TUUL only five years after they founded it can divert attention from the concrete and successful work that was accomplished in the face of such dispiriting odds.

Some historians have described the TUUL as purely an expression of party policy, and there can be no doubt that party directives mattered a great deal in the life of the TUUL.[8] Yet other historians argue that following party policy did not preclude TUUL union members from being effective and legitimate trade unionists.[9] In Chicago, party policy encouraged a more militant and democratic form of union organization than existed in most AFL locals. When workers supported TUUL organizations, they found willing and active party unionists who were often veterans of labor struggles informed by Marxist teachings offered at party schools designed for union organizers. Non-party workers in the TUUL also learned about Communist issues at work and in their union meetings—support for the unemployed, the Scottsboro case, the Soviet Union, and impending capitalist war. For that matter, individual TUUL activists did not always follow party policy or directives. Tensions between leaders' revolutionary expectations and the daily realities of the rank and file—repression by employers, the state, and groups within Chicago's organized labor; fellow workers' lack of interest and occasional hostility; and tactics that varied from the practical to the idealistic—pulled rank-and-file comrades against their leaders. Communist trade unionists were based in different industries with different work cultures. Like their fellow comrades who organized the unemployed in Chicago's neighborhoods, they did not simply follow orders from above.

There is also more to the story of the TUUL than whether or not its members followed party policy. The story of the TUUL's birth, its structure, and the challenges its organizers faced through the period of Roosevelt's policy change exposes the dramatic political, social, and economic changes rank-and-file Communists and Chicago's workers faced in the late 1920s and early 1930s. TUUL successes and failures provide a window onto the state of Chicago's labor movement; the violent nature of labor politics in the city; and workers' attempts to come to terms with welfare capitalism and state and employer repression, AFL complacency and defensiveness, and race and gender relationships at the workplace.

This chapter's examination of the TUUL in the context of the "lean" 1920s and the early Depression years reveals the difficulties inherent in organizing the unorganized. It also demonstrates TUUL activists' ability to bridge the militant period of the post–World War I years with those of the CIO's formation and growth. Activists tried to encourage workers with the notion that the TUUL offered the possibility of a revolutionary recentering of power at the point of production into the hands of traditionally underrepresented groups of unskilled workers, women, and minorities. In the process, Communist trade unionists revealed their own shortcomings, the fear and trepidation of Chicago's industrial workers, and the heavy-handed tactics of employers, established unions, and the state.

The TUUL's creation made sense to leftists soured on, and scorned by, the AFL. But carrying out the Communist party's revolutionary trade-union policy was difficult. In the process, mistakes and small victories taught much about politics and possibilities inherent in organizing in Chicago, lessons that would serve the party in the period of the CIO's formation and growth. In the meantime, Communist trade unionists faced a disjuncture between party leaders' expectations and rank-and-file experience, differences that revealed the importance of local knowledge and creative organizing tactics on the part of Chicago's Communists. In the context of trade-union conservatism and employer and state repression against labor, Communists found ways to pressure foremen, bring workers together, and extract small concessions from employers. They were not able to move large numbers of workers into their organization, however. Local party activists reassessed their tactics through the early 1930s, changed their organizing strategies, and eventually created the conditions for the TUUL to dissolve.

From the TUEL to the TUUL

Like other skilled craftsmen, Nels Kjar, a carpenter, held an AFL membership card. Unlike the majority, however, Kjar was a Communist, and unlike many Communists he supported the party's 1920s trade-union organization, the Trade Union Education League, as late as 1928 by following its policy of "boring from within" his union. Somehow he and a few others had managed to avoid expulsion from their local union for Communist beliefs and behaviors, but for Kjar this good fortune was about to run out. In 1928, from within his carpenters' Local 181, Kjar agitated against the union leaders Thomas Flynn and Charles Sands by encouraging members to reduce their "fat" salaries. For this and similar activities, Kjar was expelled. In June 1929, he wrote a "personal appeal" to the brothers of his local not to vote for Elmer Larson or Phillip Pleger in the local's upcoming election because they had worked with "socialist renegades" in expelling him and others. That August, the union's executive board brought up Kjar's friend, Nicolai Bull, on charges of distributing Kjar's appeal during voting at Wicker Park Hall. Deciding that expulsion was too severe a punishment, union leaders agreed to a suspended sentence for Bull, as long as he continued to have good behavior. For Kjar and Bull, TUEL work within AFL unions would not be easy, but they agreed it was important.[10]

Kjar and Bull's dedication to agitate through the TUEL after local unions expelled leading Communists for such behavior stood in contrast to most Communist trade unionists in organized industries, who decided they simply could not raise Communist issues inside AFL unions, a decision that would lead them to support the TUUL, a revolutionary alternative. In the building trades, general party activity suffered after non-party union leaders expelled a number of Communist unionists in addition to Kjar in the fall of 1928. In a Communist party meeting of industrial leaders, Kjar agreed with Nathan Held that since that time, "[O]ur members have fallen down on their work in the unions."[11]

In the needle trades, party forces working through the TUEL also suffered. As late as 1927, Chicago's party leaders complained that they had never established strong leadership in the trades, nor had their members established much of a cooperative relationship with progressives in the Amalgamated, International

Ladies Garment Workers, or Cap Makers' unions.[12] This sentiment was not entirely accurate: in the early 1920s, Communists provided important leadership in these unions. But at the end of 1923, trouble began. Mayer Perlstein, the ILGWU vice president, arrived in Chicago with the single mission to rid its locals of Communists. Eleven old-time party union activists were expelled, including the city party leader Dora Lifshitz. Refusing to go quietly, the group gathered two thousand ILGWU members at Ashland Auditorium to protest their expulsion. They braved gunfire aimed at the speakers' platform, where the TUEL and party leader William Z. Foster stood, but had to wait until 1925 to be readmitted.[13] One year later, party members took over the union's joint board and bucked the wishes of its international leaders by supporting New York cloakmakers' Communist-led strike. The result, according to the union's historian, Wilfred Carsel, was "a virtual state of war between the Chicago Joint Board and the International." Fights broke out at local union meetings and spilled onto the streets. A new election that year secured the right-wing leader's position back on the board. The CFL's support of the right and an injunction from the Superior Court of Cook County sealed the left wing's fate. By 1927, a small group still organized in the dress trade, but they had lost their momentum.[14]

Within the Cap Makers' Union, internal political fighting came to a head in 1927 during a lockout of the union. Communists won workers' support to lead the union but antagonized other political factions within it. When party members walked picket lines, a group of thugs, locally known as the Miller street gang, attacked them. In response, the party fraction issued a leaflet on the role of the right wing in the strike and called a meeting of all cap makers, which attracted 250 gangsters. Clarence Hathaway believed some of these gangsters were responsible for breaking windows in the building where the Jewish Communist daily *Freiheit* was published and for stabbing and beating "dozens" of comrades. In the wake of these attacks, anti-Communist unionists succeeded in breaking up the left-wing strike committee and initiating what Max Bedacht referred to as "bitter warfare" against the left wing.[15] These attacks led to a decline in the willingness of Communists in the needle trades to speak out and organize. Dora Lifshitz, at a meeting of the party's industrial committee in April 1929, observed that TUEL forces in the needle trades were "weak."[16]

In such large industries as the stockyards, where organization lagged, party members succeeded by the late 1920s in agitating through the TUEL in and around factories, but they were not so successful in one-on-one organizing or recruiting established union members into the TUEL. In 1928, party organizers held twenty neighborhood meetings around the stockyards and formed one nucleus of five members, who sent out a leaflet announcing a meeting to which 250 workers, sixty of them non-union, turned out. That same year, though, party leaders complained that the nucleus was "systematically killed" from lack of attention.[17] In March 1929, the nucleus was rebuilt when a call for a mass meeting resulted in sixty-two workers offering their names to the TUEL. At its peak, only two months later, 175 workers signed up with the TUEL, but a plan of work never got off the ground.[18]

TUEL reports were not always so grim. Between late 1921 and 1923, organizers advanced on several fronts. TUEL members published an impressive radical labor magazine, *Labor Herald;* supported a labor party based on unions; and developed a wide network of labor militants who pushed for the amalgamation of craft workers in the same industry into the same union. According to James R. Barrett, between 1922 and 1923 the TUEL succeeded in getting their amalgamation resolution adopted by "perhaps half of organized labor in the United States."[19] TUEL organizers also made inroads into the ILGWU, Amalgamated Clothing Workers', Cap Makers', Furriers', and Miners' unions. And they successfully sponsored a national amalgamation conference for railroad workers out of the ashes of the failed 1922 shop-crafts strike. This conference, held in Chicago, resulted in the gathering of 425 machinist and railroad delegates committed in some way to amalgamation.[20]

But in the immediate aftermath of Communists' domination of the Farmer-Labor party and their isolation from John Fitzpatrick and other labor progressives, such victories gave way to an unrelenting tide of conservative unionism. At its 1923 convention in Portland, Oregon, AFL leaders expelled William Dunne, a Communist organizer and credential-carrying union member. Such action, David Montgomery observes, represented the first time a person was expelled from an AFL convention based solely on their political beliefs.[21] Throughout the country, city central bodies and individual AFL unions followed suit, purging Communists from their membership rolls. Those who were not expelled often behaved like Chicago Communist machinists, who "simply dropped out of the union without telling anybody, forgetting to pay their dues."[22] If the point of the TUEL was to use the AFL to reach working people, the purges and attacks on party members rendered this strategy useless. Instead of focusing on working within established unions, the TUUL would allow Communist trade unionists an independent and wholly revolutionary organization from which to work, while still permitting activity in independent and AFL unions where the local context warranted it.

In 1928, the leader of the Comintern's industrial organization, Alexander Lozovsky, announced the Communist party's new trade-union policy in Moscow at the fourth congress of the party's international trade-union organization, the Red International of Labor Unions. While it took such leaders as Foster some time to get in line with Moscow's leadership, Edward Johanningsmeier's work shows that significant support for the new policy came from Communist trade unionists who were stymied by the AFL and those who came from an "indigenous tradition of radical industrial unionism." As early as 1924, Joseph Manley, Foster's son-in-law, an organizer of the 1919 steel strike and a participant in the 1923 Farmer-Labor party movement, criticized the TUEL policy of working within the AFL. Manley suggested the party reach out to the IWW and their dual unions, a plan Lozovsky had considered. Joseph Zack and Earl Browder also offered early critiques of the TUEL's boring-from-within strategy, as did the IWW activist Bill Haywood. Johanningsmeier rightfully suggests that the willingness of party leaders to debate new forms of radical union structures during the Third Period and Haywood's willingness to offer critiques to party officials puts the Communist party at the center of the leftist debate of how best to radicalize workers. Johanningsmeier concludes that Third Period Communist trade-union discussions linked the "tradition and outlook" of the prewar IWW with the Communist industrial movement of the 1930s more firmly than scholars have thought.[23]

In addition to the individuals Johanningsmeier traces, many of whom spent parts of their political careers in Chicago, the city's Communist trade-union leaders also agreed with the new policy. By 1928, purges from local AFL unions encouraged them to take a new turn in their work. Even though the TUEL had its start in the city, they were frustrated with their inability to work within the AFL and hoped that the TUUL would help them counter the attack that anti-Communist unionists had launched. RILU leaders changed party policy, and based on their day-to-day organizing, Chicago's trade unionists could understand why.

For this reason, at least initially, enthusiasm for the TUUL ran high. On September 19, 1929, four hundred "enthusiastic" trade unionists gathered to hear Chicago's TUUL delegates report on the Cleveland Convention. Brother Kease from the Railroad Amalgamated Committee declared that the immediate task for railroad workers was to "organize shop committees as the basis for a powerful industrial union." A food worker, Alma Polkoff, declared that "Chicago culinary workers are ready to join this movement. The . . . program . . . for the food workers is already being put into effect and every indication point[s] in the direction of success." Delegate Feingold from the needle trades reported on the "immediate application of the decisions of the convention in Chicago," and delegate Rubicki from the machinists explained that Chicago metal workers were "putting into motion the program adopted at the Cleveland convention." Herman Dorsey, an African American electrician, announced, "The building of an industrial union in the building trades with full equality for all workers regardless of race is the objective of the Trade Union Unity League and the Negro workers are going to support this movement."[24] Less than one month later, Chicago's organizers could report that fifty steel and metal workers in the city had agreed to join the TUUL's Metal Workers Industrial League.[25] Otto Wangerin, the party leader in charge of organizing railroad workers, reported that party organizers had distributed a railroad paper with TUUL union application blanks and "expected to take in many members shortly."[26] Wayne Adamson helped call a conference among food workers attended by a small number of party members but "quite a few outsiders." A few months later, Alma Polkoff reported on "great progress" made among Chinese food workers, "who must toil from 10 to 16 hours a day for 7 days a week for the small wages of $20 to $30 per month." TUUL organizers signed up over a hundred Chinese members.[27]

Not all groups were doing well, however. In November 1929, the party's industrial committee lamented small numbers at International Harvester's McCormick and Tractor plants, Western Electric, and the stockyards; the legacy of 1920s anti-unionism, segmented labor markets, and labor defeat plagued their effort. In response to Rubicki's comment that he had a hard time reaching the party's shop committee at Harvester, other industrial committee members heckled, "[T]here . . . [is] no such animal as the Harvester shop committee."[28] In the stockyards, party leaders placed a Spanish-speaking member, "Jiminez," to assist with the committee of mostly Spanish-speaking workers. These laborers came out of a small Mexican community in the Back of the Yards, largely composed of single men who had been in the city less than five years. Most had worked in the packinghouses of Omaha and Kansas City in the 1920s before settling in Chicago, so even though the city's South Side steel mills had offered Mexicans their first opportunity in the city to work in heavy industry, and a small Mexican community settled there, by the mid-1920s, their packinghouse numbers were on the rise: Mexicans were 5 percent of Swift and Armour's workforce and 3 percent of Wilson's. Rick Halpern found that within these plants, "they held the least desirable jobs, working in the hide cellars, freezers, glue houses, and fertilizer departments." He also found that as a group, Mexicans tended to be "more left-leaning and politicized than other workers." Some remembered the Mexican Revolution, were influenced by the radical campaigns of Zapata and Villa, and held membership in the Chicago affiliate of the Confederación de Trabajadores. And yet the party could not hold on to them. By mid-November, Communist organizers reported that only one and a half members belonged to the league.[29] It was clear that party trade unionists had hard work ahead of them.

How to Build the TUUL

In response to these disappointing reports, John Williamson and his organization department began writing directives for Chicago's organizers on how to build revolutionary unions. Similar to party work in Unemployed Councils, union activity was supposed to be connected to party members' everyday political activity. Talking about unions was not enough; the TUUL would be built on struggle. Such direction helped organizers establish committees and plan actions within unions and factories and allowed them to build on party resources outside factory gates.

To make up for their limited resources in Chicago and throughout the country, national Communist leaders pushed their trade unionists to develop a policy of "concentration"—a focused drive to recruit members in "the most decisive industries." Nationally, these included mine, steel, textile, marine, and auto. Once they selected particular factories for concentration, Communists were supposed to hold gate meetings, pass out literature, provide aid to striking workers, and develop a group of supportive union activists "that are genuine." In the face of a strike, the party was to offer legal assistance through the ILD and strategic help through its leading trade unionists.[30]

In Chicago, party leaders agreed to narrow their union concentration to the steel, meatpacking, and railroad industries. It was no wonder. In South Chicago and northern Indiana, a number of steel mills grew up on Lake Michigan and the Calumet River, including the world's largest, Gary Works. This Calumet region stretched over 196 square miles and included Chicago's steel communities of South Chicago, South Deering, the East Side, and Hegewish, where waves of immigrants and a small group of black migrants lived and worked for such employers as Crane Company, Republic Steel, Illinois Steel, and Wisconsin Steel. This region would lead the nation in the production of steel and iron.[31] The Union Stockyards were similarly impressive, filling one square mile, five miles southwest of the city's downtown Loop. Forming one of the largest industrial concentrations in the nation, the stockyards were home not only to the "big three" packers of Armour, Swift, and Wilson, each employing five to seven thousand men and women, but also to smaller houses such as P. D. Brennan, Roberts and Oake, Miller and Hart, Agar, Reliable, and Illinois Meat, each employing between one and five hundred workers. By the late 1940s, around thirty thousand workers labored in the Union Stockyards' slaughterhouses, processing mills, and livestock pens.[32] While not as concentrated, the city's railroad lines were also strategically important centers that had proven pivotal in building the city's labor and radical traditions.

Work would continue in the AFL unions of the milk drivers, printers, building trades, and laundry and among garment workers, but for the time being, city leaders focused on the formation of new TUUL unions.[33] To do this, city leaders called on section leaders to bring together Communists who worked in their territory's industry with those who worked in street nuclei to decide on which plants in their neighborhoods to concentrate their efforts. Each neighborhood was to pick from concentration industries if they existed, but otherwise the choice was theirs. In Chicago, the main companies Communists chose were the steel and metal plants of International Harvester, Deering, Crane, Stewart

Warner, Western Electric, and Illinois Steel; the meatpacking plants of Swift, Armour, and Omaha; the Northwestern Railroad; and the apron and dress shops of Sopkins and Sons. With the exception of Sopkins', a majority of the workforce chosen was male.[34]

Williamson's organization department outlined steps for organizing these factories. In theory, at least some party members would already be working within the chosen plants. They were the shop nuclei. Once they got non-party members to join them, party members became known as the party fraction, which one party union leader referred to as the "effective cells for the carrying on of Communist activity within the trade unions." In theory, nucleus and fraction members did not make policy but carried out plans created in counsel with section, district, and national fraction leaders. Work in these fractions was so central to Communist organizing that one Chicago resolution explained, "Without Party fractions, the TUUL cannot be built."[35]

Once organized into fractions and/or nuclei, party members were to bring workers together around concrete issues in the plant. Within factories, an "elementary" stage of organizing was the grievance committee, which was to be composed of as many workers as organizers could gather to present grievances to management. By acting on problems in the plant with broad worker support, these committees would provide a challenge to management and any AFL or independent organization already established in the plant. Party fraction members in successful grievance committees were directed to push these committees to a higher level of organization, the shop committee, which brought together delegates from throughout the factory and was intended to lay the basis for a strong TUUL. Once a shop committee formed, Communist leaders could be assured that the TUUL organization had the support of workers in the plant and that strikes would develop. To party leaders they represented "the full fighting force of the workers in a given factory and form a basis for the revolutionary industrial unions."[36] While trying to get other workers to join, shop committee members were to pay dues and affiliate with the TUUL.[37]

An article by a packinghouse worker in the Communist journal *Party Organizer* demonstrated how these structures worked in practice. A worker in one of the larger packinghouses attended a meeting of the Packinghouse Workers Industrial Union (PHWIU) and shared his grievances with the group. For the next meeting, he brought fifteen fellow workers from his department. Out of this group a committee was selected to issue a leaflet that would express their grievances. The committee also decided to write slogans on factory walls that denounced a cut in work hours and wages. Superintendents scurried around the plant washing the walls clean, but it was too late. Once workers read the slogans, they began to talk about union and the need to settle their grievances.

At the next meeting of the PHWIU, a number of workers from departments throughout the plant came together. A shop committee was in the making.[38]

In addition to organizing structures within plants, Communists drew on the social culture of ethnic workers and organized TUUL balls and dances, continuing traditions many had experienced as members of earlier progressive movements. In December 1929, Chicago's TUUL hosted a masquerade ball at the Ukrainian Workers' Home, offering "radical prizes" for the best revolutionary masks. Advertisements reported that workers who attended could expect to hear "one of the best orchestras in Chicago." Organizers in Chicago's packinghouses also hosted masquerade balls and pushed party section members to sell tickets for twenty cents apiece.[39] These gatherings provided an alternative to company-sponsored events and allowed party members to help talk up the TUUL, socialize interracially, and make contacts in a relaxed atmosphere with workers from various shops. Communist trade unionists knew that it was through these informal contacts made at dances, socials, and house parties that unions are built.

As important as union building was among Third Period priorities, it was not to impede Communists' larger project of party building. All party members learned through directives from Williamson's organizational department that if they worked in a shop, they needed to join a party nucleus and build grievance and shop committees while continually recruiting the "best elements" of the workers into the party.[40] Party leaders pushed women's recruitment at Western Electric, Majestic Radio, the stockyards, and "other important factories that employ large numbers of women and Negro women."[41] Not only would Communists be sparking a revolutionary union movement, they would also be increasing the party's own numbers of industrial workers.

Just as they would have liked for industrial workers to make their way to the party, Chicago's leaders insisted that all party members needed to join the TUUL, a warning that permeated down to the section level.[42] Leaders around the stockyards informed their members that "stockyards work is the most important of the section—every member must be involved in bringing workers into the Packinghouse Workers Industrial Union or the Party mass organizations canvassed for stockyard workers."[43] Party leaders also encouraged assistance from party fractions in auxiliary organizations and told activists in Unemployed Councils to use connections they might still have with workers in shops where they previously worked.[44]

Williamson also encouraged using the International Workers Order (IWO), a party-influenced mutual-aid society, to build the TUUL. The IWO, founded in 1930, built its membership around ethnic people who were unhappy with the health and life insurance policies that their national societies provided. Its organization ran as a nonprofit, providing an alternative to commercial insurance companies; and it supported party initiatives through social events, public statements, and letters to its members, at times taking positions that its members would not uniformly support. In 1931, Chicago's IWO organized its four hundred members into Jewish, Polish, Ukrainian, Greek, German, Rumanian, and youth branches. Williamson saw these groups as natural targets for his campaign. He explained that about four hundred IWO members were in the needle trades, for example, but the Needle Trades Workers' Industrial Union only had 165 members. Williamson instructed, "[T]hru proper work in the IWO the fraction should become the means of utilizing the IWO in order to popularize the NTWIU [Needle Trades Workers' Industrial Union] in order to get the four hundred workers into the NTWIU." The railroad organizer Otto Wangerin also saw the importance of the IWO, especially when local IWO officers agreed to give back to railroad organizers one dollar for each member they recruited to the IWO. Even though railroad brotherhoods were required to carry insurance, in the early Depression years their funds were nearly depleted, and insurance costs for workers were rapidly rising. An IWO flyer distribution in the city had quickly resulted in a number of inquiries. Wangerin thought it good to put unemployed members to work in the railroad yards as IWO organizers. In this way, he would be using the IWO to help build local TUUL resources and would be recruiting workers into the IWO.[45]

In addition to targetting work with auxiliary groups, Williamson directed section leaders to assign comrades from street nuclei around chosen factories whose "MAJOR" work would be to assist organizing workers in the factories of concentration. Once chosen, these street nuclei were to have weekly tasks, which the section committee would check on monthly.[46] To rally workers and solicit grievances, party members inside and outside the plants were directed to work together in their launching of "energetic propaganda": gate meetings, mass meetings, door-to-door canvassing, and leafleting.

Even though party leaders focused on building revolutionary unions, they sent directives concerning oppositional activity in the AFL through the entire period of the TUUL. In a 1930 article in the *Party Organizer,* Communist trade unionists learned that "concentration on building the TUUL does not mean deserting fraction work in AFL unions." Party members in AFL unions were expected to attend local meetings, where they would actively build opposition groups and raise party campaigns and issues, such as unemployment insurance, with the hope of getting union locals' support.[47]

The historian Bert Cochran finds that Communists in the auto industry did not begin to move into AFL locals and the independent union Mechanics Educational Society of America until 1933, when the RILU favored such a move. With this evidence, Cochran argues that "Moscow soothsayers" predetermined

Communists' decision. In Chicago, however, the ranks did not wait for support from Moscow's leaders to work within AFL and independent unions. To do so would have been folly in a city where the AFL and independent railroad brotherhoods had a strong presence, even in the late 1920s and early 1930s.[48] In fact, in 1931 more Chicago party unionists were members of reformist and AFL unions than of the TUUL. A report by a leading member of America's Political buro in November 1931, two years before international Communist policy encouraged AFL work, confirms that organizing in the AFL and independent unions was a focus of Third Period union work in Chicago. In addition to organizations formed under the auspices of the TUUL—the 167 members of the Metal Workers Industrial League, twenty-four members of the Food and Slaughterhouse Workers Union, eighty-four members of the Building Trades Industrial Union, 165 members of the Railway Workers Industrial League, and 450 Needle Trades Workers' Industrial Unionists—Chicago's Communists built a strong opposition movement in the printers' union and in a few needle locals. They had also built smaller groups in two painters' locals, six carpenters' locals, five metal workers' unions, and two food workers' unions. In the milk drivers' union, fifteen party members and eight non-party members succeeded in building a broad movement and putting five thousand milk drivers "into motion" against established union leaders.[49]

The structures party leaders established and industries they focused on put men at the center of their drive. Women workers were always an important part of party rhetoric during this period, but inadequate follow-up and separate organizational structures usually marginalized women activists, who nevertheless persisted within the party to push the need to organize women workers. Despite insuring they had lesser power, the party provided these women a base where they honed their organizing skills and fought battles in the labor movement—a significant accomplishment in the late 1920s and early 1930s, when political and cultural pressures pushed against women in the workplace and undermined their fight for rights as workers. In this way, the party offered an unusual space for the Woman Question to be hashed out and for women activists to be trained. Still, even in Communist circles, women found that their victories were usually of their own making.[50]

TUUL structures and strategies did not preclude women's involvement, but party organizers did. As early as 1926, the Comintern insisted that party work among women shift from a focus on housewives to one on female industrial workers, but as late as 1930, Chicago's mostly male leadership still had not made efforts to follow this directive. One Chicago women's leader berated local party officials at a district plenum for their notion that the "work of organizing women into revolutionary movement [is] a joke." She observed, "No serious discussion [of organizing women] even [occurs] in leading committees." Hoping that TUUL leaders would place a capable person in charge of women's work, she found instead that they suggested someone "loaded down with other work" and thus unable to direct attention to the work needed among women.[51]

Too often party leaders treated women's issues as a separate and not integral part of the activity in which all party activists participated. At one citywide meeting of section and unit women's-work directors, a member moved that women's work appear on every unit meeting agenda to show its importance. Katherine Erlich argued against such an approach, suggesting it was too "mechanical" and created the erroneous impression that "work among women was a separate struggle that the Party had to carry out, something apart from the daily work of the unit." Instead of isolating and generalizing women's work, Erlich argued for a more concrete approach: "When taking up recruiting, the unit should take up how all comrades will help in getting working women for the Party, from the shop of concentration and the mass organizations in the territory, how individual comrades in the shops where women are employed will recruit women for the Party."[52] Erlich's suggestions were practical but ahead of her time. Not enough party people thought this way, and it proved easier to simply make gestures. Few were willing to take the time to develop strategies focused on women. One woman leader complained to the national party leadership, "Until last week I ran around like a chicken without a head trying to get someone to work on the department with me that would work not just have their name on it."[53]

A resolution that came out of the 1930 plenum described the place of women's industrial work in Chicago's party. "The entire burden of bringing the masses of women of the working class into the Party falls on the shoulders of the women's committee which is often composed entirely of women comrades who are not trained organizationally or politically for the carrying on of Party work and who receive very little if any political guidance from the Party in its work."[54] Instead of members of TUUL shop nuclei, Communist contacts in women's organizations were responsible for the thirty-nine delegates, half of them non-Communist, who attended Chicago's TUUL Conference for Working Women. Reports on the conference sent to the women's department resulted in warm replies, whereas those sent to the TUUL went without any response.[55]

Erlich recalled similar problems relating to organizing women in industry when she explained how section leaders appointed women to women's work and then neglected them. In her section, the woman appointed to lead the area's women's work called a meeting with other women's-work directors elected from each nuclei in her section. Together they waited in vain for a citywide or section leader to come and tell them what they needed to do. The section's women's-work appointee had no idea what tasks to take up with her fellow unit directors. Erlich hoped the party would have "overcome our old methods (the bad ones) of work so that at the next plenum we will [not] have to say again that we are still working in the same old bureaucratic ways."[56]

Despite the party's neglect of women, Communist women activists argued that women workers were a vital part of the working class and needed to be organized. On behalf of the Central Committee, Pauline Rogers toured the nation and met with party leaders concerning women's work in their districts. She commented on the willingness of Communists to see the importance of organizing working-class women in terms of the effect they would have on their husbands, sons, and brothers, but she encouraged them also to see organizing women as an important goal on its own terms. Industries across the country were hiring women and paying them half the wages of men for the same work. It was true, Rogers conceded, that women did not work in some basic sectors of industries such as steel, but they did work in tin mills and aluminum plants for low wages. Rogers agreed that women's auxiliaries were important structures for organizing women, but they operated as support for male workers and did not reach into the plants where women worked.[57]

Women organizers like Rogers believed there was great potential in women's industrial work, particularly in Chicago. As early as 1930, Ukrainian and Swedish women's organizations participated in the party's call for May Day demonstrators. Several women showed their bravery and commitment when they were arrested and beaten for handing out literature in front of the gates at Majestic Radio.[58] The TUUL's 1930 conference for Chicago's working women succeeded in bringing together thirty-nine women, many of whom had never attended a meeting, to take up shop-floor questions. Even though women leaders reported that many attendees were "shy" when asked to give reports, they were encouraged by women's participation. Still, most Chicago Communists joined comrades in cities like Pittsburgh and Cleveland in viewing women's work as an aid to organizing men and not as inherently valuable.

Part of the problem was that existing structures for organizing women largely focused on housewives, not factory women. The Working Women's Federation (WWF), for example, was the party's umbrella organization intended to unite women from mass organizations behind various Communist campaigns. By 1931, one report indicated that it lacked a "definite program of action," was "merely being used as agency for bazaars and selling tickets," and was largely composed of party members from various language and mass organizations where Communists already had support. Women's Councils of Housewives and Mothers' Leagues also existed in the city, but these tended to get bogged down in internal squabbles over leadership rather than working together against "high rents, food prices, and bad conditions in the schools." The eight to ten Housewives' Councils in Chicago had no centralized program and did not coordinate their activities, as did those Analise Orleck described in New York.

Chicago's party work among women resisted turning to factory workers. It was no wonder, then, that Rogers reported: "In Chicago, the idea still prevails, even among some of the leading section functionaries, that women's work consists of building housewives' councils [instead of TUUL groups]."[59]

Thus, by 1930, some were arguing that the TUUL did not take enough interest in women or in retooling the WWF to more effectively organize industrial women. But others disagreed.[60] In the midst of the confusion, the Central Committee handed down "Directives for Work among Women," which offered a nod to women's auxiliaries in steel and coal mining but emphasized the delegate meeting, a new form of organization in other industries. Whereas in many ways, women's auxiliaries were a natural extension of the party's success organizing housewives and women, they did not offer a means to reach women in the workplace. The Central Committee believed that delegate meetings could offer Communist women an opportunity to mobilize women workers in a separate space from their male comrades (and housewife gatherings) and provide them an opportunity to recruit among women workers. Proponents of women's delegate meetings voiced their hope that "[t]he development of delegate meetings around the factories will gradually dissolve the [working women's] federation and will orientate women's work in Chicago to shops and not to women's organizations."[61]

The delegate system brought together women from a particular department in a particular factory. In Chicago, women's efforts centered on Western Electric and the stockyards. Communist organizers were to contact sympathizers and then talk with them about shop issues and the need for "united work." Once enough contacts were made, the organizer set a date for a meeting, in a private house "to guard against exposure." If a number of these contacts came to the meeting, then they would elect delegates. Ideally, the same delegates would meet regularly, report to the women who elected them, and build increasingly large groups of supporters in their workplaces. Party leaders hoped that "[t]he delegate meetings will . . . draw all the women in the given factory into active social and political life." They believed that these meetings could serve as "the school for developing cadres and drawing women into the party and into the revolutionary mass organizations and trade unions."[62]

Beginning in 1932, though Chicago's male party leaders had begun speaking more to the need of organizing women, the delegate system was not operating well. One report indicated that successful organizing among black women working in dress shops had been accomplished and that a number of shop nuclei did exist, but "OUR PARTY SECTIONS DID NOT MOBILIZE THE CONNECTIONS THAT WE HAVE FOR THE DELEGATE MEETINGS." According to the author of the report, party leaders' better attitude toward organizing women resulted in an unprecedented number of women's organizations joining with the party's Unemployed Councils during a February 4, 1932, demonstration. But such work did not translate into organization in the factories. Party members were in shops, but "no one gives a damn whether they are doing any work among the women." "No one thinks that delegate meetings are of immediate importance."[63]

When delegate organization was not neglected, it sometimes involved more community contacts than shop-floor relations, despite party leaders' warnings. Helen Kaplan reminded Chicago party activists that when this happened the meetings were too general, did not focus on department grievances, and lost the interest of working women in attendance.[64] But women found that their community contacts sometimes paid off. In 1934, women YCL organizers reached out to Polish women through a settlement house, elected a delegate, and made connections with a group of older women workers. These contacts also helped them when male party members would not. When the one male comrade at Stewart Warner was "not energetic," women relied on their own contacts and organized a meeting with women from the shop.[65] Aside from small successes such as this, Communists slowly faced the fact that Chicago's workers, men and women, were reluctant to join the party's revolutionary unions. It did not matter what form they took.

The Trials of Revolutionary Union Building

Communist leaders believed that proper guidance and leadership would result in high TUUL and party recruitment numbers and militant union activity. Chicago's workers saw things differently. Between 1929 and 1933, Chicago's political, social, and cultural character, exacerbated by the nation's economic woes, created poor conditions for the building of revolutionary unions. Communist leaders' inflated sense of what was possible, confusion, sectarianism, and varying levels of commitment among the ranks compounded difficulties created by the Depression-era atmosphere, employer policies, and workers' fears.

Communists learned quickly that the depression that devastated industrial America did not necessarily signal a revolutionary drive in the workforce. Part of the problem was workers' support of their employers' 1920s welfare capitalist plans. Employees at Crane made valves and plumbing fixtures on Chicago's southwest side under the management of its founder's son, who offered them low-priced car insurance, inexpensive land for house building, company stock, and a company counselor who helped when problems with the police or the courts threatened. Wisconsin Steel workers had access to one thousand acres of land their company opened up for crop cultivation as well as to seed kits, plants, fertilizer, and tractors provided by International Harvester. And employees at U.S. Steel enjoyed pension plans, company athletic leagues, and employee stock plans.[66] In the packinghouses of Armour, Swift, and Wilson, employers expanded earlier schemes that targeted specific populations to include all hourly workers. While their companies' programs were not identical, they tended to include company unions, foreman training, wage incentives, expanded benefits, and recreational activities.[67]

Rick Halpern and Lizabeth Cohen argue that even though these programs were intended to keep workers loyal and productive, they had unintended consequences. Halpern finds that company unions served as "schools" for workers, preparing them for the CIO; foreman training did not diminish their hegemony on the shop floor; wage incentives at times promoted cooperation among workers; and limited benefits caused frustration. Cohen argues that employer-sponsored events promoted collective worker identity. Both historians argue that the 1930s labor movement was rooted, in part, in lived experiences of these 1920s programs. And while their arguments are strong, Communist organizers in the 1920s had a more difficult time being optimistic. At Western Electric, one party organizer argued that the party would never be able to organize the workers to strike because "every worker there is a share holder."[68] Workers' investment in their jobs and the fringe benefits their companies offered may have prepared them to organize when their benefits were later taken away, but in the beginning of the Depression, job security trumped union militancy.

As factory conditions worsened, Communists readied themselves for a worker revolt. Employers at Northwestern Railroad cut workers' hours and wages and required them to be at their benches by certain times, trimming opportunities for workers to socialize.[69] A new machine in Crane's blacksmith shop replaced a number of molders and increased production, resulting in decreased wages for those who remained. Harvester workers also experienced a speedup of their work, wage cuts, and layoffs. At Illinois Steel, employers forced their employees to begin work before the official starting time without extra pay. Meanwhile, rumors that a number of mills would close throughout Chicago and the Calumet region created difficult organizing conditions. Already several mills were operating only two or three days a week. One party member complained that in the mills, each of the party's half-dozen contacts eventually moved or was laid off, once again isolating the party from the shops.[70]

Communists continued to hold to the idea that as Depression conditions wore away the illusion of company paternalism, workers would rally to the TUUL. But hard times did not automatically result in union militancy. Workers in Chicago industries clung to the hope that in the thick of the economic crisis they would not lose their jobs. Those who were able to keep their jobs were not willing to muddy company waters by complaining. A steel organizer lamented that the "wage cut has not brought about an organizing sentiment, just dissatisfaction among workers." Even Communist railroad workers bucked party directives and refused to offer union motions against wage cuts, according to Otto Wangerin, because they felt that railroad workers would not support them; organizers insisted that these workers took the cuts as a "matter of course."[71] Les Orear, a young Communist employed at the Armour plant, remembered thinking, "You had to break down this belief that the company was God and you did it by revealing all the faults and hypocrisy. You did it by convincing the people that together they were just as strong, maybe stronger, than the bosses." Cohen demonstrates that in the late 1920s and early 1930s, Chicago's workers did resist their employers through quitting, being absent, turning to family resources, and enacting what she describes as "subtle forms of collective action," but Depression conditions made them skittish about militant action. Herb March, a Communist organizer in Armour who grew up in the YCL and organized unemployed workers in Kansas City before coming to Chicago, optimistically remembered that "people . . . had gone through a real period of suffering and oppression and they were ready to revolt," but it was clear that, in part, fear held them back and overpowered sustained, organized solidarity in the early 1930s.[72]

Physical segregation of workers along ethnic and racial lines inside and outside the plant bolstered the power of employer paternalism to quell solidarity. Chicago workplaces and trades employed different mixes of ethnicities, races, and genders. Asking party organizers to use their local knowledge about these conditions, John Williamson reminded section leaders that when assigning rank-and-file members to industry they should take into account "the composition of the workers employed in the shop—American, foreign born, Women, Negro, and young workers . . . so that they can have a better approach."[73]

Fitting in with workers in a given plant was one thing, but getting men to overcome their fear of women or blacks replacing them for lower wages or rallying black and white workers to fight against racial segregation was quite another. Wayne Adamson, an industrial organizer among food workers, experienced this difficulty firsthand. Calling together workers on the TUUL's behalf, he found that nearly all supported segregation and openly opposed the league's stand on racial equality. After he condemned them for their position and promoted the party's position of black and white solidarity, the food workers still "seemed to stick with us and many of them joined our group. They did not however say whether they were convinced or not" on the race question.[74]

Racial segregation was perhaps most pronounced in the building trades, where white AFL unionists refused to organize African Americans.[75] The problem predated the party and provides a good example of a historic local union struggle that the Communist party incorporated into its trade-union efforts. The way this was done also reveals Communist tactics and the independence individual Communists often had organizing outside of the party's main campaigns.

In 1914, Edward Doty, an African American pipe fitter's assistant working in Armour, watched in vain as the AFL organized the plant's white pipe fitters. In response, he and a number of African Americans approached the organization, but as he recalled, "[T]hey looked out and saw our faces, and they slammed the door in our faces."[76]

Unable to advance in the packinghouse, Doty and other of Chicago's black technicians tried to find work independently but frequently found themselves arrested for working without a state license, which only a few blacks could acquire. Born in Mobile, Alabama, Doty came to Chicago in 1912 at the age of seventeen. When he was twenty-five, he and friends began holding training classes for fellow blacks who had been refused apprenticeships by white teachers, which resulted in the licensing of the first group of black plumbers in the city. Doty and his allies soon learned that licensing was one step, but union recognition was another. White unions still gave them the runaround, so Doty and his associates took further action.[77]

In 1926, Doty and a few fellow minority plumbers began forming organizations. By this time, Doty had been a member of the Communist party for four years. In 1926, he joined with non-party plumbers and set up the Chicago Colored Plumbers Protective Association, which they soon renamed the Cook County Plumbers Union, representing minority plumbers in their relationship with black employers (since white contractors did not provide them with any work). In 1928, he also organized the American Consolidated Trades Council (ACTC), an organization for black plumbers, steamfitters, electricians, bricklayers, lathers, plasterers, and building laborers. Although Doty was a leader in the organization and a member of the Communist party, the party did not have a clear affiliation to the ACTC at its origin. Doty was a talented local organizer who saw a problem and created a solution. While his Marxist training informed his work, the shape it took emanated from the segregated conditions black building-trades workers faced in the city. According to Doty, the organization gave black building-trades workers the ability to use "pressure against the major white unions which were discriminating against Negroes, denying them membership, denying them the right to the job, denying them the right to all privileges that all workers were entitled to."[78]

The ACTC did not come under the aegis of Chicago's Communist party until 1934. By then, Doty's tenuous relationship with the city's party had come to a breaking point. In 1928, Chicago's leaders included Doty's name among a group of black leaders who would participate in the party's Sixth World Congress in Moscow. National party leader Max Bedacht opposed the proposal, arguing that Doty did not pay dues and was not active in party work. In September 1930, Chicago's leaders once again dragged Doty's name through the mud, despite the fact that in February of that year he had organized a TUUL mass demonstration against unemployment among building-trades workers and the corruption of their "fascist" union officials. In September, however, a conflict emerged between some black Communists and Chicago's party leadership over how to organize black workers. Many black Communists argued that the party's American Negro Labor Congress (ANLC) was ineffective. Formed in 1925, the ANLC hoped to create African American unions where white unions excluded blacks. Eventually, the party envisioned, ANLC councils would join with local labor groups and form interracial labor councils. The ANLC ran forums in the city, but few members joined. Then, with the creation of the TUUL and integration of racial issues into general party and ILD work, the ANLC lost its reason for existing.[79] Several Chicago black party activists, like Sol Harper, argued that the party should focus on integrating established unions. By refusing to dismantle the ANLC, it was clear to Harper that the party "does not understand Negro work in any of its phases." As a result of his belief, Harper refused to take action against such lower-ranking members as Doty, who, like Harper and a few others, disagreed with the party's policy of continuing with the ANLC and "jim-crowing" black workers. In October 1930, Chicago's Communist Control Commission expelled Doty because he was "inactive," had a "petty bourgeois ideology," and put "financial condition above Party duties."[80]

Regardless of the conflict and expulsion, Doty hung on as secretary of the ACTC through 1932 and pushed the Illinois Federation of Labor to rule that its member unions accept black workers. On May 8, 1932, letters from H. Dorsey, chair of the ACTC and a veteran party member, and Doty arrived on the desk of Victor Olander, secretary of the Illinois Federation of Labor. Dorsey and Doty described mounting tensions in the black community. Local conferences between the white unions of plumbers and steamfitters and the ACTC over the possibility of the white unions admitting black workers resulted in white local leaders' deferring authority to their international presidents. Dorsey and Doty appealed to Olander to "use your influence in our behalf." They also asked him to attend a mass meeting at the A.M.E. Zionist church where eight hundred workers would meet to protest discrimination in the building trades. Olander responded that the federation was unwilling to interfere in the autonomy of its member unions, meaning the ACTC would have to fight alone. On May 27, three hundred workers protested the AFL and the hospital board when they refused to permit subcontractors to employ licensed, skilled, black mechanics in the building of the new Provident Hospital and Training School.[81]

By 1934, the party had clarified its relationship with the ACTC. In a meeting of the party's city leadership, Communist ACTC organizers agreed to transfer ACTC members into TUUL unions in packing, steel, metal, needle, and food; to allow fraternal delegates at both the TUUL executive board and the ACTC; and to focus more fully on the blacks' right to join the AFL on the "basis of complete equality."[82] With formal support from the party, the ACTC turned its attention to integrating building-trades employees on federal housing and South Side school projects. It also worked on relief for blacks, continuing to work within black churches and community organizations. By this time, though, ACTC leaders were apparently excluding Doty. Claude Lightfoot agreed to work with two other ACTC leaders until they were able to find "one comrade to take over the job."[83]

Despite its commitment to interracial activism in other areas, it took until 1934 for the party formally to become a part of the struggle for interracial unions in the building trades. Communist leaders' preoccupation with the ANLC prevented them from attacking racially exclusive AFL unions sooner and in different ways.[84] It did not, however, preclude their members from doing so. Chicago party leaders initially had no control over the ACTC, even though party members were in leadership positions. When Doty fell away from party circles, he remained active in the ACTC. His work and continued relations with such party leaders as Lightfoot speaks to Communists' willingness to work with non-party activists and their ability to overcome party politics. But even more than internal party developments, the story of the ACTC reveals black workers' difficulty in creating interracial unions, a situation that the AFL and Illinois Federation of Labor's own leaders exacerbated.[85]

White unionists were not solely to blame for this segmentation of the workforce. At home, workers also segregated themselves. Life in the Back of the Yards, Bronzeville, South Chicago, Cicero, and on the North and West Sides provided workers rich cultural lives. But in the 1920s and early 1930s strict lines divided racial and ethnic enclaves, and in the case of Chicago's race relations, violence backed the divisions. The bloodiest battle before the Depression occurred during the summer of 1919, but tensions surrounding this conflict persisted into the 1930s. Jack Kling, a YCL leader in Chicago, recalled the fights and arrests that surrounded YCL attempts to integrate the city's beaches and the violence that ensued when two YCL families bought homes on Peoria Street and invited "blacks and other friends" to visit them.[86]

In addition to enforcing segregation, violence prevented new forms of union organization in Chicago. When Communists tried to form a TUUL opposition in the milk drivers' AFL union among "militant milkmen," union "thugs" watched closely. Nate Schaffner, a loyal party member from 1925, was often their target. Schaffner became interested in the Communist party as a young man witnessing open-air debates on the street corners of his West Side neighborhood. As a milk-truck driver and party activist, he wanted to help build the union, but union hit men, attending meetings with guns, helped ensure the status quo.[87]

Milkmen were not alone. Thugs also terrorized Communist newspaper publishers so much that some feared printing Communist papers. Nathan Green, a party member in the needle trades, reported that three Amalgamated shop committees set up before the TUUL convention were not functioning because "in the Amalgamated everybody seems to be afraid of the terror."[88] Police beatings intimidated Communist organizers around Western Electric, and a fear of spies prevented work elsewhere because employers simply fired employees who openly pushed for new union alternatives. Even when violence was not used, union bureaucracies were often so firmly established and worked so closely with employers that it seemed impossible to get around them.[89]

In Chicago—home to Al Capone's underworld—labor politics turned to violence frequently. Union corruption and labor violence were accentuated from 1919 through 1933, during the Prohibition period. By the late 1920s, gangsters had made their way into a number of trade unions, making racketeering a profitable and violent characteristic of the city's labor scene. Beyond the milk drivers' union, where one Communist observed "machine guns on the table when the meeting is called to order" and where in 1932 a bomb shook the union headquarters, syndicate influence permeated the Motion Picture Operators' Union, the Hotel and Restaurant Employees International Alliance, and Bartenders' International League. While these were the unions best known for connections to gangs, violence for hire—whether acid, bombs, shootings, or hijackings—was, according to Barbara Newell, "tailored to various industries."[90] A North Side mob organization even offered its services to party leaders who rented offices in the same Division Street building as the mob. Steve Nelson remembered that at least one party leader thought it a good idea to befriend them, but others believed that they had enough problems without attaching themselves to gangsters. "No thanks," replied Clarence Hathaway, a city leader. "That's not our style." Communists were careful not to alienate such powerful friends, and "every once in a while an irate immigrant woman would get the floors mixed up and begin banging on the door of the loft, yelling in Polish about eviction and police brutality. The gangsters had a little peephole that they would slide open, saying, 'The Reds are one floor down.'"[91]

Of course, corrupt unions and syndicates were not the only organizations responsible for Chicago's tumultuous scene. If Chicago's Employers' Association stressed union gangsterism to smear the overall union movement, at the same time it participated in labor violence and corruption. Edward Nockels explained how this worked: members of the association met with employers who honored union contracts and offered "to supply such employers with strikebreakers, detectives, and other racketeers" to break the unions. According to Nockels, when an open-shop drive was hatched, Employers' Association members brought the state's attorney, the chief of police, and city judges into their racket and in this way ensured "the cooperation of the city authorities." Such collusion meant that Communists worked in the context of shootings, beatings, and death threats.[92]

Communist trade unionists struggled to find an adequate way of dealing with labor spies, police violence, thugs, and entrenched union bureaucracy. The main question was whether or not to openly organize as Communists. After all, they were supposed to lead workers to the revolution. How would workers know who they were if they kept their politics a secret? As early as 1930, the *Party Organizer* laid out the party's formal position on the issue, which allowed room for (mis)interpretation. "It is necessary for every Party member to be a Communist all the time, but it is not necessary for a Party member always to advertise that he is a Communist." "When organizing in a shop," members were told, "a Party member may tell a sympathetic worker that he is a Communist, but when the boss or the foreman is around, he keeps that information to himself." If Communists wanted to keep their jobs to be able to organize workers, then they had to consider the realities of labor spies, Red Squads, and anti-Communist workers who reported names and caused Communists and their supporters to be fired. Directives to rank-and-file party unionists to let sympathetic workers know their identity and to keep bosses in the dark could be tricky business.

More often than not, party activists simply denied or hid their Communist affiliation. A national party leader, Harry Shaw, admitted he could not come out as an open leader of a union movement because "leaders would have enough material to discredit me as a red, not a railroad man." That, according to Shaw, was the problem with Otto Wangerin, who directed the party's national and Chicago-based railroad campaigns from "behind the scenes." Such distance from the workers affected union work. When directed to bring together five to seven railroad workers to form a local rail committee to push for unity among the various railroad trades, Chicago's party activists had to admit they did not have enough comrades for the committee.[93]

Railroad organizers seemed paralyzed over how to lead from behind the scenes, and they were not alone. Those in the building trades were so afraid of violating their union's constitution that they avoided openly building the party and its fractions within the AFL.[94] One former Illinois Steel employee and party organizer argued, "If you want to do some work in the mill, you are not able to keep still inside. In my department I kept quiet but was fired anyway." Four leading members of the YCL in packing also learned a lesson for being too "loose" in organizing. The superintendent called each one into his office and told them they were known Communists. This time only one lost their job. Vicky Starr recalled that when organizing, Communists had to be "very underground because if you even talked union you were fired. . . . You didn't have the law which guaranteed people the right to organize. So we actually had secret meetings. Everybody had to vouch for anyone that they brought to the meeting, that they were people that we could trust, because as soon as the company found out that people were trying to organize, they would try to send in stool pigeons." Despite all this, Joe Weber, an organizer in the TUUL's Steel and Metal Workers' Industrial Union (SMWIU), remembered, "We had small underground unions" that operated through "very close-knit departmental groups." According to Weber, an organization in "department A" had "no connection" with "department B groups, except with the heads of each of these groups, so that the company stooges would not fire our people."[95]

By 1933, Communist leaders began to change opinion on their private versus public nature. In November of that year, the national leadership met and concluded that hiding the party's face in industry was a way to stab the party in the back, "creating the feeling that Communism is something to be afraid of." To one organizer at Western Electric, it also caused confusion. Putting together a secret organization meant that "half the time we didn't know what was going on in the shop."[96] But the reality of the organizers' situation still prevented many from being too public. The decision to hide party ties would later encourage anti-Communists to be suspicious of anyone who supported progressive issues, driving a wedge between the Left and Right in the city's unions. In the context of the early 1930s, however, some party members felt they had little choice.

In addition to fear of dismissal, fellow Communists' resistance, inconsistency, and apathy also contributed to the slow growth of Communist unions. National leaders complained that even though Communists worked in concentration industries, they resisted actively building TUUL unions. The problem did not stop there. Across the country, they argued, "capable comrades . . . [were] totally inactive in the unions, [and] . . . many Party functionaries do not even belong to the TUUL."[97]

Chicago's leaders warned, "If our comrades cannot get connections in the shops after working there months and years they are not yet Bolsheviks." But threats did not improve the situation. At a district convention in 1930, leaders complained that "TUUL and shop committees are practically nonexistent" and noted "resistance among Party members toward building TUUL." Party leaders berated Communists in unions who saw themselves as privileged—thinking that all party work must be done for them as opposed to by them—and who waited for party leaders to act. In a 1932 district letter, leaders' frustration was apparent. "Although we have some connections, and here and there shop nuclei, our work is not proceeding in building up shop committees, grievance committees, etc."[98]

Problem solving was difficult when party leaders could not get organizers to attend meetings. For a meeting on why Western Electric workers were inactive in the union, only one of the ten Communists concentrating there showed up.

Others did not attend a meeting for planning concentration work in the stock-yards. The International Harvester section organizer S. Yandrich wrote that even though a nucleus had been in place in Harvester since 1925, its members "seldom met." When they did, "there was no life in the nucleus, no perspective whatsoever and as a result the unit was losing members." More embarrassing than missed meetings were missed public gatherings. Leaders learned that they could not depend on party activists in stockyards and steel plants to show for mass meetings that they themselves had called.[99] Communists in metal unions had similar problems. Of the fifteen who belonged to the metal league, only three organized. Ironically, a metal organizer reported, this metal league was the only one in the TUUL that was growing.[100]

When Communists did decide to work on unions, inconsistent practices exacerbated their inability to build the TUUL. Such tendencies can be seen through the use of shop bulletins, the primary way Communists communicated with workers inside a factory. Occasionally shop bulletins served their purpose, educating workers and bringing grievance committees to life. George Patterson, a non-Communist steel worker, remembered becoming "engrossed" with Communist party leaflets. In trying to talk about the issues raised with fellow workers, Patterson found himself labeled a Communist. Regardless, he remembered that workers read party literature to keep current on labor issues. Though a few men talked openly with Patterson about these things, he quickly made friends with them because, he recalled, he "learned from them." Leaflets like the one Patterson read could get small grievances solved and bring clout to organizations. Communists learned that whether involving dirty toilets or an overbearing foreman, leaflets about shop-floor problems could have positive effects.[101]

Shop papers were problematic in part because they appeared erratically. The organization department berated section leaders because in the four months since January 1931, only one section had issued any shop bulletins. Section leaders had difficulty finding members to make stencils and run mimeograph machines, but organizers had little sympathy.[102]

Even before the TUUL's formation, shop papers had problems. According to Jack Stachel, they initially looked like trade-union papers without political content. They also claimed to be created by "workers in the plant" rather than the Communist party nucleus.[103] By 1928, leaders had corrected these circumstances. Now the problem was that the papers were going too far in the other direction. They were too theoretical and, according to party leaders, "appear[ed] completely divorced from the problems of the workers in the factories where the shop bulletin is published." Beatrice Shields, a Chicago Communist leader in workers' education, argued, "Our bulletins only speak of the Soviet Union during the time of anniversaries. The achievements of the workers in the USSR must be utilized as a constant contrast to the conditions of the shops, and as the best weapon to rally the workers to struggle for the revolutionary way out of the crisis." Shields was a sharp, dedicated political activist, but she failed to see why Communist union militants complained that union papers were too political and not practical.[104]

By the early 1930s, party leaders were again raising questions about the authorship and messages of the papers. The official position was to issue shop papers in the name of a particular Communist party nucleus in the shop. Party leaders argued, "[T]he Communist aim and identity of the paper shall not be concealed from the workers." But others believed workers would be more open to the papers if they hid the party members' authorship. A recently expelled party member, Sam Cohen, argued that the TUUL should issue the paper. At a gathering of party leaders, Dora Lifshitz explained the problem clearly: Party bulletins "are issued in the name of the CP unit, the TUUL and a lot of other things. In one bulletin you tell them to join the CP, join the union, and everything else and they don't know the difference between one and the other."[105]

Problems of tone also hurt the papers. One organization letter warned that shop papers reveal "too much of a Party approach." In 1930, Northwestern Railroad authors told workers to "abolish capitalism," and in 1932, Harvester authors instructed workers to "build department committees," but neither provided specifics. One entitled *Hart, Schaffner, and Marx Worker,* sprinkled with drawings of sickles and broken chains, called on workers to unite "against their common enemy the bosses['] class."[106] In a review of shop papers, leaders complained that the *Illinois Steel Worker* did not advertise the Steel and Metal Workers' Industrial Union but simply dealt with building a grievance committee. The bulletins included articles on the anniversary of the Russian Revolution but did not connect this event to conditions in the plant, nor did they contrast the plant's conditions to those in the Soviet Union. Revolutionary party leaders' priorities could not be those of indigenous union radicals if these rank-and-file Communist trade unionists were to win workers' support. Communist trade unionists complained about the predicament they found themselves in: "We issue a bulletin and are told to put in all the campaigns . . . [or else] you get a bawling out from the center." But when they included party campaigns, they were not safe from scolding. While occasional issues of some bulletins did a good job reporting on shop-floor problems, most found it difficult to strike a balance.[107]

In the same way that their bulletins fluctuated in tone, party members' participation in union meetings varied between those who resisted going against the tide and others who were outspoken. In one AFL painter's local, party members decided they would not push too fast, and at the reading of a resolution to attend a Communist-supported May Day rally, they did not speak up.

Even though the party's leadership warned against such behavior, it recurred. Five months later, in 1930, when the AFL and the TUUL ran opposing demonstrations, twice as many workers attended the AFL's, even though the TUUL demonstration was free and the AFL charged admission. Party leaders scorned their members who did not raise the differences between the two organizations at union meetings.[108]

In other situations, Communists went overboard in their revolutionary rhetoric and Third Period tactics. Some Chicago leaders worried that Communists had the "illusion of fighting police in battle and forgetting to organize." Occasionally when they connected with non-party members, Communists' control of bulletins, resolutions, and meeting agendas stifled non-party participation. In some industries with AFL locals, Communists refused to work because they saw the AFL as a fascist organization.[109]

As TUUL organizations grew, however, so did the tendency of Communist trade unionists to focus less on the party's political ends and more on the concrete demands of the workers. But even then, there were problems. Party leaders were concerned that by focusing too much on economic issues, Communists would lose their revolutionary appeal and fall away from the movement. In fact, once small groups formed inside the plants, Communist activists in them tended to avoid party leaders and Communist groups outside of the plant. Such neglect left city leaders uninformed about union activities and prevented Communist neighborhood organizations from supporting the TUUL in the plant. By demanding that Communist union leaders not separate trade-union work from party work, leaders hoped to check local autonomy.

These tensions pulled at Communists working in unions. They were to focus on the issues that concerned workers but not get too lost in business unionism. They also were to agitate and raise these demands to a higher level while building fighting organizations. And all the while, they were to maintain relationships with the party's district leaders.[110]

Communists' public actions revealed the strain of these tensions. At first, Communist leaders hoped that agitating would build the movement, and on May Day 1930, they organized a demonstration that would result in a citywide strike and the beginning of a strong TUUL organization. Not a single shop nucleus organized a May Day committee in its plant. Communists neglected to organize a conference to raise the strike question, and rank-and-file Communists even raised doubts about the strike strategy. Instead of a citywide stoppage and TUUL growth, some party members held noontime meetings, and one brought a small group of fellow workers to the demonstration. To party functionaries, this was a "sad picture."[111]

In 1932, after three years of organizing, TUUL leaders had little to show. That year, the Yards' TUUL still lacked leadership and active cadres. When news

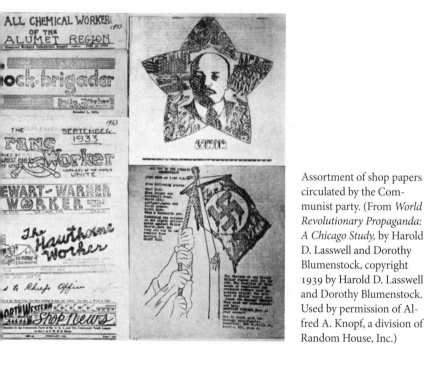

Assortment of shop papers circulated by the Communist party. (From *World Revolutionary Propaganda: A Chicago Study,* by Harold D. Lasswell and Dorothy Blumenstock, copyright 1939 by Harold D. Lasswell and Dorothy Blumenstock. Used by permission of Alfred A. Knopf, a division of Random House, Inc.)

spread of a 10-percent cut in wages, Communists in the neighborhood section got wind and created and distributed leaflets on behalf of the TUUL without informing TUUL members. Max Eastman argued that he acted without the TUUL because he "had no confidence in the TUUL," since Communists failed to build it. When the TUUL group in the stockyards called fraction meetings and invited neighborhood unit members to join, they rarely attended. According to the party's head stockyard organizer, stockyard unit meetings covered "the actual activity which must be carried on in the yards, such as visiting of contacts, discussion of conditions inside the yards." The problem, however, was that "the comrades who work in the yards do not always feel this necessity of discussing these conditions."[112] One meeting after another did not motivate party trade unionists to talk shop, nor did they encourage members to make contacts with non-party recruits.

In addition to those who were willing to organize, however, were those less interested in building a TUUL in the Yards. In one party registration, "many comrades who are working in the stockyards were discovered who were not members of the Stockyards unit but of the street units in the sections." Some Communists directed their energies away from TUUL activity even when their own workplace was being organized. The most common reason these members gave for not participating in the union drive was that they "can't afford to belong to two organizations"; paying party dues was enough. During economic hard times, union dues may have been difficult to pay, but more likely these Communist workers did not view themselves as union organizers. From the 1929 TUUL convention, when the industrial committee reported that the stockyards unit had "about 1½ members," to the end of 1932, the TUUL organization in the Yards had grown to twenty-six, including fifteen Communists. Most non-party members worked in small shops outside the party's concentration. Only two were in Armour, one in its killing department. Growth was slow and not in line with party successes in its unemployed activities.[113]

The situation among railroad workers was similar. Party activists tried to build on railroad workers' reaction to a wage cut announced at the end of January 1932. Workers did not like how lodge officials dealt with the negotiations, and many refused to pay a negotiating assessment passed on to them for the talks. The Brotherhood of Locomotive Firemen and the Brotherhood of Railroad Trainmen lost seven and eight thousand members, respectively, based on this issue. In response, Communists built an opposition movement in a few of the old unions under the auspices of a rank-and-file committee, consisting of party and non-party workers. One non-party member had participated in a railroad-union amalgamation meeting that Communists had planned back in the period of the national railroad shopmen's strike of 1922, but others who joined with him were more conservative. They were unhappy with the wage cut and the tactics of their lodge officials but, as one party official explained, were "deathly afraid of becoming connected up with any 'red' movement." Suspicious of the league's leadership, they refused to turn over leaflet funds and bulletin control to league officials. Party leaders, in turn, agreed that they would support the publishing of a few leaflets but would discourage permanent publication plans until they were able to "secure more control over it."[114]

Such tactics speak to the lack of growth of this rank-and-file group. At one of its meetings, forty-one workers showed up and passed a resolution that party members had prepared beforehand against the wage cut and for a referendum on the issue. This meeting was repeated on four other occasions in the city, each with the same result. Turnout was small, workers were unwilling to discuss, and, according to Wangerin, "little militancy [was] displayed when they were called upon to express themselves." Communist unionists' expectations and behavior likely exacerbated non-party league members' skepticism. Despite railroad workers' disgruntled state, the TUUL organization remained small. A Northwestern shop boasted eight members, and one in Burnside, six.[115]

Steel workers were also suspicious of TUUL organizers. One party organizer, Morton, had spent time organizing in Chicago's steel region and was known as a Communist among steel workers, which, according to reports, gave him a "bad reputation." Party leaders agreed that they would need new blood. The problem was that even though the SMWIU reported two hundred members in South Chicago, not a single Communist organized for the union. When they did union work, league members held mass meetings and issued leaflets. The problem with these strategies was that workers did not like coming to small public meetings. An organizer explained that one Friday night the league organized a meeting, and three workers went home "because there were not enough there." Focus on spectacular gatherings also meant less concentration on work within the mills.[116]

Meanwhile, opposition work in the AFL slogged along. An industrial report on Chicago's activity suggested that work was limited to building trades, milk drivers, needle workers, and laundry workers but that none of it was coordinated or centralized. Approximately 350 Communists worked in AFL unions, of an estimated three hundred thousand in the city. Party leaders agreed that they would have to "give a lot of attention to Chicago because it is one of the most important trade union center[s]." But the effect of purges and attacks on union activists stifled rank-and-file enthusiasm.[117]

For workers in the early years of the Depression, fear of unemployment was more tangible than revolutionary unions, and unemployed workers were more willing to act militantly than those in tenuous jobs. The party's numbers show that members were more interested in working in Unemployed Councils, where their revolutionary activities matched the party's rhetoric. One party organizer admitted that even though he was assigned to organize Western Electric work-ers, "I did not do anything in that factory because I was impressed like every-one else with the importance of unemployed work. I devoted all my time to unemployed work. Factory work is more difficult."[118] Another Western Electric organizer reported that workers from International Harvester and Crane would say to party members, "You fellows go down and fight for relief, you have an organization. You get relief. But if we have a fight in the shop, how much are we going to gain?" He had to admit, "Directly we have got more relief by our fight of the unemployed than with the employed workers."[119] The huge funeral for workers slain in the August 1931 eviction riot drew thousands, yet Com-munists working the next neighborhood, where the stockyards operated, were not able to build their organization from such successes. To Communist leaders, the overlap between the population in the Yards and those at the funeral and demonstrations should have eased this work, but it did not. Through the period, Communists recruited more unemployed than employed. Between January and May 1932, Chicago's Communists brought in 2,009 new members; 71 percent were unemployed.[120]

And yet even though Chicago's TUUL never sparked the revolution party leaders envisioned, nor did it maintain strict party discipline, it accomplished a great deal. In spite of high levels of unemployment, employer-driven open-shop drives, gangster attacks, police assaults, and sectarian party policy, effec-tive trade-union organizers emerged. Working against the conservative and exclusive traditions of AFL and independent unionists in the city, these Com-munist trade unionists got their first taste of what would be involved in building industrial unions and made important inroads—settling grievances, making contacts, creating a common voice of dissent—in several factories. Some, like Nate Schaffner, stood up against gunmen and built a broad movement of re-formers in the milk-drivers' union. Others, like Ed Doty, took the first steps toward integrating the city's building-trades unions. Such women as Katherine Erlich sparked the first serious internal party conversations about the best way to bring women workers into union organizations. There were also bright spots in the life of Chicago's TUUL. Its leaders successfully represented women gar-ment workers in a 1933 strike against Sopkins and Sons' apron and dress plants in the city.[121]

And still, by the end of 1933, party leaders faced a predicament. Conditions for working people were bad and getting worse, yet Communists' union move-ment was not able to convince workers of alternative solutions to their problems. Organizing against the grain, Communists tested a number of strategies. Their belief that their organizations had the right answers for Chicago's workers en-abled them to persist in this uphill battle from 1929 through 1933. Such work positioned them to take advantage of changes about to occur.

In 1933, Roosevelt's New Deal program changed the field of labor organizing, but not in favor of the TUUL. Party trade-union organizers began shifting tactics, abandoning the TUUL to work solely within independent unions and the AFL. In the short term, it seemed as though they abandoned their revolutionary hopes, and while they did indeed forsake any aspiration of a revolution sparked by Communist unions, in the long term it became clear that such actions laid the groundwork for future industrial union drives, with their own potential to bring about change. In any case, radical trade unionists had few options in the TUUL if they wanted to have an effect on the city's labor movement. To some, the appearance of the TUUL was an example of Communist folly. But for Communist activists interested in mobilizing America's workers, the TUUL offered real possibilities. Communists' inability to grow their alternative labor federation speaks to the state of industrial relations in the late Hoover and early Roosevelt years and to workers' social and economic state, as well as to mistaken assumptions within Chicago's local Communist organization. When the New Deal changed the political landscape and workers looked optimistically to AFL unions, Communists joined them, taking lessons learned from the TUUL with them and showing their ability to learn from their failures.

6

"Generals Are of No Use without an Army": How and Why Communists Abandoned the TUUL

Though the law had no teeth, Section 7A of the National Industrial Recovery Act (NIRA) of 1933 created the appearance of government support for union organization and thoughts among workers of minimum wages, maximum hours, and contractual protections against speedups and work hazards. All of this encouraged union-minded workers to organize. But union enthusiasts found they would have to do so against the wishes of their employers, who fought Section 7A's provisions in subtle and open ways. The resulting clash resulted in a spate of strike activity. "Man-days lost due to strikes, which had not exceeded 603,000 in any month in the first half of 1933," writes the historian Irving Bernstein, "spurted to 1,375,000 in July and to 2,378,000 in August." From heavy industry to garment workers and even the movie industry, workers demanded the right to collective bargaining. Come 1934, Bernstein notes, "anybody struck. It was not just auto parts workers in Toledo, truck drivers in Minneapolis, longshoremen in San Francisco, or mill hands in the South. It was the fashion."[1]

Chicago's Communist leaders observed workers' changed temperament as the spirit came to the city. Strikes and organizational activity were particularly strong among leather, neckwear, cleaning, upholstery, restaurant, and rubber workers, as well as metal polishers and pattern makers. The *Chicago Tribune* reported that pickets ringed 250 of Chicago's businesses in November 1933. Marshall Field, a strongly anti-union employer, relented to its skilled maintenance workers after they protested for forty weeks. A successful 1933 stockyard-handler strike revived labor organizing among stockyard workers. Such activities signaled a shift in workers' expectations: by protecting their right to form unions, a strong federal government should work for them rather than for their employers.[2]

Lizabeth Cohen's depiction of workers' search for "moral capitalism" best describes the motivation in the early Depression years that drove Chicago's workers toward the CIO, yet the city's Communist leaders viewed workers' stirrings in more revolutionary terms.[3] Communists' participation in a shoe workers' strike resulted in the building of a union and the organization of three new shop nuclei. Chicago's Communists also led 1,500 African American women out of Ben Sopkins and Sons' six apron and dress plants. In the Englewood neighborhood, a non-party worker agreed so strongly with TUUL principles that he built a TUUL group, resulting in new carpenters' and painters' locals. Communist steel activists believed that the industrial recovery bill increased their organizing potential, since, they noticed, steel workers were "more free to talk than . . . previously." Party activists in meatpacking also noted changes: stockyards workers organized departmental actions, and non-party workers wrote letters to the party shop paper linking their problems to the National Recovery Administration (NRA) and political change.[4]

Communists working in International Harvester's McCormick and Tractor works, once considered by party leaders as "no good, an element that is dead," began using shop papers effectively. In one case, they exposed a foreman's abuses and placed the paper on his desk. Encouraging this tactic elsewhere, the writers explained, "The foremen go up in steam when they read these exposures, and although they are raging with anger, they are afraid to attack anybody." Other tactics included focusing on such annoying work rules as having to attend management meetings on their own time or having to pay fines for lost safety cards. At McCormick, the organizing efforts were successful in both cases. Reporting on these small victories and others like them caused at least a handful of the forty SMWIU members from these plants to join by filling out application forms they found inside the party's shop paper.[5] While forty represents a modest success, party organizers reported that they overheard workers bragging about many more: "Some would say well about one thousand. Others say every second worker is a Communist." In the context of small victories won in various departments, this hearsay seemed to bode well for future party activity.[6] Within metal shops more broadly, Communists were winning workers' support. One leader reported six metal shops on strike; and in most struggles, Communists won leadership positions.[7]

Revolutionary union activity encouraged party leaders, but they did not abandon AFL work. In fact, attention there intensified once Congress passed the NIRA and workers joined AFL unions at unprecedented rates. At an AFL Communist fraction meeting, Jack Stachel reminded party members that while members should work in the TUUL, "at the same time more attention than ever, many times more, [needed to be given] to work among the workers in the AFL."[8] A quick check of Communist unionists indicated that the party claimed over one hundred AFL delegates to the federation's 1933 convention, 70 percent from the building trades (90 percent of whom were painters). The growth of these numbers over previous tallies among AFL workers presented future organizing possibilities.

In response to city leaders' AFL push, a Communist machinist named Jurich reported his own changed attitude. After early failed struggles in the International Association of Machinists, he and others "simply forgot that there is a machinists union and we simply let them do whatever they pleased." But since party leaders paid new attention to the AFL, Jurich reconsidered his activity and started attending union meetings and speaking out. "The first question I raised in the AFL," he recalled, "was the question of relief. My idea was that we should elect a committee in the local and demand relief for the [unemployed] workers there."[9] In response, AFL unionists started a fund to help these workers out. Such efforts made Chicago party leaders believe it was possible to revive their oppositional work in established AFL unions.

Communists' opposition also surfaced within established railroad unions. The Communist activist Reva Weinstein boasted of a newly formed concentration unit on the rails. In addition to unit members making door-to-door visits and holding open forums, section leaders established study classes. In a short time, organizers recruited two railroad workers into the party and sold one hundred copies of the *Daily Worker* at railroad gates.[10]

Workers' increased willingness to support Communists extended from Chicago's factories out into the communities that surrounded them. In the steel region, Communist speakers received "the greatest support and applause" in a debate between the Communist party and representatives from the Republican and Liberty parties. Chicago's Communists were also involved with non-party groups in a "united front" conference on unemployment in South Chicago in which 119 organizations participated, even though Communists controlled only seventeen. Still more thrilling to Communists was that the Communist nominee for chair, though disputed because of his Communist connection, in the end "carried it" and was allowed to lead.[11]

From their belief in impending revolution in 1933, leaders found workers' increased acceptance of Communist party activists a heady shift, and yet the limits of even this surge of support quickly became apparent. After three 1933 strikes, a core of Chicago's Communist trade unionists organizing the city's most important industries became convinced of dual unions' limits. Even after Communists led or supported strikes, won grievances, rallied workers, and activated members, they still remained organizationally and philosophically isolated from the majority of Chicago's workers.

Comintern leaders revealed their Popular Front strategy of working with leftist groups to defeat fascism in August 1935, but in Chicago, as in their unemployed organizations, Communist trade unionists in rail, meatpacking, and steel did not wait this long. They followed patterns similar to many other Communist trade unionists across America's urban landscape. Chicago's Communist trade unionists anticipated the dissolution of the TUUL and the movement toward a Popular Front strategy in trade-union work as early as 1932 in railroad unions and throughout 1934 in meatpacking and steel.[12]

Sources from Moscow's Comintern archive make it clear that national party leaders closely watched regional developments. Robert Cherny shows that party work in the San Francisco maritime strike served as a primary example of why Communist trade-union policy should change. Party sources also suggest that Chicago Communists' work in meatpacking moved national party leaders away from their dual-union strategy and closer to one they would perfect during the Popular Front. In any event, the dissolution of the TUUL occurred in reaction to the daily experiences of rank-and-file Communists in their organizing in factories across the country. These were realities with which Chicago's Communists were all too familiar.

Proof of Isolation

The 1933 strikes of Chicago needle workers, stock handlers, and steel workers offered Communists examples that their dual-union strategy did not widely attract pro-union workers. Whether building their own union, as in the Sopkins and steel strikes, or supporting another, as in the livestock handlers' strike, Communists could not translate their successes into effective union building, let alone party recruitment. Communists in one industry after another became convinced that to succeed, they would have to rethink their dual unions.

Claude Lightfoot led the party section that included Ben Sopkins and Sons' apron and dress plants, where women, mostly black, worked. An organizer of the unemployed, Lightfoot found that after one year of working on Chicago's South Side, Communists' Unemployed Council contacts began to pay off. Supplied with a list of potential supporters, the Needle Trades Workers' Industrial Union began a union drive there and in June 1933 took the six Sopkins plants out on strike, including its largest, which housed the company's offices. With the support of women in the plants, the NTWIU fought for increased wages, better hours, and a union contract. On the strike's third day, police attacked the striking women, pushing the *Chicago Defender* onto the strikers' side and convincing civic leaders to get involved. Strikers' support meetings brought together community leaders, politicians, and Communists to discuss the situation. At one conference, black strikers convinced Chicago Urban League leaders to allow James Ford, the Communist party's 1932 vice presidential candidate, to speak for them. Support for Ford continued into strike negotiations, when he joined the league and representatives of the *Defender* in a parley with the company on the strikers' behalf. When the company pushed Ford out of the negotiations, the strikers insisted he participate.[13]

The strike was a victory in that the women workers received wage increases, shorter hours, and the rehiring of strikers, among other concessions; yet Communists were unable to build on these successes. Party leaders insisted that members involved in the strike build the party at the same time they built the union, but Communist union activists hid their political identity in the plants as they built the union. The *Chicago Defender,* whose editors criticized Chicago police for attempting to draw attention from strikers' demands by painting them all as Communists, supported Communists' downplaying of their role: "The police are attempting to smoke-screen the issue by calling these women Communists. Suppose they are! Take some of these same policemen off of the pay roll for six months and they will be Communists too. This nation is dedicated to the principle of free speech, and it is not up to the police to change the Constitution."[14]

Communists' popularity did not translate into increased party or union membership. Strikers accepted and defended party leaders, but by the strike's end, Communists had recruited only eighteen workers. Once the strike ended, it became harder to convince workers that the party offered them much. The nine hundred women who joined the union during the strike quickly fell away. Three months afterward, party organizers called their work at Sopkins "fruitless" and tried to revive it by turning to a few female party members who had assisted during the strike, but they were unable to rebuild the NTWIU.[15]

Unlike the Sopkins strike, where Communists were in the limelight, in the stockyards Communists were isolated from skilled Irish workers' strike actions and from the bulk of white ethnic and black workers in the plants. Their isolation was due in part to the nature of the union organizations in the Yards. In 1933, three different groups—the independent Stockyards Labor Council (SLC), the AFL-affiliated Amalgamated Meat Cutters and Butcher Workmen of North America (AMC), and the TUUL-member Packinghouse Workers Industrial Union (PHWIU)—vied for labor's loyalty; and each succeeded in representing different types of workers.

As a result of the NIRA, non-Communist veterans of the 1917 to 1921 stockyard organizing drive rejuvenated the SLC, even installing their former president, Martin Murphy, at the union's helm. In its earlier days, the SLC was a militant organization that was unable to break from its craft-based structures. Thus, in 1933, veterans in the organization had little following among black workers. Also, activists in the SLC worked mostly in the half-dozen small packing plants where the World War I–era union militants were able to find work after being blacklisted from the larger plants. The SLC's strength lay in plants that employed white, ethnic workers. In early 1934, the union claimed five thousand members.[16]

Unlike the SLC's tradition of militancy, the AMC was a craft-based organization strong among the Yards' predominately Irish livestock handlers. Even though such AMC leaders as Dennis Lane had undermined members' interests in the past, workers looked to the AMC for leadership because it was the only union with an international organization and access to the CFL's resources. Yet after a decade of inaction, the AMC was poorly positioned to take advantage of workers' militancy generated by the New Deal.[17]

Rather than speaking for veteran union builders or craft-based meatpacking workers, the PHWIU represented more recent arrivals to the Chicago stockyards. After the NRA decreased the number of hours people could work and companies began to rehire, young Communists were able to get their first jobs in Chicago's plants. One of these was Herb March. Born in Brooklyn in 1913, March grew up in a Socialist environment and joined the YCL at sixteen. After his involvement in the 1929 silk strike near Paterson, New Jersey, he agreed to organize the YCL in the Southwest and then worked against lynching and unemployment in Missouri, Nebraska, and Oklahoma. Moving to Kansas City, he organized workers in meatpacking plants and assisted Unemployed Council drives. But after meeting Jane Grbac at a party gathering, he agreed in the spring of 1933 to move to her home in Chicago and begin working in the Yards.[18]

March's timing was impeccable, and his commitment and energy helped spark a movement. With March on board, a small group of YCL members, several of whom were younger women, began an intensive drive to create revolutionary industrial unions. Their experiences rallying behind the Scottsboro defendants and Angelo Herndon as well as their commitment to interracial union organizing allowed them to reach black workers, and in a short time they had some strength among African Americans in Armour's sheep and hog kills. Thus, while they did not have the numbers of the SLC, they did have a foothold in the larger Armour plant. In addition, Communists had community contacts, resources, and support beyond the plants.[19]

From the beginning of their effort, although Communists cooperated with the SLC in the smaller plants, their major interest was the larger Armour factory. But there, the AMC kept them isolated to few departments where they were ineffective. Throughout 1933, as companies found loopholes in NRA agreements and work conditions deteriorated, Communists watched plant executives step up their attacks on activists. Similar trends occurred at smaller plants. At the end of 1933, employers at the small packers Hammond and Agar fired union leaders and activists and at Robert and Oakes closed the plant and laid off their workforce.[20]

Party leaders were unwilling to accept these defeats. Calling the stockyards section the most important area of the city, Bill Gebert argued that stockyards workers not only shared a tradition of militancy and a composition that reflected the city's proletariat, but that the dominance of the industry in the city meant that Communist success there would lead to broader positive political and economic change.[21] Work in the Yards had to be revived.

In their despair, Communists found hope in a spontaneous and unsanctioned livestock handlers' strike. Unhappy over wage cuts, the exclusionary and typically conservative livestock handlers walked off the job in November 1933. The mostly Irish composition of the handlers' union meant that Communists had few contacts among the group, so Communists were able to show support only by having the PHWIU agree to walk off the job.[22] But the strategic position of the handlers, who supplied the rest of the plants with livestock, helped make their strike a success in only two days without Communists' assistance. The handlers won a 10-percent wage increase, and Communists regretted not having better relations with AFL unionists.[23]

The second time the AMC livestock handlers struck, this time over a reclassification system in the summer of 1934, Communists began to consider the consequences of their isolation. During this second strike, Communist unionists took a more active role working with the AFL. They sent a "rank-and-file committee of the AFL" to extend greetings and to offer support to win the strike, and they worked to get strike-endorsing resolutions passed in AFL unions across the city. They also sought support from the CFL. Party leaders directed Unemployed Councils to send delegations to the livestock handlers and to offer unemployed picketers to join their picket lines. Within the plants, the PHWIU raised the question of mass picketing and spreading the strike and organized department actions. A unit organizer reported that in one department two hundred workers struck for higher wages. In another, workers refused to extend their day by half an hour.[24]

Once again, party activity had a limited impact. Communists desperately wanted to spread the strike sentiment, but according to a unit organizer, they "didn't have an organized opposition in the livestock or butchers' unions."[25] In this situation, no leaflets, mass meetings, and department actions could change the strike's character.

This event represented the culmination of a series of experiences in the Yards that exposed Communists' isolation from workers. Across the Yards, Communists led successful actions against speedups, safety hazards, and the lack of rest periods, but not many workers joined their union. Rank-and-file party members began to argue that to gain members they would have to play a larger role in the reformist unions. A unit organizer wrote of learning that "it isn't enough to have a PHWIU which is weak, we need to have organized opposition movements with a concrete program of action and demands inside of existing locals of the AFL." The unit member articulated what many already realized: "[T]he largest single number of workers in the yards are members of the AFL: butchers, livestock handlers, electricians, metal men and truck drivers."[26]

Communists in steel similarly concluded that the SMWIU did not adequately allow them to reach the masses. In 1933, SMWIU party members at the Standard Steel Forging plant in Indiana Harbor led workers out on strike. The event lasted six weeks, and steel workers in the region showed them support, but party members were unable to consolidate the union. In fact, over the strike's six weeks, Communists were unable even to fully mobilize their own forces behind the effort. Language organizations failed to respond, and party members found themselves "isolated from movements in the shops." Without Communists' input, workers in Standard Forging advocated accepting partial demands. Party leaders agreed that their members needed to be politically reoriented.[27]

In addition to their problems at Standard Forging, Communists faced competition in the broader steel industry. The most serious contender was the Amalgamated Association of Iron, Steel, and Tin Workers (AA), formed in 1876 and best known among steel workers for its unsuccessful union drive in 1919. This failure convinced its leader, Mike Tighe, of the futility of mass recruiting workers, and as a result, the AA represented only a small number of the most skilled craft workers in the industry, leaving the majority of steel workers without union representation. While certainly a ghost of its postwar self, the AA of the early 1930s had the advantage of legitimacy in the eyes of the organized labor movement and among some steel workers who hoped an AA-led organizing drive could be revived.[28]

In addition to the AA, the passage of Section 7A of the NIRA led some antiunion employers in the industry to promote their own solution to the union "problem." Management in Republic, U.S. Steel, and smaller mills promoted and cooperated with company unions or Employee Representation Programs (ERPs), which, they claimed, would result in shared power between the company and its employees. Rarely did such democracy prevail.[29]

The weakness of the AA and ERPs gave inspiration to party organizers, who looked to the mills in hopes of building their union. Joe Weber was one party hopeful. A veteran of Unemployed Council struggles, in 1933 Weber was in charge of work in steel. In the summer of that year, he called a meeting at Calumet Park, and a large number of steel workers gathered. Joe Germano, a future leader of the CIO in steel and a vehement anti-Communist, remembered, "Weber was quite an orator. You had to really know the guy. If you didn't know him or felt you knew him, he could convince you; he was a very persuasive guy. He spoke to these people—he spoke to all of us—maybe half an hour or forty minutes. Everybody listened, and there was quite a bit of applause."[30] Weber's message was similar to one that appeared in a leaflet circulated among steel workers, encouraging them to join the SMWIU, a union dedicated to "organizing all workers, Negro and white, young and old, foreign born and native, skilled and unskilled on an equal basis." In suggesting that workers "remember how we fought in 1919, only to be sold out by the American Federation of Labor leaders," authors of the leaflet hoped to connect the SMWIU to the campaign of William Z. Foster and other labor radicals a generation earlier. This time, Communists hoped that built-up resentment toward the AA would pay off under the SMWIU, a union "organized and controlled by the workers from the mills."[31]

Reiterating these sentiments, Weber took the opportunity to attack Germano, standing in the crowd, for his role as an ERP representative. These were fighting words, equivalent to calling a person a company man, but Germano ably defended himself. He argued that he and other ERP followers in steel were not dupes of their employers but members of the AA in addition to the ERP who were waiting for the AA to take initiative, charter their plants, and revive a union drive. Germano insisted that the AA was his union and the union of their fathers, the only union recognized by the government since it was an AFL affiliate. Weber may have tapped into steel workers' desire for a strong union drive in steel, but Germano's words reflected most steel workers' instincts. Communists wanted their SMWIU to become an organization of the workers, but in 1933, Chicago's most union-friendly steel workers were wary of Communists and their proposals.[32]

After the ratification of the NIRA, AA leaders made little effort to organize steel workers, but it did not matter. In the first three months after the bill's ratification, sixty-eight new lodges formed. Communists watched these developments and worried. In December 1933, Chicago party leaders reported that the SMWIU was inoperative in steel and that the AFL was stronger than the TUUL.[33]

The party did see a few bright spots, however. In September 1933, organizers in Standard Forging succeeded in organizing shift meetings and bringing out almost a hundred workers to an open-air meeting. When AFL organizers tried to red-bait SMWIU organizers, workers booed them. When company men ordered workers to perform tasks they previously did not have to do, the workers participated in a four-hour stoppage. Such action forced the company to back down, inspiring a few who reportedly came "right up to the secretary of the [SMWIU] union in the shop and asked for application cards." Steel organizers also reported that in a short time, twenty-four steel workers joined the SMIU, and twenty others filed applications from various mills. The African American Communist and trade unionist Jack Reese successfully organized a work stoppage in the pickling and rolled steel departments of Youngstown Sheet and Tube, and other party activists stabilized a small SMWIU local in the American sheet and tin company.[34] Yet Communists still could not compete with the twelve new

AA lodges of four thousand members in the Chicago-Gary area. One report noted that the largest group of steel workers in South Chicago, representing 38 percent, were American-born, but only twenty American-born steel workers were party members. Even party schools set up in Gary and South Chicago around steel workers' shifts and according to topics they might find interesting could not turn around the low SMWIU numbers.[35]

By 1934, Communists recognized that good work came in small packages. In two instances, non-party workers at International Harvester used physical force to protect Communist speakers from police arrest, and workers supported party shop papers, contributing over thirty dollars for one issue at Western Electric and twenty-five for one at Harvester. Non-party workers also supported the Communist railroad paper, helping with writing and fundraising. While convincing party leaders of the potential worker support they could win, these examples did not result in union growth.[36]

Small successes sometimes faded quickly, which is what happened to Communist efforts within the AFL painter's union. Thousands of painters and paperhangers were suspended or expelled because they were unable to pay AFL dues. With the Depression decreasing the amount of work available to any painter in the city, the AFL's official policy of policing worksites and chasing away suspended and expelled unionists made a bad situation worse. TUUL activists began organizing around the right to work as members of the TUUL and readmission to the AFL without having to pay back-dues or initiation fees. In 1932, painters and paperhangers formed a TUUL local on the West Side, made union cards, and voted on demands. But this enthusiastic group, after an initial period of excitement and activity, ended up doing more talking than acting. One "veteran painter" remembered the group as "more like a club than a union."[37]

Shifting Gears

In 1934, the party listed only 2,010 TUUL members in Chicago. This was especially embarrassing when compared to the AFL's membership of between fifty-three and sixty-one thousand. In the stockyards alone, one independent union numbered over 2,500.[38] Rank-and-file Communist support for the TUUL drive did not look better. The twenty-two trade-union nuclei of 124 party members that the party claimed in 1933 jumped to thirty-seven nuclei and 253 members in 1934, but this still represented only a small fraction of the 3,303 members in the city.[39] In January 1935, Chicago's leaders reported on the status of the city's trade-union participation before enacting the shift away from the TUUL. The report indicated that 41.1 percent of members were active in unions, a significant leap from the 1930 numbers, but even at this late date only 17.7 percent were in TUUL unions, while 20.1 percent were in AFL unions and 3.3 percent in independent unions.[40]

Despite Communists' work and agitation, the AFL received a much bigger influx than the TUUL following the 1933 labor legislation. Chicago's Communists found that their isolation in steel, meatpacking, and needle work reflected a national trend. By 1934, the AFL had added five hundred thousand to its national rolls, giving it a membership of over 2.5 million workers, whereas the TUUL added only one hundred thousand, bringing its membership to 125,000.[41]

These disappointing numbers, combined with Communists' frustrating experiences, convinced party trade unionists that if they wanted to have input into mass union drives, they would have to change their strategies. Early in 1934, Communist unionists in two TUUL industries of concentration, packing and steel, began new tactics. Those in the railroad industry had been moving away from the TUUL beginning in 1932 and continued to reevaluate their strategies through the party's Popular Front shift in policy. The staggered timing of these changes demonstrates the need to consider local conditions when discussing Communist trade unionism and suggests that issues emanating from rank-and-file work were as important as party policy in determining Communist trade-union activity. National party leaders officially disbanded the TUUL in March 1935 and did not announce their shift to a Popular Front strategy until August. In the months preceding these events, Chicago's Communists learned from their experiences that to be effective trade unionists, they would have to work closely with established, recognized unions and the reformers who led them. Their mistakes, plentiful and varied as they were, provided important lessons for the period that was to follow, which would include the time of the building of the CIO.

The earliest shifts in organizing strategy occurred in the railroad industry. Initially, Communists interested in organizing railroad workers promoted a separate revolutionary union, the Railroad Industrial League. By 1932, enthusiasm for this organization had begun to wane. Party members in California explained that since most of their active organizers belonged to established craft unions, it did not make sense for them to emphasize a separate organization.[42]

That year in Chicago, a similar sentiment became apparent when railroad organizers began to build the unity movement, which was the party's attempt to bring together rank-and-file workers from twenty-one different crafts into one opposition movement. The purpose was not to destroy existing unions or to build a dual union but to welcome delegates from established unions into unity groups where unionists from all parts of the industry could join together around specific issues facing railroad workers. Leaders hoped this would also provide an opportunity to unite white and black railroad workers, a move not yet attempted in the industry. The fact that it was a separate organization that individuals and groups from established unions had to join, however, raised loyal union members' suspicion; they thought that this was going to be a divisive organization. The movement's paper, *Unity News,* worked hard to dispel such notions.[43]

One of Chicago's Communist trade unionists explained how he connected his shop to the unity movement. First, he organized workers into the AFL. Next, he formed a grievance committee and began circulating a shop paper. By the summer of 1934, he began working with the city's unity committee, bringing issues raised there back to the group.[44]

The biggest issue the unity committee faced was the consequence of railroad consolidation. Overwhelmed by huge economic losses, railroad executives appealed to the federal government for assistance. The Roosevelt administration's answer was to consolidate railroad facilities by merging lines and decreasing routes. Once services were slimmed, railroad workers would have to reorganize seniority lists and watch as thousands of co-workers received pink slips. At first, chiefs of the railroad brotherhoods seemed content to push for a dismissal wage to compensate their laid-off members. To Communists, this was not enough. They wanted to organize workers so effectively that they would be willing to strike to keep their jobs.[45]

To that end, J. E. McDonald, the national chairman of the unity movement, working in Chicago, wrote and distributed flyers explaining how essential it was for railroad workers to fight this challenge together. Chicago's workers, he believed, needed to be particularly concerned since Roosevelt's advisors had specific plans to merge facilities in the city. As soon as enough lodges supported the movement's call for a national conference on the issue, the pamphlet announced, a committee would work out the final plans.[46] In June 1935, Chicago's railroad activists reported on a number of smaller conferences of individuals representing "most [of the city's railroad] unions" (with the exception of engineers and switchmen, in whose unions battle raged over participation). Individuals participating in these conferences brought back to their lodges the question of united action against consolidation and the demand that railroad executives return employment conditions to 1931 terms, before wage cuts and speedups degraded their work. On most occasions, the lodges approved the program for united action and appointed committees to continue the work.[47]

The unity movement continued in the railroad industry even after the party shifted to Popular Front organizing strategies. In the early months of the Popular Front, leaders of the unity strategy reached out to the Railroad Employees National Pension Association, which formed as an independent opposition among railroad workers against established union leaders. The Railroad Employees National Pension Association was interested in winning a federal pension system, as opposed to the privately operated one that forced workers to be loyal to particular companies for long periods of time, gave workers no recourse to funds if they were fired prematurely, and undermined strike activity. When the Supreme Court struck down a national pension system in May 1935, Communists worked closely with left-leaning members on the Pension Association's national board and encouraged them to abandon the legalistic route they had been taking. Party members agreed that they needed to "call for a united front to force thru a national retirement system by economic or strike threat and at the same time [to] turn attention to the possibility of securing a national retirement system without legislation by direct agreement with the carriers."[48] The more conservative members of the Pension Association's board, however, were content with working through the courts and drafted what William Z. Foster referred to as "a much inferior bill" to the one the court originally turned down. Through their unity movement, party members hoped to work with the left-wing members of the Pension Association and prevail over more conservative forces.[49]

Chicago's Communists had reason to think that railroad workers would support their unity movement. Railroad workers, who tended to be cynical about the outcome of joining across craft lines, seemed to be doing just that in Chicago in 1933. Not only had Chicago railroad workers formed the National Pension Association, but they had organized a federation of thirteen crafts to fight against company unions. Party organizers also had word that stockyard switchmen were seen "running up and down waving the [Communist] pamphlet" on the issue of unity.[50] If workers were willing to join across craft, Communists speculated, they likely would do so through the unity movement.

They were wrong. It was true that trainmen's and carmen's unions passed Communist-supported resolutions. They also went on record against fascism, and the trainmen passed a resolution against war.[51] But participation of these groups' members in the unity movement remained limited: in November 1935, only 124 people were willing to work and finance the movement. Of the thirty-five party members in the group, a handful went back to the days of the National Railroad Industrial League, suggesting that not many more were picked up along the way. No important terminal had a mass circulation of *Unity News,* and only 794 people subscribed.[52]

The entrenched personal and political differences that brought tension to the Chicago office of the Communist party made working in the unity movement even more difficult. Grace King and J. E. McDonald simply did not like, agree with, or find it easy to work with Art Handle, Harry Shaw, and Otto Wangerin, party loyalty notwithstanding. When fraction meetings overturned McDonald's proposals, he simply continued to push them among workers. Shaw complained, "Other comrades, including myself, have at times failed to carry through fraction decisions but never when it related to basic political questions, and never in an effort to superimpose our opinions and ideas on a decision of a majority of the leading comrades." Interestingly, party leaders had no interest in suspending or expelling McDonald; they simply wanted him to stop working against them. Shaw recommended that McDonald leave work in Chicago to him, Handle, and Wangerin and that he move to St. Louis, where his talents might be appreciated.[53]

At the same time, leaders of established railroad unions were able to win back a wage cut and succeeded in passing the 1935 Railroad Retirement Pension Act. They also began to oppose consolidation and the dismissal wage they initially supported. Such actions increased their unions' memberships while decimating opposition movements, like the unity movement.[54]

In response to these challenges and the changed political context of the Popular Front, Communists decided that instead of continuing their organization, which required individuals and groups from craft unions to affiliate with the unity movement, they would liquidate the unity movement and work officially through railroad unions. "Because the broadest United Front can be built outside the unity movement," Shaw wrote, "and because United Front activity is the main source of establishing the broadest possible connections for our Party, this [unity] movement becomes more or less superfluous and should be abolished." Coming months after the launching of the Popular Front, this decision finally put railroad organizers in line with the new party attitude that promoted harmony and discretion among the ranks.[55]

Even before this Popular Front shift and change in railroad organizing tactics, some Communists already had abandoned Third Period sectarian styles. One railroad worker explained in early 1934 about his fellow unionists who simply would not second his union motions. Finally, after Communist self-examination, he decided he had the wrong approach. It was "no use waving a red flag in front of a bull," he acknowledged. When he and comrades took to "broadcasting our Party material in streaming headlines on the first page of . . . [a shop bulletin] hundreds of these bulletins were lying on the ground." When they highlighted shop news, however, only a few were tossed. His message was clear: "Generals are of no use without an army and we will work with the army, bringing the message of the class struggle before them." To keep party forces strong, he counseled, Communists would need to stay on the job without exposing their identity, since "bosses are organized" and ready to undermine any plans party members make.[56] Party leaders outside of the railroad industry agreed that to engage in mass work they would have to break through the "shell of sectarianism." So in the months before Communist leaders dissolved the TUUL and well before they announced the party's official shift to the Popular Front, organizers in railroad unions had already begun to pave the way.

Communists' activity in meatpacking also resulted in their leaving behind revolutionary dual unions, but again the timing and reasoning emanated from their daily work on the local level. The strength of SLC locals in small shops caused Communists to form unity groups at the end of 1933. Since joint work proved more successful than acting alone, in April 1934, party organizers began planning a joint conference of the three unions to strengthen organizing in the stockyards and to make better contacts in the different unions.[57] The following month, Communists increased their work in the reformist unions and divided thirty Communists who worked in the Yards among the SLC, the AMC, and the PHWIU. A Communist leader in meatpacking reported that "some comrades already did join the unions." Two had been members of the SLC, and two others joined the AMC. Once in the AMC, the small Communist group was still isolated from most stockyard workers, but Communists made headway in the SLC with Polish workers. Their penetration seemed so successful that Chicago's party leaders predicted, "In a period of a few weeks the SLC will be one of our organizations."[58] By November, two YCL members were elected to the SLC's executive board.[59]

Given the failures within their independent revolutionary union, Communist trade unionists began to develop new strategies to work within the reformist organizations while maintaining their own organization. This was a far cry from where they stood in early 1933. Before the NIRA, Chicago's Communist leaders ordered comrades in meatpacking to use Washington Park's open forums and party leaflets to "expose" AFL and SLC leaders who hoped to "line up the packinghouse workers in their ranks." These Communist trade unionists were to win members out of the reformist organizations and over to the Communists' union. But sentiment the NIRA raised in workers and the activities of AFL unionists in the Yards caused Communists to rethink their position.[60]

Also, Communists' ability to organize workers, especially women, only exacerbated their isolation and did not bring them the power and influence they desired. YCL officials reported that Communist "girls" built a local of the PHWIU in a department and won demands. The problem they found was that the "girls" who "basically composed" party units were "not always the decisive people in the plants." Even if they did successfully organize a work stoppage, they could not shut down the entire plant.[61] Since women did not directly influence other more powerful segments of Yards workers, the fact that Communists were able to organize them did not seem of particular importance to their leaders.

In the case of meatpacking, national party leaders discussed and supported local trade-union actions after they occurred. At a national Communist leadership meeting in August 1934, Jack Stachel explained why he supported trade unionists' move toward oppositional work within meatpacking unions. In meatpacking, he reported, "we have not a single member in the AFL." Therefore, he continued, "we had to make a decision that in the skilled departments we shall not even try to build our union, but to send them into the AFL."[62] Stachel hoped that by changing the strategies in meatpacking, the "united front would really mean something."[63] A few months later, the PHWIU completed its merger with the SLC, retaining the SLC's name and keeping a fraternal affiliation to the national PHWIU. No longer would Communists maintain a separate union for stockyard workers. Rather than remain divided and isolated, they made the first move to unite the Yards' organizations, hoping to win workers away from reformist leaders in the SLC and the AMC and to begin a real drive to organize the industry. If AMC and SLC members would not join the PHWIU, they left Communists little choice but to sign up as members of the respective unions.

For Communists in Chicago's stockyards, the decision seemed inevitable. After all, party forces were too weak to push forward alone; even the leaders could not romanticize their two small shop nuclei, which by 1934 had grown to only thirty members.[64] Communists in the industry recognized that while divisions in the three union groups caused weaknesses overall, the weakest link in the chain was the PHWIU. Party leaders speculated that the SLC had about fourteen hundred members, with a solid organization in the smaller shops and a showing in Armour's, especially among the plant's hog butchers. And while the SLC had more influence than the PHWIU, both paled in comparison to the AMC, which according to Gebert was developing such a militant campaign that groups of SLC workers were already abandoning their organization for it. The AMC had the stock handlers, butchers, electricians, and truck drivers, an increasing number of SLC members, two party members, and one member of the YCL. By joining the reformist organizations, Communists began to move away from separate structures and toward a strategy that would allow them greater influence over workers' union activities.[65]

Communists were not the only ones to support these developments. Beginning in 1934, workers supported radicals in the SLC's leadership positions. Herb March joined Martin Murphy, Frank McCarty, and Arthur Kampfert on the executive committee of the SLC. March and other Communist fraction members raised African Americans' concerns and considered the problems of the unemployed, moving the council toward a more inclusive model. While business unionists like Murphy were concerned about the direction that March and the others were taking the council, such other leaders as Kampfert and McCarty supported Communists, suggesting that their leftist strategies made sense to a growing audience. In fact, McCarty eventually joined the party. Thus Murphy was clearly overstating his case when he told a settlement-house worker that Communists had no influence in the council and that he "makes them come right up and kiss the flag every once in a while, just to make sure of them." Communists, in part, were shaping the council's direction.[66]

In the SLC Communists quickly realized, though, that in order to be "comprehensive," they needed the support of the AMC. Official ties to the AMC would also allow them to built on its increasing militancy. Thus, sometime after June 1934, Communists convinced other SLC leaders to approach the AMC to push for a united organizing drive in the Yards. YCL leaders reported in November that this unity movement "found a very good response on the part of the workers. In the AFL some people expressed agreement with the proposed unity." AFL leaders were not interested in unity or broadening their membership, however.[67] With their belief in the need to unify their movements, the AFL left Chicago party leaders no choice but to dissolve the SLC and direct its members into the AMC unions. One way or another, Communists would see to it that a drive was started in the Yards.[68]

The case of meatpacking suggests that local conditions played an essential role in determining how Communist unionists organized. Before party leaders dissolved the TUUL, rank-and-file organizers began leaving their dual union for more established, reform organizations in the stockyards. Such national leaders as Jack Stachel noted the local situation and agreed with the tactic. After the TUUL dissolved but before the Popular Front began, Chicago's Communists in meatpacking changed their strategies once again and joined forces with the AFL union they had once viewed as anathema to their cause. Party policy mattered, but so did local realities.

As did meatpackers, Communist steel workers gradually united with other unions based on common experiences. The SMWIU boasted fifteen thousand members at its height, but at its 1934 national conference in Pittsburgh, with about half that number on its rolls, its delegates argued about what to do next. They wanted desperately to mobilize workers at the bigger steel plants but found that their strength lay mostly in light industry. In 1931, party organizers in steel predicted a general steel strike. By 1934, such a stoppage had not materialized, and Communist organizers had to focus on the few mills where organizing conditions seemed favorable. The problem, of course, was that steel companies and anti-Communist workers succeeded in branding the SMWIU as a Communist outfit.[69]

These pressures help explain Chicago Communists' decision at the beginning of 1934 to join company and AFL unions in an attempt to convert them into "genuine shop committees." Party leaders counseled discretion when taking over these organizations, but they were encouraged by the possibilities.[70] George Patterson's shop was one in which this policy took effect. When the company union at South Works held its 1934 election, a number of militants were elected, including Patterson. Through the ERP, Patterson and his committee brought five issues to G. C. Thorpe, the president of the Illinois Steel Company, including a wage increase, an end to foremen's favoritism, a monthly instead of biweekly paycheck, time-and-a-half for overtime and Sunday work, and paid vacations for hourly workers. Thorpe refused these demands and the committee's call for an outside arbitrator. A few more rounds with management convinced Patterson and his fellow committeemen that they had pushed the company-union format as far as it would go. They needed a real union.[71]

What Communists referred to as a "real mass" of workers from South Works met outside the mill in August 1935 and agreed to form their own independent union, the Associated Employees (AE), which proved to be a short but successful venture. Communists numbered only fifteen in the mill but worked closely with Patterson and others in crafting the union's constitution, which directed a democratic structure, giving power to members instead of officers and opening membership to all workers at South Works. The AE held weekly meetings that featured Spanish, Polish, and Serbo-Croatian speakers, and its leaders were impressed with their success among Mexican workers, whom they assisted with work and immigration problems. Party members also encouraged the building of a women's auxiliary to help organize the men. Patterson's wife Dorothy visited workers at their homes and women at local churches to build union support. In November 1935, the AE claimed 1,300 members and by June 1936, over three thousand. That month, the AE nominated a slate to run in the ERP election, and twenty-one of those nominated won.[72]

Along the lines of the Popular Front, Communists inside and outside the plant encouraged AE members to affiliate with the AA to unify steel workers in the region and support the struggle within steel to take over its leadership, but AE members, still grousing about the union's failure in 1919, remained uninterested. Communists had a hard time convincing the AA to take an interest in the alienated AE workers in the plant. One organizer explained that AA officials were "afraid of the Communists who have applied for membership in the local union." One of the AA's leaders, a former party member who was since expelled, worked to keep his union Communist-free. Not until the Steel Workers' Organizing Committee (SWOC) came to Chicago and contacted local organizers did AE members vote to join the SWOC, beginning a new chapter in its workers' struggle.[73]

South Works was unusual in that while it had an ERP and an independent union, the AA stayed away. For those mills with an AA in place, Communists began to consider the possibility of working within the AA even before the dissolution of the TUUL. Everywhere it existed, the AA was stronger than the SMWIU; even in such anti-union companies as Republic Steel, it succeeded in building locals. Frustration over their lack of success motivated a minority group within the SMWIU to push for a new organizing policy that would allow them to work within the plants' AFL and independent unions. "If laborers thought the SMWIU was the only good union," one report argued, "they wouldn't flock to the AFL or independent unions." Dutiful party organizers like Jack Reese took his party assignment to work within the AFL organization at Youngstown Sheet and Tube. Party activists also worked with a group of one hundred at Illinois Steel, where the new steel code reduced their hours, forcing them to take home less pay. Party leaders insisted that these union activists bring the SMWIU forward as an option for the workers, but party organizers were "still hesitant . . . knowing it has a reputation of being a red union." Ignoring leaders' prodding, Communists working at Illinois Steel decided that it would be better not to alienate their fellow workers.[74]

An unsigned Communist report on steel, dated October 1934, discussed new directions Communists were taking in the industry. At that time, Chicago's Communists met with five leaders from Chicago's AA. Once there, Communists proposed a left-wing alliance inside the AA that would build toward a strike the following spring, the first step of a rank-and-file takeover. Communists hoped these leaders would use their positions in the AA to provide "official auspices" for the rank-and-file movement, which would eventually issue a left-wing newspaper.[75]

These left-leaning AA leaders agreed to consider the proposal, but Communists loyal to Third Period teachings were still not convinced they should join forces with non-Communists. "How deep can we afford to go into the movement with these people at the present time?" a Communist Chicago steel worker wondered. "Some of them are Republicans, some Democrats, some have some sort of connections with the Muste movement, not organizationally but ideologically." Such questioning reveals the pressures Communists felt during the Third Period. If they were to lead workers, then an alliance with reformist types was surely a "gamble." But how many choices did they have? Given the context, reality set in. The report's author wrote, "I think, however, that we can afford to try this out. . . . I think there is an opportunity to do something serious and there is a possibility some of these people are good types and we may really win them over in the course of the movement and make real leaders out of them." Again, the local situation forced a reevaluation of party policy.[76]

For the alliance to work, Communists had to pull members out of the SMWIU and have them work inside the AA. Even though Jack Stachel indicated that Chicago was the weakest center in terms of carrying through a merger, the city's Communists finally changed their approach.[77] Chicago's steel workers found that they were not alone. Stachel explained that frustration in dealing with the AA from the outside resulted in the "same trend among the rank and file" around the country. In district after district, Communists dissolved the steel sections of their SMWIU, transferred the union's steel members into AA locals, and began battling with the AA's national leader, Mike Tighe.[78]

Pushed by Communist steel workers, district organizations of the AA in December 1934 planned a drive to organize steel workers and agreed to hold a conference of all the country's district lodges in February. Tighe was noticeably absent from this December meeting, and just before the February conference he sent a letter threatening to expel members in all lodges that participated. Regardless, the conference went on with seventy-eight lodges represented. Tighe retaliated by expelling eighteen of them. Lodges that protested in support of the expelled found themselves in the same boat.

In response, delegations of steel workers appealed to the AA's executive board and the AFL's executive council in Washington, D.C. The AFL leader William Green listened but was unwilling to step into the fray. Reports from inside the AFL indicated there was a "hot fight" in the council on the question of steel and that John L. Lewis threatened to lead a movement of industrial unions out of the AFL and into a new federation.[79] Party leaders did not oppose new unions without question, but they feared that a dual union in steel would run into the same problems they encountered in their TUUL unions, and that workers would not support it.[80] Such developments within the AFL leadership, however, caused Communists to conclude that they would not get the AFL's help and that "steel workers must fight their own battle with whatever support they can organize from their own committees, lodges, and the rest of the working-class movement."[81]

Communists were convinced that unorganized steel workers were ready to be unionized, but they did not want to create the impression that they were pushing for this through a dual organization. Instead, a group of expelled delegates got together and, with Communist prodding, agreed to declare an emergency in the union, establish an emergency committee of the expelled, and continue to fight for their readmission through established lodges. While not formally readmitted to the AA, the emergency committee of steel workers would coordinate work of the expelled lodges. Stachel wanted rank-and-file Communists to understand, "and this is no small point," that the organizing work would have to be "carried on thru the lodges and districts," not independent and separate organizations. Already by the end of February 1935, Stachel reported, membership increased at meetings called by these rank-and-file committees.[82]

While the hope was that these rank-and-file committees would channel the energy of steel workers nationally, in Chicago, workers, including party members, stood by and waited to see what would happen between Tighe and the rank-and-file movement. City leaders proposed picking one department to popularize the rank-and-file movement, sending a delegation to the CFL for support against the expulsions, creating a leaflet to clarify issues as they arose, and placing a comrade in language organizations to organize the members. But little follow-up occurred.[83]

A summer federal district court decision helped speed the readmission of expelled lodges into the AA, but Communists' inflated Third Period hopes still allowed them to downplay the decision in favor of the argument that the rank-and-file struggle, the strength of the expelled lodges, and the feeling among the AA's own ranks resulted in the executive board taking them back.[84] When they returned, Communist leaders recognized that what they had was a "temporary truce" that could end at any moment. Tighe still fought an organizational drive and imposed heavy fines and dues payments on the newly admitted lodges. Such terms made workers feel that their reinstatement was not such a victory after all. Communists agreed but felt that the time was not right to lead a fight within the AA. They first had to regroup their forces. In any case, party organizers announced that for the time being they did not sense a "mass sentiment for union" among steel workers.[85] They agreed to lie low. Besides, a battle within the AFL was brewing. The creation of the SWOC would provide them with a new set of options.

Experiences in different industries brought Communist trade unionists to the same conclusion. The revolutionary call for separate unions would not result in a wide working-class following. They needed to work within established and trusted organizations within each industry.

Back on the Inside

Once inside the AFL, party leaders encouraged Communist ranks to take advantage of new opportunities to push for unemployment relief and champion labor militancy. Communists needed to reach out to their newest members and teach them proper methods for party work. They also needed to convince each other to attend union meetings. Work that had been largely neglected under the revolutionary union model in central and state labor councils also needed to be restarted. Most importantly, AFL union work could not remove members from their unit responsibilities. "The comrades in the trade unions cannot bring the Party and the daily issues to the membership unless they participate in the work of the units and the sections."[86]

In Chicago, Communist trade unionists quickly shifted gears. In a June 1935 report, leaders indicated that even though comrades found it difficult to rally AFL workers behind them on many party issues, on the question of unemployment insurance "they . . . attract a large number of AFL locals and keep them" through official local committees of their own unions.[87]

Party activists also agitated for support of an organizing campaign in the stockyards. Chicago's Communist trade-union commission discussed the prospects and agreed that even though international officers of the AMC supported a union drive, they did not take it seriously and instead "expect[ed] it to die out." Chicago's Communist language and trade-union leaders hoped their strategies to broaden and strengthen the drive would forestall its early death. Using contacts in the Yards' railroad unions, the community's churches, and the party's language clubs, Communists hoped to launch a real drive in meatpacking.[88]

Herb March and Frank McCarty's election as delegates to the CFL in July 1935 pushed the possibilities further, as they asked the CFL to support a drive. Frustrated with the inaction of the AMC and bitter over past political maneuvering of its leaders, Fitzpatrick allowed the body to discuss the drive, and delegates agreed to support it.[89] But AMC leaders had no intention of watching Communists force their hand, and at the drive's kickoff at a Labor Day rally at Soldier Field, union officials invited Chicago's Red Squad, whose members proceeded to arrest a number of party members and to raise fears of a Communist takeover among union members.[90]

Communists also tried to mobilize their forces within the IFL, but work was slow. The party had only five delegates to work with and a few others with whom they were "able to influence and work." Ignoring their small numbers, they put forth resolutions and looked for support wherever they could find it.[91]

Morris Childs, a leading Chicago party member, reported the success of the party's "limited forces" in getting support from "many unions" for their resolutions. In fact, he reported, "A number of these resolutions received the majority." These included a resolution against the sales tax, for trade-union unity, against the expulsion of union militants, and for the Lundeen Bill for unemployment insurance. The IFL president Reuben Soderstrom and secretary Victor Olander, however, did not want them aired and ruled these Communist motions and resolutions "defeated." Communist delegates reported that IFL leaders took voice votes, and called them as they liked.[92]

The central issue raised through the party's resolutions was the one on industrial unionism, which resulted in hours of heated debate. Victor Olander led a "passionate" offensive against it by raising the threat of Communist subversion within the unions. Dropping the name of William Z. Foster and the Communists' earlier TUEL policy of boring from within, Olander exclaimed that Communists were expelled back in the 1920s because they were destructive to the AFL. Industrial unionism would pave the way to their active participation once again. Olander accused the delegates who introduced the resolution of being "Reds." The votes for the resolution were not even counted, and instead the IFL chair announced "what he thought carried" and ruled all appeals out of order.[93]

Olander was right. Communists were drawn to industrial unionism and would fight to spark drives based on this model where they could. For the time being, the most logical place for this fight was within the AFL, where even the Communists knew a battle was brewing at its highest levels. In November 1935, a Committee of Industrial Organizations would form within the AFL and take the labor movement on a new path. Once again, Communists would have to consider their options and plan their next move. A new chapter of labor history and radical trade unionism was to be written, and Communists' Third Period activism positioned them to play an important role in both. The TUUL taught them organizing strategies, built wide networks of supporters, and pushed industrial, interracial unionism before its time. Such experiences would result in CIO leaders offering full-time organizing positions in the city's most important industries to Chicago's Communist trade unionists. Joe Weber, a party trade unionist in steel, remembered that the party's Third Period organizing resulted in "skeleton organizations in the major industries—in steel, of course, in packing, Crane company, and other places." With such structures in place, CIO organizers such as Weber swiftly moved to organize. This time, they found, Chicago's workers were eager to work with them. A revolutionary shift was under way in Chicago's labor movement. Communists were not the cause, and yet they were a crucial element.[94]

7

"Not That These Youths Are Geniuses": Young Communists Move from the Margins to the Mainstream

S. Kirson Weinberg, a student of the prominent University of Chicago sociologist Ernest Burgess, headed into the Jewish neighborhood of Lawndale to study its generation of youth drawn to the political Left in response to government's and business's inability to solve the problems caused by the Depression. Weinberg came across one young man who explained: "'I lost my job two years ago. Since then I've only worked a few days. I need money for clothes, to see a show, to help my family, to go to school. . . . The first year I hoped for the better. But no more. It's useless to hope. . . . Then someone told me about Communism. It was what I looked for. I went to a meeting. I began to think. There was no more righteous thing in the world. Why shouldn't a worker who produces an object have a share in the profits? The bosses get it all. . . . They caused the Depression and they're causing their own doom.'"[1]

Of course, not all respondents made such an easy connection between the Depression and Communism. One young high-school graduate explained that when he could not find work, his parents supported his enrollment in Crane College, where, introduced to young Socialist and Communist groups on campus, he became "'social minded.'" He found Socialists more akin to his interests because Communists were "'too rigid and too extreme; they suppressed one's individuality too much by stressing loyalty to the Party. I wanted more freedom. Besides, I didn't want to give up my religion, my family, my individual expression. Besides, I heard that upon being admitted to the bar, a morals committee could discharge one if he professed Communism. Of course, I immediately gave up that notion. I sought something milder, not as binding, looser. The only alternative was Socialism.'"[2]

While Communists' appeal was their "righteousness," Socialists attracted those who still believed in the system's viability. Weinberg's study shows a contrast between adherents of these two groups while tapping into a larger phenomenon of Depression-era youth who increasingly questioned and challenged 1920s assumptions of capitalism's stability, the ease of upward mobility, and a vapid youth culture. As across the nation, in Chicago the typical young person did not profess Communism or Socialism. Yet the messages these young radicals articulated or acted upon resonated among young people who only a few years earlier were notorious for exerting their energies on sports and fraternity and sorority gossip. Depression conditions shook young people out of their 1920s apolitical state, allowing young radicals to move out of their small, alternative enclaves into the mainstream.

The seeming collapse of capitalism and, after 1932, the increasing threat of war and fascism caused a generation of young people to question the assumptions of those who came before them. A vocal segment of the under-twenty-five-year-old demographic became uncertain that adults in leadership roles, whether school administrators, foremen, police, or politicians, had their best interests in mind and the answers to society's problems. Robert Cohen's study of the 1930s youth movement follows this ferment among college students nationally. In Chicago, youth activism spilled out of universities into factories and onto the streets. Whether students in the nation's leading universities or workers on the assembly line, these young people assessed their place in 1930s America and decided to leave the "roaring twenties" behind them.[3]

They increasingly joined in political coalitions that brought together labor, religious, and political groups to articulate the voice of young America. Working more flexibly than their adult counterparts, young activists in the 1930s found their greatest success in mobilizing against war and fascism, rallying students to question their role in universities, and organizing an American Youth Congress.

Communist youth were at the center of this ferment, at times questioning the leadership and authority of their own Communist leaders. Their flexible approach and liberal/reformist impulse became hallmarks of Popular Front coalitions and activism, but during the early years of the Depression, YCL activity, regardless of its success, remained at odds with Stalinist forces and mainstream Third Period ways.

Communist youth were willing to buck party leaders when creating coalitions, but they still strongly admired older Communists' confidence and commitment. Initially, such admiration caused young Communists to hang around their older counterparts and participate in party-sponsored initiatives of unemployed work and union building rather than develop specific youth-oriented ones. The one YCL-controlled event they did put on, a 1932 counter-Olympics, was innovative but impotent. In time, conditions of the 1930s and the YCL's student-heavy composition pushed young Communists to get creative. Beginning in 1932, they became active in a momentous antiwar movement, particularly strong at the University of Chicago, which launched the YCL into a national movement of students beginning to challenge the university and rethink their role within its walls. The challenge would result in a state-senate inquiry on Communism and, ironically, a boost in YCL activity and interest.

Unemployed, union, sport, and antiwar activity broadened the horizons of Chicago's youth, pushed them to join with people who saw the world differently than they did, and reflected a new impulse among young people to take a stand on the big questions with which Americans of all stripes were dealing, lessons that would influence adults on the Left and set the next decade's political tone.

The Depression and the YCL

Charles Hall's family moved to Chicago's North Side in 1929 and supported his older brother and, a year later, Chuck as they attended the University of Chicago. But the Depression's reality quickly set in, and economics forced Chuck and his brother to drop out because they "didn't have enough money to keep on going." Les Orear faced a similar change in his life plan. First attending college in Wisconsin, Orear was forced to leave school and get a job in Chicago to help support his family.[4] Hall and Orear represent a much larger segment of youth who by 1932 were no longer able to shield themselves from the Depression by attending university. As economic conditions worsened, young people were forced to reshape their outlooks. Some found their way to the youth branch of the Communist party, the YCL.

As a young student and leader of his Presbyterian church's youth group, Hall heard radical words his brother brought home from work. Returning home on Fullerton, Hall's older brother came upon Bughouse Square, where there was "a free-for-all where everybody who had a soapbox could get up and spout his piece." To Hall's brother, the Communists made the most sense, and he signed with the YCL, which had a branch working around the Finnish Workers' Hall on Fullerton and Halsted. After a few years working with the YCL, he got his younger brother interested; Chuck Hall joined the YCL in 1934.[5]

Orear's path to the party was different. He left college, landing a job in the plant at Armour's meatpacking company, where he came into contact with such young Communists as Herb March. Through March, Orear met young people who shared his way of thinking about the world. As he recalls, "It was the kind of people who shared an attitude, a broader vision, and so we hung around with each other." Before long, Orear became a YCL activist, with the task of crafting the group's shop paper in the Yards.[6]

During the Depression, Hall and Orear found themselves in the company of a growing and increasingly active group of people. Nationwide, the YCL claimed 2,300 in 1929, 3,000 in 1931, 3,750 in 1932, 6,000 in 1934, and 8,000 in 1935.[7] Chicago's YCL grew as well, but at a slower rate. Even though its numbers more than doubled between 1931 and 1935, YCL membership never reached the expectations of party leaders; and yet through the YCL, the party trained many of its most important future leaders and trade-union organizers.[8]

The young and daring Jack Kling was responsible for Chicago's YCL during much of the Third Period. Party leaders plucked him from New York's YCL ranks because of his leadership potential and sent him to the national party school in Cleveland. Led by Israel Amter, the Ohio district organizer; Betty Gannett, the national YCL director; and Sam Don, a youth leader, Kling immersed himself in political economy. "In a short time," Kling recalled, "the school made me aware of how little I knew about our philosophy."[9] A quick study, Kling returned to New York and organized youth sections in needle-trade unions, among unemployed groups, and in antiwar groups and demonstrations. AFL "goons" beat him, and city police clubbed him and put him in jail. By 1930, these experiences qualified him for Chicago's leading YCL post, a position he accepted grudgingly, lacking confidence in his leadership skills.[10]

In Chicago, Kling met the party activists Bill Gebert and John Williamson as well as the Chicago YCL leaders Gil Green, John Marks, and Ben Gray. Growing up in the Jewish ghetto on Chicago's West Side, where he and his family experienced the degradation of public assistance, Green was politicized on Roosevelt Road, his "university," where "one joined friends, scanned store-window displays, marveled at the glittering marquee above the new movie house, and reveled in the oratory of soapboxers." Finding himself inclined toward socialist ideas, Green accepted an invitation to a Young Communist meeting when asked by a friend's radical piano instructor. By the mid-1930s he would emerge from Chicago's ranks as a national YCL leader.[11] Marks came to Chicago from Milwaukee, where he had been a unit functionary. Twenty years old in 1931, Marks worked in a machine shop for two years before becoming a YCL organizer.[12] Like Kling, Gray was uprooted from New York, but his move was of his own doing rather than the party's. Job insecurity drove him to Chicago, where he eventually landed work as an assistant pickle-truck helper and where he came into contact with YCL activists. Jailed for his protest at a Scottsboro demonstration, Gray remembers signing his YCL membership card while locked up.[13]

As YCL leaders, Kling, Gray, and Marks were responsible for planning and overseeing Communist youth activity, recruitment, and education. They were the conduits between the party and its youth. Their leadership positions sometimes put them in difficult straits, needing to answer the demands of party leaders and of their own members, which were sometimes at odds. Through their personalities and activism, these men took on the smoothing over of rough edges, a large responsibility made even more significant by the YCL's relationship to the party. As Marks reminded party activists, "The YCL [is] not an ancillary organization—it is a section of the CP and must be regarded as such."[14]

As a section, of course, the YCL ran into the same problems that hindered other sections of the party. The most persistent one, in leaders' eyes, was its composition. In May 1930, only fifteen of the city's members were eligible for membership in the TUUL. Reporting in July that no shop nuclei existed in the YCL, Marks critically stated that the league's ten units were primarily comprised of students.[15] Not until 1932 could the YCL declare any activity in the shops, and even then it was minuscule. The small number of its 357 members who were not students or unemployed were divided in small shops and stores, the only exceptions in the city's large factories being four stockyards workers.[16] By 1935, twenty-two of the YCL's six hundred members worked in meatpacking, and while no shop nuclei existed in South Chicago's steel mills, fifty YCLers organized there through street nuclei. The YCL also had one unit in a radio department of Stewart Warner, but it had been closed down. Five of the seven activists stayed with the YCL, and the other two remained sympathizers.[17] By all accounts, union activity among young workers was not the YCL's strong suit.

Neither was work among African Americans. Even though two of the city's most charismatic African American activists, David Poindexter and Herbert Newton, worked among youth, they could not turn the tide. The YCL increased its black membership to fifty by 1932, but its organizational structure tended to isolate whites from blacks. As early as 1932, the YCL planned to build a separate youth organization for African Americans "as a bridge to the league," but they quickly found that separation of the groups did not need formal recognition: YCLers simply segregated themselves. Four of the six groups were either composed of all white members or all black members, most likely as a by-product of where members lived.[18]

Yet the fact of segregation did not prevent YCL members from taking on issues of civil rights and racial equality. YCL members showcased their antiracist position at a public trial they held at People's Auditorium in August 1932, which mirrored those held in party units throughout the country between 1930 and 1933 in an attempt to rid the party of racism and publicize its commitment to racial equality.[19] In this case, the YCL already had expelled Harry Hankin when about four hundred gathered to watch him be tried for racism. The meeting opened with the YCL's section leader explaining the importance of the fight against segregation and the need for "unity of all workers." Then the judge called for the election of a "workers' jury," before defending and prosecuting attorneys presented their cases. Was Hankin simply a product of the capitalist environment? Could he overcome his position in support of segregation? The trial reached its climax when Hankin took the stand and argued that he was "completely cleared up." But when asked if he would be ready to give his "life in the struggle for Negro rights," he was unsure. After deliberating for half an hour, the jury "endorsed the expulsion of Harry Hankin and all white chauvanism from our ranks." YCL leaders hoped this trial would have "great significance" throughout Chicago by showing white workers who "preach segregation for colored workers" that they are "enemies of the working class."[20] And while the party press made much of the trial, civil rights work never became the YCL's major emphasis. Instead, the YCL recruited most of its black members as a by-product of the party's campaign against unemployment rather than through specific work among black youth.

No record exists of women YCL members throughout the Third Period. The only groups receiving special note were trade unionists and African Americans, without indication of gender. It is not that women did not distinguish themselves among YCL activists. Vicky Starr, Jane March, and Edith Miller stood out for their bravery and leadership skills. But the party's male culture trickled into the YCL, so men became its leaders, and male party members failed to recognize the quality and quantity of female participation, practices that prepared women for the challenges they faced once they became full-fledged members.

With a membership of white students and nonworkers, YCL leaders found that their culture also chafed party leaders. In the early 1930s, leaders were perturbed at young Communists' willingness to shield political deviants in their midst. By 1931, the party and the YCL had already been through a purge of Trotskyists. Party leaders did not want to repeat it and for some time refrained from calling the rebellious and outspoken YCL leaders in their midst "Trotskyites," but eventually they did. Kling recalled, "It soon became apparent that the YCL leadership was bucking the Party on almost all policy questions. I felt that the differences were more than simply minor or mistaken views, but that the main leadership was Trotskyist in outlook, left over from the time the Trotskyites had been expelled from the Party and the YCL a few years earlier."[21] High-level meetings among Chicago's leaders confirm the independence of the YCL's leadership and their willingness to "take up action contrary to the decision that had just been made by the Party secretariat."[22] But a purge of these leading YCL activists, which resulted in their leaving the party for a national Trotskyist youth group, simply left a vacuum without changing the YCL's culture. Regular complaints of "bad attitudes," "right-wing leaders," and "bad tendencies" continued to be heard in party meetings.[23]

Upon purging themselves of supposed followers of Trotsky, YCL members increasingly reached out to young Socialists. One party member commented that the young Communists were not "oriented toward anything except the YPSL [Young People's Socialist League]." Communist leaders would have liked to interpret this orientation as subversive, but YCL members developed close and trusting relationships with young Socialists. One YCL member wrote, "their [YPSL] people here are on our side. . . . I believe the fellows are sincere." In his thinking, these good connections "lay the basis for a national congress of youth," which could focus on issues of war, homelessness, and unemployment among youth, a congress that eventually materialized in 1934 in the form of the American Youth Congress (AYC).[24]

Yet even before the AYC, Kling recalled close relations between the YCL and YPSL. YPSL leaders invited Kling to teach a class to their members on Marxism, which he did at a borrowed cottage in the Indiana Dunes on Lake Michigan. Once the school concluded, weekly classes continued in Chicago. These amicable interactions led to YPSL members refusing to follow their Socialist party leaders when they broke with Communists in the planning stage of a "Free Tom Mooney" congress that the groups were working on in a United Front fashion. The national secretary of the YPSL, George Smerkin, spoke at the congress despite the Socialist party's refusal to support it, causing his expulsion. By November 1933, the entire national leadership of the YPSL found itself in the same boat and joined the YCL. The YPSL may have been responsible for reaching out, yet it is significant that during the Third Period, the YCL was willing to work with them.[25]

Such amiable relations with Socialist leaders flew in the face of Third Period orthodoxy but were out of the party's control, since those in charge of the YCL were themselves tolerant of such relations and uninterested in factional struggle. Ben Gray was particularly opposed to factionalism. Instructed to attend party meetings as a YCL representative, Gray witnessed factional attitudes and behaviors that he felt distracted from the party's main activity. "The faction became the important thing," he remembered, "whether they would make a victory at this meeting or at that meeting, or they would isolate this guy or the other, and I could never understand it and really didn't appreciate it."[26] In one of the few district buro meetings where Gray's words are recorded, he is trying to stop early factionalism within the YCL and the party.[27]

Kling also opposed sectarianism within the YCL. In addition to his tutelage of YPSL students, he challenged Comintern leaders who accused Chicago's group as having "a rotten liberal attitude" when it came to differing political views. In 1932, he, Marks, and Green, who was already a national YCL leader, went to Moscow to "consult" and "exchange experiences" with others. Working on a resolution that dealt with the American YCL, Kling and his fellow delegates learned that Comintern leaders did not appreciate the openness Chicago's YCL showed toward Trotskyists. Kling and the others agreed that they had a liberal attitude, especially when it came to "shielding" Trotskyite members. But when told that their liberal attitude was rotten, Kling and his delegation appealed to the Comintern leader Otto Kuusinen (the former Finnish Communist party leader), to no avail.[28] Such a scolding from Comintern leaders had little effect on the activity of these YCL leaders, however, and Gil Green came before the Comintern leadership once again in October 1934 to defend the YCL's participation in the AYC. In Moscow, he found himself in the company of Raymond Guyot, a leader of the French Communist youth who had also been involved in broad-based youth movements. After three weeks of discussion, Comintern leaders decided that Green and Guyot had been right in their work all along. In this case, local activism predated international policy.[29]

Before the "correctness" of Chicago's YCL's attitude became the day's order, the proper cultivation of its members was a regular concern of party leaders. Their concern did not always translate into specific direction, however. In fact, Chicago's YCL carried on in its unorthodox manner in large part because the party paid them little daily attention. In 1931, a YCL representative scorned party leaders by reminding them that "there was no representative in the league from the Party, no daily guidance, no actual coordination between Party and league."[30] Bill Gebert admitted in private correspondence, "We did not give any attention to the league and the league membership did not rise to the height of the developments."[31] By 1932, it seemed as though relations between the YCL and party members had improved at the lower levels of the city's bureaucracy, but as one leader commented, "[T]he same can not be said of the district leadership."[32] A local activist reported in 1933 that the "league is in a serious situation. . . . Party here seems to be rather contemptuous rather than helping Jack."[33] Lack of party assistance was so well known by 1935 that F. Brown, critiquing the party's inability to grow its YCL, commented, "I am sure that if the Chicago district had assisted the YCL in all its work . . . today we would have different picture."[34]

Certainly, party and YCL forces worked on plans to institutionalize a close relationship between the groups. A series of directives outlined their theoretical working relationship. Nuclei leaders were to turn names of twenty-three-year-olds in their midst over to party leaders for YCL assignment. At the same time, leaders from all levels were to be released for full-time work guiding the YCL. Like party leaders, young Communists had the opportunity to be educated in a YCL school. Party members were to supervise student recruitment to ensure representation from "decisive factories." To show that YCL recruitment was taken seriously, leaders agreed in 1934 to print its recruitment numbers along with the party's own. For their part, YCL members were expected to attend party meetings as a way to learn procedures, policies, and plans.[35]

Yet, however well-intended these proposals, party assistance was not forthcoming. Despite plenum decisions to assign people to supervise YCL work, only one section turned in names of volunteers, and no section turned in names of younger members, even though they existed.[36] By 1934, leaders removed YCL functionaries borrowed from the party's ranks rather than bolster them and declined to support YCL members attending party schools.[37] And financial neglect of the YCL went further. When approached for any percentage of money raised from party bazaars or celebrations, the party flatly refused the YCL. Even the five-dollar weekly subsidy the party had been paying to the YCL stopped. Leaders did not want the YCL to fail, but the YCL was not its priority. Doling out their meager resources with care, party leaders left little for the YCL.[38]

Tense relations between the YCL and the party did not deter YCL members from jumping headlong into party-initiated drives. In fact, leaders regularly criticized those in the YCL for not charting their own course. Making the break was difficult for them. With little financial backing, a student-heavy base, and Third Period priorities, YCL members spent a great deal of their time meeting with one another and working on party-organized activities of Unemployed Councils and union building. When they did branch out in 1932 to organize a counter-Olympics in the city, they received little party support, and their efforts passed with little notice. Not until student activity at the University of Chicago began to take on a life of its own did the student-heavy base of the YCL begin to pay off and the liberal attitudes of its members result in new and sustainable coalitions.

The YCL in Action

Thinking back on their time as YCLers, Chuck Hall and Les Orear remembered the insularity of their groups. Hall recalled, "We put out a lot of leaflets, we did a lot of going around to [party] demonstrations. I would say we were rather a sectarian group. We were not really a part of the flow of life in the community."[39] Orear simply labeled his group "pretty inbred."[40] Their memories fit with comments of league leaders from the period. In May 1930, John Marks told party leaders, "While the YCL in the district has recently made ideological progress in its struggle against the right danger, left sectarianism, student ideology, etc., the league organizationally is completely isolated from young workers."[41] Two years later another league leader added, "The activity and life of YCL is internal. There are no specific youth activities, no development of mass struggles around youth issues. . . . Comrades don't try to take on youth features from Communist working-class point of view but bourgeois youth ideology is reflected in the ranks. . . . The YCL tries to copy too much the Party activities and Party campaigns. . . . They are trying with a weak apparatus to conduct a dozen campaigns, instead of concentrating on one or two."[42]

If in the early 1930s league members did stick closely to party activity and their numbers did not grow significantly, they nevertheless gained experience for future alliances with non-party youth where adult Communists were absent. Fighting alongside party activists, young Communists were supported in their militancy, encouraged to seek and challenge breaches of civil rights, and nurtured with the teachings of Marxism-Leninism in hopes of countering the education they received through the public schools. Their experiences with Unemployed Councils and unions revealed the underside of capitalism, reinforcing their party education and committing a solid core to a future as full-fledged activists. Gradually pulling away from the party in 1932 and after, YCL activists found their own niche challenging war and fascism. Through the auxiliary organization, the National Student League (NSL), young Communists began to break out of their isolation and into a broader scene where young people like themselves questioned the world they were about to inherit.[43]

When it came to unemployed activity, league members usually followed the lead of their elders in Unemployed Councils. Their contribution consisted largely of passing out leaflets and demonstrating. Harry Haywood recalled being joined in his arrest in front of a relief station by the YCL organizer for the Hyde Park neighborhood and a University of Chicago student who was also a YCL member.[44] Occasionally their bravery stood out. During the March 6, 1930, mass rally against unemployment, Chicago's police arrested Fred Fine, a fourteen-year-old demonstrator party leaders called "the kid." In front of a group of party leaders, police twice slapped Fine's face, called him a "dirty Jew," and asked if he would try to shoot if he had access to the officer's gun. When Fine replied, "Yes, I would," he earned the respect of leaders who sat defenseless on the bench behind him.[45]

Because YCL participation in unemployed activity did not always have a distinguishing character, Kling made sure to point out cases to party leaders when it did. One of these moments occurred in 1932 after cuts in relief resulted in a demonstration where a relief worker at the Emmerson relief station slapped a black applicant. YCL activists planned a follow-up demonstration demanding no relief cut, payment of rent, removal of the offending official, and no discrimination against youth, even though the party had not articulated offenses against young people. YCL members worked flophouses and poolrooms to turn out young people for the demonstration.

According to Kling, one thousand people, most of them African American, gathered and elected a small committee to enter the office. Once inside, relief officials refused them a hearing, and police officers prevented their leaving. In response, "a royal battle took place," writes Kling, where demonstrators smashed doors and threw rocks and bottles to counter police clubs and blackjacks. Police knocked the YCL unit organizer Edith Miller unconscious. Five of the many arrested were YCL members.[46]

After the arrests, a smaller group proceeded to the Unemployed Council office at Fortieth and Federal, where police and Red Squad officials, in Kling's words, "marched in at the point of guns." After asking women to leave, the officials, Kling recalled, "lined up the men against the walls, with hands lifted over their heads and beat hell out of them. Then they arrested the bunch. About 50 were arrested." YCL members were among the group. Before the police had control of the situation, however, a small number of activists were able to escape through a back window. They gathered block captains from councils in other territories for a late-night meeting where they organized a demonstration at the court the following morning. About four hundred showed up to the demonstration, but police were mobilized for twelve blocks around the courthouse, arresting "every worker that walked" past. Kling reported, "[Q]uite a number of YCL comrades and young workers were also arrested."[47] It was Kling's hope that such active YCL participation would build YCL numbers, and he happily reported that directly following the incident, youth attending three South Side YCL meetings showed a "splendid spirit." In one case, five new young workers showed up, having only been active in worker sport clubs, but on the whole, neither this incident nor any single Unemployed Council event resulted in a surge of membership.[48]

The same can be said of the YCL's union work, although YCL activists distinguished themselves in the packinghouse campaign in ways party activists had not. As in their work supporting Unemployed Councils, YCL activists served as resources for party unionists. Their influence is evident in shop papers, such as the piece that appeared in the May 1928 edition of the Northwestern Railroad paper, which expressed apprentices' complaint that older workers took a position against aid to youth in the shop.[49] The article calls on the apprentices to overcome divisions with older workers: "Employers are united and we should be." Military intelligence reports also note young Communist support of union drives. In one case, a University of Chicago student and member of the NSL, Stella Winn, opened her Hyde Park apartment to the TUUL's office workers' union for a "studio party," which included portrait sketches, entertainment, and dancing.[50] Similar attention and support was given in steel, metal, and meatpacking, but it was not until 1934 that the YCL could actually speak of units within industry, and even then they were concentrated in meatpacking.

YCL activists did participate in the large 1933 strike at Sopkins and Sons, and while they did not take on a role different than party leaders', their participation sometimes made strike activity a family affair.[51] One family, the Holmans, was both a party and YCL family whose members opened their home to discuss the strike. One time the police interrupted and began to separate whites from blacks, placing one Jewish leader with the blacks and a light-skinned African American with the whites. Both YCL and party members learned an important lesson on how easily race could be used to divide workers. Each group got a lecture attacking the other race. Police bungling foiled the plan to create suspicion between the groups, but the experience confirmed lessons youth learned through party readings, lectures, classes, and family discussions.[52]

By all accounts, meatpacking was the industry the YCL best served. Minutes from the party section that incorporated the stockyards indicate that as late as September 1933, party members felt a paternal urge to guide the work of YCL activists in the Yards: "Party member . . . unable to impress youth in unit with need for work and not all play. Unit to try to send additional older comrade there to guide."[53] It is unclear, however, whether this comment reflected conditions among youth in the Yards or party members' sense of self-importance, because beginning in 1933 it was members of the YCL who put in gear the packinghouse union drive. Prior to that time, party members only experienced brief moments of glory in a demonstration, rally, or organizational meeting. The arrival of Herb March and the activism of women YCLers in departments in Armour's plant began to turn the tide. Of course, March and these young women were not solely to credit. They worked hand in hand with older members scattered throughout the Yards and had Roosevelt's New Deal momentum working for them. But youth connections and attitudes made a difference.

March himself was used to a certain amount of independence in his work. Growing up in Brooklyn, he was exposed to community organizing and leftist politics at a young age. Watching neighbors come together for rent strikes and listening to street-corner meetings of radical groups, March made up his mind to become a Communist because he "didn't think it was right for some people to be poor and some people to be so damn rich." He signed up with the YCL at the age of sixteen and supported strikers in Paterson, New Jersey, where he was arrested during a silk strike. He also worked for civil rights and against unemployment in Kansas City. Quickly making his mark, March became a YCL organizer for a seven-state region in the Southwest, gaining his reputation of being "a maverick" and "hard to control." But through his direction, YCL members got jobs in Kansas City's packinghouses and began to organize workers. In the early 1930s, he married Jane Grbac from Chicago, who would organize at the University of Chicago settlement and oversee the YCL in the Back of the Yards neighborhood. Wanting to start a family with his new wife, March moved to Chicago, where he was able to land a job working in the stockyards. His experiences in Kansas City and his independent spirit served him well as he drew on party and YCL resources that had been largely stagnant before his arrival.[54]

March stands out because his energy and determination ultimately resulted in a successful meatpacking drive and because of his his promotion to director of the union's district—an indication of the importance that one highly skilled party organizer could make—but he was not alone among YCL members making a significant contribution to the drive. A core of YCL women working within the plants made headway, winning small demands and signing up members to the PHWIU. In interviews given later in his life, March emphasized the strength the PHWIU had on the sheep and hog kill in the Armour plant, decisive departments with a large number of African American workers. And while the union might have had its strongest representation in these areas, reports from the party indicate that party "units [were] basically composed of girls."[55]

One of these young women was Vicky Starr. On her family's farm, Starr became friendly with a woman who had spent time with the family for her health and now needed to return to Chicago to get an operation. Seventeen and needing work to help relieve her family's financial strain, Starr left with her for Chicago and boarded with her family in the city. Two of its members were Herb and Jane March. Through the Marches, Vicky became radicalized. "The Marches would have meetings of the YCL in the attic and they'd ask me to sit in. . . . They pointed out things to me that, in my very unsophisticated and farm-like way, I saw. . . . [YCLers] thought that instead of just thinking about ourselves we should be thinking about other people and try to get them together in a union and organize and then maybe we would have socialism where there would not be hunger, war, etc. They initiated me into a lot of political ideas and gave me material to read. We had classes and we would discuss industrial unionism, the craft unions and the history of the labor movement in this country."[56]

Politicized and ready to make change, Starr obtained a job at Armour, where she began to organize women workers. One floor below her department, a woman lost her fingers in a meat chopper that lacked safety guards. Starr and two other women organized a stoppage. Six floors participated in the sit-down, which resulted in the company adding safety equipment and women gaining an interest in the union.[57]

The YCL also made a difference in the ability of its organizers to get shop papers into the hands of stockyard workers. Drawing on their student strength, YCL organizers contacted a group from the University of Chicago to help edit and raise funds to publish the *Yards' Worker*. They also helped write other leaflets, and they distributed them at the stockyard gates before the 7 A.M. shift. Vicky Starr recalled, "They did this because we could not do so, for if we were caught giving out leaflets we would be fired."[58] Rather than publicly handing out party materials, Starr snuck papers into the plant on her person and spread them out in the washroom. "I really think we had a lot of guts," she recalled. Such antics occasionally paid off. At least two workers turned in YCL applications found inside the Yards' paper.[59]

In 1934, YCL leaders announced that they were able to "initiate a movement for united action on part of various unions in packing." According to the report, workers in the PHWIU and the Stockyards Labor Council responded well to the suggestion of unity. Some individual AFL members agreed to unity, but for a time their leaders "sabotaged" the effort. Regardless, members of the YCL persisted assigning each shop nuclei member to a particular union. Two YCL members were elected to the executive board of the SLC.[60] Despite their small numbers, YCL members made a difference in the Yards drive, gave young people union-building experience, and placed youth in leadership positions.

Their work organizing a counter-Olympics protest was not as successful. The organization that planned the protest had its beginnings in 1927, when a United Front group of Communists, Socialists, and members of the IWW founded the Labor Sports Union to encourage athletics among workers while winning them away from boss-controlled athletic organizations, where anti-union propaganda persisted. By 1929, the party purged Socialists and IWW members from the organization and affiliated it to Moscow's Red Sports International.[61] Put under the YCL's control, its members held fraction meetings to plan the organization's leadership and activities. In October 1930, the national executive board fraction of the LSU put forward Jack Kling, then living in New York, as a member of the LSU's national council. Three YCL members from Chicago and one party member were also on the slate.[62]

The idea of organizing an International Workers' Athletic Meet, or a counter-Olympics, built on a European tradition of the worker-sport movement. The historian William Baker points out how European trade unionists, long tired of the capitalist exploitation of sports, formed working-class athletic clubs and sporting events throughout the interwar era. In 1928, four million people belonged to either the Socialist Workers' Sport International or the Red Sports International. Between 1921 and 1937, these worker-sport groups participated in Olympiads and sporting events in Germany, France, Austria, Russia, Norway, and Czechoslovakia. One year before the Chicago event, over 1,400 athletes competed before more than a quarter of a million people in Vienna.[63]

The YCL and the LSU had a rich tradition of sport protest upon which to draw.[64] The problem was that the party itself did not take an interest in the campaign, and Chicago's YCL followed its lead. When counter-Olympic committee members approached Detroit's party organizer, he dismissed the national representative and told them simply to "go to the youth." Chicago's leadership similarly marginalized the campaign. Its secretariat assigned two party members to work on the campaign, but one flatly refused, and the other was only "partially active." Meanwhile, Chicago's leadership "forgot" to invite the national representatives of the counter-Olympic committee to a gathering so they could familiarize members with and encourage support for the event.[65]

Chicago's language and fraternal groups also did not provide much support. Offering lip service only, none of the groups carried out directives passed on to them by the national counter-Olympic committee. In a letter from the national committee to Earl Browder, committee members explained, "We requested appointments with the respective language bureaus for the purposes of discussing the building of the Labor Sports Union in these language organizations, but to date not a single bureau has notified us regarding their meeting dates." The committee also asked that these groups discuss workers' sports, endorse the counter-Olympics, and print the national committee's publicity in their presses, but the requests were "almost entirely ignored."[66]

The organization that should have been most engaged in this campaign, the YCL, was similarly disengaged. National leaders reported that the YCL in Detroit and Chicago had done almost no work to support the counter-Olympics. Chicago's group, in particular, ignored specific directives. In January 1932, only five YCL members were reported among the membership of the city's LSU of 450.[67] It was no wonder that national counter-Olympic organizers asked the party's Central Committee to send out a sharp letter on their behalf, assign representatives to direct the campaign, and "take the leadership of the sports' movement out of the hands of the YCL."[68]

In addition to party indifference, the LSU had problems with city officials, publicity, weather, and threats from athletic organizations. As Baker outlines, national news agencies ignored counter-Olympic news releases, and even the *Daily Worker* offered only occasional reporting. "Free Tom Mooney Runs," swimming, basketball, and soccer tournaments that were to occur in cities throughout the country as preliminary heats leading up to the Olympics met with obstacles. Boston's city officials refused permission to host a run through its city streets; Buffalo and Detroit would not allow the use of school gyms for athletes' training; a downpour stopped the race in Cleveland; and the Amateur Athletic Union threatened a lifetime ban on any athlete participating in the runs. As the date for the opening of the games approached, LSU officials learned that two German worker-athletes and five Russians, hoping to participate in the games, would not be permitted visas.[69]

These botched meets culminated at the University of Chicago's Stagg Field, the site for a poorly attended International Workers' Athletic Meet. Numbers of spectators and athletes vary in each report, but regardless they do not add up to much. While the *Daily Worker* reported that five thousand watched from the stands, at least one participant insists that numbers did not reach two thousand, despite a low, twenty-five-cent admission fee.[70]

While the number of athletes—between two and four hundred, compared to the approximately 1,500 who attended the Los Angeles Olympic games—was disappointing, their composition speaks to the significance of the event. While a large percentage were ethnic, anywhere from one-quarter to one-third were African American—a significant fact, considering that only four blacks were represented on the American track and field team in Los Angeles. As Mark Naison has shown, this commitment to black athletes became a hallmark of Communist party race work.[71]

Despite the working-class flavor of the event, and maybe because of it, Chicago's counter-Olympics did not serve as a serious alternative to the Olympic games as the LSU intended. Nor did the games do much toward freeing Tom Mooney. One indoor meeting held on the games' opening night to protest Mooney's arrest was all the organizers had to show. If William Baker is correct that the games "underscored the weakness of the workers' sport movement," he is less insightful when he suggests that they also demonstrated the "marginal position of the Communist Party."[72] In many ways the counter-Olympic demonstration was a remnant of 1920s ethnic-based activism and did not reflect the changes that were occurring within the party's base. Party members' and youth activists' lack of interest suggests that they were more invested in the campaigns that were drawing Communist activists out of the margins and into the center of political activity. Their involvement with a broad antiwar movement proved Communists were anything but marginal.

Chicago's antiwar movement blossomed overnight. Young Communists' interest in organizing on college campuses and in Chicago's communities against capitalism, war, and fascism set them apart from young people before them. Using politics and personal networks to bridge town and gown, young Communists would eventually play a leading role in the city's antiwar movement. In mobilizing this movement, they made lasting connections with youth of all political stripes and found these peers increasingly receptive to related issues of academic freedom, free speech, and civil rights.

Scholars writing on youth antiwar work tend to focus on college students' activities. Certainly such actions on campuses in the city, and especially at the University of Chicago, represented a high-water mark of party outreach and influence. But in Chicago, nonstudent youth also participated in antiwar work. One party report indicated that the YCL was building an antiwar united front in the Back of the Yards, in the Gross settlement house, among workers at the National Malleable plant, and within churches and community organizations.[73] Herb March remembered recruiting the YCL member Mary Shukshick, a Polish woman, and some Ukrainian members directly through the peace movement. Members of the YCL in the stockyards were particularly active in the antiwar movement. One attended a peace conference in Paris and agreed to report on it at a local conference on war and fascism.[74] Others served as delegates to the national antiwar organization, the American Congress against War and Fascism, where they met YCL members from the YMCA and various shops throughout the city. These YCL members also worked on building community organizations against war. One report indicated that there were "steps to build sixty-seven neighborhood committees" in such places as Albany Park, Rogers Park, the lower West Side, the West Side, the South Side, and around the university campus. In November 1934, four committees already functioned. Albany Park's organization brought together ten community groups; the one on the South Side included representatives from churches, factories, sport clubs, and mass organizations; Rogers Park's group included six churches; and one community group had representatives from the Presbyterian church, sports clubs, and revolutionary organizations.[75]

Party leaders were most interested in the antiwar work that occurred in the shops. It was the Third Period, after all, and party activists were to focus on workers and class conflict, not privileged students training to enter the middle class. Leaders' desires, however, were undermined by the attention received and activity initiated by YCL members at the University of Chicago and at other schools in the city.

A headline of the April 1932 *Daily Maroon* announced, "Communism Comes to Campus! Form Chapter of League." The league in question was the National Student League, an organization that appealed to a core of the nation's most radical students due to its disdain for liberalism, its critique of America's economic and political system, its willingness to uphold the Soviet model for emulation, and its implicit tie to the American Communist party, with its commitment to labor and unemployed struggles and its relationship to Soviet Russia. Walter Quinn, one of the University of Chicago NSL's graduate-student members, confirmed this commitment to reporters for the *Daily Maroon*, stating that the NSL was building a movement "'against the present narrow confines of the capitalistic order.'" To do this, NSL members pledged to "take the part of the worker at all opportunities, and to participate in strikes and picketing about the city."[76] It was with workers that NSL members felt a common bond, "for the holder of the Ph.D. is as unlikely to find work under the present regime of economic exploitation and capitalistic rule as is the laborer."[77]

Revolutionary rhetoric and class ideology ensured that the NSL never became a mass movement, and yet the size of its membership and the numbers who attended its open meetings reveal a larger interest in leftist politics among college students than had existed up to that time.[78] According to the *Daily Maroon*, the NSL counted seventy-five members within a few weeks of its birth. One open meeting brought in five hundred, and weekly discussion and study groups attracted thirty to forty students a session. In April 1933, the University of Chicago's NSL began publishing its own newspaper, *The Upsurge*. Its first edition sold over 450 copies, and it was selling 650 by the end of 1934.[79]

In no way did all of these members identify as Communists. In a *Daily Maroon* interview, the chairman of Chicago's NSL and YCL member Julius Hauser stated that the league was "overwhelmingly non-Communist" and that his Communist viewpoint was "but a minority here." Hauser emphasized that "Republican, Democrat, Socialist, Communist, in short any political brand of student, is invited to become a member." The only hitch was that members had to be committed to work toward a "changed social order."[80]

Of course, the party had an interest in shaping the tone and activity of the group, but its hands-off approach toward the YCL and the character of YCL members meant that YCL actions within the NSL were fairly free from direct party control. One report from 1934 indicated that the YCL had started with a campus unit of fourteen members that grew to twenty-one, but even in that unit ideological conformity was ephemeral. After all, at the University of Chicago YCL members came from different walks of life than those in the stockyards. A YCL leader explained, "There were all sorts of people in the YCL, daughters of corporation lawyers, army generals, etc., with such people in a unit, I think it is obvious that it was a difficult thing to fight for a real clear cut line on the University campus."[81]

That the NSL found any appeal at the University of Chicago speaks to the changes that college students underwent in the early Depression years. As Robert Cohen describes, 1932 was a pivotal year in the attitudes of college students across the nation. It was the first peacetime year that college enrollments fell, causing a spiral effect on campus budgets and erosion of the optimistic tenor on campuses. Cohen notes that faculty found students more interested in understanding the world around them, particularly concerned about why the Depression started and how it could be stopped. Such concerns extended beyond campus to working people and low-income students. Student confidence of the 1920s was slowly wearing away as the nation entered its third and fourth years of economic turmoil. Young people's futures were uncertain; upward mobility was not a guarantee.[82]

These national trends were reflected at the University of Chicago. Drawing on Chicago-area high schools for its student body, the university served as one road to opportunity for the city's white youth.[83] The entering class of 1932 had more fathers in middle-class occupations than classes of the 1920s, and far fewer students were self-supporting. Mary Dzuback argues that the increasingly middle-class character of Chicago's students indicates that they "expected to support themselves after they finished formal schooling, and it is highly unlikely that they perceived their higher education in isolation from these future plans."[84]

With an increased concern for the world around them, NSL students found themselves at a campus ripe for organizing. One student commented in the campus newspaper, "There seems to be no question that there is a rapidly growing radical group on this campus. And it seems to be a group willing to get out and demonstrate its beliefs. ... We hail this group of students who are sufficiently wide-awake and interested in current affairs to organize these movements, be their political affiliations what they may. They are at least sincere enough in their convictions to get out and win supporters. They are at least doing something. Undergraduates are too frequently not to be found in that category when social concerns are at stake."[85]

The University of Chicago had emerged in its earliest days as a model modern university with strong research traditions among its faculty, ties to the city's neighborhood and cultural institutions, and a liberal undergraduate education. Even before its students became more receptive to leftist ideas, a small core of its faculty delivered public lectures on Marx and Lenin, brought local leftists in for talks, and reported on their own observations of Soviet Russia. The Socialist club, the Cosmos club, a political science club, and the debate club sponsored lectures and discussions on social, economic, and political questions, but 1932 began a new era on campus where young people acted more than they talked, and they initiated their own activity rather than relying on faculty or party leaders.

Signs that students were willing to back words with action began to emerge in the spring of 1932, when the Communist party and the YCL planned an antiwar demonstration outside of the Japanese consulate in the middle of the city. Arguing against Japanese militarism and aggression in China, NSL students distributed leaflets at the University of Chicago and Northwestern University, with "several groups of students" from each campus attending. Mingling with a group of five thousand, including fifty Chinese observers, students watched as "hundreds of police on foot, horse, and motorcycle as well as squad car" battled to disperse the crowd. Police gunfire resulted in a few injuries; police arrested twenty-seven demonstrators, a few of whom were University of Chicago students.[86]

Shortly after this antiwar protest, University of Chicago students joined with other college and high-school students in a march on Samuel Insull's home, protesting his stake in the oppressive conditions in Kentucky's Harlan County coal mines. Promptly arrested by Chicago's police, these young radicals were joining in a cause with young activists on the East Coast. Students there desired to bring attention to the oppressive conditions of the striking Harlan County miners. Eighty delegates from the East headed out with supplies to aid the striking miners and witness their conditions. Stopped at the Kentucky border by a district attorney and armed deputies, the students were accused of being "revolutionists." Appeals to governors and officials in Washington did not change the outcome. Concluding that coal operators were able to "keep from the outside world the knowledge of living and working conditions of thousands of miners, citizens of the United States," one young activist spoke for a growing pool of young people who were learning lessons in corporate and state power.[87]

Shortly after the Kentucky rides and the Insull picketing, students in Chicago decided they would survey conditions in Illinois's coalfields. Some 150 Chicago students and teachers convened at the University of Chicago and began their journey to southern Illinois, but as the students experienced in Kentucky, authorities held them off. The sheriff of Browning County gripped a shotgun and declared that "no agitation is needed in Franklin County just now." This reaction was all that most of the delegation needed to turn back, but five members managed to avoid the sheriff. They were eventually arrested and, according to an NSL leader, "learned, for the first time in their lives, what the inside of a backwoods jail is like."[88]

Connections with a larger student movement and a concern for changes across society continued with the calling of the first Student Congress against War, held in Chicago in December 1932. According to military intelligence reports, two hundred elected student delegates from Chicago's high schools, colleges, and universities attended the conference. Crane Junior College sent about one hundred students and fifty teachers. Crane's night school was responsible for sixty-one of the student delegates. Tuley High School held a student assembly and elected thirty-five delegates, with almost as many teachers from that school attending. Teachers at Hyde Park High let some female students take ten minutes in classes to promote the conference. Roosevelt, Marshall, Harrison, and Lane high schools also provided delegates, along with the YMCA College, the Lewis Institute, Northwestern University, and the University of Chicago.[89]

Joining their two hundred with five hundred students from around the country, Chicago's delegates listened to Joseph Cohen of Brooklyn College, who four months earlier had attended the Amsterdam World Congress against War as the NSL delegate. He warned that "during the war years college laboratories were used for gas production; colleges were army training camps." Capitalism, he instructed, was the cause of all wars. They also heard a message sent from Theodore Dreiser and read by Henry Sloan Coffin of the Union Theological Seminary. Earl Browder and Upton Close debated the merits of pacifism, and Jane Addams and Scott Nearing lectured on how to ensure peace. At night, delegates broke into study groups and worked on militarism on campus and student and worker opposition to war.

That jeers and shouts poured forth when Jane Addams and Upton Close promoted a pacifist perspective rather than a Communist one is less intriguing than the fact that the congress, with its large non-Communist participation, went off at all. Despite their prejudice against broad movements, Chicago's Communist students were willing participants. Even Make Mills, the head of Chicago's Red Squad, commented on how readily Communists accepted non-party participants. Mills chalked up Communist self-control to the fact that "the Communist group was too yellow to make a fight on the floor." More likely, the Communist group was unwilling to alienate its new allies.[90]

Connections between college and high-school students proved to be important recruitment tools for the student movement. Quentin Young, a former YCL member, remembered living "in the shadow of the University of Chicago" as a student at Hyde Park High School, where students from the university would organize. Young recalls looking up to these who "stood the test of courage and dedication and leadership. Made me want to be that way."[91] Sometimes the connection between the university and the high-school activists was familial. Julius Hauser, an NSL leader and YCL member, was a former student at Hyde Park High; his sister Lillian, still attending high school, worked with Julius in recruiting for the Student Congress against War.[92]

Another important factor in bringing students to the antiwar cause was the nation's experience in World War I. As Robert Cohen points out, activists used lessons from the war as a message that citizens needed to prevent the country's entry into what they saw as another mistaken Armageddon. With their futures hanging in the balance, student activists increasingly questioned the values of business leaders and argued that the United States had entered the war for economic rather than moral reasons. The contemporary historian James Shotwell noted, "The tendency to find in economics the chief if not the sole cause of war has grown in the United States in recent years and has almost become an axiom in the thinking of the younger generation."[93] According to Cohen, students who grew up hearing stories of the war "felt threatened by the deterioration of international relations and the prospects of a war—a war which they knew could be even more devastating to their lives than had the Depression itself."[94]

Activism in high schools continued throughout 1933 and 1934, proving that heightened political interest was not confined to the college set. According to Chicago police arrest records, ten high-school students were arrested on the West Side on September 20, 1933, for distributing leaflets at Englewood High School, posting leaflets at Marshall High, and general "disorderly conduct." Such activity led to a demonstration organized by party and YCL groups against the German consulate the following day on Michigan Avenue, where seven people under the age of twenty were arrested.[95]

Such events provided the backdrop to a growing antiwar movement on Chicago's college campuses, spurred to action in part by Oxford University undergraduates who, in February 1933, resolved that they "will in no circumstances fight for King and Country." In May 1933, editors of the University of Chicago's student newspaper took a poll to determine student opinions on the war. Of 1,640 students responding, only 346 declared an interest in fighting in any war in which the United States participated. Over twice as many, 746, were not interested in fighting a war unless invaded, and 548 stood for peace no matter how provoked. Sentiment at the university differed from national student opinion. Nationally, more students refused to support war even in the event of an invasion than did at the University of Chicago. Still, a vibrant antiwar group coalesced at the university under the NSL's leadership.[96]

In January 1934, the University of Chicago's NSL announced its formal participation in a national student strike against war, which would occur on April 6, the anniversary of the U.S. entry into World War I. By March, the *Daily Maroon* announced that the strike would occur under a broad coalition called the United Antiwar Association, of which the NSL would be only one of the supporting groups. The united group welcomed all campus clubs and organizations and drafted a program that lent itself to inclusiveness among those opposed to war.[97]

On April 6, 1934, the United Antiwar Association called for students to leave their classes at eleven o'clock to join a parade, which would proceed around campus and stop at the Hutchins Circle. At noon, leaders would burn in effigy William Randolph Hearst for vigorously fanning the flames of war in his newspapers. Student speeches would follow the parade. In the weeks following, the committee planned a symposium on war and a two-day antiwar conference.[98] Campus newspaper reporters commented on the historic nature of this protest when they wrote, "A demonstration of this kind has not been held on the campus in recent years."[99]

Antiwar demonstration at the University of Chicago, April 13, 1935. (Chicago Historical Society, ICHi-21481, photograph: *Herald Examiner*)

The momentum from the strike resulted in wider contacts between leftist groups and antiwar groups on campus and in the community. The Student Union against War and Fascism was opened to anyone on campus who was interested in participating in demonstrations and discussions against war. On the University of Chicago's campus, the group reached out to fraternities and the general student body as well as such politically engaged groups as the Socialist club, a seminary group, the NSL, and the Cosmos club.[100]

Meanwhile, the campus's NSL affiliated with the American League against War and Fascism, where they made connections to antiwar groups in the city. Locally, these antiwar groups operated like the national American League against War and Fascism in bringing together Communist groups and prominent non-Communists opposed to war. Chicago's branch of the league included such prominent Communists as Bill Gebert but also an impressive array of non-party activists, including the University of Chicago professor Robert Morss Lovett, the Chicago Urban League's Arthur Falk, and the Socialist Ministerial Alliance's Rev. W. B. Waltmire. The organizing conference for the Chicago branch included twelve trade-union delegates, thirteen unemployed-organization delegates, fourteen labor-defense delegates, sixteen from political groups, twenty-nine from cultural organizations, eleven from fraternal organizations, three from church groups, and thirty-nine from youth organizations.[101] In this way, the antiwar movement at the University of Chicago fit within a national context of antiwar activity and antifascist movements, providing its students with information, resources, and credibility. Swept up in these movements, several of Chicago's youth activists would later risk their lives fighting against fascism in Spain.[102]

As antiwar momentum grew, the University of Chicago's administration tried to contain its student activists. When it denied permission to hold a protest in November 1934, Student Union activists proceeded anyway, resulting in the loss of their group's charter. Rather than quieting the students, however, the university's actions extended the issues. In this case, according to one Communist activist, students considered the "campaign against war and fascism more important than the trivial objections put forward by the Dean's office." Now, in the eyes of student activists, the campus was not only a place that nurtured militarism through its ROTC and research programs, but it also willingly stepped on "the most elementary rights of free speech and free assemblage."[103] Support for the Student Union quickly gathered from such groups as the debate union and the Fellowship of Socialist Christians of the Chicago Theological Seminary. Balking at the suggestion that their tuition dollars paid for "nothing more than a formal education," Chicago's student body began to discuss the need for "student rights," a new and poignant critique of the university's relationship to its students. Perhaps in an attempt to undermine the movement they saw building, the university administration did a quick turnaround and reinstated the Student Union.[104]

In the aftermath of the Student Union's fight for existence, the movement on campus against war grew and broadened. In January 1935, twelve student groups came together to discuss world peace at a campus symposium. In addition to the usual political characters, there were representatives from fraternities, the divinity school, and the campus band. The diversity of their backgrounds did not preclude a united position against war. The *Daily Maroon* reporter Wells Burnette observed, "[T]he most convincing peace poll conclusion reached by the meeting was that one hundred percent of the speakers who gave opinions on the matter would not bear arms for the United States in time of war!"[105] That April, a second national strike against war took place. This time, on the University of Chicago's campus an even broader committee, including the International Relations club, Social Problems club, YWCA, Socialist club, NSL, Research Union, Kappa Alpha Psi, and the Student League for Industrial Democracy, organized the event.[106]

And while student activism against war united the campus's small core of Communists with a broad group of the student body in a single cause, the campus and its alumni's response to an Illinois Senate investigation of Communists even more effectively speaks to the widespread acceptance of various political ideas in a college community. Although the investigation focused on professors and their teachings, the fact that Charles Walgreen's accusations of Communist influence at the university appeared only a few days after the student antiwar strike implied a broader attack on the university's politics as a whole.[107]

Ellen Schrecker and other scholars have traced back the cold-war repression of leftists in public schools and higher education to such investigations as the one instigated by the pharmacy mogul Walgreen.[108] The fact that the inquiry did not result in any firings does not lessen its oppressive tenor. Yet the overwhelming campus response to underplay his attack and to support teachings of all varieties sets this period apart from that of the 1950s and suggests some level of acceptance of the idea that the university is a place for the sharing of ideas.

Walgreen withdrew his niece, Lucille Norton, from the University of Chicago, convinced it was a hotbed of Communism. Committed to ridding the state's schools of Communist teachers, ideas, readings, and values, state senators followed Walgreen's action and launched an investigation into its schools. Led by five state senators, a committee assembled at the county commissioners' office in downtown Chicago, where Senator Charles Baker promised that his committee would "go the limit in its efforts to expose the subversive influences undermining student belief in our present form of government."[109]

Testimony at the hearings proved how overblown were Walgreen's accusations.

Walgreen himself testified that Norton's reading of the *Communist Manifesto* for her social science course convinced her that the "family as an institution was disappearing." She began questioning the values of business leaders in the country, thinking them greedy and wondering if the American system of government was the best model, inquiries that suggested critical thinking and reflected the sentiments of a growing number of people living through the Depression rather than any particular indoctrination. A few days before the hearings, Norton told a reporter that she had not been indoctrinated but had changed her mind. In response to a committee member's question about why she changed her mind, she replied that when asked she did not know what indoctrination meant and feared that it had to do with immoral sexuality. As a contemporary commented, "'The pathetic ignorance in her voice could not arouse even the hero-worshipping DAR. There were badly-concealed snickers in the room.'"[110]

Adding to the show was a "Mrs. Albert Dilling," an unabashed anti-Communist who saw Soviet intrigue everywhere. Dilling testified, "'Yes, they are all affiliated with the Communists. Professor Robert Morss Lovett, Professor Schumann, Dean Gilkey. The whole university is filled with them.'" She also went on to accuse Supreme Court Justice Louis Brandeis and Senator William Borah of being Communists.[111]

It was not hard for the university's president, Robert Hutchins, and professors Frederick Schuman, Robert Morss Lovett, and Harry Gideonse, faculty members fingered as the main agitators, to make a compelling case against indoctrination. First of all, none of them was a Communist, although Schuman and Lovett sympathized and participated in Left-supported events. Second, they ably made the argument that the university is a place where people should "discuss important problems critically, objectively, and scientifically."[112]

Support for academic freedom expanded beyond the halls of the county building. As soon as Walgreen announced his charges, students, President Hutchins, alumni, politicians, and faculty rallied to the university's cause. One *Daily Maroon* column mocked Walgreen for his exaggerated perspective. In a fictionalized telephone conversation, Walgreen inquires about the number of Communists registered at the university. When the university administrator replies "fifteen," Walgreen shouts back, "Ah! Fifteen hundred! Full of 'em." When told that his niece was enrolled in a course in the social sciences, Walgreen replies, "Aha! Socialism!"[113]

Hutchins expressed his more serious approach in a radio broadcast a few days after Walgreen's initial accusation, making clear that he did not believe that the university made Communists by permitting students to "study and talk as they please." To him, Reds were created out of a revolt against "being treated like children." Students needed to understand differences in political theory. After all, Hutchins emphasized, the Communist Party of Illinois was on the state ballot. Should not students learn about political parties running in local and national elections?[114]

Taking the probe a bit less seriously, alumni planned their own version of a Red hunt. Together with the football team, alumni agreed to carry their own "clues, tear gas, bloodhounds, red bait, and traps" to the field house, where the football team would give a preview. Following the game, a *Daily Maroon* article reported, dinner would be served and the alumni chided, "Vodka, caviar, and black bread will be conspicuously absent from the menu." The evening promised to wrap up with a report of the "red hunt investigation" and a presentation from the "professors of Moscow" in the form of the strolling friars.[115] In addition, the friars joined the fray, inviting the investigating committee to a performance of the farce "In Brains We Trust," which satirized the Walgreen accusation as well as other campus and national issues.[116]

Support from off-campus sources poured in. In one case, General Assembly-man James Monroe publicly reproached Walgreen for withdrawing his niece from the university. Arguing that he wanted his five children to "learn all there is to know about Communism, and all it leads to," Monroe called Walgreen a "foolish uncle."[117] Letters of support for the university's liberal stand and "intelligent exploration of all subjects" arrived from the Rosenwald Family Association, and testimony from Swift and Company's vice president and director and University of Chicago trustee Harold H. Swift showed the broad-based resistance to Walgreen's accusations.[118]

Since the point of the inquiry was to ferret out those who indoctrinated students and promoted violent overthrow of the system, testimony supporting academic freedom and critical inquiry were appropriate. Some leftists still criticized those who testified that no Communists taught at the university or promoted the overthrow of the system, arguing that denial seemed to justify the question. But that a significant core of faculty, administrators, students, and off-campus supporters expressed the value of a liberal education, the importance of learning about different systems of thought, and the right of faculty to hold their own political beliefs as long as they did not indoctrinate students with such beliefs speaks to the fact that the context in which student activists operated in the 1930s was more open than in the post–World War II period. In response to accusations of indoctrination, administrators were forced to articulate the belief that students were able to think for themselves and that suppression of student activism only led to more of it. This lesson came in handy in the weeks following the hearings, when the NSL lost its campus charter for displaying its banner in an off-campus rally. A few weeks later, after campus protest coalesced, the dean reinstated the group.[119]

Outside the university, antiwar work grew among the city's nonstudent youth. The success of such work culminated in the building of the AYC, an organization that grew out of a United Front movement to address youth issues. Eventually winning influence in the organization, Communist and Socialist youth joined with Boy Scouts, Girl Scouts, young Zionists, and religious groups and established contacts with youth movements that were growing around the world. Through these contacts, the YCL helped create a national youth conference and the AYC, which in 1936 participated in the first World Youth Congress in Geneva, Switzerland. The organization claimed 1.7 million members; maintained the support of Eleanor Roosevelt, state senators, and members of Roosevelt's cabinet; and backed such Communist-friendly measures as the Workers' Unemployment Insurance Bill, an antiwar resolution, and an attack on the Civilian Conservation Corps.[120]

By July 1935, the YCL was no longer an embarrassment to party leaders. Instead, Earl Browder highlighted YCL achievements in an article for the party's theoretical journal, *The Communist*. Browder asked, "How is it that the youth are making greater success than the Party with one-fourth the strength of the Party? They make twice or three times the advances in the united front that the Party generally does." According to Browder, it was "not that these youths are geniuses"; rather, it was young Communists' ability to "quickly adjust themselves to the tasks of the united front."[121] In fact, their adjustment had not been as quick as it was about to be for the rest of the party. Youth had been adjusting throughout the Third Period. The righteousness of their way was only beginning to be recognized as a model for the new order of the day.

Epilogue

In July 1935, Georgi Dimitroff, an antifascist Bulgarian revered by the Communist party for his role in a conspiracy to burn down the German Reichstag, stood before 513 delegates from sixty-five countries gathered in Moscow for the Comintern's Seventh World Congress. Dimitroff heralded the turn from the ultrasectarian Third Period to the Popular Front. In reaction to Hitler's consolidation of power in Germany, the congress agreed that Communists the world over should seek broad, cross-class alliances to unite progressive forces against fascism. As for Roosevelt, Dimitroff suggested, U.S. Communists should make distinctions between him and "the most reactionary circles of American finance capital" who were "stimulating and organizing the fascist movement in the United States."[1] For the first time in their history, Communists officially welcomed Socialists and middle-class reformers into their coalitions; they put their goal of class revolution to bed; and they busied themselves with campaigns to undermine fascism. With more room to determine their daily operations, party leaders in the United States encouraged patriotic themes and American culture in party work. Between 1935 and 1938, American Communists reinterpreted the precise meaning of the Popular Front as it related to third parties, Roosevelt's New Deal, and organizing strategies.[2] And yet their overall emphasis on antifascism resulted in successful local coalition building in antifascist campaigns, unemployed organizing, industrial union drives, civil rights activism, and a surge in party membership. As Mark Naison argues, "The Popular Front developed into a unique U.S. chemistry, a vision of a nation repudiating ethnic prejudice and class privilege and employing the strength and resilience of its common people to prevent a fascist triumph."[3]

Four years later, however, news that Stalin signed a nonaggression pact with German leaders threatened American Communists' place in these coalitions, their membership base, and any sense that they acted independently of the Soviet Union. Yet while criticism against Communists increased from all political directions, Chicago's party lost relatively few members. One and a half years later, Hitler broke the pact, and the Soviet Union became America's ally in a popular war. On the surface, the conditions of the Popular Front had been restored, but the fact of the pact and its startling consequences—German and Soviet occupation of Poland; Russian annexation of Estonia, Latvia, and Lithuania; and the Russian invasion of Finland—remained. How did Communists understand these shifts, and how did these policy changes affect their local activism? In what ways did the Third Period prepare Chicago Communists for the Popular Front, what happened to them once they got there, and what does their experience say about Communism in the United States? The purpose of this epilogue is to project, in broad strokes, the themes raised throughout this book into the Popular Front.

Soviet ties challenged Communist claims to democratic and patriotic impulses. An international gathering in Moscow planned the shift to a more American party, and throughout the Popular Front, the American party leaders Earl Browder and William Z. Foster battled before Moscow's leaders, each seeking support for their domestic and foreign policies. Stalinist purges cast a further shadow on Communists' outward appearance of openness and progressivism. And democratic centralism still ruled with a strong hand, so that when Soviet leaders agreed to a nonaggression pact with Hitler, local party members made it make sense.[4]

In important ways, the Popular Front unleashed practical politics and tactics even when Communists acted within Marxist-Leninist confines. The party's call for a Popular Front sanctioned activities that some Chicago Communists had begun in the Third Period and created new opportunities to further an agenda the party increasingly shared with liberals: racial equality, progressive coalition building, advocacy for the Soviet Union, and a belief that industrial union building through the CIO and the New Deal were important agents of social change.

In the United States, the Popular Front became more than a Communist party strategy; it was a social movement created out of the political realities of the day. By 1935, the battles that urged the National Labor Relations Act and created the CIO and that rallied groups in solidarity with Spain, Ethiopia, and China convinced liberals to look past their troubled history with Communists and use party members' organizational skills and energy for progressive causes. The second generation of immigrants who straddled the post–World War I and post–World War II Red Scares created successful coalitions and industrial drives by uniting with Communists. Welcoming their invitation into these liberal and at times middle-class circles, Communists downplayed their affiliations and got to work.

Existing local party records for the Popular Front era, published records, and firsthand accounts indicate that Communists' pragmatism and flexibility characterized these broad alliances.[5] Moscow's position was only one factor shaping the experience of rank-and-file Communists during the Popular Front.

Communists' newfound popularity made the Molotov-Ribbentrop Pact and its consequences particularly difficult for local activists. The agreement devastated Communists' allies, especially those who were Jews, intellectuals, and/or middle-class sympathizers. Yet even with the loss of some fellow travelers, the party's own forces were not seriously depleted during this year-and-a-half-long hiatus in the Popular Front. Local party experiences explain their persistence in Chicago; the Soviet Union's about-face in 1939 did not seriously affect the work of most local Communists who pushed for civil rights, fought for the unemployed, and organized industrial unions. As Claude Lightfoot stated, "From 1935 onward, the Black and labor movements became the main spark plugs igniting the engines of the struggle."[6] Ties Communists had forged in the black community, in unemployed organizing, and within the labor movement offered them local networks and concrete issues that overshadowed unpopular international twists.

And yet local Communist support of the nonaggression pact, the Soviet invasion of Poland, and war against Finland show that Chicago's Communists were not too different from those around the country in what Maurice Isserman characterizes as their "determination to carry on despite isolation and persecution, and their utter inability to admit to and act on their own doubts."[7] As a result, the period of the pact widened the circle of those who saw the tragedy in American Communists' determination to hitch their fate to Stalin and the Soviet Union and exposed one of the ironies of the supposedly ultrademocratic Popular Front: the Communist party itself was probably less democratic than in the period before. To be sure, in the months between the signing of the pact and U.S. entry into World War II, reverence for the Soviet Union and its Socialist experiment carried new ethical dimensions. Chicago's Communists faced them locally.

Becoming a More American Party

The turn to the Popular Front required a reworking of the party's organization to make it more accessible to the masses while strengthening Communists' ties to America's political traditions. The Communist leader F. Brown explained, "In brief, we must *Americanize* the Party in its form and structure, in its simplicity, in its practicality." In the place of its Bolshevik-styled apparatus, the Chicago party, under directives from above, switched to a more moderate and American form of organization. Instead of a district structure headed by secretariats and buros, the party functioned through state organizations led by secretaries and executive committees. Sections became county committees; street units became branches. The party deemphasized shop fractions, semi-secret small groups concerned with the problems of the shop floor, and eventually dissolved them, creating in their place industrial units with a broader focus on issues that faced workers as a whole.[8] Geographical areas, previously units and sections, now followed U.S. electoral-district lines, such as wards and counties, allowing the Communist party to increase the size of their local units and to more closely resemble other parties in the country. With larger branches positioned within electoral districts, Communists would look more respectable to potential recruits than they had appeared in small unit gatherings. Larger branches, moreover, would allow for more leadership to develop and for more work to be accomplished.[9]

In addition to making changes within their own internal organization, party leaders encouraged the work that had been occurring within a number of mass-based organizations. Browder explained that Communists should get involved in "Negro organizations, church organizations of all kinds, neighborhood clubs, Parent-Teachers Associations, every kind of organization, including Republican and Democratic neighborhood clubs, Townsend organizations, EPIC and Utopian and all the rest of that type of grouping." And rather than Third Period behavior, where Communists were to "try immediately to stand up and let everybody know 'here is a Communist coming to give us leadership,'" Browder informed them that they should "modestly become part of the organization, speaking to the members from the point of view of helping to solve the problems for which they come together."[10]

Chicago's party schools reflected the Popular Front's culture. Branch classrooms changed their curriculum and, instead of Third Period offerings on Marxism-Leninism, ran such topical classes as "The Problems and Issues in 1936," "Current Events," and "Who Rules the U.S.?" School organizers reported good attendance and planned summer classes for neighborhood schools on other "popular subjects."[11] Question-and-answer methods replaced formal lecture style, reportedly enhancing students' enjoyment and participation. A South Side school reported that "80 or 90 per cent of the students participated actively in the discussion."[12] Of the 347 students registered in the spring term in 1935, three-quarters were proletarian and reflected an "overwhelming majority" of young people, a significant change from Third Period student profiles. Moreover, since only six or seven of the students were party members and another forty-seven were YCL members, the schools provided the party with a means of outreach.[13]

Party leaders' more encouraging attitudes towards members' families and friends reflected other Popular Front changes. Brown encouraged fellow Communists that "[o]ne of the good qualities of a Communist is his keeping close to his dear ones and to his friends, bringing them closer to the revolutionary movement and into the Party." He argued that Communists had to learn how to become "patient and persistent" with fellow workers, friends, and family members. They had to learn how to be modest and how to "avoid breaking relations with fellow-workers and friends because of disagreements on insignificant and petty questions."[14] Thus when Relford, a Communist on Chicago's South Side, recruited his wife, daughter, and two sons, party leaders proudly reported the event.[15] By avoiding sectarianism, long meeting hours, and antifamily attitudes, leaders wanted outsiders to get close to the party. To that end, their new structures, style, and attitude made it easier for members like Relford to be "good" Communists.

Communists drew upon the culture of American democracy in their fight against fascism. The "Star-Spangled Banner" and the American flag became new additions to large Communist gatherings. Party leaders praised Thomas Jefferson and portrayed their struggle as carrying on that of Abraham Lincoln and John Brown. Earl Browder coined the phrase "Communism is twentieth-century Americanism," and Chicago's party paper, the *Midwest Daily Record*, declared itself "of the people, by the people, for the people." The *Daily Worker* also underwent significant changes, adding a daily sports page, popular-culture coverage, and a Sunday magazine that blended popular culture with American revolutionary traditions. Chicago's statewide Communist convention reportedly opened in a "blaze of color" with "America's revolutionary traditions . . . pictorially represented." Michael Gold summed up party thinking: "When you run the news of a strike alongside the news of a baseball game, you are making American workers feel at home. . . . Let's loosen up. Let's begin to prove that one can be a human being as well as a Communist. It isn't a little special sect of bookworms and soapboxers."[16]

Such changes boosted party membership. In the period from 1936 through 1938, the number of Communist districts increased from twenty-seven to almost forty, and Communists organized in forty-eight states. Membership grew from 23,760 members in October 1934 to 55,000 members by May 1938. Even smaller districts, such as those in Florida, Oklahoma, and Texas, witnessed monumental increases.[17]

Party leaders, moreover, could boast that the social composition of their ranks had improved. By 1936, a majority was employed, and a large proportion was trade unionists.[18] A 1938 breakdown of recruits showed that 22 percent were in white-collar occupations, such as teachers, doctors, social workers, psychologists, and lawyers; and Nathan Glazer estimated that by 1941, "[N]o less than

44 percent of the Party was reported as professional and white-collar." The 1937 through 1938 recruiting drive showed, moreover, that a majority of recruits now were native-born. By the party's Tenth Convention in 1939, 80 percent of the delegates were born in the United States. Among those, the party saw increases in its numbers of women and youth. Rosalyn Baxandall noted that female membership increased from 10 percent of the membership in 1930 to 50 percent by 1943. Meanwhile, the YCL increased from eight thousand in 1935 to approximately twenty thousand in 1938. Ethnic workers continued in the party's orbit through mass organizations such as the IWO, which supported the party through donations to its causes, speakers at its forums, and participation at its rallies. In 1934 the IWO numbered sixty-two thousand members and grew to 141,364 by 1938.[19]

Chicago's party experienced a similar pattern of growth: 3,303 members in 1934 became 5,750 in 1938.[20] And in 1936, Chicago's leaders reported that 70 percent of their new recruits were born in the United States.[21] Like the national party, increases among white-collar workers and intellectuals provided Chicago's Communists with connections to a broad base of supporters. Dr. Maurice Simpkin, a surgeon and IWO member, for example, often lent his home to party leaders for meetings. And a growing group of doctors and lawyers offered Communists their services at a discount. But perhaps more important was an extended network of middle-class support. Blanche Lowenthal, a "wealthy widow," for example, offered money to Communist causes and her home for functionary gatherings. An increasingly large number of writers also weaved in and out of party circles. Chicago's leftist writers and artists maintained a fluid community, joining Chicago's Repertory Group, working for the Illinois Writers' Project, and contributing to leftist publications such as the *New Anvil*. Douglas Wixson wrote of one "commune" of party supporters, Karl Marx Hof, where "cheap . . . beer was bought in quantities and sold for ten cents a glass to raise money for various causes such as the CP's workers' school." Dixon found that many of these intellectual leftists "felt themselves to be part of the movement without participating directly in Party activities."[22]

Chicago's party, like the national party, also witnessed an influx of women, yet local critics rightly charged that "we could have more women in the Party, if the men comrades did not adopt the attitude that the Party is not for women."[23] Chicago's leaders noted that women had become more active in party schools and were increasingly numerous among their recruits, but leaders' continued emphasis on male trade unionists had its effect. Of the 171 people recruited in February 1936, forty-nine were women. This ratio, running between 25 and 30 percent of new recruits, continued at least through 1938, when out of 240 South Side Recruits, sixty-one were women.[24]

Party leaders still believed that women should wait for Socialism before fighting for equality, and they opposed the Equal Rights Amendment because they believed it to be anti–working class. Although their opposition had some basis, and other liberal groups also challenged the amendment, the party's attacks were indicative of its larger attitudes concerning women's roles. Its papers tied women to beauty and housekeeping, encouraging party women to maintain societal norms of fashion and beauty. Chicago's *Midwestern Daily Record* taught women how to make the home more livable. Writers told women how to open stubborn jars, make hard sauce, and remove white spots on dark furniture. Jean Lyon wrote an article entitled "There's More than One Way to Nag." In fact, there were three ways, according to Lyon: the whining nag, the weeping nag, and the shouting nag. Each posed serious problems for their husbands. Women were advised to change their ways and make it easier for men, for example, to put their feet up on furniture. After all, Lyons consoled, women could comfort themselves "with the thought that 'at least he doesn't spit tobacco on the wall.'"[25]

While these attitudes persisted within the party, women began a dialogue on their role that challenged the notion that they were subordinate. Drawn into campaigns against the high cost of living and into union drives through women's auxiliaries, they found the Communist party receptive to their issues. Joining with such wide-ranging groups as the Parent Teachers' Association and the Packinghouse Workers Organizing Committee, Communist women began to challenge their place in the party and society at large. On March 23, 1939, the Communist activist Jane March wrote to the *Midwest Daily Record*: "'[F]illers' . . . don't mean a thing to the average woman. . . . [I]n the issue of March 10, the whole column on 'how to win husbands and influence lights' . . . who has time to remove all the chandeliers and sit under certain lights? . . . I would suggest a reader's column ask the women to write in on such subjects as problems in child care, home, food, style, trade union, club, PTA. . . . Yours for a real women's page."[26] Other women called for the paper's editors to give more space to women's biographies and argued with party leaders that too little attention was paid to women's activities in Chicago. Meanwhile, women like Jane March and Beatrice Shields, who led women's work and guided educational activity in the city, served as role models for younger party women who were having their first political experiences organizing their communities. The YCL member Yolanda Hall remembered women like Shields pushing for women's rights within the party, providing Hall a new sort of model for women's activism.[27]

The YCL provided a structure to organize and educate young radicals. Henry Winston explained that education within the league should "bring the youth to the point of understanding the need for a new society." This meant participating in "practical activity . . . a service organization, first, to the labor movement and, second, to all mankind." Winston explained that Communists needed to model themselves on Christian organizations, which "take into consideration the youthful desires of these people—sports, amusements, classes, dramatics, handicrafts, etc., and by taking as a starting point the particular interest of the youth, they in turn can build a large organization."[28]

During the Popular Front, they did just that. Reports of YCL social activities appear throughout the *Midwest Daily Record*. In April 1938, they held a Sweet Sixteen dance at the Free Sons of Israel Hall, celebrating sixteen years of YCL growth. And on October 26, 1938, the YCL announced that it would hold a Halloween Ball in the Majestic Hotel's ballroom, featuring swing music and costumes. But YCLers did more than throw parties. The Chicago YCL was also an important vehicle for organizing industry, with its own shop-floor organizations. The YCL group in meatpacking, for example, effectively aided the party group in the stockyards. This combination of socializing and political work increased the YCL's membership. In 1934, Chicago had only 325 YCL members, but by 1938 it had over two thousand.[29]

Leaders were especially proud of their work among African American youth and women. In 1939, a Harriet Tubman club on the South Side affiliated with the YCL, and another YCL affiliate, the Oliver Law club, published a leaflet hailing the Soviet Union's twenty-second anniversary. In the party branch that covered Washington Park and the University of Chicago, leaders announced that in 1938 they recruited 336 men and women. "The most important thing in our recruiting drive," the section organizer wrote, "was this: up until last year, it was almost impossible for us to recruit Negro women on the South Side of Chicago, with the exception of old women. Well, we have not stopped recruiting older women, but during the campaign we have gone out and brought into the Party many of the young women of the South Side." Of the 145 women brought in during this particular campaign, none was over forty-five years old.[30]

While party directives reframed inner party life, easing Communists' reach to broader networks of supporters, their success was not simply a result of a shift engineered in Moscow and followed by the rank and file mechanically. Chicago's Communists created strong precedents for this shift in their own work, and the success and breadth of the Popular Front depended on workers themselves. Throughout this period, workers were increasingly willing to join across ethnic and gender lines to promote class-based causes.

The Depression exposed the inability of community-based institutions to support workers who suffered in a broken economy. Slowly, Chicago's white ethnics and African Americans looked beyond their segregated communities to the government and new union structures of the CIO. Lizabeth Cohen has argued that this shift was possible because a "culture of unity" permeated Chicago's neighborhoods and workplaces. Throughout the 1920s, workers' ethnic institutions began to reflect more mainstream commercial ones. National chains made their way into Chicago's ethnic enclaves, integrating its workers into a national mass culture. No longer local and ethnic, movie theaters, grocery stores, and radio reinforced the decline of ethnic institutions and the rise of a shared cultural community. Organizations such as the CIO allowed workers to focus on their commonalities with fellow workers. The timing of such an organization allowed organizers to succeed when they placed special attention on creating a militant alliance of black and white workers. Observers noted that the "'arguments of the CIO were taking effect on the men'" because "'the presence of Negro organizers and the reputation of the UMW are tending to allay the old ideas as to discrimination by labor unions against [Negroes].'"[31] Women and families also played an important role in the CIO's bid to unite workers. And although they mostly strengthened industrial unions through their place within women's auxiliaries, the new attitude toward unity proved powerful to many women who joined unions and walked picket lines for the first time in their lives.

Reaching into racial and ethnic communities, the CIO pulled together a coalition based on workers' unity symbolized on CIO union buttons and lived in spaces such as bars, CIO corners, and meeting halls. Broadening their scope from one workplace to working people in general, CIO organizers developed campaigns in support of workers in other industries and on different worksites. Picketing, picnics, and solidarity statements sealed this workers' front. Cohen argued that "workers in different industries in Chicago similarly had come to understand that their fates were intertwined." They spoke of being a member of the CIO rather than of the Packinghouse Workers Organizing Committee, the United Electric, Radio, and Machine Workers Union, or the Steel Workers Organizing Committee. And while Cohen does not credit Communists with this development, they were central figures, furthering union workers' unity-consciousness.[32]

The culture of the Popular Front, moreover, embraced the imagination of these working people and their liberal allies. Using the phrase "laboring of American culture," Michael Denning's work explains the Popular Front phenomenon whereby workers themselves increasingly created and received American culture, a culture that seriously dealt with questions of fascism, war, work, and civil rights. Denning argues that "the phrase reminds us that the culture and politics of the Popular Front were not simply New Deal liberalism and populism. It was a social democratic culture, a culture of 'industrial democracy' and 'industrial unionism.'" Chicago workers' renditions of "Steel Strike" reinforced their common proletarian bond with their audience.[33]

A new generation of people created this workers' culture in the 1930s, and in turn, these processes reshaped their attitudes towards uniting across racial, ethnic, and political barriers. Denning argued that the culture of this working class "was marked by a sustained sense of class consciousness and a new rhetoric of class, by a new moral economy, and by the emergence of a working-class ethnic Americanism." Immigrants learned throughout the 1920s how to become American within their individual ethnic neighborhoods and by the 1930s created a second-generation ethnic, working-class culture that formed a stronghold of the Popular Front. Denning argued that "under the sign of the 'people,' the Popular Front public culture sought to forge ethnic and racial alliances, mediating between Anglo-American culture, the culture of the ethnic workers, and African-American culture, in part by reclaiming the figure of 'America' itself, imagining an Americanism that would provide a usable past for ethnic workers, who were thought of as foreigners, in terms of a series of ethnic slurs."[34]

With its growing membership and reconstructed organization, Chicago's Communist party was well positioned to participate in this new vitality. Communists successfully worked with non-party members in the Workers' Alliance, brought welfare issues before the nation, and won several battles in Chicago. They stood in support of Spain; and through their brigades, parades, and fundraisers, Communists' support for the Spanish Republic won them liberals' praise. On the South Side, party members protested Italy's invasion into Ethiopia and explained African American oppression in terms of expanding fascism, pointing out that blacks in particular encountered fascism through their lack of housing, high rents and costs of living, denials of civil rights, wage differentials, and impaired cultural development. They also tapped ethnic and racial community organizations to build on the unity represented by the CIO. Their participation in the city's major CIO drives, moreover, made Communists' commitment was central to the growth of industrial unionism.[35]

The party's own culture during the Popular Front, then, fit with that of Chicago's workforce. No longer an animal of clandestine meetings, the party adapted to the mass media and culture of the mid-to-late 1930s and 1940s. Broadcasting from local radio stations, Communists used modern technology to unite workers behind its programs and encouraged people to meet in groups to listen to scheduled shows. Communists in many ways were becoming the best examples of the new mid-1930s Popular Front Americanism.[36]

The Popular Front not only increased Communist membership among certain groups of Chicago's population, it increased the party's general prestige and support. Communist leaders noted that people began to identify themselves as Communists without actually joining the party. In 1938, Brown recognized that "tens of thousands of workers, professionals, and farmers" had "sympathetically followed our Party for the last few years," and he acknowledged that "[t]housands of these would like to be part of our family. They even call themselves Communists and act as Communists." Further acceptance of Communists was demonstrated in the 1938 *Chicago Defender* Bud Biliken parade. A student following the YCL's float, with its "Black and White Unite" and "Free the Scottsboro Boys" slogans, reported that a "wave of applause followed the float along the whole route. Old women shouted, 'Yes, free the boys!' People noted: 'Them's the Communists. They don't believe in no differences. All's alike to them.'" From this student's report, Horace Cayton and St. Clair Drake concluded that "Bronzeville demonstrated that it approved of whatever the Communists stood for in its mind."[37]

Thus, the party's heyday was framed by several factors. Rank-and-file Communists, who already began courting non-Communist progressives during the Third Period, set the stage for a more coordinated drive during the Popular Front. International directives shaping party structures allowed Communists to create an organization that more easily fit into the American landscape. And workers, forced by the Depression into new solutions, were more willing to unite across political and cultural boundaries.

Roots of the Popular Front's Decline

Coalitions formed during the Popular Front were built on somewhat unstable foundations that were eventually eroded by international and local forces. Despite the reformist nature of the Popular Front, Communists faced problems that lingered from the Third Period. How would they continue to spread their revolutionary ideology and at the same time build the party?[38] The Soviet Union handed them new problems. What effect did the Molotov-Ribbentrop Pact have on Chicago's Communists? Local experience showed that while some party members enforced Communist mandates and were unwilling to acknowledge contradictions, inconsistencies, or moral dilemmas, others wavered. Chicago's Communists remained a mixed bag even as international events brought them closer to one another and, for a time, farther from everyone else.

Communist ethnics maintained their independent streak into the Popular Front. During a *Daily Worker* drive, Chicago's leadership found that its language groups were not doing their part to raise money. When the *Ny Tid* needed money, the Scandinavian buro raised $250 in one week; but in the eight-week drive for the *Daily Worker,* they barely raised $80. The South Slav buro acted similarly. A bigger concern, however, was the way the language members separated their activities from the shop floor. Lawson complained, "We do not find the Polish Buro in packing, South Slav Buro in steel, nor the Slovaks and Lithuanians in the coal fields." Chicago party leaders wondered why such buros as the Bulgarian did not have steel organizing on their agendas; and they discovered that among the Croatian fraction, there was much quarreling about how to work in clubs and lodges, no political discussion, and no orientation to "concentration" work. Although the party's leadership would have liked all of their members to actively work in a union and belong to an organization with ties to non-party members, not all Communists had the same aspirations.[39]

Those who were enthusiastic about union building, antifascism, and civil rights work created other problems as they abandoned older projects for positions in the CIO and in broad-based coalitions. While union leadership and mass organizations were ideal ways to reach working people, Communist involvement left such other party projects as Unemployed Councils barren and disorganized. As the Ninth Party Conference restructured the party into branches and industrial units, party leaders found that they did not have enough lower leaders to see the changes through; they were preoccupied with new activities.[40] Acting within unions and mass organizations, moreover, party members did not necessarily promote Communist initiatives. Instead, leaders continually criticized their fellow Communist unionists for focusing too much on trade-union issues and for not raising political ones. While many Communist CIO organizers became known for their fighting spirit, those in the AFL were a mixed bag. Party reports explained that their three AFL representatives on the Chicago Federation of Labor's central body could not get specific programs passed because they were lax in their responsibilities and did not win non-party delegates' respect.[41]

On the one hand, party leaders were concerned with members who blended into the mass population only too well; but on the other hand, they had to repeatedly remind members, especially older ones, that the Popular Front was a period in which to rid themselves of their sectarian ways. Browder warned Communists that their behavior that substituted "revolutionary impatience and desire for overthrow of capitalism for the hard work of winning the masses for the struggle to overthrow capitalism" had to end. Party leaders did not want a few good cadres but instead hoped to use the new structure and networks to "be among the millions."[42]

The party's organizational problems proved a real nuisance for leaders and consumed their energies throughout the period. But more serious problems would plague them. When the Soviet Union and Germany entered into a nonaggression treaty in 1939, the wheels of the Popular Front screeched to a grinding halt. Antifascism had become such an integral part of the party's program that its members and leaders could not imagine the Soviet Union moving away from its no-nonsense antifascist stand, but it did. Communists all over the United States were shocked by the news and photos of Joachim von Ribbentrop, the German foreign minister, and Stalin shaking hands. British and French appeasement was one thing, but Soviet appeasement was quite another. The term "Communazi," coined by a reporter in September 1939, filled mainstream newspapers, taunting the party faithful.[43]

Whereas before the signing of the nonaggression pact, Communists could argue that they acted on the behalf of America's workers and in the interest of society as a whole, their about-face on alliances against Nazi Germany raised ethnical and political questions in intellectual and progressive communities. Communists lost their moral authority and found themselves having to explain that in fact "Communism" and "fascism" were different systems and political forces. The nonaggression pact betrayal, moreover, confirmed more conservative activists' suspicions that Communists would betray America's workers at any cost for the Soviet Union.

The *Daily Worker* tried to rationalize the pact as a blow to Nazi Germany. "By compelling Germany to sign a non-aggression pact, the Soviet Union not only tremendously limited the direction of Nazi war aims, but thereby bolstered the possibilities for peace in the world." Articles and editorials tried to convince readers that the party had not moved away from its antifascist stand but still stood for peace, freedom, and democracy. Browder himself argued that the pact "should strengthen Popular Front movements everywhere." And when war broke out in Europe, and Germany announced its intention to annex Poland, the American party went into full gear in support of Poland and the policies of Roosevelt, and against Germany.[44]

Like their counterparts on the national scene, Chicago's party leaders were eager to follow Soviet policies. They simply did not know how to interpret them, exactly. They did, however, know that they needed to defend the Soviet Union. When the staff of the Socialist *Jewish Daily Forward* organized an anti-Soviet meeting, Communists showed up to "expose speakers." At their own open-air meeting on St. Louis and Roosevelt Road, in the heart of a Jewish community, a Jewish Communist newspaper editor reportedly spoke to two thousand people who applauded as the speaker explained "how the Soviet German Pact was an aid to peace."[45] At least publicly, the party minimized the hypocrisy of the new Soviet policy, and for a short time they sought comfort in their Popular Front–type campaign to "Save Poland." In their grand style, Chicago's party organized a rally in defense of Polish independence which included Catholic priests, Jewish rabbis, and Chicago's civic and trade-union Polish leaders.[46]

On September 11, however, word reached national party leaders that Moscow was critical of the Polish government, insisted that the war was imperialist, and prohibited the American party from taking a side. American leaders quickly made an embarrassing about-face on the whole situation. Chicago leaders followed suit. On September 15, two days before the Soviets invaded Poland, Chicago's party paper announced a talk by Gebert, billed for "Chicago Poles who want to get the lowdown on the Nazi invasion of Poland." The party seemed unwilling to let go of its antifascist appeal, yet there were new developments in need of clarification: the role of Britain, France, and *the Polish government* in the situation. One can only imagine the response that Bill Gebert faced in his September 15 talk at Koscuisko Hall. Speaking in Polish to former party supporters, Gebert must have seemed like quite a traitor. Certainly Polish and South Slav workers in the city's stockyards and steel mills thought so. In these places, Communist organizers worked furiously to put down "embittered" opposition groups that linked them to the CIO as a whole and threatened to destroy their union drives. One Communist organizer reported on his difficulties holding Ukrainian and South Slav steel workers in line, "notwithstanding the fact that they were CP members or sympathizers of long standing." Work in the packinghouses was no better. Members of the Packinghouse Workers Organizing Committee's Polish American Committee had been raising money for Polish people and were understandably reeling from the recent turn of events.[47]

Chicago's progressive Jewish community, which had supported the party in the past, seethed with anger. Even though the party press hailed the Soviet Union as liberators of Eastern European Jews, Chicago's community understood that endorsing the pact meant turning their backs on Germany's and Poland's Jews, who were suffering a horrible fate. Party leaders noted that the circulation of their paper declined exclusively in Jewish neighborhoods, where Communists faced off against rabbis who delivered anti-Soviet messages to their congregations. One rabbi canceled a Communist speaker at his synagogue, and reports indicated that in the city's temples Jewish leaders distributed anti-Soviet articles by James Waterman Wise, the son of the noted New York rabbi Stephen Wise, who had been a party member until the pact.[48]

For many in and around the party, the Soviet Union's new policies and actions were indefensible. Members of the League for Peace and Democracy and the ILD, not to mention those in Jewish locals of the IWO, gave Chicago party leaders "particular difficulty," according to reports. Ben Gold, the international president of the Furriers Union, came to assist the Chicago union officials Abe Feinglass and Lewis Goldstein with what an informant described as a "crack up in that union due to the revolt of the radical Jewish members, who are threatening to secede on account of the Nazi-Soviet pact." An FBI agent reported, "The radical Jews apparently cannot stomach the implications of Stalin's cooperation with Hitler."[49] Soviet policies had backed the city's leaders into a corner. An FBI informant reported: "Among themselves, many of the American Communist leaders deplore the Non-Aggression pact entered into between Hitler and Stalin, as it has created considerable discontent in the American Party membership. However, they are doing their best to justify the Pact."[50]

Harvey Klehr argues that the Comintern helped the American party through the crisis of the period, but national and Chicago leaders also relied on their instincts and political realities.[51] While the Comintern sent word on how it wanted the American party to speak about the war and capitalism, Earl Browder balked when it came to immediately breaking with Roosevelt.[52] On the local level, Chicago leaders' dislike of Soviet policy caused some to advise their members to downplay unpopular policies and focus on local issues. William Patterson suggested that Communists would improve their influence among African Americans "if they would at least temporarily concentrate on other than war issues—such as relief, WPA, housing, equal rights, anti-lynching bills."[53] Concrete popular campaigns were where most party members felt comfortable. Herb March, the packinghouse union organizer, recalled how practical work overshadowed the ugly reality of Soviet foreign policy: "[The Nazi-Soviet pact] was difficult to defend—of course . . . these things didn't become . . . big . . . in the union because we were busy getting full recognition."[54] A letter from national party leaders showed that these impulses to downplay unpopular Soviet policies were not unique to Chicago. In general, party members were "too hesitant" when it came to "defending the peace policy of Soviet Russia." National leaders lamented that "in many instances comrades have remained silent even in the face of savage attacks against Soviet Russia by non-Party elements."[55]

The international turn of events unleashed terror at home against Communists at all levels. When Browder was arrested on false passport charges, Chicago's party leaders who had also traveled on fake passports suffered from what one informant described as a "serious case of the nerves." Meanwhile, the Dies Committee, the precursor to the House Committee on Un-American Activities established in May 1938 and chaired by Martin Dies, began to harass Communists and their former supporters from the League for Peace and Democracy, the American Student Union, and other such organizations. State and local governments also participated in the attack, indicting Communists under criminal syndicalist laws. An FBI informant reported on the mood of Chicago's party leaders: "There is no doubt that the CP leadership is greatly frightened at the turn of events. The leadership of today does not seem to have half the courage and energy of the leaders of twenty years ago, who openly fought every effort . . . to force them out of business or underground."[56]

Certainly, there was now more to lose than ever before, and Communist trade unionists understood this all too well. CIO momentum was building throughout the city, and party trade unionists were at its center. It is no wonder that John L. Lewis sent a surge of fear through party ranks when he made anti-Communist remarks at a CIO convention in Detroit. Word of Lewis's attack spread through Chicago's steel and packinghouse locals, and rumors surfaced that Sam Levin, vice president of the Amalgamated Clothing Workers' Union, was "conducting a whispering campaign against CIO leaders suspected of being Party members or sympathizers." Feverishly, William Z. Foster worked at the national level to keep CIO leaders from kicking Communists out of their union positions, and local Chicago Communists made their rounds to party unionists trying to lessen their panic. Regardless, key union activists began distancing themselves from the party.[57]

But generally speaking, despite such embarrassing shifts, ethical dilemmas, and ensuing attacks, party members remained loyal. Maurice Isserman explained that "[t]hose who stayed may not have been happy, and may have looked back wistfully on the golden days of Popular Front respectability. But they stayed." They felt, Isserman argued, that "this was a testing period in which they would have to prove their mettle." Chuck Hall remembered the period of the pact as "very confusing." Yet he believed that "it was a necessity for the Soviet Union to make that pact. . . . It was a self-defense to try and stop the invasion of the Soviet Union." Appeasement at Munich convinced him and other Communists that Western powers could not be relied upon for support against fascist aggression. While aligning their own interests with the safety of the Soviet Union, many Communists rationalized Soviet realpolitik, making themselves anathema to those committed to fascism's defeat.[58] FBI estimates of party membership indicate that approximately five thousand remained on Chicago's rolls during the period of the pact. Out of its 1938 membership of 5,750, only 13 percent of Chicago's members left, just under national rates of desertion. To the majority of Chicago's party members, Communism was more than any particular policy; it was a way of life, not easily disregarded.[59]

As time passed, state leaders began to reorganize the party for more public attacks and anti-Communist purges. Because they feared that they might have to go underground, they required state leaders to strengthen their secret apparatus and prepare for the party's illegality. Work would remain in a few trusted hands. Only one party member would be responsible for the organization, and only two or three leading members would know who that person was. Fred Brown and J. Peters prepared the secret work nationally, while Jack Parker trained Chicago's leaders on how to safeguard their members. Branches were to be led by members who were not in any immediate danger of prosecution and who worked outside of industry. Group meetings would occur early in the evening and away from union halls, and then the information would be transferred to the people working in industry.[60]

The party's position was morally and politically damaging, yet the new political context created an opening for Communists to tap into a popular peace sentiment. Among youth, Communists directed attention to the unfair draft and raised the possibility of increasing relief agencies' resources by cutting war spending. At the University of Chicago, Communists facilitated a coalition of eleven student groups into a Keep America Out of War Congress.[61] Communists also reenergized their campaign against the high cost of living to fight against war profiteers. By the summer of 1940, Chicago's Communists focused on organizing a nationwide peace mobilization and found some support in unions, fraternal benefit organizations, ethnic churches, and among students. To help popularize their effort, fur-shop representatives and a significant number of

National Maritime Union folks showed up to rally at the Chicago Stadium on Labor Day in 1940. The Communist Rev. John R. Thompson chaired the rally and led a committee that formed in its aftermath to carry national antiwar activity to Washington.[62] The new American Peace Mobilization (APM) worked for a national peace policy. With the slogan "For a People's Peace," the APM confronted those involved in war preparations with leaflets, pamphlets, and posters in opposition to war and organized a speakers' bureau with members who addressed trade-union meetings. In February the Illinois Communist party printed 250,000 leaflets in opposition to the Lend Lease Bill. Branches throughout Chicago issued their own leaflets. Mary Gordon, the leader of the APM work in Chicago, stated that more than seventy new groups were organized in February and that finally Communist party branches were working on these projects. Harry Haywood estimated that the APM "consisted of over 6,000 delegates representing the 12,000,000 people in trade unions, youth organizations, women's clubs, and Black groups." While Jewish neighborhoods were difficult to approach for obvious reasons, Italian and black neighborhoods proved more receptive. And by early 1941, state leaders were again talking about the improved work in the Midwest.[63]

Even as international shifts threatened local coalition activity and forced local leaders to pour their energies into the APM, many Popular Front projects stayed alive throughout this period. Although the symbolism of the Nazi-Soviet pact decimated Communists' contacts in middle-class and intellectual circles, by 1939 the momentum of the Popular Front and rank-and-file Communist activity focused on the CIO, welfare rights, and combating racial discrimination. The new membership brought into the party during the early years of the Popular Front carried their dedication to these causes across the period of the pact, and the war would bring eventually bring them back into the mainstream.

Local party activity thrived during the Popular Front, party membership grew to its highest numbers, and a new composite of Communists succeeded in initiating strong local movements. But the organization's dependency on Soviet shifts exposed its vulnerability. After 1939, Communists would have an increasingly difficult time convincing a new generation of activists of their ideals. And yet the ability of party members to sustain their leadership in local movements suggests that, regardless of the historic period, the story of America's Communists is best understood when it is framed in a local context.

Notes

Introduction

1. Harold D. Lasswell and Dorothy Blumenstock, *World Revolutionary Propaganda: A Chicago Study* (New York: Alfred A. Knopf, 1939), 212–14 (quote on 213).

2. Ibid., 214.

3. Irving Howe and Lewis Coser, *The American Communist Party: A Critical History* (New York: Praeger Books, 1962), 217, 226.

4. Third Period theory taught that the first period of postwar development was revolutionary, lasting until 1923. It was followed by one of capitalist stabilization, which ended in 1928. See Isaac Deutscher, *The Prophet Outcast Trotsky: 1929–1940* (London: Oxford University Press, 1963), 38–40; and R. Palme Dutt, *Fascism and Social Revolution: A Study of the Economics and Politics of the Extreme Stages of Capitalism in Decay* (1934; reprint, San Francisco: Proletarian Publishers, 1974).

5. Howe and Coser, *American Communist Party*, 175–235. Works that discuss the Third Period from a national perspective include Theodore Draper, *American Communism and Soviet Russia* (1960; reprint, New York: Vintage Books, 1986), 405–41; Howe and Coser, *American Communist Party*, 175–272; Harvey Klehr, *The Heyday of American Communism: The Depression Decade* (New York: Basic Books, 1984), 28–166; and Mark Solomon, *The Cry Was Unity: Communists and African Americans, 1917–1936* (Jackson: University Press of Mississippi, 1998), 95–230.

6. This interpretation was originally advanced by ten studies sponsored by the Fund for the Republic, beginning in 1953, on various aspects of "Communism in American Life." The published works include Daniel Aaron, *Writers on the Left: Episodes in American Literary Communism* (New York: Harcourt, Brace, and World, 1961); Clinton Lawrence Rossiter, *Marxism: The View from America* (New York: Harcourt, Brace, and World, 1960); Frank S. Meyer, *The Moulding of Communists: The Training of the Communist Cadre* (New York: Harcourt, Brace, and World, 1961); Ralph Lord Roy, *Communism and the Churches* (New York: Harcourt, Brace, and World, 1960); David A. Shannon,

The Decline of American Communism: A History of the Communist Party of the United States since 1945 (New York: Harcourt, Brace, and World, 1959); Nathan Glazer, *The Social Basis of American Communism* (New York: Harcourt, Brace, and World, 1961); Robert W. Iversen, *The Communists and the Schools* (New York: Harcourt, Brace, and World, 1959); and Theodore Draper, *The Roots of American Communism* (1957; reprint, Chicago: Ivan Dee Inc., 1985). See also Klehr, *Heyday of American Communism;* Bert Cochran, *Labor and Communism: The Conflict That Shaped American Unions* (Princeton, N.J.: Princeton University Press, 1977); Howe and Coser, *American Communist Party;* and Harvey Klehr and John Earl Haynes, *The American Communist Movement: Storming Heaven Itself* (New York: Twayne Press, 1992). This perspective recently has been pursued in a Yale University Press series, which includes Harvey Klehr, John Earl Haynes, and Fridrikh Igorevich Firsov, *The Secret World of American Communism* (New Haven, Conn.: Yale University Press, 1995); and Harvey Klehr, John Earl Haynes, and Kyrill M. Anderson, *The Soviet World of American Communism* (New Haven, Conn.: Yale University Press, 1998). See also Vernon Pedersen, *The Communist Party in Maryland, 1919–57* (Urbana: University of Illinois Press, 2001); and John Earl Haynes and Harvey Klehr, "The Historiography of American Communism: An Unsettled Field," *Labour History Review* 68.1 (April 2003): 61–78. A similar interpretation from a different political perspective has been expressed by Bryan D. Palmer, "Rethinking the Historiography of United States Communism," *American Communist History* 2.2 (2003): 139–73.

7. Draper, *American Communism and Soviet Russia,* 440.

8. Ibid., 4 (first quote); Klehr, Haynes, and Anderson, *Soviet World of American Communism,* 5 (second quote); Haynes and Klehr, "Historiography of American Communism," 61–78.

9. Historical autobiographies reflecting this perspective include Steve Nelson, James R. Barrett, and Rob Ruck, *Steve Nelson, American Radical* (Pittsburgh: University of Pittsburgh Press, 1981); Nell Irvin Painter, *The Narrative of Hosea Hudson* (Cambridge, Mass.: Harvard University Press, 1979); Dorothy Ray Healey and Maurice Isserman, *California Red: A Life in the American Communist Party* (Urbana: University of Illinois Press, 1990); Al Richmond, *A Long View from the Left: Memoirs of an American Revolutionist* (Boston: Houghton Mifflin, 1973); George Charney, *A Long Journey* (Chicago: Quadrangle Books, 1968); and Junius Scales and Richard Nickson, *Cause at Heart: A Former Communist Remembers* (Athens: University of Georgia Press, 1987). Important national studies include Maurice Isserman, *Which Side Were You On? The American Communist Party during the Second World War* (1982; reprint, Urbana: University of Illinois Press, 1993); Fraser Ottanelli, *The Communist Party of the United States: From the Depression to World War II* (New Brunswick, N.J.: Rutgers University Press, 1991); and Paul Buhle, *Marxism in the USA from 1870 to the Present Day* (London: Verso, 1987), 121–220. The best local and industry studies include Mark Naison, *Communists in Harlem during the Depression* (Urbana: University of Illinois Press, 1983); Robin Kelley, *Hammer and Hoe: Alabama Communists during the Depression* (Chapel Hill: University of North Carolina Press, 1990); Roger Keeran, *The Communist Party and the Auto Workers Unions* (Bloomington: Indiana University Press, 1980); and Joshua Freeman, *In Transit: The Transport Workers Union in New York City, 1933–1966* (New

York: Oxford University Press, 1986). Paul Lyons, *Philadelphia Communists, 1936–1956* (Philadelphia: Temple University Press, 1982), is less successful. For a critique of these interpretations, see Theodore Draper, "American Communism Revisited," *New York Review of Books,* 9 May 1985, 32–37; and Theodore Draper, "The Popular Front Revisited," *New York Review of Books,* 30 May 1985, 79–81.

10. Palmer, "Rethinking the Historiography," 171.

11. Randi Storch, "'The Realities of the Situation': Revolutionary Discipline and Everyday Political Life in Chicago's Communist Party, 1928–1935," *Labor: Studies in Working-Class History in the Americas* 1.3 (2004): 19–44.

12. When I did my research in Moscow, the archive was called the Russian Center for the Preservation and Study of Documents of Recent History (RTsKhIDNI). It has since changed its name to the Russian State Archive of Social and Political History (RGASPI). U.S. Communist party sources continue until the Comintern's dissolution in 1943, but local records become almost nonexistent after 1935. The CPUSA's collection (fond 515) is now available to researchers on microfilm at the Library of Congress. See Randi Storch, "Moscow's Archives and the New History of the Communist Party of the United States," *Perspectives* (October 2000): 44–50; and John Earl Haynes, "The American Communist Party Records on Microfilm," *Continuity* 26 (Spring 2003): 21–26. When I refer to sources from this archive throughout the study, I abbreviate the archive to RTsKhIDNI. I then list the source by fond (f.), opis (op.), delo (d.), and listok (l.).

13. Scholarly studies include Harvey Klehr and Ronald Radosh, *The Amerasia Spy Case: Prelude to McCarthyism* (Chapel Hill: University of North Carolina Press, 1996); John Earl Haynes, *Red Scare or Red Menace? American Communism and Anticommunism in the Cold War Era* (Chicago: Ivan R. Dee, 1996); Klehr, Haynes, and Firsov, *Secret World of American Communism;* Klehr, Haynes, and Anderson, *Soviet World of American Communism;* John Earl Haynes and Harvey Klehr, *Venona: Decoding Soviet Espionage in America* (New Haven, Conn.: Yale University Press, 1999); Pedersen, *Communist Party in Maryland;* and Allen Weinstein and Alexander Vassiliev, *The Haunted Wood* (New York: Modern Library, 2000). James G. Ryan, "Socialist Triumph as a Family Value: Earl Browder and Soviet Espionage," *American Communist History* 2 (2002): 125–42, does not appear to be purposely sensationalist, but without contextualizing espionage activity, Ryan furthers these ends. Important exceptions of recent works that do not fall into this category include James R. Barrett, *William Z. Foster and the Tragedy of American Radicalism* (Urbana: University of Illinois Press, 1999); and Solomon, *Cry Was Unity.* Sensationalized popular press stories include James Sherr, "How Stalin Infiltrated America," *New York Times,* 27 April 1997; George Will, "The Discrediting of the U.S. Left," *(New Orleans) Times-Picayune,* 21 April 1995, B7; and Cal Thomas, "Who Was Right?" *(New Orleans) Times-Picayune,* 14 April 1995, B7.

14. Lizabeth Cohen, *Making a New Deal: Industrial Workers in Chicago, 1919–1939* (Cambridge: Cambridge University Press, 1990); Robert McElvaine, *The Great Depression: America, 1929–1941* (New York: Times Books, 1984); Irving Bernstein, *The Lean Years: A History of the American Worker, 1920–1933* (Boston: Houghton Mifflin, 1960); Irving Bernstein, *The Turbulent Years: A History of the American Worker, 1933–1941* (Boston: Houghton Mifflin, 1970).

15. The most problematic methodology is found in works published in the Yale series listed in n.6 above. Relying on particular episodes taken out of context, these scholars provoke rather than explain. Other methods with less serious flaws that still have limited explanatory power include such single-industry studies as Keeran, *Communist Party and the Auto Workers Union;* Freeman, *In Transit;* Howard Kimeldorf, *Reds or Rackets? The Making of Radical and Conservative Unions on the Waterfront* (Berkeley: University of California Press, 1988); and Max Gordon, "The Communists and the Drive to Organize Steel, 1936," *Labor History* 23.2 (Spring 1982): 254–65; such historical autobiographies as Nelson, Barrett, and Ruck, *Steve Nelson;* Painter, *Narrative of Hosea Hudson;* and Healey and Isserman, *California Red;* such national studies as Isserman, *Which Side Were You On?;* and Ottanelli, *Communist Party of the United States;* such single-group studies as Kate Weigand, *Red Feminism: American Communism and the Making of American Feminism* (Baltimore: Johns Hopkins University Press, 2001); and Solomon, *Cry Was Unity.* While a community-study method provides the best model for looking at this movement, it does not always succeed. Two excellent community studies include Naison, *Communists in Harlem;* and Kelley, *Hammer and Hoe.* A more problematic one is Pedersen, *Communist Party in Maryland.*

Chapter 1: Sam Hammersmark's Chicago

1. *Daily Worker,* 7 June 1938, 6.

2. Harold M. Mayer and Richard Wade, *Chicago: Growth of a Metropolis* (Chicago: University of Chicago Press, 1969), 3–192; William Cronon, *Nature's Metropolis: Chicago and the Great West* (New York: W. W. Norton, 1991); Bessie Louise Pierce, *A History of Chicago: The Rise of a Modern City* vol. 3 (New York: Alfred Knopf, 1957), 64–233.

3. Melvin G. Holli and Peter Jones, eds., *Ethnic Chicago* (Grand Rapids, Mich.: W. B. Eerdmans Pub. Co., 1981); Victor Greene "'Becoming American': The Role of Ethnic Leaders—Swedes, Poles, Italians, Jews," and Edward R. Kantowicz, "Polish Chicago: Survival through Solidarity," in *The Ethnic Frontier: Essays in the History of Group Survival in Chicago and the Midwest,* ed. Peter d'A. Jones and Melvin G. Holli (Grand Rapids, Mich.: Wm. Eerdmans Publishing Co., 1977), 143–75 and 180–209; Youngsoo Bae, *Labor in Retreat: Class and Community among Men's Clothing Workers of Chicago, 1871–1929* (Albany: State University of New York Press, 2001), 23–32; Mayer and Wade, *Chicago,* 62–70, 117–92.

4. John T. McGreevy, *Parish Boundaries: The Catholic Encounter with Race in the Twentieth-Century Urban North* (Chicago: University of Chicago Press, 1996); James R. Barrett, *Work and Community in the Jungle: Chicago's Packinghouse Workers, 1894–1922* (Urbana: University of Illinois Press, 1987), 73–90; Lizabeth Cohen, *Making a New Deal: Industrial Workers in Chicago, 1919–1939* (Cambridge: Cambridge University Press, 1990), 21–52; Robert Slayton, *Back of the Yards: The Making of a Local Democracy* (Chicago: Chicago University Press, 1986), 147; Bae, *Labor in Retreat,* 32–45.

5. William Adelman, *Haymarket Revisited* (Chicago: Illinois Labor History Society, 1976), 3; Bruce C. Nelson, *Beyond the Martyrs: A Social History of Chicago's Anarchists, 1870–1900* (New Brunswick, N.J.: Rutgers University Press, 1988), 21; Ellen Skerrett, "The

Catholic Dimension," in *The Irish in Chicago,* ed. Lawrence J. McCaffrey, Elen Skerrett, Michael F. Funchion, and Charles Fanning (Urbana: University of Illinois Press, 1987), 22–60.

6. Nelson, *Beyond the Martyrs,* 21–23; Cohen, *Making a New Deal,* 12–52; Barrett, *Work and Community in the Jungle,* 36–58; Eric L. Hirsch, *Urban Revolt: Ethnic Politics in the Nineteenth-Century Chicago Labor Movement* (Berkeley: University of California Press, 1990), 5–10.

7. Quoted in Rick Halpern, *Down on the Killing Floor: Black and White Workers in Chicago's Packinghouses, 1904–54* (Urbana: Illinois University Press, 1997), 24.

8. Richard Schneirov, "Chicago's Great Upheaval of 1877," *Chicago History* 9.1 (1980): 3–17; Barrett, *Work and Community in the Jungle,* 121; Paul Avrich, *The Haymarket Tragedy* (Princeton, N.J.: Princeton University Press, 1984), 28–33; Hirsch, *Urban Revolt,* 23–31.

9. Richard Schneirov, *Labor and Urban Politics: Class Conflict and the Origins of Modern Liberalism in Chicago, 1864–1897* (Urbana: University of Illinois Press, 1998), 53–63, 81–86, 173–79; Nelson, *Beyond the Martyrs,* 24–26; Avrich, *Haymarket Tragedy,* 39–52; Hirsch, *Urban Revolt,* 44.

10. Avrich, *Haymarket Tragedy,* 85; Nelson, *Beyond the Martyrs,* 80.

11. Nelson, *Beyond the Martyrs,* 80–152; Hartmut Keil and John B. Jentz, eds., *German Workers in Chicago: A Documentary History of Working-Class Culture from 1850 to World War I* (Urbana: University of Illinois Press, 1988), 258–59; Bruce Nelson, "Dancing and Picnicking Anarchists? The Movement below the Martyred Leadership," in *Haymarket Scrapbook,* ed. Dave Roediger and Franklin Rosemont (Chicago: Charles Kerr, 1986), 76–79; Avrich, *Haymarket Tragedy,* 86.

12. Avrich, *Haymarket Tragedy,* 90; Nelson, *Beyond the Martyrs,* 82–98; Roediger and Rosemont, *Haymarket Scrapbook,* 11–110.

13. Nelson, *Beyond the Martyrs,* 27–51; Hirsch, *Urban Revolt,* 54–62; Schneirov, *Labor and Urban Politics,* 76–81, 87–94, 110–15, 145–52; Richard Schneirov, "'An Injury to One Is the Concern of All': The Knights of Labor in the Haymarket Era," in Roediger and Rosemont, *Haymarket Scrapbook,* 81–83.

14. Adelman, *Haymarket Revisited,* 14–17; Nelson, *Beyond the Martyrs,* 177–200; Hirsch, *Urban Revolt,* 43–85; Schneirov, *Labor and Urban Politics,* 32–40, 204–5.

15. *Daily Worker,* 30 September 1957, 5, 7; Keil and Jentz, *German Workers in Chicago,* 193–94; Hirsch, *Urban Revolt,* 73–78; Nelson, *Beyond the Martyrs,* 177–200; Schneirov, *Labor and Urban Politics,* 248–55.

16. *Daily Worker,* 30 September 1957, 5, 7; Bruce C. Nelson, "Revival and Upheaval: Religion, Irreligion, and Chicago's Working Class in 1886," *Journal of Social History* 25.2 (1991): 233–53.

17. Schneirov, *Labor and Urban Politics,* 335–43; Nick Salvatore, *Eugene V. Debs: Citizen and Socialist* (Urbana: University of Illinois Press, 1982), 127–46; Ralph Chaplin, *Wobbly: The Rough and Tumble Story of an American Radical* (Chicago: University of Chicago Press, 1948), 3–14.

18. *Daily Worker,* 30 September 1957, 5, 7; Carolyn Ashbaugh, *Lucy Parsons, American Revolutionary* (Chicago: Charles Kerr Publishing Company, 1976), 234; James Weinstein,

Ambiguous Legacy: The Left in American Politics (New York: New View Points, 1975), 1–8; Salvatore, *Eugene V. Debs,* 183–219.

19. James Weinstein, *The Decline of Socialism in America, 1912–1925* (New York: Monthly Review Press, 1967), 9–12; Salvatore, *Eugene V. Debs,* 205–12; Melvyn Dubofsky, *We Shall Be All: A History of the Industrial Workers of the World* (Chicago: Quadrangle Books, 1969); Joyce Kornbluth, ed., *Rebel Voices: An IWW Anthology* (Ann Arbor: University of Michigan Press, 1964).

20. Weinstein, *Decline of Socialism in America,* 13–14; James R. Barrett, *William Z. Foster and the Tragedy of American Radicalism* (Urbana: University of Illinois Press, 1999), 43–70; William Z. Foster, *From Bryan to Stalin* (New York: International Publishers, 1937), 58–72.

21. *Daily Worker,* 30 September 1957, 5, 7; *Midwest Daily Record,* 9 May 1938.

22. William Z. Foster, *American Trade Unionism: Principles, Organization, Strategy, Tactics* (New York: International Publishers, 1947), 18; Barrett, *William Z. Foster,* 58–66; Foster, *From Bryan to Stalin,* 58–85.

23. Untitled newspaper clipping in Jack Kling Papers, Chicago Historical Society. Foster, *From Bryan to Stalin,* 82; John Keiser, "John Fitzpatrick and Progressive Unionism, 1915–1925" (Ph.D. dissertation, Northwestern University, 1965), 1–34; Barrett, *William Z. Foster,* 74.

24. Chicago teachers were among Fitzpatrick's most important allies in this coup. See Robert L. Reid, ed., *Battleground: The Autobiography of Margaret A. Haley* (Urbana: University of Illinois Press, 1982), 90–93.

25. Keiser, "John Fitzpatrick," 22–35; Elizabeth McKillen, *Chicago, Labor, and the Rush for a Democratic Diplomacy* (Ithaca, N.Y.: Cornell University Press, 1995), 46–48; Barrett, *William Z. Foster,* 74.

26. Foster, *From Bryan to Stalin,* 98–99; Barrett, *Work and Community in the Jungle,* 188–231; Halpern, *Down on the Killing Floor,* 44–72; David Brody, *Butcher Workmen: A Study of Unionization* (Cambridge, Mass.: Harvard University Press, 1964), 81–83, 75–127.

27. Barrett, *William Z. Foster,* 83–101; William Z. Foster, *Great Steel Strike and Its Lessons* (New York: B. W. Huebsch, 1920); Keiser, "John Fitzpatrick," 42–64; Robert K. Murray, *Red Scare: A Study in National Hysteria, 1919–1920* (Minneapolis: Minnesota University Press, 1955), 135–52.

28. Murray, *Red Scare,* 211–81; Alan Dawley, *Struggles for Justice: Social Responsibility and the Liberal State* (Cambridge, Mass.: Belknap Press, 1991), 218–53.

29. Barrett, *Work and Community in the Jungle,* 98; William Tuttle, *Race Riot: Chicago in the Red Summer of 1919* (New York: Atheneum Books, 1970); Halpern, *Down on the Killing Floor,* 65–72; McKillen, *Chicago, Labor, and the Rush for a Democratic Diplomacy,* 86–96; Keiser, "John Fitzpatrick," 95–105.

30. Theodore Draper, *The Roots of American Communism* (1957; reprint, Chicago: Ivan Dee Inc., 1985), 153–73; Weinstein, *Decline of Socialism in America,* 234–57; James P. Cannon, *The First Ten Years of American Communism* (New York: Lyle Stuart, 1962), 16–17, 41–46; Arne Swabeck, "When Theory Collides with Facts Let's Re-Write History," *Progressive Labor* (May 1969): 25–38.

31. Kevin McDermott and Jeremy Agnew, *The Comintern: A History of International Communism from Lenin to Stalin* (New York: St. Martin's Press, 1997), 41–80.

32. Fernando Claudin, *The Communist Movement: From Comintern to Cominform* (New York: Monthly Review Press, 1975), 21–24. See also McDermott and Agnew, *Comintern;* Harvey Klehr, *The Heyday of American Communism: The Depression Decade* (New York: Basic Books, 1984), 5–27; Barrett, *William Z. Foster,* 111 (quote).

33. "Party Structure," *Party Organizer* (hereafter *PO*) 4 (May 1931): 6–7; District Committee Meeting, 27–28 January 1934, RTsKhIDNI, f. 515, op. 1, d. 3581, ll. 2–4; "District Leadership and Guidance," *PO* 4 (February 1931): 6–8; "Building the Party Apparatus," *PO* 2 (May–June 1928): 11–13; Robert Jay Alperin, "Organization in the Communist Party, U.S.A., 1931–1938" (Ph.D. dissertation, Northwestern University, 1959), 70–150; J. Peters, *The Communist Party, a Manual on Organization* (New York: Workers Library Publishers, 1935).

34. The largest sections only began to have organizational secretaries beginning around 1932 to cope with party growth. Where no secretary existed, the section organizer took over that work. Directives on Future Handling of Party Records and Statistics, n.d. [1933], RTsKhIDNI, f. 515, op. 1, d. 3264, ll. 12–13; District Secretariat Minutes, 14 February 1933, d. 3258, l. 106; Organization Department Letter, n.d., d. 2113, l. 100; Organization Department Letter, 11 November 1930, l. 69; Tasks of Section Organizational Secretary, n.d. [1932], d. 2466, l. 147.

35. "District Leadership and Guidance: How the District Buro Should Function," *PO* 4 (February 1931): 6; Alperin, "Organization in the Communist Party," esp. 70–150; Klehr, *Heyday of American Communism,* 5–7; District Organization Department Letters, 3 October 1931, RTsKhIDNI, f. 515, op. 1, d. 2466, l. 107; 22 September 1931, d. 2466, l. 100; n.d. [1930], d. 2113, l. 101; 5 September 1930, l. 33; 29 August 1930, ll. 50–52; 21 March 1931, d. 2466, l. 36; Section 2 Organization Department Letter, 15 March 1934, d. 3590, l. 22; "Functioning Unit Buros," *PO* 4 (April 1931): 5–7; "Material for Party Structure Classes," *PO* 4 (April 1931): 28–32; "How to Organize Agitprop Work in the Party Unit," *PO* 3 (February 1930): 3–5.

36. Chicago's first TUEL meeting turned out four hundred workers, strongest among those working in the railroad, needle, metal, building, and printing trades. J. W. Johnstone, "The League in Chicago," *Labor Herald* (April 1922): 29.

37. Barrett, *William Z. Foster,* 103–14; Draper, *Roots of American Communism,* 320–22.

38. Foster, *From Bryan to Stalin,* 160.

39. Barrett, *William Z. Foster,* 102–10; Foster, *From Bryan to Stalin,* 156–63.

40. *Midwest Daily Record,* 9 May 1938; Solon De Leon, *The American Labor Who's Who* (New York: Hanford Press, 1925), 129.

41. Draper, *Roots of American Communism,* 14.

42. De Leon, *American Labor Who's Who,* 237, 62, 185, 41, 225, 64; Interview with Vittorio Vidali, n.d. [1984], Oral History of the American Left, 17, Tamiment Institute Library, New York University; Paul Buhle, *Marxism in the USA: From 1870 to the Present Day* (New York: Verso Press, 1987), 127–30; Nathan Glazer, *The Social Basis of American Communism* (New York: Harcourt, Brace, and World, 1961), 13–46.

43. Interview with Vittorio Vidali, 17.

44. Foreign Language Press Survey, *Scandia*, 21 April 1923.

45. Barrett, *William Z. Foster*, 111–13; De Leon, *American Labor Who's Who*, 64.

46. Charles Shipman, *It Had to Be Revolution: Memoirs of an American Radical* (Ithaca, N.Y.: Cornell University Press, 1993), 134–36.

47. Ibid., 139.

48. Michael Gold describes a "proletarian intellectual" in "The Communists Meet," *New Republic*, 15 June 1932, 117. See also Barrett, *William Z. Foster*, 115; Rober A. Bruns, *The Damndest Radical: The Life and World of Ben Reitman, Chicago's Celebrated Social Reformer, Hobo King, and Whorehouse Physician* (Urbana: University of Illinois Press, 1987), 230–51; Harry Haywood, *Black Bolshevik: Autobiography of an Afro-American Communist* (Chicago: Liberator Press, 1978), 115, 129.

49. *Daily Worker*, 30 September 1957, 5, 7; newsclipping, n.d., Jack Kling Papers, Chicago Historical Society; Peter Filado interview with Gil Green, 23 January 1991, Tamiment Institute Library, New York University; John Williamson, *Dangerous Scot: The Life and Work of an American "Undesirable"* (New York: International Publishers, 1969), 92.

50. Steve Nelson, James R. Barrett, and Rob Ruck, *Steve Nelson, American Radical* (Pittsburgh: University of Pittsburgh Press, 1981), 66 (quote).

51. Martin Abern to Jay Lovestone, 9 December 1925, RTsKhIDNI, f. 515, op. 1, d. 556, l. 61 (quote); see also ll. 60 and 62; Draper, *Roots of American Communism*, 154–57, 190–92; Buhle, *Marxism in the USA*, 135–37; Glazer, *Social Basis of American Communism*, 46–58.

52. Martin Abern to Jay Lovestone, 9 December 1925, RTsKhIDNI, f. 515, op. 1, d. 556, l. 58; Glazer, *Social Basis of American Communism*, 52; Draper, *Roots of American Communism*, 186–88.

53. Martin Abern to Jay Lovestone, 9 December 1925, RTsKhIDNI, f. 515, op. 1, d. 556, l. 58.

54. Ibid.

55. "Situation in Chicago," n.d. [1925], RTsKhIDNI, f. 515, op. 1, d. 556, ll. 7–76.

56. Ibid.; Martin Abern to Jay Lovestone, 14 November 1925, RTsKhIDNI, d. 556, l. 43.

57. Minutes, 25 October 1925, RTsKhIDNI, f. 515, op., 1, d. 556, l. 33; Kate Weigand, *Red Feminism: American Communism and the Making of Women's Liberation* (Baltimore: Johns Hopkins University Press, 2001), 16–20.

58. 9 December 1926, RTsKhIDNI, f. 515, op. 1, d. 671, l. 50; Women's Work Report, 1926, d. 1157, l. 12; Martin Abern to Jay Lovestone, 9 December 1925, RTsKhINDI, d. 556, l. 58 (quote).

59. Haywood, *Black Bolshevik*, 129 (quote); Paul Young, "Race, Class and Radicalism in Chicago, 1914–1936" (Ph.D. dissertation, University of Iowa, 2001), 155–73; Mark Solomon, *The Cry Was Unity: Communists and African Americans, 1917–1936* (Jackson: University Press of Mississippi, 1998), 3–21.

60. Haywood, *Black Bolshevik*, 139.

61. Draper, *American Communism*, 331–32; Solomon, *Cry Was Unity*, 52–67; Philip S.

Foner and James S. Allen, eds., *American Communism and Black Americans: A Documentary History, 1919–1929* (Philadelphia: Temple University Press, 1987), 109–29.

62. Draper, *American Communism,* 24–28 (quote on 20); David Kirby, "Zimmerwald and the Origins of the Third International," and Kevin McDermott, "The History of the Comintern in Light of New Documents," in *International Communism and the Communist International, 1919–1943,* ed. Tim Rees and Andrew Thorpe (Manchester: Manchester University Press, 1998), 15–30 and 31–40; Kevin McDermott and Jeremy Agnew, *The Comintern: A History of International Communism from Lenin to Stalin* (New York: St. Martin's Press, 1997), 1–80.

63. Communication Number 11, 2 March 1925, RTsKhIDNI, f. 515, op. 1, d. 556 (first quote); Letter to Jay from Shannon, n.d., RtsKhIDNI, f. 515, op. 1, d. 1036, l. 122 (second quote); Cannon, *First Ten Years of American Communism,* 117–27; Barrett, *William Z. Foster,* 148–62.

64. William Z. Foster and James Cannon, "Statements on Our Labor Party Policy," n.d., f. 534, op. 7, d. 464, l. 54 (quote); Cannon, *First Ten Years of American Communism,* 129–31; Barrett, *William Z. Foster,* 123–25 and 136–39; McKillen, *Chicago, Labor, and the Rush for a Democratic Diplomacy,* 193–213; Draper, *American Communism,* 29–51; William Z. Foster, "An Open Letter to John Fitzpatrick," *Labor Herald* (January 1924): 6–8, 26; William Dunne, "Workers and Farmers on the March," *Labor Herald* (April 1924): 38–40; Earl Browder, "Chicago, St. Paul, Cleveland," *Labor Herald* (August 1924): 166–68.

65. Party Building, December 1927, RTsKhIDNI, f. 515, op. 1, d. 1159, ll. 9–16.

Chapter 2: Revolutionary Recruitment

1. Report of Bill Gebert on 13th CC Plenum and Tasks, 6 September 1931, RTsKhIDNI, f. 515 op. 1, d. 2455, l. 96.

2. On Jews and middle-class groups in the party, see Nathan Glazer, *The Social Basis of American Communism* (New York: Harcourt, Brace, and World, 1961), 130–68.

3. The Communist party underwent a number of name changes in its early years, including Workers Party of America, Workers (Communist Party), and Communist Party of the USA. I refer to it throughout as the Communist party. John Williamson, *Dangerous Scot: The Life and Work of an American "Undesirable"* (New York: International Publishers, 1969), 29 (quote); Bernard Johnpoll and Harvey Klehr, eds., *Biographical Dictionary of the American Left* (Westport, Conn.: Greenwood Press, 1986), 418.

4. Robert S. McElvaine, *The Great Depression: America 1929–1941* (New York: Times Books, 1984); Maury Klein, *Rainbow's End: The Crash of 1929* (Oxford: Oxford University Press, 2001); Frances Fox Piven and Richard A. Cloward, *Regulating the Poor: The Functioning of Public Welfare* (New York: Vintage Books, 1971), 58; Albert Prago, "The Organization of the Unemployed and the Role of Radicals, 1929–1935" (Ph.D. dissertation, Union Graduate School, 1976), 30 and 174; Frank Folsom, *America before Welfare* (New York: New York University Press, 1991), 231–37.

5. These figures are from Lizabeth Cohen, *Making a New Deal: Industrial Workers in Chicago, 1919–1939* (Cambridge: Cambridge University Press, 1990), 217 and 241.

6. Rick Halpern, *Down on the Killing Floor: Black and White Workers in Chicago's*

Packinghouses, 1904–1954 (Urbana: University of Illinois Press, 1997), 98–112; Cohen, *Making a New Deal*, 213–50; Claude Lightfoot, *From Chicago's Slums to World Politics: Autobiography of Claude M. Lightfoot* (New York: Outlook Publishers, 1987), 38–54; Horace Cayton and St. Clair Drake, *Black Metropolis: A Study of Negro Life in a Northern City*, 2 vols., 2d ed. (New York: Harper and Row, 1962); Report of the Head Resident on the Neighborhood and Unemployment Emergency, 1930–1931, folder 1930, Graham Taylor Papers, Newberry Library (quote); Lester V. Chandler, *America's Greatest Depression, 1929–1941* (New York: Harper and Row, 1970), 45.

7. District Eight Org. Letter, 7 February 1931, RTsKhIDNI, f. 515, op. 1, d. 2466, l. 14.

8. District Eight Org. Letter, 11 August 1932, RTsKhIDNI, f. 515, op. 1, d. 2870, l. 84 (quote).

9. In 1928, there were 1,100 in the district, which included Milwaukee, St. Louis, southern Illinois, and Indianapolis. In 1931, New York's district reported 2,346 members. That year, only 1,692 of Chicago's members filled out complete registrations, but party records indicate that membership reached 1,963. Organizational Status of the CPUSA, 1932, RTsKhIDNI, f. 515, op. 1, d. 2618, l. 95.

10. Ibid., 98.

11. Analysis for Recruiting and Dues for the Month of November 1934, n.d., RTsKhIDNI, f. 515, op. 1, d. 3591, l. 39.

12. Harvey Klehr, *The Heyday of American Communism: The Depression Decade* (New York: Basic Books, 1984), 153; Glazer, *Social Basis of American Communism*, 101.

13. In July only 611 members paid their dues. Letter to Comrades from Frankfeld, 2 September 1930, RTsKhIDNI, f. 515, op. 1, d. 1956, l. 48.

14. Glazer, *Social Basis of American Communism*, 212–13 n.28; "Build the Party thru Recruiting New Members," n.d. [1930], RTsKhIDNI, f. 515, op. 1, d. 2113, l. 48; District Organization Department Letter, 12 October 1930, l. 55; 3 April 1931, d. 2466, ll. 39–40.

15. J. Williamson, "The Party Nucleus—A Factor in the Class Struggle," speech at Plenum of District Committee, 29–30 March 1931, RTsKhIDNI, f. 515, op. 1, d. 2455, l. 17.

16. Glazer, *Social Basis of American Communism*, 122.

17. "Build the Party thru Recruiting New Members," n.d. [1930], RTsKhIDNI, f. 515, op. 1, d. 2113, l. 48. See also Report on Recruiting Drive in Chicago District, Williamson to District Buro, 5 April 1932, d. 2874, l. 209.

18. Ibid.

19. Organization Department Letter, 28 October 1930, RTsKhIDNI, f. 515, op. 1, d. 2113, l. 59. For national trends, see Klehr, *Heyday of American Communism*, 156–60. The *Party Organizer* regularly reported on national fluctuation problems as well.

20. Report on Recruiting Drive in Chicago District, Williamson to District Buro, 5 April 1932, RTsKhIDNI, f. 515, op. 1, d. 2874, ll. 208–10 (quote on 209); Monthly Recruiting Bulletin, August 1934, d. 3591, ll. 24–26.

21. Organization Department Letter, 3 April 1931, RTsKhIDNI, f. 515, op. 1, d. 2466, ll. 39–40.

22. "Give More Personal Guidance," *PO* 5 (November–December 1932): 21–23.

23. Minutes of the District Buro, 26 March 1931, RTsKhIDNI, f. 515, op. 1, d. 2457, l. 26; 15 May 1931, l. 51; Report of Commission Investigating Sections 5–11–12, n.d., d. 3853, l. 48; Party Registration—1931, n.d., d. 2464, ll. 93–104.

24. Klehr, *Heyday of American Communism,* 161–62; Glazer, *Social Basis of American Communism,* 38–89, 100–101.

25. National unemployment figures can be found in Irving Bernstein, *The Lean Years: A History of the American Worker, 1920–1933* (Boston: Houghton Mifflin, 1960), 316–17. Louis Wirth and Margaret Furez, eds., *Local Community Fact Book, 1938* (Chicago: Chicago Recreation Commission, 1938), indicate that 14.02 percent of Chicagoans were on relief in 1934. For national party trends, see Klehr, *Heyday of American Communism,* 161; and Robert J. Alperin, "Organization in the Communist Party, U.S.A., 1931–1938" (Ph.D. dissertation, Northwestern University, 1959), 58. For Chicago, see Party Registration—1931, n.d., RTsKhIDNI, f. 515, op. 1, d. 2464, l. 93; "Notes on the Recruiting Drive in District Eight," *PO* 4 (December 1931): 11–13; "Party Recruitment Drive," *PO* 5 (January 1932): 13–15.

26. This registration covered the district, which includes an area larger than Chicago. Although the registration has statistical inconsistencies, it provides the best reflection of Chicago's membership currently available for this period. The party's separation of "housewives" from "workers" reveals their bias and does not mean that these housewives were not members of the working class, although the party treated them as though they were the bourgeoisie. On housewives as an ambiguous category of analysis, see Christine Stansell, *City of Women: Sex and Class in New York, 1789–1860* (New York: Knopf, 1986); Eric Olin Wright, "Rethinking, Once Again, the Concept of Class Structure," in *The Debate on Classes,* ed. E. O. Wright (London: Verso, 1989), 269–348.

27. For the percentage of Chicago's Communist trade-union membership, I divided the total number of Chicago's Communists who claimed union membership (396) by the total number of Chicago's Communists who provided information to party leaders during their 1931 registration (1,692). I based my national party statistics on Robert Alperin's research, which indicated that the party had a total of 14,475 members. Of these Communists, 2,300 belonged to unions. Of union members in the national party, 28 percent were in the AFL and 72 percent in the TUUL, whereas Chicago's party had 52 percent in the reformist unions and 48 percent in the TUUL. Alperin, "Organization in the Communist Party," 49, 57; Party Registration—1931, n.d., RTsKhIDNI, f. 515, op. 1, d. 2464, l. 95.

28. Chicago's party culture and the particular campaigns that explain these high proportions are discussed in chapters 3–5 and 7.

29. U.S. Bureau of the Census, *Fifteenth Census of the United States: 1930, Population,* vol. 3, pt. 1 (Washington, D.C.: Government Printing Office, 1932), 656; Party Registration—1931, n.d., RTsKhIDNI, f. 515, op. 1, d. 2464, ll. 93–104; Organizational Status of CPUSA, d. 2618, ll. 95–96. New York's black Communists represented 3.1 percent of their membership, whereas Chicago's black members represented 24.3 percent. See Mark Naison, *Communists in Harlem during the Depression* (Urbana: University of Illinois Press, 1983), 68. See also Robin Kelley, *Hammer and Hoe: Alabama Communists*

during the Great Depression (Chapel Hill: University of North Carolina Press, 1990), 17, 33. Thanks to Glenda Gilmore for sharing her research on Birmingham's African American membership.

30. Glazer, *Social Basis of American Communism,* 169–84.

31. Section 2 Organization Letter, 29 March 1932, RTsKhIDNI, f. 515, op. 1, d. 2882, l. 38; "New Tasks Brought Out by Membership Study," *PO* 6 (January 1933): 24; J. Peters, "A Study of Fluctuation in the Chicago District," *PO* 7 (October 1934): 20–25.

32. Glazer, *Social Basis of American Communism,* 176.

33. These conflicts will be discussed in the next chapter.

34. Party Registration—1931, n.d., RTsKhIDNI, f. 515, op. 1, d. 2464, ll. 93–104; U.S. Bureau of the Census, *Fifteenth Census of the United States,* 636, 638, 640.

35. The largest groups in Chicago missing from party categories were the Irish and the Swedes. Given the Swedes' importance to Chicago's party, most likely a large percentage of the miscellaneous category included them. The lack of Irish participation is more difficult to explain, since party records are silent on the issue. Of those party members born in another country, 64 percent were citizens of the United States. See Party Registration—1931, n.d., RTsKhIDNI, f. 515, op. 1, d. 2464, l. 93. Klehr states that the 1931 registration of the party showed that half of the immigrant members were citizens, and two-thirds of the party was foreign-born. In Chicago, less were foreign-born, comparatively, and more, 66 percent, were citizens. See Klehr, *Heyday of American Communism,* 162. Also see Glazer, *Social Basis of American Communism,* 38–89, for comparative national party figures.

36. Data Cards, n.d., RTsKhIDNI, f. 515, op. 1, d. 4129; Klehr, *Heyday of American Communism,* 6. For a time, Charles Karenic edited *Rovnost L'udu* (Equality of the people), an ethnic newspaper begun in 1906, which ran until 1935, when it changed its name to *Ludovy Dennik* (The people's daily).

37. Steve Nelson, James R. Barrett, and Rob Ruck, *Steve Nelson, American Radical* (Pittsburgh: University of Pittsburgh Press, 1981), 46.

38. Membership Report, 13 November 1931, RTsKhIDNI, f. 515, op. 1, d. 2464, l. 58; Party Registration—1931, n.d., ll. 93–104; Roger Keeran, "The International Workers Order and the Origins of the CIO," *Labor History* 30.3 (1989): 385–408; Roger Keeran, "National Groups and the Popular Front: The Case of the IWO," *Journal of American Ethnic History* 14.3 (Spring 1995): 23–29.

39. Nelson, Barrett, and Ruck, *Steve Nelson,* 85 (quote). The November 1929 edition of the ILD's *Labor Defender* lists greetings from twenty-eight ILD branches in Chicago (244–45).

40. District Buro Minutes, 16 October 1931, RTsKhIDNI, f. 515, op. 1, d. 2457, l. 108.

41. "Study of Fluctuation in the Chicago District," *PO* 7 (October 1934): 20–25; "How Are the Convention Decisions Being Carried into Life?" *PO* 7 (July 1934): 4–6. See also Minutes of Org. Department, 26 December 1931, RTsKhIDNI, f. 515, op. 1, d. 2464, ll. 77–78; Party Registration—1931, n.d., ll. 93–104.

42. Michael Denning, *The Cultural Front: The Laboring of American Culture in the Twentieth Century* (London: Verso Books, 1996), 205.

43. "Paintings against War," *Left Front* (September–October 1933): 10.

44. Bettina Drew, *Nelson Algren: A Life on the Wild Side* (Austin: Texas University Press, 1989), 50–52; "Midwest Club Notes—Chicago," *Left Front* (May–June 1934): 21; Richard Wright, *Black Boy: American Hunger* (New York: Harper Perennial, 1993), 372.

45. Drew, *Nelson Algren*, 76.

46. Quoted in ibid., 77.

47. Wright, *Black Boy*, 381, 406.

48. Denning, *Cultural Front*, 210.

49. "Henri Barbusse to Visit Chicago" and "The Midwest John Reed Conference," *Left Front* (September–October 1933): 11.

50. "Midwest Club Notes—Chicago," *Left Front* (May–June 1934): 21.

51. On clubs throughout the country, see Denning, *Cultural Front*, 205–11.

52. Wright, *Black Boy*, 379–86; Denning, *Cultural Front*, 210.

53. Quoted in Douglas Wixson, *Worker-Writer in America: Jack Conroy and the Tradition of Midwestern Literary Radicalism, 1898–1990* (Urbana: University of Illinois Press, 1994), 287.

54. Quoted in Drew, *Nelson Algren*, 77.

55. Quoted in ibid., 77.

56. Hazel Rowley, *Richard Wright: The Life and Times* (New York: Henry Holt, 2001), 80–81 (quote); Wright, *Black Boy*, 387–90.

57. Quoted in Rowley, *Richard Wright*, 287.

58. Klehr, *Heyday of American Communism*, 81–83; Wright, *Black Boy*, 391 (quote).

59. Party Registration, n.d. [1931], RTsKhIDNI, f. 515, op. 1, d. 2464, ll. 93–104.

60. District Organization Department Letter, 17 November 1930, RTsKhIDNI, f. 515, op. 1, d. 2113, l. 72.

61. Minutes of the Women's Committee, 15 May 1930, RTsKhIDNI, f. 515, op. 1, d. 2115, ll. 24–25. See also Christine Ellis interview in *Rank and File: Personal Histories by Working-Class Organizers*, ed. Alice Lynd and Staughton Lynd (Boston: Beacon Press, 1973), 10–33.

62. Report of Chicago District on Work among Women, n.d., RTsKhIDNI, f. 515, op. 1, d. 2110, ll. 12–17. On the organization of a federation of working women's organizations, see Anna David to Jack Stachel, 29 February 1928, d. 1334, l. 11.

63. Report of Chicago District on Work among Women, n.d., RTsKhIDNI, f. 515, op. 1, d. 2110, ll. 12–17. On the party's inability to find a head for the district women's department, see Minutes of District Political Committee, 23 May 1929, d. 1773, l. 1; Report of the District Organizer, n.d., d. 1416, l. 83. On Chicago women's role in the Gastonia drive, see *The Activizer*, October 1929, d. 1777, ll. 28–30.

64. Letter from Section 7 Organizer, 19 May 1934, RTsKhIDNI, f. 515, op. 1, d. 3587, l. 139 (quote); Randi Storch, "'They Could Stay in the Toilet and Play with the Babies': Women's Personnel and Political Struggles within the CPUSA," paper presented at the Social Science History Association Conference, 20 November 2004, Chicago; Sharon Hartman Strom, "Challenging 'Woman's Place': Feminism, the Left, and Industrial Unionism in the 1930s," *Feminist Studies* 9.2 (1983): 359–86; Elizabeth Faue, "'Dynamo of Change': Gender and Solidarity in the American Labour Movement of the 1930s," *Gender and History* 1.2 (1989): 138–58.

65. Elizabeth Faue, "Paths of Unionization: Community, Bureaucracy, and Gender in the Minnesota Labor Movement of the 1930s," and Patricia Cooper, "The Faces of Gender: Sex Segregation and Work Relations at Philco, 1928–1938," in *Work Engendered: Toward a New History of American Labor,* ed. Ava Baron (Ithaca, N.Y.: Cornell University Press, 1991), 296–319 and 320–50; Alice Kessler-Harris, *In Pursuit of Equity: Men, Women, and the Quest for Economic Citizenship in Twentieth-Century America* (Oxford: Oxford University Press, 2001).

66. Lydia Sargent, ed., *Women and Revolution* (Boston: South End Press, 1981), ix–xxxi; Van Gosse, "'To Organize in Every Neighborhood, in Every Home': The Gender Politics of American Communists between the Wars," *Radical History Review* 50 (Spring 1991): 109–42; Robert Schaffer, "Women and the Communist Party USA, 1930–1940," *Socialist Review* 45 (May 1979): 73–118; Rosalyn Baxandall, "The Question Seldom Asked: Women and the CPUSA," in *New Studies in the Politics and Culture of U.S. Communism,* ed. Michael Brown (New York: Monthly Review, 1993), 141–62; Kate Weigand, *Red Feminism: American Communism and the Making of Women's Liberation* (Baltimore: Johns Hopkins University Press, 2001), 28–64. For a discussion of the Communist party's construction of gender, see chapter 3 of this volume.

67. Election Flyer, Illinois Communist Party folder, vertical files, Tamiment Institute Library, New York University; Minutes of Secretariat Meeting, 3 February 1939, RTsKh-IDNI, f. 515, op. 1, d. 2109, l. 102; Minutes of District Secretariat, 24 August 1932, d. 2866, l. 105; *Workers' Voice,* 15 October 1932, 2; U.S. Military Intelligence Department Reports, Surveillance of Radicals in the United States, Microfilm, reel 29, frame 468 (hereafter USMI-SRUS); Minutes of the Polcom, 9 November 1929, d. 1773, l. 29; *Negro Champion,* 3 November 1928, 1 (quote).

68. Edith Margo, "The South Side Sees Red," *Left Front* (January–February 1934): 4; Harry Haywood, *Black Bolshevik: Autobiography of an Afro-American Communist* (Chicago: Liberator Press, 1978), 300, 312–14.

69. Wright, *Black Boy,* 346–51; Haywood, *Black Bolshevik,* 101, 115, 129; Horace Cayton and St. Clair Drake, *Black Metropolis: A Study of Negro Life in a Northern City* (1945; reprint, New York: Harper and Row, 1966), 603; Roger Bruns, *The Damndest Radical: The Life and Times of Ben Reitmann* (Urbana: University of Illinois Press, 1987), 246–48; Harold Gosnell, *Negro Politicians: The Rise of Negro Politics in Chicago* (Chicago: University of Chicago Press, 1967), 328–31, 337.

70. District Plenum, 19–20 December 1931, RTsKhIDNI, f. 515, op. 1, d. 2464, ll. 70–74; n.d., d. 2115, l. 26.

71. See map; Minutes of the District Secretariat, 20 September 1932, RTsKhIDNI, f. 515, op. 1, d. 2866, ll. 115–16; Resolution on the Results of the Elections and the Next Tasks, n.d., d. 2869, ll. 23–25; Conference Discussion, 6 September 1931, d. 2455, l. 54. See precinct map indicating Communist support in box 50, folder 3, Ernest Burgess Papers, Regenstein Library, University of Chicago; thanks to James R. Barrett for bringing this source to my attention. For a general discussion of black voting patterns, see William J. Grimshaw, *Bitter Fruit: Black Politics and the Chicago Machine, 1931–1991* (Chicago: University of Chicago Press, 1992).

72. Organization Department Letter, 4 June 1931, RTsKhIDNI, f. 515, op. 1, d. 2466, ll. 75–76; Section 7 Organization Letter, 11 October 1933, d. 3267, l. 122; Minutes of PolBuro Meeting, 17 August 1930, d. 2109, ll. 45–46; Report on Labor Day Demonstration, 2 September 1930, d. 2110, ll. 59–63.

73. Allan H. Spear, *Black Chicago: The Making of a Negro Ghetto, 1890–1920* (Chicago: University of Chicago Press, 1967), 148–49. See also Wright, *Black Boy*, 331–32; Cayton and Drake, *Black Metropolis;* Haywood, *Black Bolshevik*, 86–88; Roger Horowitz, *"Negro and White, Unite and Fight!": A Social History of Industrial Unionism in Meatpacking, 1930–1990* (Urbana: University of Illinois Press, 1997), 61–67; Rick Halpern, *Down on the Killing Floor: Black and White Workers in Chicago's Packinghouses, 1904–1954* (Urbana: University of Illinois Press, 1997), 105–12; James R. Barrett, *Work and Community in the Jungle: Chicago's Packinghouse Workers, 1894–1922* (Urbana: University of Illinois Press, 1987), 208; Cohen, *Making a New Deal*, 33–38.

74. For good descriptions of the Back of the Yards in the 1920s and 1930s, see Robert Slayton, *Back of the Yards: The Making of a Local Democracy* (Chicago: University of Chicago Press, 1986), 3–15; Thomas J. Jablonsky, *Pride in the Jungle: Community and Everyday Life in Back of the Yards Chicago* (Baltimore: Johns Hopkins University Press, 1993), 1–25; Horowitz, *"Negro and White, Unite and Fight!"* 61–63, 67–68; Halpern, *Down on the Killing Floor*, 10–12, 21–22, 66–67, 81–82, 155–58; Scott Nearing, "The Jungle," *Labor Defender* (September 1928): 188 (quote). See also *Negro Champion*, 27 October 1928, 5.

75. Christopher Reed, *The Chicago NAACP and the Rise of Black Professional Leadership, 1910–1966* (Bloomington: Indiana University Press, 1997), 72–89; Beth Bates, *Pullman Porters and the Rise of Protest Politics in Black America, 1925–1945* (Chapel Hill: University of North Carolina Press, 2001); District Organization Department Letter, 11 November 1930, RTsKhIDNI, f. 515 op. 1, d. 2113, l. 67; Section 7 Organization Letter, 7 December 1933, d. 3267, l. 129; M. Childs to Wolfe, 17 March 1928, d. 1334, l. 24; Browder to Secretariat, 15 January 1929, d. 1652, ll. 59–60.

76. Haywood, *Black Bolshevik*, 55.

77. Ibid., 1, 3.

78. Ibid., 5; William Tuttle, *Race Riot: Chicago in the Red Summer of 1919* (New York: Atheneum Books, 1970).

79. Haywood, *Black Bolshevik*, 99.

80. Ibid., 100, 117.

81. Ibid., 117–18.

82. Ibid., 83; Wright, *Black Boy*, 415–16.

83. Wright, *Black Boy*, 419–22; Rowley, *Nelson Algren*, 98.

84. Wright, *Black Boy*, 371–72; Rowley, *Nelson Algren*, 74. On 24 June 1933, the editor of the *Chicago Defender* asked whether Communists had it right concerning religion. The responses from its non-party readers were decidedly mixed.

85. Wright, *Black Boy*, 372.

86. Ibid., 372–90; Rowley, *Nelson Algren*, 79–80.

87. Wright, *Black Boy*, 387–89; Rowley, *Nelson Algren*, 80–81.

88. Quoted in Rowley, *Nelson Algren,* 97.

89. William Patterson, *The Man Who Cried Genocide: An Autobiography* (New York: International Publishers, 1971), 148.

90. Gosnell, *Negro Politicians,* 345.

91. David Poindexter quoted in ibid., 345–46; Jim Klein and Julia Reichart, interview with Claude Lightfoot for *Seeing Red,* 9 October 1978, 11 (second quote), Tamiment Institute Library, New York University.

92. Jim Klein and Julia Reichart, interview with Claude Lightfoot, 11, Tamiment Institute Library, New York University; Claude Lightfoot, *Chicago Slums to World Politics: Autobiography of Claude M. Lightfoot* (New York: New Outlook Publishers, 1980), 33–34.

93. Jim Klein and Julia Reichart, interview with Claude Lightfoot, 11, Tamiment Institute Library, New York University.

94. Wirth and Furez, *Local Community Fact Book,* 24, 28, 31; District Organization Department Letter, 15 September 1930, RTsKhIDNI, f. 515, op. 1, d. 2113, l. 41; 15 December 1930, d. 2113, l. 82; 13 September 1932, d. 2882, l. 144.

95. Wirth and Furez, *Local Community Fact Book,* 24, 28, 31.

96. District Organization Letter, 15 September 1930, RTsKhIDNI, f. 515, op. 1, d. 2113, l. 41; Clarence Hathaway to Max Bedacht, 17 October 1929, d. 1652, ll. 121–23; Mary Cygan, "The Polish-American Left," and Maria Woroby, "The Ukrainian Immigrant Left in the United States," in *The Immigrant Left in the United States,* ed. Paul Buhle and Dan Georgakas (Albany: State University of New York Press, 1996), 148–84 and 185–206. For voting patterns among Chicago's Polish groups, see Edward R. Kantowicz, *Polish-American Politics in Chicago, 1888–1940* (Chicago: University of Chicago Press, 1975).

97. Party Registration—1931, RTsKhIDNI, f. 515, op. 1, d. 2464, l. 93; District Organization Department Meeting, 9 November 1932, d. 2882, l. 169; Minutes of District Secretariat, 12 April 1933, d. 3258, l. 131, and 29 June 1933, l. 141. See also Paul Buhle, "Themes in American Jewish Radicalism," in *The Immigrant Left in the United States,* ed. Paul Buhle and Dan Georgakas (Albany: State University of New York Press, 1996), 77–118; Irving Howe, *World of Our Fathers* (New York: Harcourt Brace Jovanovich, 1976); Paul Buhle, "Jews and American Communism: The Cultural Question," *Radical History Review* 23 (Spring 1980): 9–36; Irving Cutler, *The Jews of Chicago: From Shtetl to Suburb* (Urbana: University of Illinois Press, 1996), 233–38; Glazer, *Social Basis of American Communism,* 130–44.

98. "A Radical Woman: The Life and Labors of Mollie West," *The (Chicago) Reader* 22.28 (16 April 1993): 20.

99. Section 4 Organization Letter, 1 August 1932, RTsKhIDNI, f. 515, op. 1, d. 2882, l. 128; Letter from District Organizer, 25 July 1930, d. 1956, l. 46; Minutes of PolBuro, 17 August 1930, d. 2109, ll. 45–46; Report on Labor Day Demonstration, 2 September 1930, d. 2110, l. 61. On the Dil Pickle, see Haywood, *Black Bolshevik,* 115, 129; and James R. Barrett, *William Z. Foster and the Tragedy of American Radicalism* (Urbana: University of Illinois Press, 1999), 73.

100. Wirth and Furez, *Local Community Fact Book,* 6, 7, 8; Edith Abott, *The Tenements of Chicago, 1908–1935* (New York: Arno Press, 1970), 106–10.

101. Ten Year Anniversary Festival with Bazaar, 1918–1928, Workers Lyceum, in possession of author, translated from Swedish by Janne Hereitis. Thanks to the late Steve Sapolsky for lending this source.

102. Report, 10 November 1932, reel 29, frame 464, USMI-SRUS; Henry Bengston, *On the Left in America: Memoirs of the Scandinavian-American Labor Movement* (Carbondale: Southern Illinois University Press, 1999), 202.

103. Jack Spiegel, interviews with the author, 28 May 1994 and 4 May 1996; Robert McClory, "The Incurable Radical," *The (Chicago) Reader* 13.2 (14 October 1983): 8, 9, 34, and 36.

104. Jack Spiegel, interviews with the author, 28 May 1994 and 4 May 1996; McClory, "Incurable Radical," 8, 9, 34, and 36.

105. Jack Kling, *Where the Action Is: Memoirs of a U.S. Communist* (New York: New Outlook Publishers, 1985), 6. The title of Kling's gang is telling; the term "pineapple" was a euphemism for homemade bombs. See Barbara Newell, *Chicago and the Labor Movement: Metropolitan Unionism in the 1930s* (Urbana: University of Illinois Press, 1961), 80.

106. Kling, *Where the Action Is,* 6–7.

107. Ibid., 17.

108. Party Registration—1931, RTsKhIDNI, f. 515, op. 1, d. 2464, l. 93.

Chapter 3: "True Revolutionaries"

1. The specific charges are not documented but most likely have to do with Poindexter's reluctance to publicly attack "Negro reformists" as party leaders directed. See Conference Notes, n.d., RTsKhIDNI, f. 515, op. 1, d. 3581, l. 87.

2. The first account can be found in Hazel Rowley, *Richard Wright: The Life and Times* (New York: Henry Holt, 2001), 100–101. The second is in Mark Solomon, *The Cry Was Unity: Communists and African Americans, 1917–1936* (Jackson: University Press of Mississippi, 1998), 161. Solomon dates the trial to 1932 based on an interview with Claude Lightfoot, but Haywood did not get to Chicago until two years later.

3. Harry Haywood, *Black Bolshevik: Autobiography of an Afro-American Communist* (Chicago: Liberator Press, 1978), 441–42.

4. F. Bury to J. Mackovich, trans. J. F. Schiffel, 23 March [n.y.], RTsKhIDNI, f. 515, op. 1, d. 3052, l. 53.

5. Jim Klein and Julia Reichart, interview with Carl Hirsch for *Seeing Red,* 13 October 1978, 6–8, Tamiment Institute Library, New York University.

6. Richard Wright, *Black Boy: American Hunger* (New York: Harper Perennial, 1993), 346–47; Solomon, *Cry Was Unity,* 46–47; *Chicago Tribune,* 4 August 1932, 34.

7. Rowley, *Richard Wright,* 65; Wright, *Black Boy,* 346.

8. Jim Klein and Julia Reichart, interview with Carl Hirsch, 15 October 1978, 11.

9. J. Williamson, "The Party Nucleus—A Factor in the Class Struggle," 29–30 March 1931, RTsKhIDNI, f. 515, op. 1, d. 2455, l. 21.

10. Harvey Klehr, *The Heyday of American Communism: The Depression Decade* (New York: Basic Books, 1984), 156–57, suggests that Communist leaders clung to their eso-

teric language because they believed it was the only way to express the science of Marx-ism-Leninism, but the pervasive use of Russian symbols in dress as well as language suggests more of a cultural affinity and desire to directly connect themselves to Russia's successful revolution than his explanation implies.

11. Organization Letter, 14 March 1931, RTsKhIDNI, f. 515, op. 1, d. 2466, l. 33.

12. Weekly Organization Letter, 26–30 December 1930, RTsKhIDNI, f. 515, op. 1, d. 2113, l. 89.

13. Ibid.; Organization Letter, 7 February 1931, RTsKhIDNI, f. 515, op., 1, d. 2466, 1. 6.

14. Applications in RTsKhIDNI, f. 515, d. 4143 and 4144. Andrea Graziosi found that in 1931 the American party received over a hundred thousand appeals to emigrate to the Soviet Union. See Andrea Graziosi, *A New Peculiar State: Explorations in Soviet History, 1917–1937* (Westport, Conn.: Praeger, 2000), 228.

15. Jim Klein and Julia Reichart, interview with Ben Gray for *Seeing Red,* 8–9, Tami-ment Institute Library, New York University.

16. Ibid., 13. See, for example, "Workers! Don't Let Bosses Attack the Soviet Union!" *Labor Unity,* 29 November 1930, 2. In the December 1934 issue of *Labor Unity,* Steve Rubicki, the TUUL leader in Chicago, criticized the paper's editors for sending him "a Soviet Pictoral" instead of a paper that "gives us guidance and the line for our work. . . . The Secretaries of our Local Unions," he complained, "refuse to take this magazine and I'll be damned if I can convince them to do so." The paper's editors responded that they "do not apologize" for the issue and that it is the job of *Labor Unity* to "discuss the achievements and victories of the workers of the Soviet Union."

17. Claude Lightfoot, *Chicago Slums to World Politics: Autobiography of Claude M. Lightfoot* (New York: New Outlook Publishers, 1980), 11.

18. Jim Klein and Julia Reichart, interview with Carl Hirsch, 3; see also Jack Kling, *Where the Action Is: Memoirs of a U.S. Communist* (New York: New Outlook Publishers, 1985), 17.

19. Jim Klein and Julia Reichart, interview with Ben Gray, 11.

20. Report at District Plenum, 29–30 March 1931, RTsKhIDNI, f. 515, op. 1 d. 2455, l. 20.

21. From 1928 through 1935, anywhere from ten to thirty Communist periodicals were published in Chicago. See Harold D. Lasswell and Dorothy Blumenstock, *World Revolutionary Propaganda: A Chicago Study* (New York: Alfred A. Knopf, 1939), 58–71; Klehr, *Heyday of American Communism,* 166; Org. Department Questionnaire for Dis-trict 8, 10 October 1930, section 2, box 8, file 35, Earl Browder Papers, Syracuse Univer-sity Library, Special Collections, Research Center, Syracuse, N.Y. See also *Labor Unity,* 31 January 1931, 1, which describes a Chicago meeting where twenty-five literature agents pledged to hook ten thousand new readers on the paper.

22. "The District School," in *The Activizer: Official Organ of Section Three,* October 1929, RTsKhIDNI, f. 515, op. 1, d. 1777, l. 28; Org. Letter, 7 April 1932, d. 2870. l. 35. In the summer of 1931, the district school was held at the Finnish Workers camp outside Waukegan; see Organization Letter, 4 June 1931, d. 2466, l. 76.

23. DC Secretariat to Agitprop CC, 1 December 1932, RTsKhIDNI, f. 515, op. 1, d. 2876, l. 137.

24. District 8 Letter, 1 July 1932, RTsKhIDNI, f. 515, op. 1, d. 2870, l. 72.

25. Section 7 Letter, 7 December 1933, RTsKhIDNI, f. 515, op. 1, d. 3267, l. 130.

26. DC Secretariat to Agitprop CC, 1 December 1932, RTsKhIDNI, f. 515, op. 1, d. 2876, l. 137; Italian Buro Report, n.d., d. 2337, l. 132.

27. 10 January 1933, USMI-SRUS; Section 6 Organization Letter, 7 December 1932, RTsKhIDNI, f. 515, op. 1, d. 2882, l. 222; Section 5 Organizational Directives, 17 November through 24 November 1932, f. 515, op. 1, d. 2870, l. 118.

28. Organization Letter, 21 December 1929, RTsKhIDNI, f. 515, op. 1, d. 1777, l. 38.

29. District Buro Minutes, 8 December 1932, RTsKhIDNI, f. 515, op. 1, d. 2866, l. 85.

30. Section 5 Organization Directives, 17 November through 24 November 1932, RTsKhIDNI, f. 515, op. 1, d. 2870, l. 118.

31. "How to Get Signatures for Nominating Petitions," n.d., RTsKhIDNI, f. 515, op. 1, d. 2112, ll. 65–66; AgitProp Conference, 19 April 1929, d. 1775, l. 8; Minutes of AgitProp, 20 April 1929, l. 5–6.

32. Minutes Secretariat Meeting, 27 January 1929, RTsKhIDNI, f. 515, op. 1, d. 1775, l. 47; District Organization Department Letter, 4 June 1931, d. 2466, l. 76; Minutes of District Buro, 26 November 1932, d. 2866, ll. 83–84; Haywood, *Black Bolshevik,* 155–65, 200–206.

33. Mary Templin, "Revolutionary Girl, Militant Housewife, Antifascist Mother, and More: The Representation of Women in American Communist Women's Journals of the 1930s," *Centennial Review* 41.3 (1997): 625–33.

34. Eric D. Weitz, *Creating German Communism: 1890–1990* (Princeton, N.J.: Princeton University Press, 1997), 188–232; Joyce Kornbluth, ed., *Rebel Voices: An IWW Anthology* (Ann Arbor: University of Michigan Press, 1964).

35. Weitz, *Creating German Communism,* 189.

36. Elizabeth Faue, *Community of Suffering and Struggle: Women, Men, and the Labor Movement in Minneapolis, 1915–1945* (Chapel Hill: University of North Carolina Press, 1991), 69–125; Alice Kessler-Harris, *In Pursuit of Equity: Women, Men, and the Quest for Economic Citizenship in the Twentieth Century* (Oxford: Oxford University Press, 2001).

37. Van Gosse, "'To Organize in Every Neighborhood, in Every Home': The Gender Politics of American Communists between the Wars," *Radical History Review* 50 (1991): 108–41.

38. These images appear in each issue of *Working Woman.*

39. Annelise Orleck, *Common Sense and a Little Fire: Women and Working-Class Politics in the United States* (Chapel Hill: University of North Carolina Press, 1995).

40. See *Working Woman,* July 1931, 1; June 1931, 1; August 1931, 1.

41. Kessler-Harris, *In Pursuit of Equity;* Linda Gordon, *The Moral Property of Women: A History of Birth Control Politics in America* (Urbana: University of Illinois Press, 2002);

Nancy Woloch, *Muller v. Oregon: A Brief History with Documents* (Boston: Bedford Press, 1996).

42. They also argued that Republican and Democratic platforms and policies did not support women. *Working Woman,* June 1931, 4; August 1931, 7; June 1940, 4; Robert Shaffer, "Women and the Communist Party, USA, 1930–1940," *Socialist Review* 45 (May–June 1979): 84.

43. District Disciplinary Decisions, March 1933, RTsKhIDNI, f. 515, op. 1, d. 3264, l. 18. See also District Disciplinary Decisions, July 1933, d. 3264.

44. John Williamson, *Dangerous Scot: The Life and Work of an American "Undesirable"* (New York: International Publishers, 1969), 92.

45. Christine Ellis interview in *Rank and File: Personal Histories by Working-Class Organizers,* ed. Alice Lynd and Staughton Lynd (Boston: Beacon Press, 1973), 24 (in Chicago, Christine Ellis was known as Katherine Erlich).

46. Kate Weigand, *Red Feminism: American Communism and the Making of Women's Liberation* (Baltimore: Johns Hopkins University Press, 2001), 15–27.

47. Lasswell and Blumenstock, *World Revolutionary Propaganda,* 44.

48. Report on May Day Demonstration, 5 May 1930, RTsKhIDNI, f. 515, op. 1, d. 2110, l. 2; Carolyn Ashbaugh, *Lucy Parsons: American Revolutionary* (Chicago: Charles Kerr, 1976), 253.

49. For a detailed history of Red Squads, see Frank Donner, *Protectors of Privilege: Red Squads and Police Repression in Urban America* (Berkeley: University of California Press, 1990). For examples of police attacks at party offices, see M. C. to PolBuro, 6 September 1935, RTsKhIDNI, f. 515, op. 1, d. 3859, ll. 68–69; Johnny to Browder, 16 November 1931, d. 2460, l. 112; Report of Labor Day Demonstration, 5 May 1930, d. 2110, l. 63; Letter from K. E. Heikkine, 26 October 1929, d. 1652, l. 126.

50. Organizational Department Letter, 25 September 1931, RTsKhIDNI, f. 515, op. 1, d. 2466, l. 106.

51. Haywood, *Black Bolshevik,* 444; *Daily Worker,* 29 September 1932; Rowley, *Richard Wright,* 96; "The Atlanta Six," *Labor Defender* (August 1930): 154.

52. Lasswell and Bluenstock, *World Revolutionary Propaganda,* 47; *Chicago Needle Worker,* March 1928, RTsKhIDNI, f. 515, op. 1, d. 1526, l. 3; Organizational Department Letter, 28 February 1931, d. 2466, l. 23; Section 4 Organization letter, 15 December 1931, d. 2472, l .90.

53. The Soviet policy is explained in Joseph Stalin, *Marxism and the National Question: Selected Writings and Speeches* (New York: International Publishers, 1942). Good discussions of how this policy was understood in the American context can be found in Solomon, *Cry Was Unity,* 68–89; and Haywood, *Black Bolshevik,* 218–35.

54. "Outline for Discussion on the Right to Self Determination," n.d., RTsKhIDNI, f. 515 op. 1, d. 3269, ll. 84–85; Haywood, *Black Bolshevik,* 552–54; Philip S. Foner and Herbert Shapiro, eds., *American Communism and Black Americans: A Documentary History, 1930–1934* (Philadelphia: Temple University Press, 1991), 14–16, 41–42, 63–70, 85–86.

55. Section 7 Organization Letter, 7 December 1933, RTsKhIDNI, f. 515, op. 1, d. 3267, l. 129 (quote); James Goodman, *Stories of Scottsboro* (New York: Random House, 1994).

For party involvement with the Scottsboro case in Harlem, see Mark Naison, *Communists in Harlem during the Depression* (Urbana: University of Illinois Press, 1983), 57–89. For Birmingham, see Robin Kelley, *Hammer and Hoe: Alabama Communists during the Great Depression* (Chapel Hill: University of North Carolina Press, 1990), 78–91.

56. St. Clair Drake and Horace Cayton, *Black Metropolis: A Study of Negro Life in a Northern City* (New York: Harper and Row, 1962), 86, 736 (quote), 737; Section 2 Organization Letter, 7 November 1933, RTsKhIDNI, f. 515, op. 1, d. 3267, l. 70; Section 1 Organization Letter, 5 April 1932, d. 2870, l. 31; Lightfoot, *Chicago Slums to World Politics*, 42–44.

57. Letter from P. Camel to the *Daily Worker*, 18 January 1934, RTsKhIDNI, f. 515, op. 1, d. 3587, l. 62.

58. Solomon, *Cry Was Unity*, 173; Lightfoot, *Chicago Slums to World Politics*, 53–54; Drake and Cayton, *Black Metropolis*, 129–73.

59. *Chicago Defender*, 1 July 1933, 15 (quote); Demsey J. Travis, *An Autobiography of Black Chicago* (Chicago: Urban Research Institute, 1981), 48.

60. For a fuller discussion of expulsions during the Third Period, see Randi Storch, "'The Realities of the Situation': Revolutionary Discipline and Everyday Political Life in Chicago's Communist Party, 1928–1935," *Labor: Studies in Working-Class History in the Americas* 1.3 (Fall 2004): 19–44.

61. Minutes of District Convention, 7–8 June 1930, RTsKhIDNI, f. 515, op. 1, d. 2107, l. 5.

62. Jim Klein and Julia Reichart, interview with Ben Gray.

63. Minutes of District Plenum, 11 May 1930, RTsKhIDNI, f. 515, op. 1, d. 2108, l. 2.

64. "Control of How Party Instructions Are Carried Out," *PO* 3 (1930): 14–15; "Regular Party Work," *PO* 3 (March 1930): 13.

65. District Disciplinary Decisions, March 1933, RTsKhIDNI, f. 515, op. 1, d. 3264, l. 19; District Disciplinary Decisions, October–November 1932, d. 2870, l. 123.

66. Organization Letter, 4 November 1930, RTsKhIDNI, f. 515, op. 1, d. 2113, ll. 64–65; Directives on Future Handling of Party Records and Statistics, n.d. [1933], d. 3264, l. 12.

67. District Disciplinary Decisions, March 1933, RTsKhIDNI, f. 515, op. 1, d. 3264.

68. Al Glotzer interviewed by Jon Bloom, 13–21 December 1983, Oral History of the American Left, Tamiment Institute Library, New York University.

69. Theodore Draper, *American Communism and Soviet Russia* (New York: Vintage Books, 1986), 357–76, 374 (quote).

70. James P. Cannon, *The First Ten Years of American Communism: Report of a Participant* (New York: Lyle Stuart, 1962), 222–26; Draper, *American Communism and Soviet Russia*, 357–76; James R. Barrett, *William Z. Foster and the Tragedy of American Radicalism* (Urbana: University of Illinois Press, 1999), 153–55.

71. Appeal to the CEC against the "Resolution on Organization" Adopted by the Chicago District Polburo Appeal by M. Childs, N. Green, Wm. Simmons, Leo Fisher, Nels Kjar, Dora Lifshitz, Steve Rubicki, 29 September 1928, RTsKhIDNI, f. 515, op. 1, d. 1334, l. 99.

72. Joe Giganti to Polcom, 24 January 1929, RTsKhIDNI, f. 515, op. 1, d. 1640, l. 5; Tom O'Flaherty, the Communist editor of the *Voice of Labor,* city editor of the *Daily Worker,* and journalist and founder of *Labor Defender,* was also expelled for "refusing to join in the hue and cry against Trotsky." See Tom O'Flaherty to Jack Conroy, 9 June 1931, Jack Conroy Papers, Newberry Library, Chicago.

73. Minutes of District PolCom, 10 February 1929, f. 515, op. 1, d. 1773, l. 20.

74. District Political Committee Minutes, 10 February 1929, RTsKhIDNI, f. 515, op. 1, d. 1773, ll. 120–21; To CEC Plenum, 13 December 1928, l. 144; To CEC Plenum, 24 December 1928, l. 146; Appeal to CEC, 29 September 1928, l. 99; Draper, *American Communism and Soviet Russia,* 357–76; Klehr, *Heyday of American Communism,* 7–10. Party leaders also noted that Jews were more sympathetic to these splinter groups than were any other racial or ethnic group. See Hathaway to Lovestone, 12 August 1929, d. 1652, ll. 100–109.

75. Minutes of the District Convention, 7–8 June 1930, RTsKhIDNI, f. 515, op. 1, d. 2107, ll. 2–12; Minutes of the PolCom Meeting, 15 March 1930, d. 2109, l. 14.

76. Isaac Deutscher, *The Prophet Outcast Trotsky: 1929–1940* (London: Oxford University Press, 1963), 39. For a detailed party analysis of social fascism, see R. Palme Dutt, *Fascism and Social Revolution: A Study of the Economics and Politics of the Extreme Stages of Capitalism Decay* (1934; reprint, San Fransicso: Proletarian Publishers, 1974).

77. Deutscher, *Prophet Outcast Trotsky,* 38. For a good discussion of Third Period terms, see Kevin McDermott and Jeremy Agnew, *The Comintern: A History of International Communism from Lenin to Stalin* (New York: St. Martin's Press, 1997), 68–73 and 81–119.

78. Klehr, *Heyday of American Communism,* 13; Harvey Klehr and John Haynes, *The American Communist Movement: Storming Heaven Itself* (New York: Twayne Press, 1992), 69–73.

79. Jack Spiegel, interview with the author, Chicago, 4 August 1996.

80. *Northwestern Shop News,* April 1931, RTsKhIDNI, f. 515, op. 1, d. 2474, l. 7.

81. Chicago Foreign Language Press Survey, *Radnik,* 31 October 1928 and 26 February 1929.

82. Chicago Foreign Language Press Survey, *Otthon,* 29 March 1931; *Rassviet,* 19 December 1933.

83. District Organization Department Letter, 5 September 1930, RTsKhIDNI, f. 515, op. 1, d. 2113, l. 33.

84. District Organization Department Letter, 29 November 1930, RTsKhIDNI, f. 515 op. 1, d. 2113, l. 76.

85. District Organization Letter, 7 February 1931, RTsKhIDNI, f. 515, op. 1, d. 2466, l. 15; 2 December 1931, l. 132; 19 June 1931, l. 80.

86. District Organization Department Letter, 26 June 1931, RTsKhIDNI, f. 515, op. 1, d. 2466, l. 85.

87. District Organization Department Letter, 26 January 1931, RTsKhIDNI, f. 515, op. 1, d. 2466, l. 8; District Organization Department Letter, 22 October 1931, d. 2466, l. 119; Resolution Adopted at the Section 5 Conference, 19 December 1930, d. 2110, ll. 78–82; District Organization Letter, 28 October 1930, ll. 59–60.

88. District Organization Letter, 16 July 1931, RTsKhIDNI, f. 515, op. 1, d. 2466, l. 91; 31 July 1931, l. 87.

89. District Organization Department Letter, 19 June 1931, RTsKhIDNI, f. 515, op. 1, d. 2466, l. 80.

90. Weekly Organization Letter, 26–30 December 1930, RTsKhIDNI, f. 515, op. 1, d. 2113, l. 89; Minutes of the District Secretariat, 14 February 1933, d. 3258, l. 106; District 8 Letter, 9 September 1932, d. 2870, l. 93; District Organization Department Letter, 21 May 1931, d. 2466, l. 71.

91. Minutes of Organization Department, 17 October 1931, RTsKhIDNI, f. 515, op. 1, d. 2464, l. 42; Minutes of Section Committee Meeting, 5 October 1931, d. 2472, ll. 13–14.

92. District Organization Department Letter, 31 July 1933, RTsKhIDNI, f. 515 op. 1, d. 3267, l. 234; District Organization Department Letter, 15 September 1930, d. 2113, l. 42; Letter to Potkin from Section Organization Department, 29 January 1932, d. 2874, l. 27.

93. Minutes of the Secretariat, 23 October 1934, RTsKhIDNI, f. 515, op. 1, d. 3581, l. 61.

94. Resolution on First Half of Three Months Plan of Work, 30 May 1931, RTsKh-IDNI, f. 515, op. 1, d. 2457, l. 59. Out of ninety-three units in the first half of 1931, ten had study groups.

95. Minutes of Section 11, 7 February 1934, RTsKhIDNI, f. 515, op. 1, d. 3587, l. 30; Letter to Organization Committee from Section 7, 19 May 1934, d. 3587, l. 139.

96. Report of Commission Investigating Sections 5–11–12, n.d., RTsKhIDNI, f. 515, op. 1, d. 3853, l. 50; Plan of Action for Building the TUUL in Chicago, n.d. [1930], d. 2113, l. 99; District Organization Department Letter, 12 October 1930, ll. 53–55; Letter to Central Committee from Organization Department of the District, 12 February 1932, d. 2874, l. 79.

97. Minutes of the Lithuanian Central Buro, 16 October 1931, RTsKhIDNI, f. 515, op. 1, d. 2532, l. 25; F. Borich to Jugoslav Buro, n.d., f. 515, op. 1, d. 2021, l. 64.

98. S. Zinich, "The Right Wing Danger in Foreign Language Organizations and Our Tasks," RTsKhIDNI, f. 515, op. 1, d. 1816, ll. 11–16.

99. Letter to Hathaway, n.d., RTsKhIDNI, f. 515, op. 1, d. 1683, l. 73.

100. Letter to Finnish Buro, 1933, RTsKhIDNI, f. 515, op. 1, d. 3265, l. 273; Clarence Hathaway to William Kruse, 12 August 1929, f. 515, op. 1, d. 1652, ll. 100–109.

101. Minutes of the Conference on the Lithuanian Question, 3 March 1931, RTsKh-IDNI, f. 515, op. 1, d. 2532, l. 12.

102. Language Commission to Comrade Loyen, 14 March 1933, RTsKhIDNI, f. 515, op. 1, d. 3176, l. 36.

103. "On Fighting White Chauvinism," *PO* 5 (May 1931): 14–16; "Resolution of the Central Committee, USA, on Negro Work," *Daily Worker,* 23 March 1931; Solomon, *Cry Was Unity,* 129–46; Naison, *Communists in Harlem during the Depression,* 46–48; Klehr, *Heyday of American Communism,* 327–30.

104. Statement and Decision on the Situation in the Editorial Staff of Vilnis, n.d., RTsKhIDNI, f. 515, op. 1, d. 2532, l. 57; On the Fight against the Opportunists in the

Lithuanian Fraction, f. 515, op. 1, d. 2532, l. 71; Minutes of the Lithuanian Fraction, 19 June 1931, f. 515, op. 1, d. 2532.

105. P. Camel, Letter to the editor, *Daily Worker,* 18 January 1934, RTsKhIDNI, f. 515, op. 1, d. 3587, ll. 60–65.

106. Decisions of DCC, August–October 1933, RTsKhIDNI, f. 515, op. 1, d. 3264, l. 24; Decisions for April and May 1934, d. 3052, l. 21.

107. On race relations in Chicago, see Jim Grossman, *Land of Hope: Chicago, Black Southerners and the Great Migration* (Chicago: University of Chicago Press, 1989), 161–80 and 259–65; St. Clair Drake and Horace Cayton, *Black Metropolis: A Study of Negro Life in a Northern City* (New York: Harper and Row, 1962), 65–76, 129–73; Allan H. Spear, *Black Chicago: The Making of a Negro Ghetto, 1890–1920* (Chicago: University of Chicago Press, 1967), 201–29.

108. P. Camel, Letter to the editor, *Daily Worker,* 18 January 1934, RTsKhIDNI, f. 515, op. 1, d. 3587, ll. 60–65.

109. S. Zinich to P. Smith, 6 December 1929, RTsKhIDNI, f. 515, op. 1, d. 1683, ll. 56–57.

110. Letter to District Eight from Members of the Scandinavian Fraction, 24 July 1934, f. 515, op. 1, d. 3587, ll. 207–11.

111. John Mackovich to the Central Committee, 13 April 1929, RTsKhIDNI, f. 515, op. 1, d. 1712, ll. 25–26.

112. On the Ukrainian Labor Home, 10 October 1930, RTsKhIDNI, f. 515, op. 1, d. 2047, ll. 62–64.

113. Organization Department Questionnaire for District Eight, 10 October 1930, series 2, box 8, file 35, Earl Browder Papers, Syracuse University Library, Special Collections, Research Center, Syracuse, N.Y.

114. South Slavic Fraction to Language Department, 17 April 1930, RTsKhIDNI, f. 515, op. 1, d. 2021, l. 84.

115. Language Department of the Central Committee to Loyen, RTsKhIDNI, f. 515, op. 1, d. 2021, ll. 88–89.

116. Minutes of Lettish Bureau, 7 October 1930, RTsKhIDNI, f. 515, op. 1, d. 2160, l. 3.

117. Gebert to Browder, 6 March 1931, RTsKhIDNI, f. 515, op. 1, d. 2277, l. 11.

118. Report of the Subcommittee to Investigate the Work of Language Buros, June 1935, RTsKhIDNI, f. 515, op. 1, d. 3858, l. 229; Minutes of District Eight Convention, 7–8 June 1930, f. 515, op. 1, d. 2107, l. 9.

119. Klehr, *Heyday of American Communism,* 163 (quote); Nathan Glazer, *The Social Basis of American Communism* (New York: Harcourt, Brace, and World, 1961), 62–63.

120. S. Zinich, "The Right Wing Danger in Foreign Language Groups and Our Tasks," RTsKhIDNI, f. 515, op. 1, d. 1816, ll. 11–16.

121. Minutes of the Language Buro, December 1930, RTsKhIDNI, f. 515, op. 1, d. 2109, l. 117.

122. Central Committee, Language Department, to John Mackovich, 8 January 1930, RTsKhIDNI, f. 515, op. 1, d. 2021, l. 9.

123. I. Garelick to Lovestone, 11 January 1929, RTsKhIDNI, f. 515, op. 1, d. 1652, ll. 53–55; District Organization Department Letter, 21 May 1931, d. 2466, l. 71.

124. Zinich to Alpi, 7 January 1930, RTsKhIDNI, f. 515, op. 1, d. 2021, l. 7; Zinich to Alpi, 2 January 1930, d. 2021, l. 3.

125. Zinich to Alpi, 7 January 1930, RTsKhIDNI, f. 515. op. 1, d. 2021, l. 7.

126. Gebert to Alpi, 8 February 1931, d. 2021, l. 51; Zinich to Alpi, 7 January 1930, d. 2021, l. 7.

127. John Mackovich to Central Control Committee, 13 April 1929, RTsKhIDNI, f. 515, op. 1, d. 1712, l. 25.

128. Gebert to Kovis, 11 December 1930, RTsKhIDNI, f. 515, op. 1, d. 2112, l. 63.

129. Chicago Foreign Language Press Survey, *Rassviet,* 19 December 1933.

130. Verblin Speech at District Buro, 24 February 1933, RTsKhIDNI, f. 515, op. 1, d. 3258, ll. 40–45, 42 (quote).

131. To Earl from Bill, 5 August 1933, RTsKhIDNI, f. 515, op. 1, d. 3265, l. 208.

132. District Buro Minutes, 24 February 1933, RTsKhIDNI, f. 515, op. 1, d. 3258, l. 38; Decisions on Disciplinary Cases for April and May 1933, d. 3264, l. 23; Decisions on Disciplinary Cases of January 1934, d. 3586, l. 2; see also Bill to Earl, 5 August 1933, l. 208.

133. Appeal to the CEC against the "Resolution on Organization" Adopted by the Chicago District Polburo Appeal by M. Childs, N. Green, Wm. Simons, Leo Fisher, Nels Kjar, Dora Lifshitz, Steve Rubicki, 29 September 1928, RTsKhIDNI, f. 515, op. 1, d. 1334, l. 99; District Plenum, 11 May 1930, d. 2108.

134. Letter, 22 March 1929, RTsKhIDNI, f. 515, op. 1, d. 1652, l. 73.

135. Gebert letter, n.d., 1931, RTsKhIDNI, f. 515, op. 1, d. 2460, l. 57; Gebert summary, 6 September 1931, f. 515, op. 1, d. 2455, l. 96; 17 June 1931, d. 2457, l. 73.

136. Wm. Mauseth to Lovestone, 11 January 1929, RTsKhIDNI, f. 515, op. 1, d. 1652, l. 51.

137. Ibid.

138. Nels Kjar to Lovestone, 18 January 1929, RTsKhIDNI, f. 515, op. 1, d. 1652, l. 65.

139. Wm. Mauseth to Lovestone, 11 January 1929, RTsKhIDNI, f. 515, op. 1, d. 1652, l. 51; Paul Buhle, interview with Joseph Giganti, 26 July 1983, Oral History of the American Left, Tamiment Institute Library, New York University.

140. The two in 1933 had only joined the party four months earlier.

141. Minutes of Polburo, 1 February 1931, RTsKhIDNI, f. 515, op. 1, d. 2457, ll. 10–11. For other readmissions, see Secretariat Minutes, 29 December 1932, d. 2866, l. 44; District Committee Decisions, October–November 1932, d. 2870, l. 123.

142. Tony Martin, *Race First: The Ideological and Organizational Struggles of Marcus Garvey and the Universal Negro Improvement Association* (Westport, Conn: Greenwood Press, 1976), 221–72; Wilson Record, *The Negro and the Communist Party* (Chapel Hill: University of North Carolina Press, 1951), 39–43.

143. Record, *Negro and the Communist Party,* 39–43; Gosnell, *Negro Politicians,* 338–39.

144. Statement of Sol Harper on the Letter of A. Schultz and Marie Houston, n.d, RTsKhIDNI, f. 515, op. 1, d. 2047, ll. 85–94; Sol Harper to Max Bedacht, 20 September 1930, d. 1956, l. 60; Minutes of District Convention, 7–8 June 1930, d. 2107, ll. 8; Minutes of the PolBuro, 17 August 1930, d. 2109, l. 46.

145. Michael Gold, "The Negro Reds of Chicago," part 1, *Daily Worker*, 9 September 1932; Robin Kelley, *Race Rebels: Culture, Politics, and the Black Working Class* (New York: Free Press, 1994), 117.

146. Beth Bates, *Pullman Porters and the Rise of Protest Politics in Black America, 1925–1945* (Chapel Hill: University of North Carolina Press, 2001), 214–15 (first quote); District Political Committee Minutes, 17 August 1929, RTsKhIDNI, f. 515, op. 1, d. 1773, ll. 22–23 (second quote); Section 4 Minutes, 25 May 1931, d. 2472, l. 62; Letter from Section 4 leadership to Units, 24 June 1931, l. 76; Gosnell, *Negro Politicians*, 337–38.

147. District Discipline Committee, February and March 1935, RTsKhIDNI, f. 515, op. 1, d. 3860, l. 5 (first quote); Danny Duncan Collum, ed., *"This Ain't Ethiopia, but It'll Do": African Americans in the Spanish Civil War* (New York: G. K. Hall and Co., 1992), 14 (second quote); Minutes of the Negro Committee, 8 November 1929, d. 1775, l. 39; Gosnell, *Negro Politicians*, 342.

148. District Organization Department to Secretariat Central Committee, 12 February 1932, RTsKhIDNI, f. 515, op. 1, d. 2874, ll. 79–80; District Buro Minutes, 4 February 1932, d. 2866, l. 29 (quote).

149. Section 2 Organization Letter, 14 February 1933, RTsKhIDNI, f. 515, op. 1, d. 3267, l. 9; Minutes District PolCom, 10 February 1929, d. 1773, l. 23; Statement of Sol Harper on the Letter of A. Schultz and Marie Houston, d. 2047, ll. 85–87.

Chapter 4: Red Relief

1. Edith Margo, "The South Side Sees Red," *Left Front* (January–February 1934): 4–6.

2. Ibid., 5.

3. Accounts of this event are taken from ibid.; Gebert to Browder, 11 August 1931, RTsKhIDNI, f. 515, op. 1, d. 2460, l. 52; Harry Haywood, *Black Bolshevik: Autobiography of an Afro-American Communist* (New York: Liberator Press, 1978), 442–43; Harold Lasswell and Dorothy Blumenstock, *World Revolutionary Propaganda: A Chicago Study* (New York: Alfred A. Knopf, 1939), 196–204; Michael Gold, "The Negro Reds of Chicago," part 2, *Daily Worker*, 15 September 1932; Paul Clinton Young, "Race, Class, and Radicalism in Chicago, 1914–1936" (Ph.D. dissertation, University of Iowa, 2001), 212–14; Claude Lightfoot, *Chicago Slums to World Politics: Autobiography of Claude M. Lightfoot* (New York: New Outlook Publishers, 1980), 41–42.

4. People were able to view the guarded bodies of O'Neil and Grey for a week. Estell Armstrong, Frank Armstrong's wife, refused to allow her husband's body to be used by the Unemployed Council in this way. See Young, "Race, Class, and Radicalism in Chicago," 215–16; *Chicago Defender*, 15 August 1931; Lasswell and Blumenstock, *World Revolutionary Propaganda*, 201–4 (quote on 201).

5. Report of Bill Gebert at the 13th Central Committee Plenum, 6 September 1931, RTsKhIDNI, f. 515, op. 1, d. 2455, l. 96; Haywood, *Black Bolshevik*, 442–43, Lightfoot,

Chicago Slums to World Politics, 42; Lasswell and Blumenstock, *World Revolutionary Propaganda,* 201–4; Harold Gosnell, *Negro Politicians: The Rise of Negro Politics in Chicago* (Chicago: University of Chicago Press, 1967), 330–31.

6. James Lorence, *Organizing the Unemployed: Community and Union Activists in the Industrial Heartland* (Albany: State University of New York Press, 1996); Robin Kelley, *Hammer and Hoe: Alabama Communists during the Great Depression* (Chapel Hill: University of North Carolina Press, 1990); Robin Kelley, "A New War in Dixie: Communists and the Unemployed in Birmingham, Alabama, 1930–1933," *Labor History* 30.3 (Summer 1989): 367–84; Mark Naison, *Communists in Harlem during the Depression* (Urbana: University of Illinois Press, 1983), 31–57. See also Roy Rosenzweig, "Organizing the Unemployed: The Early Years of the Great Depression, 1929–1933," *Radical America* 10 (July–August 1976): 47–60; and Daniel Leab, "United We Eat: The Creation and Organization of the Unemployed Councils in 1930," *Labor History* 8.3 (Fall 1967): 300–315.

7. Lizabeth Cohen, *Making a New Deal: Industrial Workers in Chicago, 1919–1939* (Cambridge: Cambridge University Press, 1990).

8. Steve Nelson, James Barrett, and Rob Ruck, *Steve Nelson, American Radical* (Pittsburgh: University of Pittsburgh Press, 1981), 76.

9. Helen Seymour, "The Organized Unemployed" (M.A. thesis, University of Chicago, 1937), 9–11; Albert Prago, "The Organization of the Unemployed and the Role of the Radicals, 1929–1935" (Ph.D. dissertation, Union Graduate School, 1976), 56–62, 71; Franklin Folsom, *America before Welfare* (New York: New York University Press, 1991), 232–44; Nelson, Barrett, and Ruck, *Steve Nelson,* 74.

10. District Resolution on TUUL, n.d., RTsKhIDNI, f. 515, op. 1, d. 2109, ll. 83–85.

11. Prago, "Organization of the Unemployed," 56–57 and 71. For the TUUL as a guide to Unemployed Councils, see Sergei Malyshev, *Unemployed Councils in St. Petersburg in 1906* (New York: Workers' Library Publishers, 1931). See also Seymour, "Organized Unemployed," 10–11; Rosenzweig, "Organizing the Unemployed," 52; Minutes of District Plenum, 11 May 1930, RTsKhIDNI, f. 515, op. 1, d. 2106, l. 6; District Resolution on TUUL, n.d., d. 2109, l. 83.

12. "Organize for the Fight against Unemployment and Starvation!" *Labor Unity* (22 February 1930): 1.

13. Statement on the March 6th Demonstration, n.d., RTsKhIDNI, f. 515, op. 1., d. 2109; Nelson, Barrett, and Ruck, *Steve Nelson,* 81–85; William Z. Foster, *History of the Communist Party of the United States* (New York: International Publishers, 1952), 281–82. The *Herald Examiner,* 7 March 1930, reported a mere seven hundred marchers, while the *Chicago Tribune,* 7 March 1930, did not offer a specific number. The staggering inconsistency between Communist estimates and non-party reports is typical of Communist overestimation and anti-Communist underestimation.

14. Leab, "United We Eat," 300–315. Leab argues that this demonstration was the high point of party influence, but in Chicago, this is clearly only the beginning. District Buro Minutes, 29 June 1929, RTsKhIDNI, f. 515, op. 1, d. 1775, l. 13; Statement on the March 6th Demonstration, d. 2109. For descriptions of other March 6 demonstrations, see Prago, "Organization of the Unemployed," 71–88.

15. Prago, "Organization of the Unemployed," 99–100; Nelson, Barrett, and Ruck, *Steve Nelson*, 75–76 (quote on 76).

16. Prago, "Organization of the Unemployed," 99–102; Folsom, *America before Welfare*, 256–66; Harvey Klehr, *The Heyday of American Communism: The Depression Decade* (New York: Basic Books, 1984), 49–51; Lorence, *Organizing the Unemployed*.

17. Klehr, *Heyday of American Communism*, 54–55.

18. *Hunger Fighter*, 27 February 1932, 4.

19. *Hunger Fighter*, 23 April 1932, 2.

20. Nelson, Barrett, and Ruck, *Steve Nelson*, 75.

21. Unemployed Insurance Campaign, 29 November 1930, RTsKhIDNI, f. 515, op. 1, d. 2113, ll. 77–80; Organization Department Letter, 28 February 1931 and 7 March 1931, d. 2466, l. 25 and l. 28, respectively; Minutes of Polburo Meeting, 9 November 1930, d. 2109, l. 65; Section 6 Newsletter, 27 June 1932, d. 2870, l. 69; Secretariat Minutes, 2 August 1932, d. 2866, l. 97; Secretariat Minutes, 7 September 1932, d. 2866, l. 107, and 29 September 1932, l. 115; Secretariat Minutes, 22 November 1932 and 29 December 1932, ll. 134–35 and l. 145, respectively; Section 1 Organization Letter, 29 March 1932, d. 2882, l. 4.

22. Minutes of the District Committee, 3 October 1931, RTsKhIDNI, f. 515, op. 1, d. 2460, l. 119; Minutes of the Political Buro, 9 January 1931, d. 2457, l. 1; Minutes of the District Committee, 6 April 1931, d. 2457, l. 36; Minutes of Political Buro, 1 February 1931, d. 2457, l. 11.

23. Jack Spiegel, interview with the author, Chicago, 4 August 1996; *Hunger Fighter*, 18 June 1932, 4.

24. District Buro Minutes, 1 April 1932, RTsKhIDNI, f. 515, op. 1, d. 2866, l. 47; Organization Letter, 1 July 1932, d. 2870, l. 71.

25. Party Registration—1931, RTsKhIDNI, f. 515, op. 1, d. 2464, l. 93; fractions in Section 4 consisted of three comrades in each council. See Section 4's Organization Letter, 5 May 1931, d. 2472, l. 52.

26. District Plenum, 6 September 1931, d. 2455, l. 77; Section 6 Organization Letter, 27 June 1932, d. 2870, l. 69; Organization Letter, 25 September 1931, d. 2457, l. 96; *Hunger Fighter*, 26 March 1932.

27. Enlarged District Committee Meeting, 6 September 1931, RTsKhIDNI, f. 515, op. 1, d. 2455, l. 77.

28. District Convention Minutes, 7–8 June 1930, RTsKhIDNI, f. 515, op. 1, d. 2107, ll. 2–12; G. P., "Local Struggles and the Building of Unemployed Councils in Preparation for the Hunger March," *PO* 5 (January 1932): 9–10.

29. District Convention, 7–8 June 1930, RTsKhIDNI, f. 515, op. 1, d. 2107, l. 4 (quote).

30. Resolution of District Eight Buro, adopted 4 March 1931, RTsKhIDNI, f. 515, op. 1, d. 2457, l. 19.

31. Interview with Ben Gray, Oral History of the American Left, Tamiment Institute Library, New York University.

32. Ibid.

33. Ibid.; Edwin H. Sutherland and Harvey J. Locke, *Twenty Thousand Homeless*

Men: A Study of Unemployed Men in the Chicago Shelters (New York: Arno Press, 1971): 24–34.

34. Quoted in Robert W. Beasley, "Care of Destitute Unattached Men in Chicago with Special Reference to the Depression Period Beginning in 1930" (M.A. thesis, University of Chicago, 1933), 74.

35. Car Kolins, interview with researcher, box 132, folder 2, Ernest Burgess Papers, University of Chicago Special Collections.

36. *Hunger Fighter,* 23 January 1932.

37. *Hunger Fighter,* 26 December 1931 and 18 June 1932.

38. Interview with Ben Gray.

39. *Hunger Fighter,* 13 February 1932, 2.

40. Frances Fox Piven and Richard A. Cloward, *Poor People's Movements: Why They Succeed, How They Fail* (New York: Pantheon Books, 1977), 59.

41. *Hunger Fighter,* 7 May 1932, 2; District Buro Minutes, 1 April 1932, RTsKhIDNI, f. 515, op. 1, d. 2866, l. 47.

42. *Hunger Fighter,* 21 May 1932, 2.

43. Beasley, "Care of Destitute Unattached Men," 73.

44. District Buro Minutes, 1 April 1932, RTsKhIDNI, f. 515, op. 1, d. 2866, l. 47.

45. Gebert Report on February 25th Demonstration, 27 February 1931, RTsKhIDNI, f. 2460, ll. 1–2.

46. Gosnell, *Negro Politicians,* 321 and 329.

47. The streetcar riot activity resulted in blacks getting about twenty-five jobs in their first action on September 16 and fifty in their second action in October. See Christopher Reed, *The Chicago NAACP and the Rise of Black Professional Leadership, 1910–1966* (Bloomington: Indiana University Press, 1997), 73–74, 81–84; Lightfoot, *Chicago's Slums to World Politics,* 33–35; Young, "Race, Class, and Radicalism in Chicago," 191–92.

48. Letter from District Organizer to Comrades, 25 July 1930, RTsKhIDNI, f. 515, op. 1, d. 1956, ll. 45–46; District Organization Letter, 14 September 1933, d. 3267, l. 112; Michael Gold, "The Negro Reds of Chicago," part 1, *Daily Worker,* 9 September 1932.

49. Lightfoot, *Chicago's Slums to World Politics,* 38–42 (quote on 31); Beth Bates, "A New Crowd Challenges the Agenda of the Old Guard in the NAACP, 1933–1941," *American Historical Review* 102.2 (1997): 340–77; Gosnell, *Negro Politicians,* 328; Gold, "Negro Reds of Chicago," part 1.

50. Section 4 Minutes, 25 May 1931, RTsKhIDNI, f. 515, op. 1, d. 2472, l. 62; Letter from Section 4 leadership to units, 24 June 1931, l. 76; Minutes of the District Political Committee, 17 August 1929, d. 1773, ll. 22–23; Interviews with Todd Tate, 1 and 2 October 1985, and with Richard Saunders, 13 September 1985, United Packinghouse Workers Oral History Project, Wisconsin State Historical Society, Madison (hereafter UPWAOHP); Rick Halpern, *Down on the Killing Floor: Black and White Workers in Chicago's Packinghouses, 1904–54* (Urbana: University of Illinois Press, 1997), 111–12.

51. Quoted in Hazel Rowley, *Richard Wright: The Life and Times* (New York: Henry Holt, 2001), 96.

52. Lasswell and Blumenstock, *World Revolutionary Propaganda,* 170–71; Lightfoot, *Chicago's Slums to World Politics,* 38–39.

53. Gebert to Browder, 11 August 1931, RTsKhIDNI, f. 515, op. 1, d. 2460, l. 52.

54. Ibid.; Max Naiman interview, in Studs Terkel, *Hard Times* (New York: Avon Books, 1971), 468–72.

55. Quoted in Halpern, *Down on the Killing Floor*, 110; "We Must Draw Negro Workers into the Mass Organizations and the Party," *PO* 9 (November 1931): 27–28; Cohen, *Making a New Deal*, 266.

56. Cohen, *Making a New Deal*, 266. Also see Robert Asher, "The Influence of the Chicago Workers' Committee on Unemployment upon the Administration of Relief, 1931–1934" (M.A. thesis, University of Chicago, 1934), 41; and Gosnell, *Negro Politicians*, 322.

57. Gosnell, *Negro Politicians*, 336–42; Michael Goldfield, "Race and the CIO: Reply to Critics," *International Labor and Working-Class History* 46 (Fall 1994): 142–60.

58. *Chicago Whip*, 1 August 1931, and *Chicago Defender*, 14 January 1933, quoted in Gosnell, *Negro Politicians*, 321 and 341. See also Stephen Tallackson, "The *Chicago Defender* and Its Reaction to the Communist Movement in the Depression Era" (M.A. thesis, University of Chicago, 1967), 62–63.

59. Horace R. Cayton, "The Black Bugs," *The Nation*, 9 September 1931, 255.

60. Horace Cayton and St. Clair Drake, *Black Metropolis: A Study of Negro Life in a Northern City* (New York: Harper and Row, 1962), 86–87; Yates quoted in Danny Duncan Collum, ed., *"This Ain't Ethiopia, but It'll Do": African Americans in the Spanish Civil War* (New York: G. K. Hall, 1992), 13; Dempsey Travis, *An Autobiography of Black Chicago* (Chicago: Urban Research Institute, 1981), 48. In 1934, Reverend Austin invited Angelo Herndon to speak to his South Side congregation at the Pilgrim Baptist Church. Herndon was on a national tour, newly released from a Georgia prison. Over three thousand people turned out and cheered Herndon on. In addition to support for Herndon, however, was the loud applause and cheers the crowd gave to Reverend Austin when he proclaimed that "any man who does not want freedom is either a fool or an idiot, and if to want freedom is to be a Communist, then I am a Communist, and will be till I die." Communism, he added, "means simply the brotherhood of man and as far as I can see Jesus Christ was the greatest Communist of them all." According to the *Defender*, "For fully five minutes the crowd stood and cheered." See *Chicago Defender*, 22 September 1934, 1; and Beth Bates, *Pullman Porters and the Rise of Protest Politics in Black America, 1925–1945* (Chapel Hill: University of North Carolina Press, 2001), 124.

61. Cayton, "The Black Bugs," 255–56.

62. A good example of mainstream anti-Communist propaganda occurred on 1 May 1933, when five bombs exploded in the city. The papers immediately pinned the event on "the Reds," even though a conflict with the Teamsters was later revealed as the cause. A front-page article in the *Chicago Daily Tribune* on 1 May 1933, "May Day Bombs Jar City," reported that "the five bombings were part of a May Day red demonstration." Deputy Chief of Detectives William Blaul ordered detective-bureau squads to arrest "all known reds and other agitators." One day later, the *Tribune* reported that union racketeers were to blame. Communists expressed their frustration with such false accusations but were pleased that most Chicagoans in 1933 did not ever believe the Reds

were to blame. See Lawrence Lipton to Freeman, 1 May 1933, RTsKhIDNI, f. 515, op. 1, d. 3265, ll. 130–33.

63. See the council's first platform in Folsom, *America before Welfare*, 263; and in John Williamson, *Dangerous Scot: The Life and Work of an American "Undesirable"* (New York: International Publishers, 1969), 80–93.

64. Minutes of the Polburo, 1 February 1931 and 13 February 1931, RTsKhIDNI, f. 515, op. 1, d. 2457, l. 9 and l. 13.

65. Louis Wirth and Margaret Furez, eds., *Local Community Fact Book: 1938* (Chicago: Chicago Recreation Commission, 1938), 61.

66. Section 2 Organization Letter, 11 November 1931, RTsKhIDNI, f. 515, op. 1, d. 2113, l. 69; Minutes of Section 2 Committee, 20 February 1933, f. 515, op. 1, d. 3267, l. 11; Section 2 Newsletter, 20 March 1933, l. 19; 20 April 1932, d. 2882, l. 46.

67. Quoted in Halpern, *Down on the Killing Floor*, 110.

68. Gebert to Browder, 11 August 1931, RTsKhIDNI, f. 515, op. 1, d. 2460, l. 57; Edith Abbott, *The Tenements of Chicago, 1908–1935* (Chicago: University of Chicago Press, 1936), 442.

69. Gebert quotes Cermak as saying that "'Chicago is ready and willing to feed the hungry and lodge the homeless who are orderly and gentlemanly. For the disrespective and riotous we have built jails and penitentiaries.'" After the demonstrations, Gebert claimed that Cermak "didn't dare to make this statement, he made a statement that evictions will be stopped and that there are funds to feed the unemployed, because at that time we were at the height of a broad mass movement that they would not dare to evoke." Gebert's Report on 13th CC Plenum and Tasks, 6 September 1931, RTsKhIDNI, f. 515, op. 1, d. 2455, l. 35; To Committee of Unemployed from A. J. Cermak, Mayor, 1 November 1932, d. 2876, l. 86; Piven and Cloward, *Poor People's Movements*, 55; and Abbott, *Tenements of Chicago*, 442, 444, 458–64. Abbott also describes unfilled promises that city officials had been making before the "riot."

70. Charity organizations paid rent for one month not to exceed fifteen dollars (although the median rent paid by repeaters to renter's court was $18.88), usually given after evictions occurred and the family had found a new place to live. Abbott, *Tenements of Chicago*, 426–76; Piven and Cloward, *Poor People's Movements*, 54; and Seymour, "Organized Unemployed," 2.

71. Interview with Ben Gray.

72. Cohen, *Making a New Deal*, 213–50.

73. Letter to Member Agencies from the Council of Social Agencies of Chicago, 15 October 1932, General Papers 1923–35, University of Chicago Settlement Collection, Chicago Historical Society.

74. *Hunger Fighter*, 23 April 1932, 1.

75. Moss to Johnson, 16 August 1932, Folder August–November 1932, Raymond Hilliard Papers, Chicago Historical Society.

76. "Wicker Park Conference," 21 July 1932 through 19 January 1933, box 1932, Graham Taylor Papers, Newberry Library, Chicago; District Organization Letter, 15 September 1932, RTsKhIDNI, d. 2870, l. 94.

77. *Hunger Fighter,* 4 July 1932; Moss to Johnson, 16 August 1932, Folder August–November 1932, Raymond Hilliard Papers, Chicago Historical Society.

78. *Hunger Fighter,* 12 March 1932.

79. Jack Kling to Gil Green [ca. 1932], RTsKhIDNI, f. 515, op. 1, d. 2876, ll. 192–94; Piven and Cloward, *Poor People's Movements,* 59.

80. District Organization Letter, 31 July 1931, RTsKhIDNI, f. 515, op. 1, d. 2466, l. 95.

81. Chicago Civil Liberties Committee Special Bulletin, Report on Police Brutality at Humboldt Park Demonstration, 22 November 1932, Section 2, no folder number, Raymond Hilliard Papers, Chicago Historical Society.

82. Moss to Allman, 28 November 1932, Folder August–November 1932, Raymond Hilliard Papers, Chicago Historical Society.

83. Vernon Pedersen argues that "Communists normally refused to apply for parade permits during the Third Period, partially as a matter of principle but mainly to provoke confrontations with the authorities." Evidence shows that this was not the case in Chicago. Regardless, the city's police provoked confrontation. Vernon Pedersen, *The Communist Party in Maryland, 1919–1957* (Urbana: University of Illinois Press, 2001), 48; Lasswell and Blumenstock, *World Revolutionary Propaganda,* 172.

84. Steve Rosen, interview with Irving Meyers, Radical Jewish Elders Project, Spertus Library, Chicago.

85. Ibid.

86. Ibid.

87. Director to Illinois Emergency Relief Commission, 8 October 1932, Folder August–November 1932, Raymond Hilliard Papers, Chicago Historical Society.

88. Louis McCann to Moss, 9 December 1932, Folder December 1932–November 1933, Raymond Hilliard Papers, Chicago Historical Society.

89. Meeting of Subcommittee on Relief and Service of Advisory Board of Cook County Bureau of Public Welfare, 11 January 1933 (quote); Jennie Greenspan to Moss, 13 January 1933, Folder December 1932–January 1933, Raymond Hilliard Papers, Chicago Historical Society; Beth Schulman, "The Workers Are Finding a Voice: The Chicago Workers' Committee and the Relief Struggles of 1932," unpublished paper, box 6, folder 12, Frank McCullough Papers, Chicago Historical Society; Cohen, *Making a New Deal,* 264–65.

90. District Convention Discussion, 6 September 1931, RTsKhIDNI, f. 515, op. 1, d. 2455, l. 73.

91. Borders was a resident of the Chicago Commons settlement house and would later become a chief of the Bureau of Supply of the United Nations Relief and Rehabilitation Administration in 1944. Frank McCulloch, born to a family from the reform tradition, eventually became chairman of the National Labor Relations Board in 1961. These two men guided the organization that eventually joined with the Communist Councils into the Workers' Alliance. See Judith Ann Trolander, *Settlement Houses and the Great Depression* (Detroit: Wayne State University Press, 1975), 92–93. See also Asher, "Influence of the Chicago Workers' Committee," 9–14.

92. Trolander, *Settlement Houses,* 95; Cohen, *Making a New Deal,* 264. By mid-1932, the CWC had about sixty locals.

93. Section 4 Organization Letters, 7 February 1933 and 20 February 1933, RTsKh-IDNI, f. 515, op. 1, d. 3267, l. 78 and l. 82; Williamson, *Dangerous Scot,* 83–85.

94. Agent's Report, 10 November 1932, reel 29, frame 464, USMI-SRUS; Williamson, *Dangerous Scot,* 83–85.

95. The protest, incidentally, resulted in a $6.3 million loan from the federal government's Reconstruction Finance Corporation to the city. Rally organizers claimed victory. Trolander, *Settlement Houses,* 97; Asher, "Influence of the Chicago Workers' Committee," 20–22; Cohen, *Making a New Deal,* 264–65. They also took credit for increases in unemployment funds in November 1931 after their staged county hunger march. The 1932 march was organized by the Unemployed Councils and the CWC.

96. Browder to Gebert, 11 August 1931, RTsKhIDNI, f. 515, op. 1, d. 2460, l. 57; District Buro Minutes, 17 June 1931, RTsKhIDNI, f. 515, op. 1, d. 2457, l. 73; Jack Spiegel, interview with the author, Chicago, 4 August 1996.

97. Annie Gosenpud, "The History of the Chicago Worker's Committee on Unemployment, Local #24," 1932, box 144, folder 7, Ernest Burgess Papers, University of Chicago Special Collections.

98. G. P., "Local Struggles and the Building of Unemployed Councils," 9–10.

99. Bill Gebert, "United Front from Below," n.d., RTsKhIDNI, f. 515, op. 1, d. 2873, ll. 53–67; John Williamson, "Defeat the 50 Percent Relief Cut in Chicago," n.d., ll. 72–71; District Organization Department Letter, 13 September 1930, d. 2109, ll. 52–54.

100. Enlarged District Committee Meeting, 6 September 1931, RTsKhIDNI, f. 515, op. 1, d. 2455, l. 53.

101. District Control Decisions, October–November 1932, RtsKhIDNI, f. 515, op. 1, d. 2870, ll. 123–25.

102. District Disciplinary Decisions, March 1933, RTsKhIDNI, f. 515, op. 1, d. 3264, l. 18.

103. Ibid.

104. Van Gosse, "'To Organize in Every Neighborhood, in Every Home': The Gender Politics of American Communists between the Wars," *Radical History Review* 50 (Spring 1991): 109–41; Robert Shaffer, "Women and the Communist Party, USA, 1930–1940," *Socialist Review* 45 (May 1979): 73–118; Rosalyn Baxandall, "The Question Seldom Asked: Women and the CPUSA," in *New Studies in the Politics and Culture of U.S. Communism,* ed. Michael E. Brown, Randy Martin, Frank Rosengarten, and George Snedeker (New York: Monthly Press Review, 1993), 141–62.

105. Report on Women's Work in District Buro Meeting, 3 November 1931, RTsKh-IDNI, f. 515, op. 1, d. 2457, l. 132; Margaret Keller, Women's Work Director, to Damon, 11 February 1933, RTsKhIDNI, f. 515, op. 1, d. 3265, ll. 39–40.

106. Draft Letter to the American Party on the Work among Women, 10 October 1932, RTsKhIDNI, f. 515, op. 1, d. 2618, l. 164; Letter to Comrades, 10 November 1932, l. 160.

107. Organization Letter, 1 July 1932, RTsKhIDNI, f. 515, op. 1, d. 2870, l. 71.

108. Margaret Keller to Damon, 11 February 1933, RTsKhIDNI, f. 515, op. 1, d. 3265, ll. 39–40; District Buro Minutes, 10 December 1931, f. 515, op. 1, d. 2457, l. 152; "Organize the Work among Women!" *PO* 5 (March 1932): 26–27.

109. Chicago Board of Elections, 1930 and 1932 election ledger, recap sheets, Chicago. Michael Gold offers a description of the party's 1932 nominating convention in "The Communists Meet," *New Republic*, 15 June 1932, 117–19.

110. For election returns, see election-return books, Election Board Office, Chicago. In a city of over three million, eleven thousand votes points to the fact that the party was a fairly marginalized political organization. And yet their ability to garner over eleven thousand votes for a presidential candidate and over thirty thousand for a congressional candidate suggests that they had an increasingly strong base—what sociologists refer to as a "mobilization potential," or the group of individuals "predisposed to participate in a social movement." Their ability to grow their mobilization potential throughout the Third Period would lead to a large spike in their membership rolls and in their ability to move large groups into action. See Bert Klandermans, "The Social Construction of Protest and Multiorganizational Fields," in *Frontiers in Social Movement Theory*, ed. Aldon Morris and Carol McClurg (New Haven, Conn.: Yale University Press, 1992), 77–103 (quote on 80); Sidney Tarrow, *Power in Social Movement: Social Movements, Collective Action, and Politics* (Cambridge: Cambridge University Press, 1994). Thanks to Herb Haines for introducing me to this literature.

111. Cohen, *Making a New Deal*, 265; Abbott, *Tenements of Chicago*, 434. There were 3,993 Writs of Restitution in 1929. Asher, "Influence of the Chicago Workers' Committee," 23; Piven and Cloward, *Poor People's Movements*, 66.

112. Folsom, *America before Welfare*, 416; Herbert Benjamin, "Unity on the Unemployed Field," *The Communist* (April 1936): 327–36.

113. I. Amter, "The National Congress for Unemployment and Social Insurance—and After," *The Communist* (January 1935): 33–44.

114. "Minutes of the District Buro," 14 May 1935, RTsKhIDNI, f. 515, op. 1, d. 3855, ll. 17–19; "To the Central Committee," 15 May 1934, d. 3858, l. 174; "Report of K. L. on Relief Situation," 4 May 1935, d. 3855, l. 21; "Report on Unemployed Work," n.d. [December 1935], d. 3859, ll. 235–41; "Minutes of District Buro," 18 May 1935, d. 3855, l. 26.

115. Cohen, *Making a New Deal*, 320.

Chapter 5: "Abolish Capitalism"

1. Minutes of the PolBuro, 28 August 1929, RTsKhIDNI, f. 515, op. 1, d. 1773, l. 16. Chicago leaders predicted that they would send seventy-five delegates, but a convention report indicates that Illinois sent sixty-six. See "Chic Sends 75 Delegates to Cleveland," *Labor Unity*, 24 August 1929, 1; and "Composition of Convention," *Labor Unity*, 14 September 1929, 4.

2. Gebert's Speech on the 13th Central Committee Plenum and Tasks, 6 September 1931, RTsKhIDNI, f. 515, op. 1, d. 2455, l. 47.

3. Nationwide union membership reached a peak of 5,047,800, or 19.4 percent, in 1920. By 1929 there were 3,442,600 members, or 10.2 percent. At a low point of unionization in the country, Chicago's percentage of unionized members was still higher than the national average was when it was at its peak. And while 22 percent of Chicago's overall workforce was unionized, one study showed that an even higher percentage—32

percent—of its manufacturing and mechanical industries had union representation. See C. Lawrence Christenson, *Collective Bargaining in Chicago, 1929–1930: A Study of the Economic Significance of the Industrial Location of Trade Unionism* (Chicago: University of Chicago Press, 1933), 2; Irving Bernstein, *The Lean Years: A History of the American Worker, 1920–1933* (Boston: Houghton Mifflin, 1960), 84.

4. Bernstein, *Lean Years*, 86–87.

5. Oscar D. Hutton Jr., "The Negro Worker and the Labor Unions in Chicago" (M.A. thesis, University of Chicago, 1939), 2–60; Lizabeth Cohen, *Making a New Deal: Industrial Workers in Chicago, 1919–1939* (Cambridge: Cambridge University Press, 1990), 42, 45; Earl Browder, "Reactionaries Smashing Ladies Garment Workers," *Labor Herald* (November 1923): 13–16; J. W. Johnstone, "Reaction in Needle Trades," *Labor Herald* (February 1924): 25–27; Barbara Warne Newell, *Chicago and the Labor Movement: Metropolitan Unionism in the 1930s* (Urbana: University of Illinois Press, 1961), 239–40.

6. Newell, *Chicago and the Labor Movement*, 29–30; Richard Schneirov and Thomas J. Suhrbur, *Union Brotherhood, Union Town: The History of the Carpenters' Union of Chicago, 1863–1987* (Carbondale: Southern Illinois University Press, 1988), 114–15; "Jobless Carpenters Fight Union Fakers," *Hunger Fighter*, 26 December 1931.

7. Plan of Action for Building the TUUL in Chicago, n.d., RTsKhIDNI, f. 515, op. 1, d. 2113, l. 96.

8. Some examples of this approach can be found in Bert Cochran, *Labor and Communism: The Conflict That Shaped American Unions* (Princeton, N.J.: Princeton University Press, 1977); Theodore Draper, *American Communism and Soviet Russia* (New York: Vintage Books, 1986); and Irving Howe and Lewis Coser, *The American Communist Party* (New York: Praeger, 1962).

9. Roger Keeran, *The Communist Party and the Auto Workers Union* (Bloomington: Indiana University Press, 1980); Fraser Ottanelli, *The Communist Party of the United States: From the Depression to World War II* (New Brunswick, N.J.: Rutgers University Press, 1991), 20–28.

10. A personal appeal from Nels Kjar, expelled member of Local 181, June 1929; Trial Boards, CDC expulsions of Cpers, 1929–31, research notes from Steven Sapolsky, in the author's possession. On the popularity of the TUEL position in Chicago's building trades in the early 1920s, see Arne Swabeck, "The Building Trades Problem," and Joe Peterson, "Towards Unity in the Building Trades," *Labor Herald* (June 1922): 1–5 and 7–9. On opposition to Chicago's Carpenters' District Council leadership, see Schneirov and Suhrbur, *Union Brotherhood*, 111–12.

11. Minutes of the District Industrial Committee, 30 September 1929, RTsKhIDNI, f. 515, op. 1, d. 1775, ll. 33–34.

12. Max Bedacht to Lovestone, 12 October 1927, RTsKhIDNI, f. 515, op. 1, d. 1036, l. 58.

13. Browder, "Reactionaries Smashing Ladies Garment Workers," 13–16; James R. Barrett, *William Z. Foster and the Tragedy of American Radicalism* (Urbana: University of Illinois Press, 1999), 126–27.

14. Carsel gives a detailed description of the struggle between the Left and the Right in Chicago's Ladies' Garment Workers Union. See Wilfred Carsel, *A History of the Chi-*

cago Ladies' Garment Workers' Union (Chicago: Random House, 1940), 174–92 (quote on 184).

15. Max Bedacht to CEC, 30 July 1928, RTsKhIDNI, f. 515, op. 1, d. 1334, l. 82.

16. Minutes Meeting of District Industrial Committee, 6 April 1929, RTsKhIDNI, f. 515, op. 1, d. 1775, l. 3.

17. The CEC Answer to Appeal Made to the CEC by Childs, Lifshitz, Rubicki, Fisher, and Swabeck against Election of Sklar as Org Sec, n.d. [1928], RTsKhIDNI, f. 515, op. 1, d. 1334, ll. 43–45.

18. Minutes of the District Industrial Committee, 30 March 1929, RTsKhIDNI, f. 515, op. 1, d. 1775, l. 2; "Preparations for the TUEL Convention in the Various Districts," *Labor Unity*, 4 May 1929.

19. Barrett, *William Z. Foster*, 126.

20. Ibid., 126–31; David Montgomery, *The Fall of the House of Labor: The Workplace, the State, and American Labor Activism, 1865–1925* (Cambridge: Cambridge University Press, 1987), 434.

21. Montgomery, *Fall of the House of Labor*, 433–34; Barrett, *William Z. Foster*, 140–42.

22. Minutes of the District Industrial Committee, 30 September 1929, RTsKhIDNI, f. 515, op. 1, d. 1775, l. 34; Montgomery, *Fall of the House of Labor*, 433–34.

23. Edward Johanningsmeier, "The Trade Union Unity League: American Communists and the Transition to Industrial Unionism, 1928–1934," *Labor History* 42.2 (2001): 159–77.

24. "Hear Reports on Convention in Chicago," *Labor Unity*, 28 September 1929, 2.

25. Report on Metal Workers, 15 October 1929, Earl Browder Papers, Syracuse University Library, Special Collections, Research Center, Syracuse, N.Y.

26. Minutes of the District Industrial Committee, 30 September 1929, RTsKhIDNI, f. 515, op. 1, d. 1775, l. 34.

27. Minutes of the District Industrial Committee, 30 September 1929, RTsKhIDNI, f. 515, op. 1, d. 1775, l. 35. See also "Food Workers League Going Full Speed," *Labor Unity*, 5 October 1929, 1; and "Chicago Food Workers League Making Good Gains in Stockyards," *Labor Unity*, 4 January 1930, 1.

28. Minutes of the District Industrial Committee, 30 September 1929, RTsKhIDNI, f. 515, op. 1, d. 1775, l. 34.

29. Minutes of the District Industrial Committee, 16 November 1929, RTsKhIDNI, f. 515, op. 1, d. 1775, l. 43; Rick Halpern, *Down on the Killing Floor: Black and White Workers in Chicago's Packinghouses, 1904–54* (Urbana: University of Illinois Press, 1997), 81–82.

30. Section 4 Organization Letter, RTsKhIDNI, 17 June 1931, d. 2472, l. 71 (quote); District Eight Organization Letter, 3 April 1931, d. 2466, l. 32; "Concentration—A Means of Winning the Workers in the Key Industries," *PO* 2 (February 1933), 5; "The Shop—A Center of Mass Activity," *PO* 2 (February 1933), 1–4; Keeran, *Communist Party and the Auto Workers Union*, 80–81; Ottanelli, *Communist Party of the United States*, 24.

31. Cohen, *Making a New Deal*, 21–27; James Carl Kollros, "Creating a Steel Workers Union in the Calumet Region, 1933 to 1945" (Ph.D. dissertation, University of Illinois at Chicago, 1998), 22–33.

32. "General Statistics for Standard Metropolitan Areas, by Industry," *Census of Manufactures: 1947*, vol. 3 (Washington, D.C.: Government Printing Office, 1950), 183; Rick Halpern and Roger Horowitz, *Meatpackers: An Oral History of Black Packinghouse Workers and Their Struggle for Racial and Economic Equality* (New York: Monthly Review Press, 1999), 27; Theodore Purcell, *The Worker Speaks His Mind on Company and Union* (Cambridge, Mass.: Harvard University Press, 1954), 3–4; Halpern, *Down on the Killing Floor*, 7–43.

33. Within steel, a minority group formed and pushed to "organize the workers into the organizations they want to organize into." In other words, they opposed the dual unionism of the Steel and Metal Workers' Industrial Union and applied pressure on party leaders to continue organizing within the AFL. They argued, "There are a great many workers who will fight even tho they are in the AFL. . . . [I]t is suicide to say that the [AFL] workers can't organize." Minority Group of Steel and Metal Workers Conference, n.d., RTsKhIDNI, f. 534, op. 7, d. 508, ll. 100–101.

34. Smaller drives were organized in Hart, Schaffner, and Marx; Majestic; Jones Foundry and Rubber Factory; and Oppenheimer. See Organization Letter, 30 April 1931, RTsKhIDNI, f. 515, op. 1, d. 2466, l. 55; Organization Letter, 7 April 1932, d. 2870, l. 34; Section 4 Organization Letter, 29 October 1931 and 25 May 1931, d. 2472, ll. 83 and 63; Section 1 Organization Letter, 19 May 1931, 3 June 1931, and 15 July 1931, d. 2472. ll. 1, 2, and 4; Section 2 Minutes, 19 October 1931, d. 2472, ll. 17–18; Section 5 Organization Letter, 22 December 1931, d. 2472, l. 107; Organization Chart, n.d., d. 2460, l. 123, Report on Chicago, 22 November 1933, f. 534, op. 7, d. 507, l. 251; Plan of Work for Stock Yards Section, n.d. [1933], RTsKhIDNI, f. 515, op. 1, d. 3267, l. 242.

35. Jack Johnstone, "Problems of the Trade Union Fractions," *PO* 1 (April 1927): 11–12; "The Party Fractions in the Trade Unions," *PO* 3 (February 1930): 5–7; O. Piatnitsky, "Trade Union Fractions," *PO* 2 (July–August 1928): 10–11; Harvey Levenstein, *Communism, Anti-Communism, and the CIO* (Westport, Conn.: Greenwood Press, 1981), 18; District Resolution on TUUL, n.d. [1930], RTsKhIDNI, f. 515, op. 1, d. 2109, ll. 81–86.

36. "Organizing Shop Committees," *PO* 3 (February 1930): 7–9; "What Are Shop Committees?" *Labor Unity*, 19 April 1930. The shop committee harkens to the 1917–22 shop-floor struggles of labor discussed in Montgomery, *Fall of the House of Labor*, 411–64.

37. "The Basic Units of the Party," *PO* 3 (February 1930): 10–11.

38. "Experiences in Building a Department Committee in a Large Plant," *PO* 6 (March–April 1933): 4–6.

39. Bruce Nelson, "Dancing and Picnicking Anarchists? The Movement below the Martyred Leadership," in *Haymarket Scrapbook*, ed. Dave Roediger and Franklin Rosemont (Chicago: Charles Kerr, 1986), 76–79; "Chicago TUUL Ball," *Labor Unity*, 21 December 1929, 2; Section 2 Organization Letter, RTsKhIDNI, f. 515, op. 1, d. 3590, l. 21.

40. "Methods of Work in Factory," n.d. [1931], RTsKhIDNI, f. 515, op. 1, d. 2466, l. 49.

41. Directives for Work among Women, to the Chicago District from CC Rep., n.d., RTsKhIDNI, f. 515, op., 1, d. 2345, ll. 145–46.

42. Minutes of the District Industrial Committee, 30 September 1929, RTsKhIDNI, f. 515, op. 1, d. 1775, l. 34.

43. Calendar Plan of Work for District 8, 3–7 December 1930, RTsKhIDNI, d. 2108, ll. 19–28; Section 2 Organization Letter, 2 December 1932, d. 2882, l. 57.

44. "Announce a Big Conference for Chicago Sunday," *Labor Unity,* 9 November 1929, 3.

45. William Discussion at Plenum, 6 September 1931, RTsKhIDNI, f. 515, op. 1, d. 2455, l. 67; Otto Wangerin to Bill, 17 February 1932, d. 2999, l. 5; Roger Keeran, "The International Workers Order and the Origins of the CIO," *Labor History* 30.3 (1989): 385–408.

46. Methods of Work in the Factory, Outline Created by Organization Department, 1931, RTsKhIDNI, f. 515, op. 1, d. 2466, l. 50.

47. "The Party Fractions in the Trade Unions," *PO* 3 (February 1930): 5–7.

48. Cochran, *Labor and Communism,* 71 (quote); Christenson, *Collective Bargaining in Chicago,* 1–29; Newell, *Chicago and the Labor Movement,* 24–32.

49. Cochran, *Labor and Communism,* 71–77; Smith to Browder and other members of the Polburo, 11 November 1931, RTsKhIDNI, f. 515, op. 1, d. 2548, ll. 84–85; Minority Groups in AFL, 11 November 1931, d. 2464, l. 60; MC and Block comments, district conference, n.d., d. 3256, ll. 155, 217–21; Three Month Review of Plenum Tasks, 1931, d. 2455, l. 27. U.S. party leaders were not of one mind about what to do with the AFL. See Barrett, *William Z. Foster,* 176, 192–93.

50. Robert Shaffer, "Women and the Communist Party, USA, 1930–1940," *Socialist Review* 9.3 (May–June 1979): 73–118; Analise Orleck, *Common Sense and a Little Fire: Women and Working-Class Politics in the United States* (Chapel Hill: University of North Carolina Press, 1995), 215–49; Rosalyn Baxandall, "The Question Seldom Asked: Women and the CPUSA," in *New Studies in the Politics and Culture of U.S. Communism,* ed. Michael E. Brown, Randy Martin, Frank Rosengarten, and George Snedeker (New York: Monthly Review Press, 1993), 144–48.

51. Smith comments at District Plenum, 11 May 1930, RTsKhIDNI, f. 515, op. 1, d. 2108, l. 6.

52. "Experiences in Work among Women," n.d. [1932], RTsKhIDNI, f. 515, op. 1, d. 2876, l. 212.

53. Keller to Damon, 26 September 1932, RTsKhIDNI, f. 515, op. 1, d. 2875, ll. 104–6.

54. District Plenum Resolution, 11 May 1930, RTsKhIDNI, f. 515, op. 1, d. 2108, l. 13.

55. Helen Kaplan, Report of Chicago District on Work among Women, n.d., RTsKhIDNI, f. 515, op. 1, d. 2110, ll. 12–17.

56. "Experiences in Work among Women," n.d. [1932], RTsKhIDNI, f. 515, op. 1, d. 2876, ll. 212–14.

57. Pauline Rogers, Report on Tour, 7 October–13 December, RTsKhIDNI, f. 515, op. 1, d. 2244, ll. 83–88.

58. Minutes of Polburo, 3 May 1930, f. 515, op. 1, d. 2109, ll. 31, 33.

59. Pauline Rogers, Report on Tour, 7 October–13 December 1931, f. 515, op. 1, d.

2244, ll. 83–88 (quote on 84). On the New York Housewives' Councils, see Orleck, *Common Sense and a Little Fire*, 215–49; Minutes of District Women's Committee, 15 May 1930, d. 2115, l. 24.

60. Helen Kaplan, Report of Chicago District on Work among Women, n.d., RTsKhIDNI, f. 515, op., d. 2110, ll. 12–17.

61. Directives for Work among Women, n.d., RTsKhIDNI, f. 515, op. 1, d. 2345, ll. 145–46; Pauline Rogers, Report on Tour, 7 October–13 December 1931, d. 2244, ll. 83–88.

62. Unsigned letter to Comrades, 10 October 1932, RTsKhIDNI, f. 515, op. 1, d. 2618, ll. 160–63.

63. To Department for Work among Women, CC, 16 February 1932, RTsKhIDNI, f. 515, op. 1, d. 2874, l. 87.

64. Helen Kaplan comments, n.d., RTsKhIDNI, f. 515, op. 1, d. 3256, l. 45.

65. Letter to Organization Department of CC from Unsigned, marked Chicago, 18 June 1934, RTsKhIDNI, f. 515, op. 1, d. 3587, l. 167.

66. Kollros, "Creating a Steel Workers Union," 66–67, 72–73; Cohen, *Making a New Deal*, 237–38; James McIntyre, "History of Wisconsin Steel Works," typescript, 1951, 51, Southeast Chicago Historical Society.

67. Cohen, *Making a New Deal*, 162–83; Halpern, *Down on the Killing Floor*, 85–95.

68. Cohen, *Making a New Deal*, 183–211; Halpern, *Down on the Killing Floor*, 85–95; "Shop Nuclei at Work on May Day Demonstration," *PO* 3.4 (June–July 1930): 8–10.

69. *C and NW Worker*, April and May–June 1931, RTsKhIDNI, f. 515, op. 1, d. 2474, ll. 5, 8–10.

70. Minutes of the District Buro, 11 April 1931, RTsKhIDNI, f. 515, op. 1, d. 2457, l. 32; *Crane Organizer*, July 1931, d. 2474, ll. 11–12; *Harvester Worker*, April 1931, d. 2474, ll. 24–26; Morton Report on Steel, 22 January 1932, d. 2866, l. 19; "Shop Paper Reviews," *PO* 5 (November–December 1932): 42–44; Sotos Section 6 Discussion, 6 September 1931, d. 2455, l. 70.

71. Otto Wangerin to Bill, 17 February 1932, RTsKhIDNI, f. 515, op. 1, d. 2999, l. 2.

72. Cohen, *Making a New Deal*, 196–201 (quote on 201); District Buro Minutes, 23 October 1931, RTsKhIDNI, f. 515, op. 1, d. 2457, l. 112; Interviews with Vicky Starr and Herb March, UPWAOHP.

73. "Methods of Work in Factory—Outline Prepared by Organization Department 1931," RTsKhIDNI, f. 515, op. 1, 2466, l. 150. See also Gebert's Speech on the 13th Central Committee Plenum and Tasks, 6 September 1931, d. 2455, l. 45.

74. Minutes of the District Industrial, 30 September 1929, RTsKhIDNI, f. 515, op. 1, d. 1775, l. 35.

75. Hutton, "Negro Worker and the Labor Unions in Chicago," 16–24; Paul Young, "Race, Class, and Radicalism in Chicago, 1914–1936" (Ph.D. dissertation, University of Iowa, 2001), 1–49.

76. Herbert Hill, interview with Edward Doty, 2 November 1967, in the author's possession. Thanks to Steve Sapolsky for sharing this source.

77. Ibid. According to Doty, a police order ruled that only the licensed plumbers of Local 130 could work in the city. They were all white. See also Harry Haywood, *Black*

Bolshevik: Autobiography of an Afro-American Communist (Chicago: Liberator Press, 1978), 129–30.

78. Herbert Hill, interview with Edward Doty.

79. The ANLC had one near success in Chicago in 1926 when one hundred black women walked off their jobs at a stuffed-date factory protesting pay cuts and assembly-line speedups. Fitzpatrick of the Chicago Federation invited the strike leader, Jannie Warnettas, and Fort-Whiteman of the ANLC to a meeting, but strikebreakers and violence broke the strike, and the CFL never chartered a union for the women. See *Daily Worker*, 5, 9, 18, and 23 October 1926. On the ANLC, see Young, "Race, Class, and Radicalism in Chicago," 174–79; Mark Solomon, *The Cry Was Unity: Communists and African Americans, 1917–36* (Jackson: University Press of Mississippi, 1998), 52–67.

80. Minutes of the Polburo, 26 September 1930, RTsKhIDNI, d. 2109, l. 59; Minutes of Control Committee, 30 October 1930, d. 2116, l. 16.

81. Letters from American Consolidated Trades Council to Victor Olander, 8 May 1932, 12 May 1932, 30 August 1932, Victor Olander Papers, box "Negroes and Rights," Chicago Historical Society; Protest Statement of the American Consolidated Trades Council, 27 May 1932, Victor Olander Papers, box "Negroes and Rights," Chicago Historical Society. Thanks to Steve Sapolsky for identifying these materials.

82. Minutes of District Buro, 16 February 1834, RTsKhIDNI, f. 515, op. 1, d. 3581, l. 10.

83. Minutes of Buro Meeting, 27 April 1934, RTsKhIDNI, f. 515, op. 1, d. 3581, ll. 26–27; Minutes of PolBuro, 26 September 1930, d. 2109, l. 59; Letter to CEC, 6 July 1928, d. 1334, l. 48; Jack Kling, *Where the Action Is: Memoirs of a U.S. Communist* (New York: New Outlook Publishers, 1985), 22. Claude Lightfoot claims that Doty asked him to take over responsibilities of the organization and that Doty remained active in the organization. See Claude Lightfoot, *Chicago Slums to World Politics: Autobiography of Claude M. Lightfoot* (New York: New Outlook Publishers, 1980), 49.

84. The ANLC dissolved in 1930, only to be replaced by the League of Struggle for Negro Rights, which was plagued with many of the same problems that hindered the ANLC. See Haywood, *Black Bolshevik*, 439.

85. In 1938 the electricians finally admitted African Americans, and in 1947 the plumbers followed suit. Doty became the first black officer in the plumbers' union in the early 1950s. See Haywood, *Black Bolshevik*, 131.

86. William Tuttle, *Race Riot: Chicago in the Red Summer of 1919* (New York: Atheneum Books, 1970); Kling, *Where the Action Is*, 24.

87. Video recording of Schaffner's ninetieth birthday celebration in Chicago, Chicago Radical Elder's Project, Spertus Library and Museum; Newell, *Chicago and the Labor Movement*, 79–88; David Scott Witwer, *Corruption and Reform in the Teamsters Union* (Urbana: University of Illinois Press, 2003), 84–93; MC comments, district conference, n.d., RTsKhIDNI, f. 515, op. 1, d. 3256, l. 155.

88. Minutes of the District Industrial Committee, 30 September 1929, RTsKhIDNI, f. 515, op. 1, d. 1775, l. 35; Newell, *Chicago and the Labor Movement*, 80.

89. Discussion at District Convention, n.d. [1933], RTsKhIDNI, f. 515, op. 1, d. 3256, ll. 217–26; Otto Wangerin to Bill, 17 February 1932, d. 2999, l. 2.

90. Newell, *Chicago and the Labor Movement*, 79–88; Witwer, *Corruption and Reform in the Teamsters Union*, 84–93; MC comments, district conference, n.d., RTsKhIDNI, f. 515, op. 1, d. 3256, l. 155; Irving Bernstein, *The Turbulent Years: A History of the American Worker, 1933–1941* (Boston: Houghton Mifflin, 1969), 123–24.

91. Steve Nelson, James R. Barrett, and Rob Ruck, *Steve Nelson: American Radical* (Pittsburgh: University of Pittsburgh Press, 1981), 73.

92. Ibid.; Barbara Newell, *Chicago and the Labor Movement*, 79–88; Witwer, *Corruption and Reform in the Teamsters Union*, 84–93; John Williamson, *Dangerous Scot: The Life and Work of an American "Undesirable"* (New York: International Publishers, 1969), 81.

93. Report of Tour by Shaw, 1933, RTsKkIDNI, f. 534, op. 7, d. 509, l. 46; Report on Railroad by Shaw, 9 March 1933, d. 507.

94. Ed Starr's comments, n.d. [1933], d. 3256, l. 85; Report of Stachel to AFL Fraction Meeting, 9 September 1933, RTsKhIDNI, f. 534, op. 7, d. 515, ll. 1–23.

95. Report of M. F. to Buro on YCL, 30 November 1934, RTsKhIDNI, f. 515, op. 1, d. 3655, ll. 51–62; Joe Webber, interview with Toni Gilpin, 3 January 1981, in the author's possession; Stella Nowicki interview in Alice Lynd and Staughton Lynd, eds., *Rank and File: Personal Histories by Working-Class Organizers* (Boston: Beacon Press, 1973), 75.

96. Tucker at District Conference, n.d. [1933], RTsKhIDNI, f. 515, op. 1, d. 3256, l. 94.

97. "Building the Trade Union Unity League," *PO* 3 (May 1930): 10–11; "The Work of Our Trade Union Fractions," *PO* 3 (June–July 1930): 21–22; "Rooting the Party in the Shops," *PO* 4 (November 1931): 11; "Every Factory a Fortress of Communism" *PO* 4 (September–October 1931): 1–6.

98. Organization Department Letter, 9 June 1932, RTsKhIDNI, f. 515, op. 1, d. 2870, ll. 57–61; District Buro Minutes, 22 January 1932, d. 2866, l. 19.

99. AgitProp Letter, 13 April 1931, RTsKhIDNI, f. 515, op. 1, d. 2466, ll. 46–48; PolCom Minutes, 26 April 1930, d. 2109, l. 24–29, and 3 May 1930, ll. 30–35.

100. District 8 Convention, 7–8 June 1930, RTsKhIDNI, f. 515, op. 1, d. 2107, l. 4; District Buro Minutes, 19 March 1932, d. 2866, ll. 40–42; PolCom Minutes, 19 April 1930, d. 2109, l. 22; District Plenum Minutes, 11 May 1930, d. 2108, l. 4; Plan of Action for Building the TUUL, n.d. [December 1930], d. 2113, ll. 96–100; Organization Department Letter, 9 June 1932, d. 2870, ll. 57–61; District Buro Minutes, 22 January 1932, d. 2866, l. 19; Discussion at District Conference, n.d. [1933], d. 3256, ll. 89–92; S. Yandrich, "Open Letter an Instrument for Penetration into Basic Industries," *PO* 11–12 (March 1934): 22–23; Organization Department Letter, 4 November 1930, d. 2113, l. 64.

101. George Patterson Autobiography, Chicago Historical Society; Tucker at District Plenum, n.d., RTsKHIDNI, f. 515, op. 1, d. 3256, l. 89.

102. Agit Prop to all Section and Unit Agit Prop Directors, 13 April 1931, RTsKhIDNI, f. 515, op. 1, d. 2466, l. 46.

103. A good example of this is the *Deering Worker* (November 1926).

104. Beatrice Shields, "Training Forces in the Chicago District," *PO* 7 (February 1934): 24–28; Jack Stachel, "Our Factory Nuclei," *PO* 2 (May–June 1928): 5–10. For party re-

views of Chicago shop papers, see *PO* 5 (April 1933); Shop Paper Reviews, *PO* 5 (September–October 1932) and (November–December 1932).

105. Report on Shop Papers, n.d. [1930], RTsKhIDNI, f. 515, op. 1, d. 2115, ll. 2–7; Lifshitz Discussion at District Plenum, n.d., d. 3256, l. 48.

106. *Hart, Schaffner, and Marx Worker,* March 1933, RTsKhIDNI, f. 515, op. 1, d. 3270, ll. 4–5; *Stockyards Worker,* March 1933, ll. 6–7 back; *NW Shop News,* May 1928, d. 1418, l. 17; *Kahn Worker,* December 1932, d. 2730, l. 59; *Decker Worker,* December 1932, l. 61.

107. *PO* 5 (November–December 1932); District Buro Minutes, 22 January 1932, RTsKhIDNI, f. 515, op. 1, d. 2866, l. 19; "Shop Paper Editor," *PO* 5 (November–December 1932): 42–44; PolCom Minutes, 19 April 1930, d. 2109, l. 22; Letter to the Editor in Section 4 of *Stewart Warner Worker* from B. Shields, 24 January 1934, d. 3587, l. 221–22; PolBuro Meeting, 9 January 1931, d. 2457, l. 7.

108. PolCom Minutes, 26 April 1930, RTsKhIDNI, f. 515, op. 1, d. 2109, l. 24; Labor Day Report, 2 September 1930, d. 2110, ll. 59–63.

109. Otto Wangerin to Bill, 17 February 1932, f. 515, op. 1, d. 2999, ll. 2–5.

110. "The Party Fractions in the Trade Unions," *PO* 3 (February 1930): 5–7; "On Building Shop Nuclei," *PO* 4 (December 1931): 16–17; "On the Functioning of Trade Union Fractions," *PO* 5 (February 1932): 18–19; "AgitProp Work," *PO* 5 (February 1932): 25–27; District 8 Convention, 7–8 June 1930, RTsKhIDNI, f. 515, op. 1, d. 2107, ll. 2–12; Calendar Plan of Work for District 8, Adopted 3–7 December 1930, d. 2108, l. 26; Organization Letter, n.d. [1930], d. 2113, ll. 47–49; District Buro Minutes, 28 October 1932, d. 2866, ll. 75–78.

111. "Shop Nuclei at Work on May Day Demonstration," *PO* 3 (June–July 1930): 8–10.

112. Sam Economo to E. Browder, 20 September 1932, RTsKhIDNI, f. 515, op. 1, d. 2875, ll. 63–64.

113. Eastman to Comrades, 27 July 1931, RTsKhIDNI, f. 515, op. 1, d. 2875, ll. 56–57 (first quote); Report from Sam Economo, 20 September 1932, d. 2875, ll. 63–64 (second, third, and fourth quotes); Industrial Committee Minutes, 16 November 1929, d. 1775, l. 43 (fifth quote); District Organization Department to Section 2's Committee, 4 November 1931, d. 2466, ll. 121–22; J. W. of the District Secretariat to Secretariat of the CC, 10 December 1932, d. 2876, l. 162; District Buro Minutes, 25 March 1932, d. 2866, ll. 43–45; Secretariat Minutes, 8 October 1932, d. 2866, l. 122; District Organization Department Minutes, 10 September 1932, d. 2875, l. 161; Samuels Report on Yards, 2 September 1932, d. 2866, l. 65; District Buro Minutes, 2 September 1932, d. 2875, l. 161; Lifshitz Discussion on Stockyards, n.d., d. 3256, ll. 47–50; Halpern, *Down on the Killing Floor,* 111–16; Cohen, *Making a New Deal,* 296.

114. Otto Wangerin to Bill, 2 February 1932, RTsKhIDNI, f. 515, op. 1, d. 2999, ll. 2–5.

115. Ibid.

116. District Buro Minutes, 2 October 1931, RTsKhIDNI, f. 515, op. 1, d. 2457, l. 100; District Buro Minutes, 28 October 1932, d. 2866, ll. 75–77; Morton Report on Steel, 22 January 1932, d. 2866, l. 19; Brown Report at District Plenum, n.d., d. 3256, l. 193.

117. Report on Chicago, 22 November 1933, RTsKhIDNI, f. 515, op. 1, d. 3337, l. 43.

118. Morton Discussion, 6 September 1931, RTsKhIDNI, f. 515. op. 1, d. 2455, l. 73.

119. Tucker Discussion at District Conference, n.d. [1933], RTsKhIDNI, f. 515, op. 1, d. 3256, l. 93.

120. Organizational Status of the CP of the USA, 20 August 1932, RTsKhIDNI, f. 515, op. 1, d. 2618, l. 99.

121. See chapter 6 for details on this strike.

Chapter 6: "Generals Are of No Use without an Army"

1. Irving Bernstein, *The Turbulent Years: A History of the American Worker, 1933–1941* (Boston: Houghton Mifflin, 1969), 172–74, 316; Robert Zeiger, *The CIO: 1935–1955* (Chapel Hill: University of North Carolina Press, 1995), 15–16.

2. Barbara Newell, *Chicago and the Labor Movement* (Urbana: University of Illinois Press, 1961), 44–53; Lizabeth Cohen, *Making a New Deal: Industrial Workers in Chicago, 1919–1939* (Cambridge: Cambridge University Press, 1990), 293–301; James Carl Kollros, "Creating a Steel Workers Union in the Calumet Region, 1933 to 1945" (Ph.D. dissertation, University of Illinois at Chicago, 1998), 119–24.

3. Cohen, *Making a New Deal*.

4. "Developing New Cadres in Concentration Industries in Chicago," *PO* 5 (July 1933): 23; Section 7 Committee Minutes, 14 August, 1933, RTsKhIDNI, f. 515, op. 1, d. 3267, l. 111.

5. Section 7 Committee Minutes, 14 August, 1933, RTsKhIDNI, f. 515, op. 1, d. 3267, l. 111.

6. A McCormick Worker, "Actual Experiences in Building the Party in International Harvester Co." *PO* 7 (September 1934): 9–12.

7. Bill to Earl, 5 August 1933, RTsKhIDNI, f. 515, op. 1, d. 3265, l. 211.

8. Stachel Report to AFL Fraction Meeting, 9 September 1933, RTsKhIDNI, f. 534, op. 7, d. 515, ll. 1–23; Bert Cochran, *Labor and Communism: The Conflict That Shaped American Unions* (Princeton, N.J.: Princeton University Press, 1977), 71–77; James R. Barrett, *William Z. Foster and the Tragedy of American Radicalism* (Urbana: University of Illinois Press, 1999), 176–77; Robert Cherny, "Prelude to the Popular Front: The Communist Party in California, 1931–35," *American Communist History* 1.1 (2002): 5–42.

9. Jurich at District Plenum, n.d. [1933], RTsKhIDNI, f. 515, op. 1, d. 3256, l. 16.

10. Reva Weinstein, "Chicago Section Learns about Railroad Concentration," *PO* 7 (April 1934): 6–7.

11. J. Williams, "Change Methods of Work," *PO* 6 (August–September 1933): 8–9.

12. Fraser Ottanelli, *The Communist Party of the United States: From the Depression to World War II* (New Brunswick, N.J.: Rutgers University Press, 1991), 49–80; Bruce Nelson, *Workers on the Waterfront: Seamen, Longshoremen, and Unionism in the 1930s* (Urbana: University of Illinois Press, 1988), 103–26; Cherny, "Prelude to the Popular

Front," 5–42; Roger Keeran, *The Communist Party and the Auto Workers Union* (Bloomington: Indiana University Press, 1980), 121–47.

13. "The Sopkins Case," *Chicago Defender*, 1 July 1933; Harold Gosnell, *Negro Politicians: The Rise of Negro Politics in Chicago* (Chicago: University of Chicago Press, 1967), 334–36; Mark Solomon, *The Cry Was Unity: Communists and African Americans, 1917–1936* (Jackson: University Press of Mississippi, 1998), 251; Beth Bates, *Pullman Porters and the Rise of Protest Politics in Black America, 1925–1945* (Chapel Hill: University of North Carolina Press, 2001), 120–21. In addition to Lightfoot and Ford, the party's leading YCL organizer, Gil Green, helped organize Sopkins (and was arrested for his activity). See Gil Green, *Cold War Fugitive: A Personal Story of the McCarthy Years* (New York: International Publishers, 1984), 43.

14. *Chicago Defender*, 24 June, 1 July (quote), 8 July, and 24 July 1933; Thyra Edwards, "Let Us Have More Like Mr. Sopkins," *Crisis* 42.3 (March 1935): 72; *Daily Worker*, 15 August 1933.

15. J. Williams, "Change Methods of Work," *PO* 6 (August–September 1933): 32–35; "Party Concentration Lays Basis of NTWIU Lead in Strike," *PO* 6 (August–September 1933): 47. The National Textile Codes, implemented after the strike, likely improved work conditions and lessened workers' support for the NTWIU and the Communist party. See Gosnell, *Negro Politicians*, 334–36.

16. Rick Halpern, *Down on the Killing Floor: Black and White Workers in Chicago's Packinghouses, 1904–54* (Urbana: University of Illinois Press, 1997), 112–19; Roger Horowitz, *"Negro and White, Unite and Fight!": A Social History of Industrial Unionism and Meatpacking, 1930–1990* (Urbana: University of Illinois Press, 1997), 69–70; David Brody, *The Butcher Workmen: A Study of Unionization* (Cambridge, Mass.: Harvard University Press, 1964), 153, 161–62.

17. Brody, *Butcher Workmen*, 153–57; Halpern, *Down on the Killing Floor*, 114–15.

18. Halpern, *Down on the Killing Floor*, 113–14; Horowitz, *"Negro and White, Unite and Fight!"* 68–69; Interviews with Herb March, 15 July 1985 and 21 October 1986, UPWAOHP; Herb March, interview with the author, Madison, Wis., 5 October 1995; Cohen, *Making a New Deal*, 320.

19. Interviews with Herb March, 15 July 1985 and 21 October 1986, UPWAOHP; Halpern, *Down on the Killing Floor*, 113–14; Horowitz, *"Negro and White, Unite and Fight!"* 68–69.

20. Halpern, *Down on the Killing Floor*, 116–19.

21. Bill Gebert, "The Party in the Chicago Stockyards," *PO* 7 (April 1934): 1–4.

22. See breakdown of party composition in chapter 1.

23. Letter to Stachel, 7 December 1933, RTsKhIDNI, f. 515, op. 1, d. 3265, l. 313; Gosnell, *Negro Politicians*, 333–34.

24. A Unit Organizer, "How the Party Units in the Chicago Stockyards Worked in the Strike," *PO* 7 (September 1934): 7–9; District Buro Minutes, 27 July 1934, RTsKhIDNI, f. 515, op. 1, d. 3581, l. 34.

25. A Unit Organizer, "How the Party Units in the Chicago Stockyards Worked in the Strike," *PO* 7 (September 1934): 7–9.

26. District Buro Minutes, 27 July 1934, RTsKhIDNI, f. 515, op. 1, d. 3581, l. 34.

27. Kollros, "Creating a Steel Workers Union," 137; B. Gebert, "Mass Struggle in the Chicago District and Tasks of the Party," *Communist* 12 (December 1933), 1190; D. M., "How Two Units Were Established in the Steel Mills," *PO* 6 (December 1933): 9; "Change Methods of Work," *PO* 6 (August–September 1933): 32–34; Steel Report, 19 October 1933, RTsKhIDNI, f. 534, op. 7, d. 507, l. 187; District Buro Minutes, 26 December 1933, f. 515, op. 1, d. 3258, l. 91 (quote).

28. Cohen, *Making a New Deal,* 294; Minority Group of Steel and Metal Workers Conference, n.d., RTsKhIDNI, f. 534, op. 7, d. 508, ll. 100–101; Kollros, "Creating a Steel Workers Union," 124–26.

29. Kollros, "Creating a Steel Workers Union," 119–23; Cohen, *Making a New Deal,* 172–73, 190–91.

30. Joseph Germano Autobiography, Southeast Chicago Historical Society; Kollros, "Creating a Steel Workers Union," 138; Joe Weber, interview with Toni Gilpin, 3 January 1981, in the author's possession.

31. Leaflet, "Steel Workers!" n.d. [1933], RTsKhIDNI, f. 534, op. 7, d. 508, l. 89.

32. Joseph Germano Autobiography.

33. District Buro Minutes, 26 December 1933, RTsKhIDNI, f. 515, op. 1, d. 3258, l. 91; Steel Report, 19 October 1933, f. 534, op. 7, d. 507. l. 187; "Williamson's Report on Extent to Which District Plan of Concentration in Steel Industry Accomplished," 1 September 1933, d. 3258, ll. 70–75.

34. "Williamson's Report on Extent to Which District Plan of Concentration in Steel Industry Accomplished," 1 September 1933, d. 3258, ll. 70–75; Jack Reese interview in *Rank and File: Personal Histories by Working-Class Organizers,* ed. Alice Lynd and Staughton Lynd (Boston: Beacon Press, 1973), 98–100.

35. Kollros, "Creating a Steel Workers Union," 125–26; B. S., "Developing New Cadres in Concentration Industries," *PO* 6 (December 1933): 23–25; Staughton Lynd, "The Possibility of Radicalism in the Early 1930s: The Case of Steel," *Radical America* 5.6 (1972): 38.

36. Bill to Earl, 5 August 1933, RTsKhIDNI, f. 515, op. 1, d. 3265, l. 211; Report of Section 7, n.d., d. 3267, l. 114; A McCormick Worker, "Actual Experiences in Building the Party in International Harvester Co." *PO* 7 (September 1934): 9–12; Minutes, National Committee Meeting, 19 September 1933, RTsKhIDNI, f. 534, op. 7, d. 509, ll. 1–3.

37. A Veteran Painter, "Chicago Painters Win a Victory," *Labor Unity* (March 1934): 13–15.

38. Draft Resolution of the Plenary Session of the Chicago District Committee of the CPUSA on the Economic and Political Situation and the Tasks of the Party, n.d., RTsKhIDNI, f. 515, op. 1, d. 2108, ll. 29–41; Organization Letter, 22 February 1932, d. 2882, l. 73; Newell, *Chicago and the Labor Movement,* 198.

39. P. Frankfeld, "Organization Department Questionnaire for District 8," 10 October 1930, series 2, box 8, file 35, Earl Browder Papers, Syracuse University Library, Special Collections, Research Center, Syracuse, N.Y.

40. John Lawson to CC, 8 January 1935, RTsKhIDNI, f. 515, op. 1, d. 3858, l. 4.

41. Harvey Levenstein, *Communism, Anti-Communism, and the CIO* (Westport,

Conn.: Greenwood Press, 1981), 24; Harvey Klehr, *The Heyday of American Communism: The Depression Decade* (New York: Basic Books, 1984), 123–25.

42. "Shop Paper Reviews," *PO* 5 (July 1932): 20.

43. National Committee Meeting, 19 September 1933, RTsKhIDNI, f. 537, op. 7, d. 509, ll. 1–3.

44. "Report of Work on the ___ Railroad," *PO* 8 (February 1935): 6–8.

45. Bernstein, *Turbulent Years,* 207; Report on RR, n.d., RTsKhIDNI, f. 515, op. 1, d. 3855, ll. 42–46; Summary of Proceedings of Conference of Railroad Fractions with Representatives from Northern States East of Mississippi River, 30 June 1935, d. 3917, l. 5; Shaw Speech on RR, 19 November 1935, d. 3917, ll. 18–19.

46. J. E. McDonald, "Railroad Brotherhoods Unity Movement Monthly Newsletter," March 1935, RTsKhIDNI, f. 515, op. 1, d. 3917, l. 3; Letter from J. E. McDonald, Jas. Miller, L. Metzl, J. E. Waddell, for the Committee, 1 March 1935, d. 3917, l. 1.

47. Summary of Conference Proceeding of Fractions with Reps from Northern States East of Mississippi in Cleveland, 30 June 1935, RTsKhIDNI, f. 515, op. 1, d. 3917, ll. 5–6.

48. Ibid., 5.

49. Report on RR, n.d., RTsKhIDNI, f. 515, op. 1, d., 3855, ll. 42–46; Art Handle discussion on RR Question, n.d., l. 49; Shaw Speech on RR, 19 November 1935, d. 3917, ll. 15–34; Reed Richardson, *The Locomotive Engineer, 1863–1963* (Ann Arbor: University of Michigan Press, 1963), 392–97; William Z. Foster, *American Trade Unionism: Principles, Organization, Strategy, Tactics* (New York: International Publishers, 1947), 264 (quote). On earlier work within the pension association, see J. O'Neil, "Railroad Pensions," *Labor Unity* (May 1932): 20–21; H. Shaw, "Railroad Reformists and Pensions," *Labor Unity* (December 1933): 20–21.

50. District Buro Minutes, 18 June 1935, RTsKhIDNI, f. 515, op. 1, d. 3855, ll. 41–50.

51. Report by Shaw, 19 November 1935, RtsKhIDNI, f. 515, op. 1, d. 3917, ll. 15–34.

52. Ibid.

53. Report on Railroad, n.d., RTsKhIDNI, f. 515, op. 1, d. 3855, ll. 41–46; Grace King, "Discussion on RR Question," n.d., ll. 47–48; Art Handle, "Discussion on RR Question," ll. 49; "Motions and Proposals on RR Report," l. 50.

54. Summary of Proceedings of Conference of Railroad Fractions with Representatives from Northern States East of Mississippi River, 30 June 1935, d. 3917, ll. 5–6.

55. Shaw Report on R.R., 19 November 1935, RTsKhIDNI, f. 515, op. 1, d. 3917, ll. 15–34 (quote on 23).

56. "Report of Work on the ___ Railroad," *PO* 8 (February 1935): 6–8.

57. Organization Letter to Stockyards Section, 1 August 1933, RTsKhIDNI, f. 515, op. 1, d. 3267, l. 235; Bill Gebert, "The Party in the Chicago Stockyards," *PO* 7 (April 1934): 1–4.

58. District Buro Minutes, 25 May 1934, RTsKhIDNI, f. 515, op. 1, d. 3581, ll. 12–13; A Unit Organizer, "How the Party Units in the Chicago Stockyards Worked in the Strike," *PO* 7 (September 1934): 7–9.

59. Report of M. F. to the Buro on YCL, 30 November 1934, RTsKhIDNI, f. 515, op. 1, d. 3655, l. 52.

60. Plan of Work for Stockyards Section for Six Months, n.d. [1933], RTsKhIDNI, f. 515, op. 1, d. 3267, l. 242 (both quotes); J. Rubin, "The Struggles in the Packinghouses," *Labor Unity* (January 1934): 29–30.

61. Report of M. F. to the Buro on YCL, 30 November 1934, RTsKhIDNI, f. 515, op. 1, d. 3655, l. 52.

62. PolBuro Minutes, 16 August 1934, RTsKhIDNI, f. 515, op. 1, d. 3449.

63. Ibid.

64. District Buro Minutes, 13 May 1934, RTsKhIDNI, f. 515, op. 1, d. 3581, ll. 12–13.

65. District Buro Minutes, 25 May 1934, RTsKhIDNI, f. 515, op. 1, d. 3581, ll. 12–13; "How the Party Units in the Chicago Stockyards Worked in the Strike," *PO* 7 (September 1934): 7–9.

66. Interview with Martin Murphy, 10 May 1934, folder 15, Mary McDowell Papers, Chicago Historical Society.

67. Report by M. F. to the Buro on YCL, 30 November 1934, RTsKhIDNI, f. 515, op. 1, d. 3655, l. 52.

68. The exact date of the dissolution is unclear. Halpern, *Down on the Killing Floor*, 123; District Buro Minutes, 19 October 1934, RTsKhIDNI, f. 515, op. 1, d. 3581, ll. 43–44; A Woman Packinghouse Worker, "Concentration in the Chicago Stockyards," *PO* 7 (May–June 1934): 55–57; Stella Nowicki interview in Lynd and Lynd, *Rank and File*, 75.

69. "Ed Wieck's Report on the National Convention of the Steel and Metal Workers Industrial Convention," 3–5 August 1934, Ed Wieck Papers, Walter Reuther Library, Detroit; "Williamson's Report on Extent to Which District Plan of Concentration in Steel Industry Accomplished," 1 September 1933, RTsKhIDNI, f. 515, op. 1, d. 3258, ll. 70–75; Lynd, "Possibility of Radicalism in the Early 1930s," 48.

70. TUUL Minutes, 5 March 1934, RTsKhIDNI, f. 534, op. 7, d. 520, l. 7; Max Gordon, "The Communists and the Drive to Organize Steel, 1936," *Labor History* 23.2 (1982): 258; Bill Gebert, "Growth of Company Unionism—and Our Tasks," *Labor Unity* (October 1934): 13–15.

71. Kollros, "Creating a Steel Workers Union," 165–77; George Patterson interview in Lynd and Lynd, *Rank and File*, 91–97.

72. George Patterson interview in Lynd and Lynd, *Rank and File*, 91–97; Kollros, "Creating a Steel Workers Union," 165–77.

73. Situation in Steel, 18 October 1935, RTsKhIDNI, f. 515, op. 1, d. 3855, ll. 96–101.

74. Minority Group of Steel and Metal Workers Conference, n.d., RTsKhIDNI, f. 534, op. 7, d. 508, l. 100–101 (quote); Jack Reese interview in Lynd and Lynd, *Rank and File*, 97–105. Reese's organizing style is described in Ruth Needleman, *Black Freedom Fighters in Steel: The Struggle for Democratic Unionism* (Ithaca, N.Y.: Cornell University Press, 2003), 190–92.

75. Report on Steel, 4 October 1934, RTsKhIDNI, f. 515, op. 1, d. 3449, l. 110; Minority Group of Steel and Metal Workers Conference, n.d., f. 534, op. 7, d. 508, ll. 100–101.

76. Report on Steel, 4 October 1934, RTsKhIDNI, f. 515, op. 1, d. 3449, l. 110.

77. Steel and Metal Report, 3 December 1934, RTsKhIDNI, f. 534, op. 7, d. 520, l. 53; Report, 5 March 1934, d. 520, l. 6; Report by M. F. to Buro on YCL, 30 November 1934, f. 515, op. 1, d. 3655, ll. 51–62; Report on Steel, 4 October 1934, d. 3449, l. 110.

78. Jack Stachel, "The Fight of the Steel Workers for Their Union," *The Communist* (June 1935): 489; Jack Reese interview in Lynd and Lynd, *Rank and File,* 97–105.

79. Jack Stachel, "Reorganization of the TUUL," 26 February 1935, RTsKhIDNI, f. 515, op. 1, d. 3910, l. 14.

80. Stachel, "Fight of the Steel Workers," 495.

81. Jack Stachel, "Steel Report," 25 February 1935, RTsKhIDNI, f. 515, op. 1, d. 3910, l. 12.

82. Stachel, "Fight of the Steel Workers," 483–99.

83. District Buro Meeting, 18 May 1935, RTsKhIDNI, f. 515, op. 1, d. 3885, l. 28.

84. The case, *Riverside Lodge 164, Ohio, Joseph Clair, President, vs. Amalgamated Association of Iron, Steel, and Tin Workers of North America,* and the events surrounding it are deftly explained in Carroll Daugherty, Melvin G. De Chazeau, and Samuel Stratton, *The Economics of the Iron and Steel Industry,* vol. 2 (New York: McGraw Hill, 1937), 959–69.

85. Stueben, "The Present Situation in Steel and Our Tasks," 2 August 1935, RTsKh-IDNI, f. 515, op. 1, d. 3914, l. 32; Report on Steel, n.d., d. 3921, l. 28; Report to John Lawson to District Committee, 21 September 1935, d. 3854, ll. 15–19; Kollros, "Creating a Steel Workers Union," 127.

86. L. Toth, "Build the Party in the Trade Unions," *PO* 8 (May 1935): 4–7.

87. Report on AFL National Committee Meeting, 17 June 1935, RTsKhIDNI, f. 534, op. 7, d. 525, l. 5.

88. Report by Comrade Smith for Trade Union Commission on Packing, n.d., RTsKh-IDNI, f. 515, op. 1, d. 3855, l. 57; Stella Nowicki interview in Lynd and Lynd, *Rank and File,* 74–78; Brody, *Butcher Workmen,* 159–62.

89. Halpern, *Down on the Killing Floor,* 123–25.

90. Report of John Lawson to District Committee, 21 September 1935, RTsKhIDNI, f. 515, op. 1, d. 3854, ll. 15–23.

91. M. C. [Morris Childs] to Political Buro, 17 September 1935, RTsKhIDNI, f. 515, op. 1, d. 3859, l. 89.

92. Ibid.

93. Morris Childs to P. Buro, 17 September 1935, RTsKhIDNI, f. 515, op. 1, d. 3859, l. 89.

94. Joe Weber, interview with Toni Gilpin, in the author's possession; Cohen, *Making a New Deal,* 310–13; Bernstein, *Turbulent Years,* 123–24.

Chapter 7: "Not That These Youths Are Geniuses"

1. Quoted in S. Kirson Weinberg, "Jewish Youth in the Lawndale Community: A Sociological Study," Paper for Sociology 269, box 139, folder 4, Ernest Burgess Papers, Department of Special Collections, Joseph Regenstein Library, University of Chicago.

2. Ibid.

3. Robert Cohen, *When the Old Left Was Young: Student Radicals and America's First Mass Student Movement, 1929–1941* (Oxford: Oxford University Press, 1993).

4. Chuck Hall, interview with the author, Chicago, 11 January 2000; Les Orear, interview with the author, Chicago, 13 January 2000.

5. Chuck Hall, interview with the author.

6. Les Orear, interview with the author.

7. Harvey Klehr, *The Heyday of American Communism: The Depression Decade* (New York: Basic Books, 1984), 307.

8. Minutes of District Buro Meeting, 26 June 1931, RTsKhIDNI, f. 515, op. 1, d. 2457, l. 76; Taylor Report on YCL at District Buro Meeting, 8 January 1932, d. 2866, ll. 14–16; J. Lawson to Org. Central Committee, 8 January 1935, d. 3858, ll. 3–7.

9. Jack Kling, *Where the Action Is: Memoirs of a U.S. Communist* (New York: New Outlook Publishers, 1985), 11.

10. Ibid., 11–16.

11. This piano instructor, Rudolph Leibich, performed at party affairs. He also arranged music for workers' choruses and performances. Green attended his friend's piano lessons at Leibich's house and voraciously read from his library, which was filled with socialist works. Gil Green, *Cold War Fugitive: A Personal Story of the McCarthy Years* (New York: International Publishers, 1984), 7–17.

12. Data Card, 1931, RTsKhIDNI, f. 515, op. 1, d. 4129.

13. Jim Klein and Julia Reichart, interview with Ben Gray for *Seeing Red*, Tamiment Institute Library, New York University.

14. Minutes of the District Plenum, 11 May 1930, RTsKhIDNI, f. 515, op. 1, d. 2108, l. 4.

15. Ibid.; Minutes of Buro, 10 July 1930, d. 2109, ll. 43–44.

16. YCL District Buro Meeting, 8 January 1932, RTsKhIDNI, f. 515, op. 1, d. 2866, ll. 14–16.

17. J. Lawson to the Org. Central Committee, 8 January 1935, RTsKhIDNI, f. 515, op. 1, d. 3858; Report of M. F. to the Buro on YCL, 30 November 1934, d. 3584, ll. 68–79.

18. Minutes of the Buro, 10 July 1930, RTsKhIDNI, f. 515, op. 1, d. 2109, ll. 43–44; Section 2 Committee Minutes, 6 March 1933, d. 3267, l. 16.

19. Klehr, *Heyday of American Communism,* 328–30; Mark Solomon, *The Cry Was Unity: Communists and African Americans, 1917–1936* (Jackson: University Press of Mississippi, 1998), 139–44; Mark Naison, *Communists in Harlem during the Depression* (Urbana: University of Illinois Press, 1983), 46–48. For more on this trial in Chicago, see Randi Storch, "'The Realities of the Situation': Revolutionary Discipline and Everyday Political Life in Chicago's Communist Party, 1928–1935," *Labor: Studies in Working-Class History in the Americas* 1.3 (Fall 2004): 19–44.

20. *Hunger Fighter,* 6 August 1932, 4.

21. Kling, *Where the Action Is,* 16–17.

22. Minutes of Secretariat, 3 March 1930, RTsKhIDNI, f. 515, op. 1, d. 2109, l. 105.

23. Minutes of District Buro, 20 September 1931, RTsKhIDNI, f. 515, op. 1, d. 2457, l. 153; Minutes of District Buro, 8 January 1932, d. 2866, ll. 14–16; Charlie to Johnny, 5 May 1933, d. 3265, l. 143.

24. Charlie to Johnny, 5 May 1933, RTsKhIDNI, f. 515, op. 1, d. 3265, l. 143.

25. Klehr, *Heyday of American Communism*, 101–2; Kling, *Where the Action Is*, 19; Letter to Organizational Department from District, 10 November 1933, RTsKhIDNI, f. 515, op. 1, d. 3265, l. 285.

26. Jim Klein and Julia Reichart, interview with Ben Gray.

27. Minutes of the District Buro, 26 June 1931, RTsKhIDNI, f. 515, op. 1, d. 2457, l. 76.

28. Kling, *Where the Action Is*, 30; Green, *Cold War Fugitive*, 49–50.

29. Fraser Ottanelli, *The Communist Party of the United States: From the Depression to World War II* (New Brunswick, N.J.: Rutgers University Press, 1991), 62–63.

30. Minutes of the District Buro, 26 June 1931, RTsKhIDNI, f. 515, op. 1, d. 2457, l. 76. See also Minutes of the District Plenum, 6 September 1931, d. 2455, ll. 32–47.

31. Gebert to Browder, 11 August 1931, RTsKhIDNI, f. 515, op. 1, d. 2460, ll. 51–57.

32. Taylor Report on YCL at District Buro Meeting, 8 January 1932, RTsKhIDNI, f. 515, op. 1, d. 2866, ll. 14–16.

33. Charlie to Dave, 5 May 1933, RTsKhIDNI, f. 515, op. 1, d. 3265, l. 143.

34. F. Brown, "Check Up on Organization," *PO* 8 (March 1935): 13.

35. Minutes of the Secretariat, 3 February 1930, RTsKhIDNI, f. 515, op. 1, d. 2109, ll. 101–5; Organization Department Letter, 14 February 1931, d. 2466, l. 20; Organization Letter, 25 April 1931, d. 2466, l. 54; Organization Letter, 25 September 1931, d. 2466, ll. 105–6; Tom Johnson to Pol Buro, 3 October 1931, d. 2460, ll. 93–98; Minutes of the District Buro, 13 July 1934, d. 3581, l. 31.

36. Organization Letter, 15 May 1931, RTsKhIDNI, f. 515, op. 1, d. 2466, l. 65.

37. Minutes of the District Buro, 26 January 1934, RTsKhIDNI, f. 515, op. 1, d. 3581, l. 7; Jack Kling to the Central Committee, 27 December 1932, d. 2974, l. 17.

38. Jack Kling to the Organization Department of the CEC, 7 December 1931, RTsKhIDNI, f. 515, op. 1, d. 2314, l. 100.

39. Chuck Hall, interview with the author.

40. Les Orear, interview with the author.

41. Minutes of District Plenum, 11 May 1930, RTsKhIDNI, f. 515, op. 1, d. 2108, l. 4.

42. Taylor Report on YCL at District Buro Meeting, 8 January 1932, RTsKhIDNI, f. 515, op. 1, d. 2866, ll. 14–16.

43. Cohen, *When the Old Left Was Young*, 39–41.

44. Harry Haywood, *Black Bolshevik: Autobiography of an Afro-American Communist* (Chicago: Liberator Press, 1978), 445.

45. Steve Nelson, James R. Barrett, and Rob Ruck, *Steve Nelson, American Radical* (Pittsburgh: University of Pittsburgh Press, 1981), 82–83.

46. Jack Kling to Gil Green, n.d. [1932], RTsKhIDNI, f. 515, op. 1, d. 2876; ll. 192–93.

47. Ibid.

48. Ibid.

49. *NWRR Shop News*, May 1928, RTsKhIDNI, f. 515, op. 1, d. 1418, ll. 17–18.

50. Memo on the Office Workers Union as an Affiliate of the Trade Union Unity League, 17 January 1934, reel 29, frames 1025–26, USMI-SRUS.

51. This family support was not the case for many party members with children or for the parents of YCL members. In fact, complaints from leaders suggested that a significant number of members kept their children away from party activity. On the importance of family networks in supporting the Left, see Elizabeth Faue and Kathleen A. Brown, "Social Bonds, Sexual Politics, and Political Community on the U.S. Left, 1920s to 1940s," *Left History* 7.1 (2000): 9–45.

52. Kling, *Where the Action Is,* 27–28.

53. Minutes of Section 2 Meeting, 10 September 1933, RTsKhIDNI, f. 515, op. 1, d. 3267, l. 46.

54. Interview with Herb March, 21 October 1986, UPWAOHP.

55. Ibid.; Report of M. F. to the Buro on YCL, 30 November 1934, RTsKhIDNI, f. 515, op. 1, d. 3584, ll. 68–79.

56. Stella Nowicki interview in *Rank and File: Personal Histories by Working-Class Organizers,* ed. Alice Lynd and Staughton Lynd (Boston: Beacon Press, 1973), 70–71.

57. Ibid., 72.

58. Stella Nowicki interview in Lynd and Lynd, *Rank and File,* 76.

59. Ibid.; Ann Doubilet, "The Young Communist League and Women Workers in the Packinghouse Unions in Chicago, 1933–1937, a Study in Tactics," Labor History Seminar Paper for Dr. J. Carrol Moody, 1972, 11, in the author's possession; Report of M. F. to the Buro on YCL, 30 November 1934, RTsKhIDNI, f. 515, op. 1, d. 3584, ll. 68–79.

60. Report of M. F. to the Buro on the YCL, 30 November 1934, RTsKhIDNI, f. 515, op. 1, d. 3584, ll. 68–79.

61. Theodore Draper, *American Communism and Soviet Russia* (New York: Vintage Press, 1986), 179–80; William Baker, "Muscular Marxism and the Chicago Counter-Olympics of 1932," in *The New American Sport History,* ed. S. W. Pope (Urbana: University of Illinois Press, 1997), 284–99; Si Gerson, "The Workers Sport Movement: Six Years of Workers Sport in the USA," *International Press Correspondence,* 19 January 1933, 60.

62. Minutes of LSU National Executive Board Fraction, 23 October 1930, RTsKhIDNI, f. 515, op. 1, d. 2208, ll. 40–41.

63. William Baker, "Muscular Marxism and the Chicago Counter-Olympics of 1932," 285.

64. Chicago's YCL organized "vote Communist street runs" and marathon races to draw attention to various political causes. See, for example, *Workers' Voice,* 15 October 1932.

65. A. Harris, S. Siporin, and E. Becker, Counter-Olympic Fraction, to Earl Browder, 20 May 1932, RTsKhIDNI, f. 515, op. 1, d. 3053, ll. 40–41.

66. Ibid.

67. Taylor Report on the YCL at District Buro Meeting, 8 January 1932, RTsKhIDNI, f. 515, op. 1, d. 2866, ll. 14–16.

68. A. Harris, S. Siporin, and E. Becker, Counter-Olympic Fraction, to Earl Browder, 20 May 1932, RTsKhIDNI, f. 515, op. 1, d, 3053, ll. 40–41.

69. Baker, "Muscular Marxism and the Chicago Counter-Olympics of 1932," 289–91.

70. Ibid., 292.

71. Ibid., 294; Mark Naison, "Lefties and Righties: The Communist Party and Sports during the Great Depression," *Radical America* 13 (July–August 1979): 47–59.

72. Baker, "Muscular Marxism and the Chicago Counter-Olympics of 1932," 293–94.

73. Report of M. F. to the Buro on YCL, 30 November 1934, RTsKhIDNI, f. 515, op. 1, d. 3655, ll. 55–56.

74. Ibid.

75. Ibid.

76. Quoted in Cohen, *When the Old Left Was Young,* 39–41.

77. *Daily Maroon,* 15 April 1932.

78. Cohen, *When the Old Left Was Young,* xiii–xx.

79. *Daily Maroon,* 27 April 1933; Report of M. F. to the Buro on YCL, 30 November 1934, RTsKhIDNI, f. 515, op. 1, d. 3655, ll. 51–62.

80. *Daily Maroon,* 24 May 1933.

81. Report of M. F. to the Buro on YCL, 30 November 1934, RTsKhIDNI, f. 515, op. 1, d. 3655, l. 59.

82. Cohen, *When the Old Left Was Young,* 15–21.

83. In 1932, only 1.4 percent of the entering class was African American, compared to 26 percent Jewish students and 72.3 percent gentile students; .3 percent were described as "other." Mary Ann Dzuback, *Robert M. Hutchins: Portrait of an Educator* (Chicago: University of Chicago Press, 1991), 286.

84. Ibid., 146.

85. *Daily Maroon,* 17 May 1932.

86. J. Williamson to Secretariat CC, 15 March 1932, RTsKhIDNI, f. 515, op. 1, d. 2874, ll. 164–65.

87. James Wechsler, *Revolt on the Campus* (Seattle: University of Washington Press, 1973), 105.

88. Ibid., 108.

89. Report of Student Congress against War Held at Mandel Hall, University of Chicago, 28–29 December 1932, reel 29, frame 572, USMI-SRUS.

90. Report of M. F. to the Buro on YCL, 30 November 1934, RTsKhIDNI, f. 515, op. 1, d. 3655, ll. 51–62.

91. Interview with Quentin Young, Radical Elders Project, Spertus Jewish Museum, Chicago.

92. Memo, 10 March 1933, reel 29, frame 17, USMI-SRUS.

93. Quoted in Cohen, *When the Old Left Was Young,* 82; see also "Program and Resolutions of the Student Congress against War," in *Publications Relating to Student Congress against War* (Chicago: Student Congress against War, 1932).

94. Cohen, *When the Old Left Was Young,* 85.

95. Communists Arrests in Chicago, September 1933, reel 29, frame 906, USMI-SRUS.

96. *Daily Maroon,* 9 May 1933.

97. *Daily Maroon,* 25 January 1934 and 7 March 1934.

98. *Daily Maroon,* 6 April 1934.

99. *Daily Maroon,* 4 April 1934.

100. *Daily Maroon,* 17 October 1934.

101. Memo, 2 October 1934, reel 30, frames 82–87, USMI-SRUS.

102. See, for example, *Daily Maroon,* 19 April 1934. On Chicago's Spanish Civil War recruits, see Randi Storch, "Shades of Red: The Communist Party and Chicago's Workers, 1928–1939" (Ph.D. dissertation, University of Illinois at Urbana-Champaign, 1998), 207–12.

103. *Upsurge,* 20 November 1934.

104. *Upsurge,* 5 December 1934. These arguments predate Berkeley's 1960s free-speech movement by thirty years yet make the same connection between students' rights to political activism and free speech.

105. *Daily Maroon,* 31 January 1935.

106. *Daily Maroon,* 12 April 1935.

107. Robert Coven, "Red Maroons," *Chicago History* 21 (Spring–Summer 1992): 20–37.

108. Ellen Schrecker, *No Ivory Tower: McCarthyism and the Universities* (Oxford: Oxford University Press, 1986), 70.

109. *Daily Maroon,* 2 May 1935; *Chicago Daily Tribune,* 14 May 1935, 1.

110. Quoted in Wechsler, *Revolt on the Campus,* 263. See also Nelson E. Hewitt, *How "Red" Is the University of Chicago?* (Chicago: Advisory Associates, 1935).

111. Quoted in Wechsler, *Revolt on the Campus,* 263; Schrecker, *No Ivory Tower,* 70; Coven, "Red Maroons," 37; *Daily Maroon,* 29 May 1934.

112. *Daily Maroon,* 14 May 1935.

113. *Daily Maroon,* 16 April 1935.

114. *Daily Maroon,* 19 April 1935.

115. *Daily Maroon,* 1 May 1935.

116. *Daily Maroon,* 16 May 1935.

117. *Daily Maroon,* 25 April 1935.

118. *Daily Maroon,* 14 May 1935 and 24 May 1935; *Chicago Daily Tribune,* 14 May 1935, 1.

119. *Daily Maroon,* 5 June 1935.

120. Kling, *Where the Action Is,* 26; Klehr, *Heyday of American Communism,* 320.

121. Earl Browder, "Recent Political Developments and Some Problems of the United Front," *The Communist* (July 1935): 617–18.

Epilogue

1. Georgi Dimitroff, *The United Front: The Struggle against War and Fascism* (New York: International Publishers, 1938), 99–100 (quote on 99).

2. Ibid., 9–93, 169–71, and 197–216; Fraser Ottanelli, *The Communist Party of the United States: From the Depression to World War II* (New Brunswick, N.J.: Rutgers University Press, 1991), 83–135.

3. Mark Naison, "Remaking America: Communists and Liberals in the Popular Front," in *New Studies in the Politics and Culture of U.S. Communism,* ed. Michael E. Brown, Randy Martin, Frank Rosengarten, and George Snedeker (New York: Monthly Review Press, 1993), 45–73 (quote on 47). Michael Denning, *The Cultural Front: The Laboring of American Culture in the Twentieth Century* (New York: Verso, 1997), develops this argument more fully. For insights into the conflicts and contradictions within the congress, see Kevin McDermott and Jeremy Agnew, *The Comintern: A History of International Communism from Lenin to Stalin* (New York: St. Martin's Press, 1997), 120–57. Fernando Claudin, *The Communist Movement: From Comintern to Cominform* (New York: Monthly Review Press, 1975), 174–82, argues that the burden of the shift lay with Soviet foreign-policy requirements. Jane Degras, ed., *The Communist International, 1919–1943: Documents,* vol. 3 (London: Frank Cass, 1971), reprints documents from the congress. Ottanelli, *Communist Party of the United States,* 83–105, discusses how the shift affected the American party.

4. James G. Ryan, *Earl Browder: The Failure of American Communism* (Tuscaloosa: University of Alabama Press, 1997), 159–69, 235–36; Edward Johanningsmeier, *Forging American Communism: The Life of William Z. Foster* (Princeton, N.J.: Princeton University Press, 1994), 272–313; James R. Barrett, *William Z. Foster and the Tragedy of American Communism* (Urbana: University of Illinois Press, 2000), chap. 10.

5. See examples in Gary Gerstle, *Working-Class Americanism: The Politics of Labor in a Textile City, 1914–1960* (Cambridge: Cambridge University Press, 1989); Naison, "Remaking America," 45–73; Randi Storch, "Shades of Red: The Communist Party and Chicago's Workers, 1928–1939" (Ph.D. dissertation, University of Illinois at Urbana-Champaign, 1998), 196–311; Rick Halperin, *Down on the Killing Floor: Black and White Workers in Chicago's Packinghouses, 1904–54* (Urbana: University of Illinois Press, 1997), 179–82.

6. Claude Lightfoot, *Chicago Slums to World Politics: Autobiography of Claude M. Lightfoot* (New York: New Outlook Publishers, 1980), 69.

7. Maurice Isserman, *Which Side Were You On? The American Communist Party during the Second World War* (1982; reprint, Urbana: University of Illinois Press, 1993), 54.

8. Robert Jay Alperin, "Organization in the Communist Party, USA, 1931–1938" (Ph.D. dissertation, Northwestern University, 1959), 45, 74–75; F. Brown, "New Forms of Party Organization Help Us Win the Masses," *PO* 10 (July–August 1936): 6–11 (quote on 11); E. Brown, "Ward Branches in Chicago District," *PO* 10 (June 1936): 18–21; "The Party Branch and Its Relationship to the Community," issued by the Educational Department of the Communist Party, n.d. [1943], CP of USA (IL), Tamiment Institute Library, New York University.

9. Harvey Klehr, *The Heyday of American Communism: The Depression Decade* (New York: Basic Books, 1984), 369–70; Alperin, "Organization in the Communist Party," 109, 119, 129–34; Max Steinberg, "Organize to Strengthen and Build the Party," *PO* 11 (January 1937): 11–14; Fred Brown, "Essential Problems of Organization," *PO* 12 (May 1938): 3–10; M. Gordon, "Experiences in a Chicago Party Ward Branch," *PO* 10 (May 1936): 26–28.

10. Townsend organizations formed to support the physician Francis Townsend's

Old Age Revolving Pension plan, and EPIC was Upton Sinclair's political organization dedicated to Ending Poverty in California. Earl Browder, "Win the Masses in *Their Organizations*," *PO* 9 (December 1935): 16–18.

11. District Buro Minutes, 17 April 1935, RTsKhIDNI, f. 515, op. 1, d. 3855, l. 5; 2 February 1934, l. 8; B. Shields to Bittleman, n.d. [1935], d. 3859, l. 1. On the location of the school and bookstore, see G. R. Carpenter to Assistant Chief of Staff, War Department, 4 September 1940, reel 31, frames 251–54, USMI-SRUS; Beatrice Shields, "Develop Party Cadres in Chicago," *The Communist* (February 1936): 165.

12. Frank Meyer, "Section Schools in Chicago," *PO* 9 (October 1936): 29. See also Alperin, "Organization in the Communist Party," 217–31; and Monthly Recruiting Bulletin, August 1934, RTsKhIDNI, f. 515, op. 1, d. 3591, ll. 24–26. For the low attendance at section schools throughout the city before the change in curriculum, see Minutes of AgitProp Directors, 19 October 1935, d. 3857, ll. 7–10.

13. Alperin, "Organization in the Communist Party," 221. See also Frank Meyer, "Section Schools in Chicago," *PO* 9 (October 1936): 29. Work with non-party members in the school also made Communists vulnerable to government spies. G. R. Carpenter to Assistant Chief of Staff, War Department, 4 September 1940, reel 31, frames 251–52, USMI-SRUS; Agitprop Director's Meeting, 25 May 1935, RTsKhIDNI, f. 515, op. 1, d. 3857, ll. 4–6.

14. Fred Brown, "The Importance of the Recruiting Drive," *The Communist* (October 1937): 915–24 (quote on 921–22).

15. William Carter and Ann Nowell, "Chicago's South Side Advances," *PO* 11 (January 1938): 31.

16. Gold quoted in Naison, "Remaking America," 48; *Midwest Daily Record*, 12 February 1938 and 13 May 1938; Alexander Bittleman, "Historic View of the Struggle for Democracy," *The Communist* (August 1938): 711–21; Earl Browder, "Concerning America's Revolutionary Traditions," *The Communist* (December 1938): 1079–85; Earl Browder, "America and the CI—Relationship and History," *The Communist* (March 1939): 209; F. Brown, "Let the Masses Know Our Party," *PO* 11 (October 1937): 15–18; S. L., "Bringing Forward C.P. Literature," *PO* 11 (September 1937): 37–38.

17. Alperin, "Organization in the Communist Party," 49; Isserman, *Which Side Were You On?* 18–19, 205; Fred Brown, "The Importance of the Present Recruiting Drive for the Future of Our Party," *The Communist* (October 1937): 915–24 (quote on 920); Nathan Glazer, *The Social Basis of American Communism* (New York: Harcourt, Brace, and World, 1961), 92. Some estimate the 1938 membership of the party at seventy-five thousand. This is probably due to the addition of YCL members to the total. See Klehr, *Heyday of American Communism,* 378. It may also be due to the party's own overestimation. See "The January 1938 Registration—An Analysis and Conclusion," *PO* 12 (June 1938): 1–6.

18. Nathan Glazer makes the point, though, that "even in industries where the Party had a powerful base, it did not have what might be called a mass membership." Glazer, *Social Basis of American Communism,* 114.

19. Klehr, *Heyday of American Communism,* 378–85; Glazer, *Social Basis of American Communism,* 117; Ottanelli, *Communist Party of the United States,* 128; F. Brown,

"Check-Up on Organization," *PO* 9 (March 1935): 14; Rosalyn Baxandall, "The Question Seldom Asked: Women and the CPUSA," in *New Studies in the Politics and Culture of U.S. Communism*, ed. Michael E. Brown, Randy Martin, Frank Rosengarten, and George Snedeker (New York: Monthly Review Press, 1993), 156.

20. Chicago's membership statistics become more difficult to access in this period. These are from "Comparative Status of Membership on July 1, 1935," 13–14 July 1935, RTsKhIDNI, f. 515, op. 1, d. 3859, l. 14; "The January Registration—An Analysis and Conclusion," *PO* 12 (June 1938): 1–6; Captain G. R. Carpenter to Assistant Chief of Staff, War Department, 22 October 1940, reel 31, frame 292, USMI-SRUS. For trends of party growth, see table 2.1 in chapter 2 of this volume.

21. Morris Childs, "Forging Unity against Reaction in Illinois," *The Communist* (August 1936): 783.

22. Captain G. R. Carpenter to Assistant Chief of Staff, War Department, 16 November 1939, reel 31, frames 26–29; 26 April 1940, reel 31, frames 121–22, USMI-SRUS; Douglas Wixson, *Worker-Writer in America: Jack Conroy and the Tradition of Midwestern Literary Radicalism, 1898–1990* (Urbana: University of Illinois Press, 1994), 451.

23. H. Pollack, "The Recruiting Drive in the Columbus Section," *PO* 8 (February 1935): 14.

24. Major H. E. Maguire to Assistant Chief of Staff, War Department, 7 April 1937, reel 30, frame 398, USMI-SRUS; Lt. Col. A. L. Hamblen to Assistant Chief of Staff, War Department, 15 October 1938, reel 30, frame 663.

25. Jean Lyon, "There's More than One Way to Nag," *Woman Today* (April 1937): 19; Ruth Garvin, "Face and Figure," *Midwest Daily Record,* 12 August 1939, 8; 7 October 1939, 8; and 14 August 1939, 8.

26. *Midwest Daily Record,* 23 March 1939, 3.

27. *Midwest Daily Record,* 18 September 1939, 4; Yolanda Hall, interview with the author, Chicago, 13 March 1998.

28. Harry Winston, "An Understanding of the YCL Convention," *PO* 10 (July 1937): 17.

29. *Midwest Daily Record,* 30 April 1938, 26 October 1938, and 7 December 1938; "The January Registration—An Analysis and Conclusion," *PO* 12 (June 1938): 1–6; G. R. Carpenter to Assistant Chief of Staff, War Department, 22 October 1940, reel 31, frame 292, USMI-SRUS. Morris Childs claimed that over 70 percent of the Chicago district's recruits were under thirty-five years of age in 1936. See Morris Childs, "Forging Unity against Reaction in Illinois," 783.

30. *Midwest Daily Record,* 26 October 1939, 5; 2 November 1939, 4; Bill Carter, "Planning and Organization Brought Results," *PO* 12 (April 1938): 33.

31. Quoted in Lizabeth Cohen, *Making a New Deal: Industrial Workers in Chicago, 1919–1939* (Cambridge: Cambridge University Press, 1990), 336.

32. Ibid., 345. Many of the central CIO figures pushing for workers' unity discussed in Cohen's book were party members or close sympathizers.

33. Denning, *Cultural Front,* xvi–xvii.

34. Ibid., 9.

35. For a more detailed discussion of these activities, see Storch, "Shades of Red," 155–311. On party support for Ethiopia in Alabama, see Robin Kelley, *Hammer and*

Hoe: Alabama Communists During the Great Depression (Chapel Hill: University of North Carolina Press, 1990), 107, 123. On support and activism in Harlem, see Mark Naison, *Communists in Harlem during the Depression* (Urbana: University of Illinois Press, 1983), 138–40, 155–58.

36. "Let's Get on the Radio," *PO* 10 (February 1936): 31–32; "The Radio—The Voice of Mass Agitation," *PO* 10 (April 1936): 31; "Utilize the Radio," *PO* 10 (June 1936): 1.

37. Brown, "Importance of the Present Recruiting Drive," 915–924 (quote on 920); Horace Cayton and St. Clair Drake, *Black Metropolis: A Study of Negro Life in a Northern City* (New York: Harcourt and Brace, 1945), 737.

38. G. R. Carpenter to Assistant Chief of Staff, War Department, 10 September 1940, reel 31, frames 264–67, USMI-SRUS; "Organization Letter—Section 2," 15 March 1934, RTsKhIDNI, f. 515, op. 1, d. 3590, l. 22; "Monthly Recruiting Bulletin," October 1934, d. 3591, ll. 32–34; "Monthly Recruiting Bulletin," November 1934, ll. 36–37.

39. Report of John Lawson, 21 September 1935, RTsKhIDNI, f. 515, op. 1, d. 3854, ll. 15–23; Report of Investigation Commission, Street Unit 405, n.d. [1935], d. 3853, ll. 24–25; Report for Investigation Commission—Street Unit 106, ll. 45–50; Report of Commission Investigating Sections 5, 11, 12, ll. 45–50. In several neighborhoods, Communist party members resisted joining organizations such as the Italian Citizens club and the Negro Citizens club, even though leaders insisted that connections to mass organizations were essential during this period.

40. Brown, "Importance of the Present Recruiting Drive," 915–24.

41. G. R. Carpenter to Assistant Chief of Staff, War Department, 18 June 1940, reel 31, frames 153–55, USMI-SRUS; Report of John Lawson, 21 September 1935, RTsKhIDNI, f. 515, op. 1, d. 3854, ll. 15–23.

42. Earl Browder, "United Front: The Key to Our New Tactical Orientation," *The Communist* (December 1935): 1075–1129 (quote on 1122).

43. Ottanelli, *Communist Party of the United States,* 159–189; Isserman, *Which Side Were You On?* 32–54.

44. *Midwest Daily Record,* 5, 9, and 15 September 1939.

45. *Midwest Daily Record,* 2 September 1939.

46. *Midwest Daily Record,* 5, 9, and 12 September 1939.

47. *Midwest Daily Record,* 15 September 1939, 2; Memo, 29 September 1939, reel 30, frame 931; and 25 October 1939, reel 31, frame 16, USMI-SRUS; Herb March interview with Roger Horowitz, 15 July 1974, UPWAOHP.

48. *Midwest Daily Record,* 3 October 1939; Memo, 30 September 1939, reel 30, frame 931, USMI-SRUS.

49. G. R. Carpenter to Assistant Chief of Staff, War Department, 7 November 1939, reel 31, frames 14–19, and 30 November 1939, reel 31, frames 31–33, USMI-SRUS.

50. G. R. Carpenter to Assistant Chief of Staff, War Department, 12 November 1940, reel 31, frames 301–3, and 11 October 1939, reel 30, frame 941, USMI-SRUS.

51. Harvey Klehr, *The Heyday of American Communism: The Depression Decade* (New York: Basic Books, 1984), 386–409.

52. Ottanelli, *Communist Party of the United States,* 191–94.

53. G. R. Carpenter to Assistant Chief of Staff, War Department, 7 November 1939,

reel 31, frames 14–19, 30 November 1939, reel 31, frames 31–33, and 26 March 1940, reel 31, frame 100 (quote), USMI-SRUS.

54. Herb March, interview with Roger Horowitz, 15 July 1974, UPWAOHP. On the independent tendencies of party trade unionists during the Popular Front generally, see Harvey Levenstein, *Communism, Anti-Communism, and the CIO* (Westport Conn.: Greenwood Press, 1981), 40–46; Ottanelli, *Communist Party in the United States,* 146–48; James R. Barrett, *William Z. Foster and the Tragedy of American Communism* (Urbana: University of Illinois Press, 1999), 207–8.

55. G. R. Carpenter to Assistant Chief of Staff, War Department, 12 November 1940, reel 31, frames 301–3, USMI-SRUS.

56. Memo, 18 December 1939, reel 31, frame 52, USMI-SRUS.

57. Memo, 19 October 1939, reel 31, frame 13, and 2 November 1939, reel 31, frame 16, USMI-SRUS.

58. Isserman, *Which Side Were You On?* 37 (first quote); Chuck Hall, interview with the author, 11 January 2000, Chicago (second quote); Dorothy Ray Healey and Maurice Isserman, *California Red: A Life in the American Communist Party* (Urbana: University of Illinois Press, 1990), 82. See also Harry Haywood, *Black Bolshevik: Autobiography of an Afro-American Communist* (Chicago: Liberator Press, 1978), 496.

59. G. R. Carpenter to Assistant Chief of Staff, War Department, 22 October 1940, reel 31, frame 292, USMI-SRUS.

60. G. R. Carpenter to Assistant Chief of Staff, War Department, 16 November 1939, reel 31, frames 26–29. On secret work, see 21 December 1939, reel 31, frames 60–62, and 9 January 1940, reel 31, frames 69–72, USMI-SRUS.

61. *Daily Maroon,* 2 November 1939. On national student activism in this period, see Robert Cohen, *When the Old Left Was Young: Student Radicals and America's First Mass Student Movement, 1929–1941* (New York: Oxford University Press, 1993), 278–307.

62. *Midwest Daily Reader,* 25 August, 28 October, 7 November, and 11 November 1939; G. R. Carpenter to Assistant Chief of Staff, War Department, 7 November 1939, reel 31, frames 9–16; 8 January 1941, reel 31, frame 410; 21 February 1941, reel 31, frames 465–66; 12 November 1940, reel 31, frames 301–3; 1 November 1940, reel 31, frames 295–98; 10 September 1940, reel 31, frames 264–67; "Confidential War Memo," 30 July 1940, reel 31, frame 327, USMI-SRUS.

63. G. R. Carpenter to Assistant Chief of Staff, War Department, 18 January 1941, reel 31, frames 428–31; 26 January 1941, reel 31, frames 434–37; 8 February 1941, reel 31, frames 455–58; 14 February 1941, reel 31, frames 461–63, USMI-SRUS; Haywood, *Black Bolshevik,* 496. While the party made inroads into the peace movement, the right wing had them beat. Philip Jenkins, *Hoods and Shirts: The Extreme Right in Pennsylvania, 1925–1950* (Chapel Hill: University of North Carolina Press, 1997), has excellent descriptions of the various right-wing movements and how they coalesced during the 1940–41 period.

Index

RANDI STORCH is an associate professor of history at the State University of New York at Cortland. She has published articles in *American Labor and the Cold War, The Enyclopedia of Chicago History,* and *Labor: Studies in Working-Class History in the Americas.*

THE WORKING CLASS IN AMERICAN HISTORY

On the Line: Essays in the History of Auto Work *Edited by Nelson Lichtenstein and Stephen Meyer III*

Upheaval in the Quiet Zone: A History of Hospital Workers' Union, Local 1199 *Leon Fink and Brian Greenberg*

Labor's Flaming Youth: Telephone Operators and Worker Militancy, 1878–1923 *Stephen H. Norwood*

Another Civil War: Labor, Capital, and the State in the Anthracite Regions of Pennsylvania, 1840–68 *Grace Palladino*

Coal, Class, and Color: Blacks in Southern West Virginia, 1915–32 *Joe William Trotter, Jr.*

For Democracy, Workers, and God: Labor Song-Poems and Labor Protest, 1865–95 *Clark D. Halker*

Dishing It Out: Waitresses and Their Unions in the Twentieth Century *Dorothy Sue Cobble*

The Spirit of 1848: German Immigrants, Labor Conflict, and the Coming of the Civil War *Bruce Levine*

Working Women of Collar City: Gender, Class, and Community in Troy, New York, 1864–86 *Carole Turbin*

Southern Labor and Black Civil Rights: Organizing Memphis Workers *Michael K. Honey*

Radicals of the Worst Sort: Laboring Women in Lawrence, Massachusetts, 1860–1912 *Ardis Cameron*

Producers, Proletarians, and Politicians: Workers and Party Politics in Evansville and New Albany, Indiana, 1850–87 *Lawrence M. Lipin*

The New Left and Labor in the 1960s *Peter B. Levy*

The Making of Western Labor Radicalism: Denver's Organized Workers, 1878–1905 *David Brundage*

In Search of the Working Class: Essays in American Labor History and Political Culture *Leon Fink*

Lawyers against Labor: From Individual Rights to Corporate Liberalism *Daniel R. Ernst*

"We Are All Leaders": The Alternative Unionism of the Early 1930s *Edited by Staughton Lynd*

The Female Economy: The Millinery and Dressmaking Trades, 1860–1930 *Wendy Gamber*

"Negro and White, Unite and Fight!": A Social History of Industrial Unionism in Meatpacking, 1930–90 *Roger Horowitz*

Power at Odds: The 1922 National Railroad Shopmen's Strike *Colin J. Davis*

The Common Ground of Womanhood: Class, Gender, and Working Girls' Clubs, 1884–1928 *Priscilla Murolo*

Marching Together: Women of the Brotherhood of Sleeping Car Porters *Melinda Chateauvert*

Down on the Killing Floor: Black and White Workers in Chicago's Packinghouses, 1904–54 *Rick Halpern*

Labor and Urban Politics: Class Conflict and the Origins of Modern Liberalism in Chicago, 1864–97 *Richard Schneirov*

All That Glitters: Class, Conflict, and Community in Cripple Creek *Elizabeth Jameson*

Waterfront Workers: New Perspectives on Race and Class *Edited by Calvin Winslow*

Labor Histories: Class, Politics, and the Working-Class Experience *Edited by Eric Arnesen, Julie Greene, and Bruce Laurie*

The University of Illinois Press
is a founding member of the
Association of American University Presses.

Composed in 10.5/13 Adobe Minion Pro
with Meta display
at the University of Illinois Press
Manufactured by Thomson-Shore, Inc.

University of Illinois Press
1325 South Oak Street
Champaign, IL 61820-6903
www.press.uillinois.edu

7366